Lincoln Christian College

S0-FSO-138

WITHDRAWN
University of
Illinois Library
at Urbana-Champaign

Addresses and Papers
of
John R. Mott

GENERAL PREFACE

✤✤✤

MANY FRIENDS in different parts of the world have during recent years expressed their desire that I write the story of my life and their conviction that I should do so. The preparation of an auto- biography has never appealed to me or to my family. However, the attention which I have devoted to the thorough examination of my somewhat voluminous archives has convinced me that it may be my duty to make available invaluable source material bearing on the origin and development of the world-wide Christian movements which it has been my privilege to help establish and develop. The personal records of my extensive and repeated journeys to all parts of the world have added much that is essential. If advantage is ever to be taken of the light which such foundation records shed upon these significant ecumenical movements there is no time to be lost.

It has been my opportunity to be intimately related to the begin- nings and development of the Student Volunteer Movement for Foreign Missions, the World's Student Christian Federation, the International Missionary Council, the Young Men's Christian Asso- ciation, and the modern ecumenical movement, together with various auxiliary or tributary bodies. It has seemed wise, therefore, to devote much attention, in the unsettled period of the Second World War and its aftermath, to assembling and classifying the essential source data, much of which has long been out of print. It early became evident that at least one volume for each movement would be necessary. A final volume is devoted to my papers and addresses which served a wider range of interest than that of any one of the movements to which a full volume is devoted.

NEW YORK, 1947 JOHN R. MOTT

ADDRESSES AND PAPERS
OF
JOHN R. MOTT

The Young Men's Christian Association

Parts 4, 5, 6

ADDRESSES AND PAPERS
OF
JOHN R. MOTT

Volume Four

The Young Men's
Christian Association

NEW YORK

ASSOCIATION PRESS

1947

COPYRIGHT, 1947, BY
THE INTERNATIONAL COMMITTEE OF
YOUNG MEN'S CHRISTIAN ASSOCIATIONS

137

PRINTED IN THE UNITED STATES OF AMERICA

267
M 92
v. 4

Allenson

$60.00/set

21 May 71

THIS VOLUME AND THE VOLUME THAT PRECEDES
ARE DEDICATED TO SIR GEORGE WILLIAMS, THE
FOUNDER OF THE YOUNG MEN'S CHRISTIAN
ASSOCIATION; TO RICHARD C. MORSE, THE WISE
AND FAR-SIGHTED GENERAL SECRETARY OF THE
INTERNATIONAL COMMITTEE FOR NEARLY HALF A
CENTURY; TO CLEVELAND H. DODGE, MY CHAIR-
MAN (FROM THE BEGINNING OF MY LIFE SERVICE
TO THE END OF HIS LIFE), WISE COUNSELOR
AND FAITHFUL FRIEND; TO H. H. PRINCE OSCAR
BERNADOTTE OF SWEDEN, THE MOST INFLUENTIAL
ASSOCIATION LAYMAN ON THE EUROPEAN CON-
TINENT; TO K. T. PAUL OF INDIA, AND FLETCHER
S. BROCKMAN AND DAVID YUI OF CHINA, AMONG
THE RANKING ASSOCIATION STATESMEN OF THE
ASSOCIATION BROTHERHOOD.

39639

CONTENTS

✦✦✦

VOLUME FOUR

THE YOUNG MEN'S CHRISTIAN ASSOCIATION

PART FOUR

PART FIVE

PART SIX

INTRODUCTION

FOR SIXTY YEARS I have sustained a continuous relation to the Young Men's Christian Association. This began in my undergraduate days, when, in 1886, at Cornell University, I was elected president of the Association. It was the experiences there which led to my being chosen in 1888 to become one of the two traveling secretaries of the Student Department of the International Committee of the Association Movement. Three years later I was made senior secretary of the department and held this position for nearly twenty-five years. Within five years I was also brought into a position of major responsibility for the Foreign Department of the International Committee, popularly known as World Service, and continued to carry this until 1915. That same year, after having twice declined the call, I accepted the general secretaryship of the International Committee and continued to discharge its duties until 1928, or shortly beyond the retirement age. During the closing years of this period the extensive reorganization of the International Committee was effected, resulting in the creation of the National Council, the general secretaryship of which I occupied during the initial period, 1924-1928, that is, until the time of my retirement.

Shortly before the termination of my forty years' (1888-1928) service of the North American International Committee, I was elected, at the World's Conference of the Young Men's Christian Associations held at Helsingfors, Finland, in 1926, to become President of the World's Alliance and Chairman of the World's Committee of Young Men's Christian Associations, and have continued to serve in this capacity up to the present time.

Volumes III and IV of the *Addresses and Papers* are devoted to source materials bearing successively on the various fields and phases of the Young Men's Christian Association to which I have been related from 1886 up to the present time (1946). These embrace countless official and unofficial records, conference proceedings, personal report letters, articles in periodicals, public addresses at conventions, institutes, retreats, and on lectureship foundations.

The assembling, sifting, and studying of this large body of experience across the world bears conclusive evidence that this period of sixty years has been one of great creative character.

Within this period the Young Men's Christian Association has become literally a world-wide Christian brotherhood, having spread from less than a score of countries, confined almost entirely to Western and Northern Europe and Anglo-Saxon America, to over seventy lands of Europe, the Latin as well as the Anglo-Saxon Americas, Asia, Africa, and the Pacific Island world. The membership of some hundreds of thousands has grown to over 2,000,000 of regular members, not to mention other millions who were members in their boyhood and young manhood. Racially the Association has been rapidly transformed, having drawn into its fellowship the youth of many peoples in the Orient as well as the Occident. In this period, also, the financial resources of the Movement have increased from fourteen million to over two hundred and seventy million dollars.

Vastly more important than the numerical and material expansion of the Association Movement has been its unique contribution in liberating and calling into action the comparatively latent lay forces of Christianity and relating these to the ever-expanding plans of the Kingdom of Christ.

It would be difficult to overstate the highly multiplying influence of the Association through its Student and Boys' Departments in raising up young men for the leadership, clerical and lay, of the Christian forces.

As an evangelizing force, as a vital means of developing reasonable faith and full-orbed character, and as a highly effective agency in bringing the principles and power of Christ to bear on the wide range of human relationships, the Association has won a place of unique distinction.

Even more significant than these and other services has been the ecumenical development and influence of the Association. From decade to decade it has drawn together increasingly in membership, in fellowship and in action, as has no other religious oragnization, the future leaders of the three great Communions—the Protestant, the Eastern Orthodox, and the Roman Catholic.

NEW YORK, 1947   JOHN R. MOTT

THE WAR WORK OF THE AMERICAN YOUNG MEN'S CHRISTIAN ASSOCIATIONS IN CONNECTION WITH THE FIRST WORLD WAR

THE WAR WORK OF THE AMERICAN YOUNG MEN'S CHRISTIAN ASSOCIATIONS IN CONNECTION WITH THE FIRST WORLD WAR

✦✦✦

LAUNCHING THE WAR WORK COUNCIL

PROCEEDINGS OF THE GARDEN CITY CONFERENCE, APRIL 10, 1917, AND SUBSEQUENT ACTION BY THE INTERNATIONAL COMMITTEE OF THE YOUNG MEN'S CHRISTIAN ASSOCIATION

AT THE INVITATION of the International Committee, conveyed by John R. Mott, General Secretary, representative Association men met at the Garden City Hotel to confer on possible service by the Young Men's Christian Association in connection with the proposed mobilization of troops.

After opening devotional exercises led by Mr. Wilder, Dr. Mott stated the purpose of the Conference, referring to the colossal extent of the World War and the final entry into the conflict of the United States. He said the consequent opportunity confronting the American Associations summons them first, to a larger task than any previously undertaken; second, to a task which must be done very thoroughly; third, to undertake the work in a thoroughly united fashion; and fourth, to do something which will be pronouncedly Christian, spiritual, and unselfish.

SCOPE OF THE WORK

Acting as Chairman, Dr. Mott stated the general topic proposed for discussion: "In the light of the present situation, what is the scope of the work the Association should undertake?"

1. as to the classes of men whom the Association is to serve;
2. as to the phases of service which should receive chief emphasis: (a) in the Camps, (b) outside Camps;
3. as to equipment;
4. as to personnel;
5. as to organization.

743

I. In discussing the first division—Classes of men whom the Association is to serve—the statement was made that so far as information is available at present, the armed forces of the nation will include about 1,417,000 men, as follows:

ARMY

National Guard	440,000	
Army	280,000	
Volunteers	500,000	
		1,220,000

NAVY

Reserve	15,000	
Navy	150,000	
Marine Corps	30,000	
	195,000	
Additional	2,000	
		197,000

GRAND TOTAL	1,417,000 men

There should be included in this consideration also men who are drilling in preparation for enlistment.

Other classes not directly in military service, but naturally to be considered in this connection are, those in attendance at Boys' Training Camps (probably to be omitted this year), and industrial groups more or less directly related to war needs, such as workers in munitions, shipbuilding, armaments, military clothing, and transportation. Among this latter group Associations are already doing considerable work along lines suggested by the Industrial Department of the International Committee, and greater opportunities will doubtless follow under war conditions, as it is estimated that this group will include 7,000,000 workers. It was suggested also that in the present emergency there is necessity for a special program of work with boys, in the light of the experience of Europe.

II. Taking up the second division—Phases of service which should receive chief emphasis: (a) in Camps—Mr. Tichenor outlined the methods of army Y.M.C.A. work which are the result of the experience of the Association. A building or tent should be provided which will serve as the center for the Association's work among about 5,000 men. This building is to be manned by a staff of five, one of whom should be comparable in experience and ability to the general secretary of an Association having from 800 to 1,500 members. Two of his associates should be men of experience as employed

officers of the Young Men's Christian Association, and at least one
of the other two associates may be a man of proven Christian character and of demonstrated capacity in leadership and religious work,
who has not had experience as an employed officer.

The discussion of the activities in a typical camp was under the
heads of religious, educational, and physical work. Mr. Tichenor
announced that considerable attention would be given to the methods
of camp work in the manual now being printed, in which army Association work is discussed in detail. In the consideration of religious
work, reference was made to the importance of emphasizing the great
value of friendly contact with enlisted men through organized volunteer effort. In the Ohio Camp last year near Columbus, several leading business men volunteered for this service for short periods. Wise
evangelistic effort, under the best possible leadership, and careful fol-
low-up methods were urged. Reference was made to the opportunity
the Association has to minimize the tendency to a spirit of hate.

A discussion of the educational activities possible in camp indicated that these should be undertaken after the camp has settled into
its routine. A possible course suggested was one for preparing men
to take the examination for a commission. Mr. Mehaffey read a
communication from the educational director of the Boston Association, offering the co-operation of the Northeastern College in any
educational project attempted in that vicinity. It was suggested that
lectures on national life and the national spirit and similar topics might
help men to keep high their ideals.

In considering physical activities possible in camp work, a number
of helpful suggestions were made by Dr. John Brown, who spoke of
the Association's experience in Canada. He referred to the importance of social and recreational features and warned against too
frequent use of motion pictures.

It was the consensus of opinion that the Association should make
no attempt in camp toward "conditioning" men, and in this connection
Mr. Calhoun made a timely suggestion that the Association should be
careful not to attempt to do things for which the Army already has
provided approved methods.

Turning to the second subdivision—work with men outside the
camps was considered as including men in transit and also men temporarily in cities on furlough or leave. Canadian experience has
shown the value of having a secretary accompany troop trains and
transports. This man provides reading matter and writing materials
and has many opportunities for helpful friendliness. Referring to
the experience of the Railroad Associations, Mr. Moore told of the
hospitality which they had extended to troops en route; this had
taken the form of giving them the use of the baths and swimming

pools, and providing lunches, in some instances. This type of work is possible for any city or Railroad Association when troops are in transit through its community. Another phase of work, not yet developed in this country, requires the opening of large headquarters near railroad terminals and providing lodging and refreshments there. This work will be similar in type to that now done by the navy Associations in this country. There is also an opportunity in some cities for the local Association to relate itself helpfully to men who may be stationed in armories for longer or shorter periods.

III. The third main division of the topic, Equipment, was opened by a discussion of the type of building or center most desirable. The standard "monitor" type as developed on the Mexican border was commended as likely to be usually the most satisfactory. Large tents may be practicable for temporary use under some conditions. The buildings proposed for camp work are 40 x 120 feet. Canadian experience proved the usefulness of a group of tents in summer camps, equipped so that one might be used for assemblies, another for reading and writing, another for the canteen, etc. Canadian experience also developed a type of work in which most of the activities were concentrated at the center of the camp, rather than having a number of centers through the camp. It was felt, however, that for our own camps, a building for each brigade (or about 5,600 men) would be preferable, if practicable. In this connection it must be considered whether or not the summer camp and the winter camp will be on the same site.

In discussing the advisability of the Association operating a canteen, reference was made to the Canadian Camp Manual (section V, page 8) in which the advantages and disadvantages were concisely stated. It seemed to be the judgment of the Conference that conditions in the camp should determine whether or not the Association should undertake to run a canteen. Reference was made to some Canadian camps and practically all the English camps, where ladies had volunteered in large numbers to serve in the Association canteens.

IV. The Conference reassembled after luncheon for the afternoon session, which was opened by a hymn and prayer. The fourth phase of the discussion, Personnel, was then taken up and the qualities requisite for camp work leadership were discussed. It is estimated that 1,000 men will be needed in Association service in camps, by the end of the present year, on the basis of the mobilization of 1,000,000 troops. Mr. Reeder referred to Association experience on the Mexican border and emphasized the need for a generous willingness on the part of employed officers to release or designate for camp work some of their best men, not simply those who "could be spared." Mr. Calhoun referred to the embarrassment of some of the younger secretaries in Canada because of the fact that soldiers were impatient of men of military age not in khaki.

Mr. Cook emphasized the value of attempting to secure for service in camps college men who had some volunteer experience in Association work, alumni as well as undergraduates. Reference was made to the response of the colleges of the country to the need of the war work abroad and to the necessity for training from among their ranks only the strongest men for service here. Mr. Lee, from the standpoint of his experience on the Mexican border, urged that stronger men be sent for camp work than were secured at that time.

In considering possible methods of training inexperienced men for Association service in camp, Dr. Burt and Dr. Doggett suggested possible brief training courses in the Association colleges and summer schools. The securing of capable leadership for Association work in camps was felt to be of the highest importance, because the field there includes picked men and if 1,000,000 troops are mobilized, is larger than the entire Association membership of the country. It was suggested that a number of strong ministers might be secured for camp work for blocks of their time, and that former employed officers as well as strong Christian businessmen might be willing to undertake such service.

V. In discussion of the fifth head, Organization, a statement was made by Dr. Mott concerning a proposed War Work Council, directly responsible to the International Committee, of which the chairman would be Mr. William Sloane, chairman of the present Army and Navy Department of the International Committee. He then asked Mr. Tichenor to present a proposed plan of organization for the work under such a council. This plan contemplates the division of the country into six departments, identical with the divisions made by the War Department, namely, Northeastern, Eastern, Southeastern, Central, Southern, and Western. In each of these departments would be placed a department or division secretary, who would keep in close touch with the general commanding that department. Under the division secretary would be district secretaries as required, and under each district secretary, camp secretaries, each responsible for the direction and co-ordination of Association work in a camp. Under each camp secretary would be building secretaries, each of whom would be responsible for the promotion of the work in a single building, and would have associated with him a staff of about four men. This building and this staff would serve a brigade, or about 5,600 men. The ratio of one secretary to each 1,000 men is desirable.

RESOLUTIONS

Mr. Messer, chairman of the Committee on Resolutions, presented its report, and moved its adoption. The items of the report were then taken up seriatim. As a result of very thoroughgoing discussion and some amendment, modifications were voted in the Resolutions as at first presented. On motion of John W. Cook, the Preamble and the Resolutions were then adopted unanimously, as presented in the following "Important Announcement Regarding Association War Work."

Following a discussion on possible methods of securing funds, Dr. Fisher urged that the Associations have in mind what ought to be done by them later in the event of universal military service.

Dr. Mott in closing the Conference urged that every man present take the initiative on his return to his field and push vigorously for the successful accomplishment of the projects proposed by the Conference.

It was stated that the resolutions adopted by the Conference would be sent to the members of the Conference after the meeting of the International Committee on April 12, and that the minutes or report of the Conference would be forwarded later.

The Conference adjourned at 9:00 P.M.

(signed) JOHN R. MOTT,
Chairman of the Conference

E. W. HEARNE ⎱ Secretaries of the
B. C. POND   ⎰ Conference.

IMPORTANT ANNOUNCEMENT REGARDING ASSOCIATION WAR WORK

To the Local, State, and International Officers of
   The Young Men's Christian Associations of America:

Within recent days it has become apparent that the Association Movement of America is on the threshold of one of the greatest opportunities which have come to it in all its history—the opportunity of serving 1,000,000 or more of the flower of the manhood of the country, who are being called to the colors. Other classes of young men who are to be related in an indispensable way to the war plans of the nation will also require the practical and Christian ministry of the Associations. All Association leaders recognize at once that we are summoned as an organization to do a large work. At present the total membership of the American Associations is less than 750,000 and we have found that it is a truly great undertaking to serve them. Suddenly, we are confronted with the task of helping to promote the physical, mental, and spiritual welfare of an even greater number of men and that under most difficult conditions. We are summoned also to do a thorough work as well as an extensive work. Why should we not aspire to make this the finest piece of unselfish and constructive service which our Associations have ever rendered? When we think of our vast equipment and financial resources, our trained leadership, our vital relationship to the Churches whose servants we are, the extensive and fruitful experience which the American Associations have had in the Spanish War and in the recent work on the Mexican border, as well as in the large numbers of training camps and prisoner-of-war camps in Europe, Asia, and Africa—when we think of all this, does not the country have the right to expect that we will do a more efficient and fruitful work in the task now before us than we have hitherto accomplished? To this end, we are summoned to do a united work. There is so much to do, the difficulties are so many and so great, and the time at the longest will be so short that no effort and strength should be lost through divided counsels or lack of concerted plans.

As soon as practicable after the general military policy of the government was announced, a special conference of Association leaders was summoned and held on April 10 at Garden City, Long Island. Because of the shortness of the time in which the gathering had to be assembled, it was impossible to insure the presence of delegates from the most remote parts of the country but the personnel included a thoroughly representative body of the local, state, and international executive officers of the Movement. Nearly all the principal local and state organizations were represented and likewise the various departments of the International Committee. Those who were present regard the day thus spent together as a truly momentous occasion. After full discussion we were able to formulate and arrive at a unanimous agreement upon the following:

PREAMBLE

The Young Men's Christian Associations, with the approval of the government of the United States and with the co-operation of the officers of the army and navy, during the past nineteen years (including the periods of the Spanish-American War and the mobilization upon the Mexican border) have helpfully served the men of the army and navy. The Associations are also doing a large and successful work in the armies of Europe, Asia, and Africa and among the prisoners of war. Inasmuch as we now face the concentration in the United States of large bodies of men in training and mobilization camps as well as a large increase of the regular army and navy, therefore, be it

Resolved:

1. That the Young Men's Christian Association Movement of America should undertake, in a comprehensive and united way, to promote the physical, mental, social, and spiritual welfare of the one million and more men of the military and naval forces of the United States, and in doing this the Associations should continue to co-operate with other civic, social, philanthropic, and religious movements. They should also particularly seek to strengthen the hands of the Chaplains' Corps and to serve the Churches.

2. That there should be raised a fund of at least $3,000,000 to meet the necessary expenses involved in serving the men of the army and navy in state and national camps during the year 1917, and that a War Work Council of Young Men's Christian Associations, responsible to the International Committee, should undertake, with the co-operation of the state committees, the raising of this fund during the next thirty days.

    a. The War Work Council should distribute responsibility among the various states, cities, and districts for raising the necessary funds.

    b. The War Work Council should mobilize the Association forces, international, state, and local, in raising the funds and conducting the work contemplated.

    c. The War Work funds and accounts should be kept separate from those of the International and state committees.

    d. The War Work Council, in consultation with the state committees and International Committee, should prepare a budget and apportion, upon an equitable basis, the funds received. The Council should also establish an accounting and audit system for all expenditures of the War Work funds.

3. That the Associations should augment greatly their efforts on behalf of men and boys in the industries which are so essential to the military and naval success of the United States and the Allied countries.

4. That the American Associations should continue their practical and helpful service in the prisoner-of-war and training camps in

the war zones of Europe, Asia, and Africa, calling for an estimated budget this year of $2,000,000.

5. That the Association Movement should enlarge its plans so as to minister to interned aliens on lines followed in the prisoner-of-war camps abroad.

6. That the Associations be called upon to do all in their power to promote studies in citizenship and to inspire men and boys with true patriotism and in so doing to emphasize the principles of international good will and of the Kingdom of God, on which alone an enduring world order can be based.

7. That, in view of the unusual demands now confronting the young manhood of our nation, the Associations should redouble their efforts to make available their organization, leadership, and equipment in developing young men and boys in character, physical vitality, and mental efficiency.

The foregoing recommendations drawn up in this informal and unofficial Conference were intended as recommendations to the International Committee as well as to the various state and local Associations. The following day the Army and Navy Committee of the International Committee which has from the beginning furnished such indispensable leadership in all Association work on behalf of the army and navy, gave full consideration to the principal suggestions. They drew up resolutions and on the following day, April 12, presented them at a largely attended meeting of the International Committee. This business was made the order of the day and after thorough discussion the International Committee adopted the following resolutions:

1. That the International Committee appoint a War Work Council of at least 100 men which shall formulate and carry out plans for the service to be rendered by the Association Movement among the men in the United States Army and Navy and likewise deal with other important phases of the Association opportunity and responsibility in the United States occasioned by the war. This Council shall be directly responsible to the International Committee and report to it from month to month.

2. That the War Work Council be instructed to make an effort to secure in the near future a fund of at least $3,000,000 for the carrying out of its purposes and plans for the year 1917.

It is urgently important that the entire fund be subscribed during the next thirty days. It is hoped that, so far as possible, it will be made payable before July 1, but where absolutely necessary subscriptions could be paid in part or in full as late as October 1.

We assume that it is not necessary to emphasize that this whole undertaking should be a pronouncedly Christian and spiritual undertaking, because were it otherwise it would be without interest and appeal to all true Association leaders. Let us humbly, yet earnestly, desire and resolve to render a finer and more unselfish service to Christ and the Churches than ever before through bringing all our agencies and means to bear in a prompt, efficient, and truly worthy way upon the lives of the one million and more young men who are gathering under the colors.

Very sincerely yours,

JOHN R. MOTT,
General Secretary, International Committee of
Young Men's Christian Associations

EXTRACTS FROM THE MINUTES OF THE FIRST MEETING OF THE WAR WORK COUNCIL, HELD IN NEW YORK CITY, APRIL 28, 1917

Mr. Sloane, Chairman of the Army and Navy Department of the International Committee, called the meeting to order and asked Mr. Messer of Chicago to lead in prayer.

Mr. Sloane stated that there had been many historic meetings of the Association but that there would probably be none of greater significance than this. The Association today was confronted with the greatest opportunity of its existence and judging from past experience, as well as from the developments of the past few days, the opportunity was going to be met successfully. Today, while this meeting was being held here, our Congress at Washington was considering measures which would transform the young men of the nation into a vast army. These young men represented unparalleled opportunity and need for the Association. In this national and Association crisis the Association Movement was fortunate in having at its head a general secretary who commanded the fullest confidence, not only of the whole country but of the government at Washington as well. At this point, Mr. Sloane called on Dr. Mott, who was asked to report on the steps which had been taken leading up to the appointment of the War Work Council, and outline the proposed organization.

Dr. Mott stated that when it was seen that the break with the Central Powers was inevitable it became clear that this would mean a greatly increased responsibility for the Association. Within a few hours after the formal rupture of diplomatic relations, a telegram had been sent to the President tendering him the support and co-operation of the Association Movement. A few days later a visit was made to the Secretary of War and to the Secretary of the Navy, and pledges were made of our readiness to co-operate to the fullest extent. It was gratifying that Association leaders all over the country assumed the same patriotic attitude, and immediately scores of letters came in to the International Committee with offers of co-operation and with suggestions in regard to the practical service which the Association could render. In order to make possible the largest service to the country, and to avoid unnecessary duplication and loss of effort, it was the sense of all that a conference of the most accessible leaders should be held to study the situation and to determine what steps should be taken to meet the need and opportunity. It was at once seen that unless the Association forces could get together the work could not be efficiently done. But if all the state, local, and international forces would unite, and thus speak with one voice to the country and to the government as well as to the Association's constituency, then the unique opportunity confronting the Movement could be successfully met.

The International Committee seemed to be the natural body to call the leaders together and there was held at Garden City, Long Island, on April 10, a meeting of the most available leaders of the state, local, and international work. At this conference it was decided to recommend to the International Committee the appointment of a War Work Council representing the whole Movement, with full authority to organize and carry forward a war work program that would fully meet the need of the nation in this world crisis.

The Army and Navy Committee of the International Committee considered carefully the proposals of the informal conference at Garden City and made three specific recommendations to the International Committee. The International Committee, at a largely attended meeting, adopted these recommendations and appointed the suggested War Work Council, naming at first 104 laymen. The printed letter giving these resolutions and the names of the men appointed has been seen by all those present. It was gratifying that, out of the 104 persons appointed, only four had declined to accept. This meeting today was the first session of this War Work Council.

Dr. Mott stated that he was sure they would all be glad to know that, parallel with this work which we are called upon to do in the United States, we would continue to carry on abroad the unique service which the Association was rendering to the soldiers at the front, in the training camps, and in the prisoner-of-war camps. This work would not at present come under the jurisdiction of this War

Work Council, though who could tell when the two would have to be united!

In counsel with various members of the new War Work Council and with other Association leaders, it was recognized that we ought to act immediately, without waiting for the formal meeting and organization of the Council, and not to let the present opportunity slip. So, pending a meeting of the War Work Council, advances had been made along a number of lines. For example, there had been constituted the nucleus of the Finance Committee, several secretaries had been provisionally called to serve the war work, and groups of workers had outlined plans and programs for carrying on the various activities. These would all be reported today in detail and the action taken was subject in all cases to the approval of the War Work Council.

Conference had also been had with the government, including the President and the Secretary of War. Dr. Mott stated that he had had two interviews with the President and that it was difficult to express too strongly the President's appreciation of the Association and of the work to be undertaken.

Dr. Mott then read the following letter just received from the President:

THE WHITE HOUSE, WASHINGTON, April 25, 1917

MY DEAR DOCTOR MOTT:

May I not, in view of the approaching meeting of the War Work Council, express to you the very high value I have attached to the work which has been accomplished by the Young Men's Christian Association in behalf of our own army and navy as well as in behalf of the prisoners of war and the men in the training camps of Europe, and may I not express also my sincere personal interest in the large plans of the War Work Council for the work which is still ahead of the Association?

Cordially and faithfully yours,

(Signed) WOODROW WILSON

Another matter was in regard to the status of Association workers in the mobilization of the young men of the country. It was desired that the hundreds of young men who would be called to the service of the Association should not appear as slackers or be regarded as trying to evade military obligations. Here again the President gave an expression to his keen appreciation of the importance and value of the Association work and an official order is shortly expected. As this order defining the status of secretaries engaged in Association war work has not yet been promulgated, however, Mr. Mott requested that the matter be regarded as confidential.

At this point Mr. Tichenor was asked to report on recent negotiations with the Secretary of War. He stated that Secretary Baker had recently appointed a Committee on Training Camp Activities, naming as chairman Mr. Raymond B. Fosdick and making Dr. Mott a member of the committee, with the understanding that when Dr. Mott could not attend meetings Mr. Tichenor would act as his proxy. As a result of the investigations and recommendations of this committee, the Secretary of War had decided to turn over to the Association the recreational activities in the training camps. Many other organizations were trying to get into these camps, but the Secretary of War stated that he had decided to have only the Association.

PLAN OF ORGANIZATION

Dr. Mott stated briefly the plan suggested for the formal organization of the War Work Council.

FINANCE BUREAU

Dr. Mott explained that one of the things which it had been necessary to do in advance of this first meeting of the council was to secure a director and comptroller for the Finance Bureau. A call had been extended to Mr. Whitford, General Secretary at Buffalo, to become the director of the Finance Bureau and to Mr. Hammond, General Secretary at the Bedford Branch, Brooklyn, to become comptroller.

REPORT OF THE DIRECTOR

Mr. Whitford presented the following report, which, after discussion, was unanimously adopted:

The Bureau of Finance of the War Work Council is responsible for

1. the promotion of the nationwide canvass for the $3,000,000 fund;
2. the general supervision of the collection of the funds and the forwarding of funds to the headquarters of the War Work Council;
3. the conduct and control of the financial operations of the War Work Council as represented by financial records and disbursements.

RELIGIOUS WORK BUREAU

Mr. Wilder, Senior Secretary of the Religious Work Department of the International Committee, reported on the religious work to be carried on in the camps. All phases of Association activities were important, but none were so important as those related to meeting the moral and spiritual needs of the soldiers. To be convinced of this one had only to read the recent report which Dr. Exner had prepared and published on conditions in and surrounding the camps along the Mexican border. As senior secretary of the Religious Work Department, he had consulted with Dr. Mott as well as with a group of Church leaders and a program of activities had been worked out, including religious meetings, united prayer, Bible study, music, quiet rooms for personal devotion, Bible circulation, camp visitors from among clergymen, Christian workers, etc. He called attention to the remarkable success which had followed the use of the War Roll in England, where he had been related to the religious work of the Association in the British army. The War Roll was composed of those who pledged themselves to serve, not only their King and their country, but God and Christ as well. Tens of thousands had signed this Roll, including not only the soldiers but members of their families at home.

RESOLUTIONS ADOPTED AT THE JOINT COMMITTEE MEETING OF REPRESENTATIVES OF THE FEDERAL COUNCIL OF THE CHURCHES OF CHRIST IN AMERICA AND OF THE WAR WORK COUNCIL OF THE YOUNG MEN'S CHRISTIAN ASSOCIATIONS
PRINCETON CLUB, APRIL 21, 1917

I

That the committee responsible for choosing the men to direct Association work in the camps and the committee responsible for choosing the chaplains shall take such steps as may be necessary to acquaint new workers, both Association secretaries and chaplains, with the relationships which should exist between them to insure the best results.

II

That the practice of regular and thorough conference on the part of the chaplains and the Association secretaries in the different camps regarding matters of common concern be encouraged and promoted.

III

That the Administrative Committee of the Federal Council and the War Work Council of the Young Men's Christian Associations shall each appoint a conference committee of five men to meet as occasion may require to insure the best understanding.

Upon motion the foregoing resolutions were adopted by the Council and the Chairman was given authority to name a conference committee of five men to meet and co-operate with a similar committee from the Federal Council.

REPORT OF THE NOMINATING COMMITTEE

At the opening of the afternoon session the Chairman called for a report of the Nominating Committee, which submitted the following nominations:

OFFICERS

Chairman, William Sloane
Vice-Chairman, William Fellowes Morgan
Treasurer, Cleveland H. Dodge
Assistant Treasurer, (To be chosen by the Finance Committee and Treasurer)
Recording Secretary, Walter T. Diack
General Secretary, John R. Mott
Associate General Secretaries, Fletcher S. Brockman, John S. Tichenor, Charles R. Towson

EXECUTIVE COMMITTEE

William Sloane, Chairman
William Fellowes Morgan, Vice-Chairman
Richard M. Colgate
Lewis A. Crossett
Walter T. Diack
Cleveland H. Dodge
Ralph W. Harbison
John Sherman Hoyt
William G. Low, Jr.
George W. Perkins
Harold Pratt
John L. Severance
W. P. Sidley
F. Louis Slade

CO-OPERATING COMMITTEE

Dr. Peter Ainslee, Baltimore, Maryland
Dr. Clarence A. Barbour, Rochester, New York
Dean Charles R. Brown, New Haven, Connecticut
Bishop Charles S. Burch, New York, New York
Dr. S. Parkes Cadman, Brooklyn, New York

Bishop Earl Cranston, Washington, D. C.
Dr. S. H. Greene, Washington, D. C.
Bishop Eugene R. Hendrix, Kansas City, Missouri
Bishop William Lawrence, Boston, Massachusetts
President W. D. Mackenzie, Hartford, Connecticut
Dr. Wm. H. Roberts, Philadelphia, Pennsylvania
Dr. Robert E. Speer, New York, New York
President J. Ross Stevenson, Princeton, New Jersey
Dr. J. Timothy Stone, Chicago, Illinois
Dr. George W. Truett, Dallas, Texas
Dr. James I. Vance, Nashville, Tennessee
Bishop Luther B. Wilson, New York, New York

Signed: WILLIAM SLOANE, *Chairman*
JOHN R. MOTT, *General Secretary*
G. I. BABCOCK, *Temporary Recording Secretary*

124 EAST 28TH STREET, NEW YORK

THE OPPORTUNITY OF THE HOUR IN RUSSIA AND OTHER COUNTRIES OF EUROPE

ADDRESS BY JOHN R. MOTT AT THE BOSTON CITY CLUB, OCTOBER 11, 1917

Mr. Chairman and Gentlemen:

Our attention has been directed in language both moving and adequate, to those great unbroken lines of devotion and sacrifice, even unto death, lines bound into the lives of doubtless every one of us by bonds of kindred or affection or common service, lines that will yet expand again and again through these coming momentous months.

It has been my duty seriously to study at very close range this ever enlarging host of enlisted men of the various warring nations. Since the war began I have made four extended journeys to the warring countries, three of which took me to the nations of both sides of the struggle. Those multitudes of men and boys—I say boys advisedly, because some of these armies in the early stages, and some in the later stages, have reminded me more of boys than of men— these multitudes of men and boys are with me by day and by night. Often I find myself awakened with reflections concerning what I have seen and experienced, as I have put my life, not professionally, I trust, but sympathetically, alongside of the lives of our brothers in our own and in other armies and navies.

When I returned from my first journey to those fighting countries I stated that there were 17,000,000 men and boys under arms. When you recall that in no previous war have more than 2,000,000 men been lined up against each other in aggressive warfare, the colossal dimensions of this struggle even at that time, December, 1914, were apparent. When I came back from the next journey I stated that the number under the colors of these fighting nations had expanded to between 26,000,000 and 27,000,000. I returned only recently from my fourth journey, and in my judgment the number of men now in the various arms of the services of these nations, excluding the terrific losses that have tinged the intervening months, is more nearly 40,000,000 than 35,000,000. I think I could show that they number at least 38,000,000. Again I remind you that in no previous war have more than 2,000,000 men been arrayed against each other in combat. Here are nearly twenty times as many still under these colors.

Who are these men? They are the flower of the strongest nations of Europe, northern Africa, southern Asia, Australasia, and North America. Whom do they represent? They represent populations which aggregate two-thirds of the human race. How are they chosen? By the two most rigid selective processes to which men are ever subjected, one of which is the process of conscription—and some of us know what that meant on the Continent, and we know what it means in its best form and process in our own country in these days. There has been nothing like it in the history of nations. The other process is the working of the voluntary principle and that has been working in every nation, and where you would least expect it. For example, at the end of my first journey to Germany since the war began I was told that the number of men and boys there who had already volunteered, in addition to those conscripted, was over 1,600,000. Say what you or I may in a depreciative sense of any other nation now at war, we cannot lay at the doors of this fighting nation the charge of disloyalty or lack of devotion to the cause, even unto death.

Where are these men? Our attention has been called to one line of them in that great arc of field and human blood that reaches from the English Channel 360 miles to the Swiss mountains. I see that line now as I have touched it at different points before; and I see today that steadily and startlingly waving line on the eastern front, stretching from the Baltic down to the Carpathians and across the plains of Armenia, and on again into the Caucasus. I see that zigzag line which has been worked at what a cost, up and down the Austrian and Italian Alps. I see that more attenuated line that skirts the Suez Canal and is pushed across the Arabian Desert today almost up to the gates of Jerusalem. I see that giant wedge that has been driven into the heart of the Balkan States, and from which we shall hear much more in these coming months. I see another wedge, with its dripping, bloody point that has been crowded across the mud plains of Mesopotamia, and in these days even pushed upon Baghdad toward us. And behind these unending trenches, first, second, third, and communicating trenches, in many hundreds of reserve or depot camps, I see yet other millions ready to go into their first struggle, or their tenth struggle, or their thirtieth battle. Behind these, in countless garrison cities and towns that I have visited in peaceful country retreats, in city parks, I see other millions in preparation, and I see countless battleships, cruisers, destroyers, submarines, navy yards, and naval reserves, and countless hundreds of thousands of men in these other arms of the service on which we so much depend.

These tens of millions I have mingled with, and I think I know them. If I were asked to describe them I would say that all of these men are serious, none of them more so than the men who try to give you the opposite impression. I would say, likewise, of those men, that they are more free from cant and hypocrisy than any other bodies of men on earth. They have stripped off the veneer. They see things as they are. They are dealing with realities. They have counted the cost. They are ready to pay it. I would say, also, of these men that they are needy, none more so than those who at first might not admit it. They have their physical needs, and there are some physical needs that even our most generous government cannot adequately supply, and they well know it. These men also have mental needs. Oh, the tragedy of the mental anguish of multitudes of men at the front today, judging by the lists I see and the questionnaires they use in some of these armies, of men who without wise guidance, put up in front of this present situation, and with the prices they are paying, are unable to answer their own questions! Then, there are the moral and spiritual needs. One of the great writers has said that there are in each man heights not only that lay hold of highest heaven, but also depths that lay hold of deepest hell. I have looked down into the darkest abyss of moral collapse and despair among men of these different countries, and, thank God, I have followed these men up into the greatest heights of attainment in character with which I am familiar among young men of our generation. These men today are accessible in every army of the many fighting nations, unless it be the Turkish army, and I hope soon that that will be open. Not only so, but in each of these nations the men are responsive—oh, how responsive—wherever the hand of sympathy and brotherhood and comradeship is extended to them.

When our own country came to the break with Germany, that very day I sent a telegram to President Wilson, placing at his disposal all the leadership and organization and facilities of the Young Men's Christian Association. A few days later I went to Washington to see him, and the Secretary of War and the Secretary of the Navy, and reassured them in explicit terms of our desire to serve these men in every way in our power. The President and these two secretaries told me that we should get ready for large things. But no man in those days in April said to me that we should be serving more than 1,000,000 men by Christmas. So, with our Mexican border experience in mind, where it had cost us on the average three dollars a man to serve the men eight months, we said, "We need in round figures $3,000,000," and lodged the appeal with the American people who never fail us. But they knew our requirements better than we, apparently by intuition, because they responded with subscriptions that aggregated more nearly $5,000,000. They were right, because within a few days we shall have expended virtually that entire sum, and that on the American troops of both arms of the service on this side of the water.

We were told we might be serving by Christmas at the maximum 1,000,000 men in uniform and under the colors of our army, but actually we are serving more nearly 1,500,000 such men, and we are not yet at the end of the year. We have nearly three months left. Nobody told us that we should probably have to be serving many of our men over in France by January 1, 1918. It is not for me even to hint at military secrets today; but I could say that the number of our men now in France and England is far greater than most people realize, and the number will rapidly increase. Of this there is no question whatever. Thus, we have suddenly been called upon to face up, in rendering an adequate service to this much larger number of our men and boys. If there are two more calls of the draft by next July as most leaders think there may be, we shall be ministering to over 2,500,000 American soldiers and sailors. We would not be wise, in the judgment of the best military and naval advisers, to get ready for anything less than this.

This means that we have to gather a fund for expenditure among America's troops on this side of the Atlantic alone before next July of $11,000,000; and for the men who will be overseas, for the same period, a fund of not less than $12,000,000; or a total of $23,000,000, to serve what will be a maximum, perchance, of 2,500,000 men. Someone says, "That figures out about ten dollars a man." Yes, it does. But nobody who has examined what we have been called upon to do by the military and naval authorities of our nation, who know the facts, would have us pare this down by a single dollar. If any man is skeptical, let him examine the range of the needs that we are obliged to meet among these men; let him examine the variety of the agencies that we must place at their disposal; let him remind himself, likewise, of the purpose which has rallied these men under our colors; let him also recall the motive which animates these men; and, above all, let him remember the spirit which leads these men, without complaint and without reservation, to dedicate their lives, even unto death, for us; and where is the man so small that he will say to spend anything less than ten dollars on any one of these men?

After what I have seen in the trenches, and in these camps; after what I have heard in the homes from which these men have gone, never will you see me listen without bitter protest to anybody who would hint at economies in this great and unselfish service. Happily, I do not find the people who suggest it.

This is a great undertaking. But I remind you that on top of this we have had other great burdens of responsibility placed upon us that we cannot escape, and that we do not wish to escape. I have just returned from Russia, and I deeply resent certain imputations and strictures and charges being made in this country by good patriots of the United States with reference to Russia. I detect an element of impatience and of quick and hasty judgment and of criticism concerning our ally, Russia. That is not the way to treat an ally. The time of times to be true to an ally is in the darkest hour of that ally's life. What nation have you ever read about or seen that simultaneously had to deal with these four processes: In the first place, to engage in the greatest war the world has ever known. Surely Russia has done that. She has maintained her line there now for over three years, alone. She has not had, as the splendid army of France has had, at one elbow, England, Canada, Australia, and now the United States, and at the other elbow, Italy. There she has stood, alone, in great isolation. In the second place, she has been engaged in the greatest political revolution of modern times. I think of none greater in ancient or middle times. A revolution that has swung them from an extreme, a dark and cruel autocracy, out into the full stream of a democratic republic. In the third place, she has been occupied with the most bewildering and remarkable social revolution which has ever engaged any nation. I make no exception. Russia today with easy hand is laying hold of the most obstinate social facts, which have baffled other nations which she is putting to shame—the United States,

France, England, and Germany—in her courageous and fearless treatment of these social problems. Be she misguided, as she may be with reference to her suggested remedies for some of the evils, she is yet squarely facing them. In the fourth place, contrary to general knowledge, Russia is now in the midst of the most striking religious revolution which has swept over any great people since the Reformation—a revolution which I see clearly is bringing religious tolerance for Jew, Protestant, Catholic, and Mohammedan, as well as the Greek Orthodox—a revolution that is democratizing even the great Greek Orthodox Church, which was so recently the instrument of autocracy. I have no disposition to criticize a nation that is simultaneously dealing with all those four things. Our country is finding its hands filling up fast with the first of them. It does not become any of us to speak uncharitably with reference to a nation that must deal with all of them.

But, you say, what about the Russian army and navy? Well, it is the greatest that has ever been assembled. They have called since the war began 16,200,000. I frankly admit that the Russian army today, and the Russian navy, have shown signs, and still show signs of demoralization. But I am not at all surprised, and you will not be after I have mentioned the causes for the demoralization of the Russian army and navy. As I mention these things, ask yourselves this question, what army is there on earth that would not be demoralized if it had to deal with all of these causes? Now, notice them. In the first place, war-tiredness. The Russian army and navy are tired. Every army and navy save those of America are now war-tired. They don't disguise the fact when you talk with them. The Russian army and navy have a right to be tired. They have lain in the trenches in the Pripet marshes and the neighboring network of marshes along that whole front, and along the plains that are before Galicia and those inaccessible heights of the Carpathians, in the trenches of the Caucasus, and in the tablelands of Rumania, and they have laid away already over 3,000,000 Russian men and boys who have given up their lives. They have had 2,000,000 so shattered by wounds and diseases that they can never fight again. You see those men everywhere, all over Russia. They have 2,500,000 other men who are today languishing in the prison war camps of Germany, Bulgaria, Turkey, and Austria, many of which I have visited in the last two years. There is scarcely a Russian home I visited, all across ancient Russia or Siberia, across which the dark shadow has not fallen at least once since this war began. I say Russia has a right to be tired, and the Russians are not hypocrites enough to say that they are not.

In the second place, this war is working into their minds the consciousness and the certain knowledge that they have been betrayed by their government in high places. Before the line broke, at least three war ministries betrayed their men at the front and on the waters. When I was in Russia on one of my visits one war ministry had passed the word down that they were not to shoot more than two shells per gun per day, although they had ample ammunition in reserve, and although the men were put up against German batteries that at that time were shooting more than 3,600 shells per day. My friend, Dr. Hurd, who was among the Russian armies at that time, told me the other day, coming back on the cruiser from the expedition on which President Wilson sent us to Russia, that he had seen 100,000 men go into a fight and only 10,000 come out alive. He told me that multitudes of these men, without ammunition, had put their bodies up against some of the finest artillery that was then in the war. Do you wonder, when things like these are true and when such things happened, that there has come into the great Russian army distrust and uncertainty, and therefore weakness and collapse? They would be less than human if such were not the case.

Notice a third cause of this demoralization. The minds of the Russian soldiers and sailors have been flooded with the most fascinating ideas that can come into men's minds—the ideas of the Russian revolution. We cannot very well put ourselves into the position those men were in before the revolution, even those of us who visited Russia in the old days. We cannot take this in. But I think we may imagine it. Suppose there had come to millions of men in this country for the first time ideas like light instead of darkness. Well have the Russians been called a dark people; they are 80 per cent illiterate. Suddenly there comes noonday light, and every man now is to have an education. What an alluring thought. Notice also, that the idea of liberty instead of slavery has been put into their minds. Slavery is a weak word with which to characterize the situation under the autocracy, because they had ostensible liberty, but only in name, and not the form and not the reality. Now they hear the shackles breaking at their feet in pieces, never to be re-formed. Then notice this idea: plenty instead of poverty. What do those two ideas not connote to every one of us who has been in Russia? And now, to think that they are to have plenty—these men who have felt grinding poverty, multitudes who have not known what it was to have one satisfying meal a day. You fill their minds suddenly with all of these ideas, and is it strange that they are bewildered and that they are responsive to them?

On top of these, let me mention the main cause of the demoralization of the Russian army and navy—the masterly German intrigue propaganda. I use the word "masterly" with reflection. There has been nothing like it, and I hope there will be nothing like it again. But we do well to sit at their feet in point of thoroughness in dealing with the psychological factor in war, notwithstanding all their blunders. The day the Russian line broke in Russia not hundreds, but thousands of German emissaries were on hand. Many were right there in Finland. I saw them. A year ago last summer I saw them —because they were there then. There were many more than some have thought. Many more than we thought were in Sweden. And, incongruous as it seems to you today, many were right in the trenches —all fraternizing; and there were many other thousands already in Russia. Now notice. The line breaks; the death penalty is immediately abolished all over Russia. Every policeman, from the Atlantic to the Pacific Ocean, is discharged, and 180,000,000 start on a great, long holiday. The Germans are there, with some of their wisest leaders. They have millions at their disposal. They buy up the newspapers. They start other papers. They circulate tens of millions of pamphlets and leaflets. I have in my office leaflets that they fired with the guns over into the trenches.

They had hundreds of skilled and able speakers. I went down one day on the streets of Petrograd and with the help of a few friends counted 200 meetings being held. There was a small gathering here, being addressed by one of these German emissaries, and a small gathering farther on, and crowds lining the street until we came to the park, where there were nine or ten thousand people.

We had a skilled interpreter, who moved among these groups, and brought back to me samples of the kind of things that were being spread in their minds — such arguments as these: "Germany fought you when you had the Czar. You have abolished the Czar. Why fight longer? Why not be brothers?" Or, this idea, which they were spreading in all of these meetings: "The land is now going to be divided. These great estates are going to be given up. Why don't you get home and take your share?" At one time an assistant minister of Russia told me that there were 2,000,000 men who had not deserted, but who took home leave. Notice this idea: They said in all of these meetings, and they are saying it still in Russia, that this is a war of the capitalists of England and France, and that that is the main reason why the United States has come in; that some of these main agitators, hundreds of them, came into Russia not from Finland or Germany, but from the United States of America, many of them with American passports.

I ask you, with causes like these working, is it surprising that the Russian army crumbles, and crumples? I should not believe my intellectual processes if it were not so. And I say it is our fault if we permit these processes to go on without doing what it is obvious we should do.

The mission on which I went to Russia, of which Senator Root was the chairman, and General Scott, late Chief of Staff of the army, and others were members, was a diplomatic mission. It is not fitting that I should speak today of that mission. We did not go on a religious mission. But we had not gone far before we found this demoralization of the army, and, regardless of our religious views, we came unanimously to the conclusion, that what the Russian army and navy needs is that which the Young Men's Christian Association is supplying in the American, English, and Canadian armies. That was our unanimous conclusion. So, by the time we reached Petrograd, Senator Root said, "Mr. Mott, I want you to take this up with the authorities, military, naval, and civil, in Russia, and likewise with the ecclesiastical leaders." Before we got to Petrograd, we found that some of our discerning American secretaries, whom we had had over there for three years working among the enemy prisoners, not being able to stand it any longer, seeing this demoralization and knowing the Association principles, had said, "We must see if we cannot do something in this army," so that in places as far removed as Turkestan in the south, Petrograd on the north, and Siberia on the eastern front, they were trying out their plans. I have brought here with me the report of an interview of one of these young Americans, twenty-four years old, from one of our American colleges, who went over there. I want to read you this. We came to the Winter Palace one day, where our mission was entertained, that palace in front of which the cannon were trained on the thousands of peasants when they came forward that Christmas holiday, and where their blood flowed crimson—in that palace we were lodged, with the red flag of the revolution above it, and there I had my conferences with the soldiers and the officers. A soldier, who came all the way from Turkestan, wanted to see me, but I was out, and one of our attaches took down his conversation, the substance of which I will now read:

INTERVIEW WITH BASIL MILES, SECRETARY OF THE SPECIAL DIPLOMATIC MISSION, FORMERLY IN CHARGE OF EMBASSY RELIEF WORK IN RUSSIA, WITH THE RUSSIAN PRIVATE SOLDIER, STEMPACH, OF THE ARMY OF TURKESTAN

On June 20, Mr. Stempach came to the Winter Palace with a letter from the office of the Young Men's Christian Association, explaining that he had been in Turkestan and knew about the work being done there by the Young Men's Christian Association secretary, D. A. Davis.

Since about March 1, Mr. Davis has been working with Russian soldiers. In three months he has got in touch with 25,000 men. Stempach states that the organization of games, movies, theatricals, lectures, classes, etc., is so well-established that it needs only intermittent attention from Mr. Davis. Headquarters are at Tashkend and other centers are Samarkand, Bokhara, Andijan, Chernaieff, Kanshaka, etc. Mr. Davis organized Russian general committees, with subcommittees for each regiment. They have organized sports and games, four grades of classes commencing with grammar, reading, and writing, private theatricals, lectures, moving pictures, and welfare work. Of the 25,000 men in Turkestan, Stempach stated that the regimental committees had been able to make attendance and participation compulsory.

Stempach volunteered the statement that because of this work he believed the discipline of the army of Turkestan was the best in revolutionary Russia.

When questioned, Stempach seemed confident this work could be extended to the troops in European Russia, and suggested that as Turkestan no longer required Mr. Davis' permanent attention, he might commence work in Russia. Mr. Davis now speaks pretty good Russian.

By this you see what can be done in the entire Russian army. The general in command in Turkestan was so much impressed with what had been done in our army that he sent our man to Petrograd to get permission to spread this work along the whole front. Similar experiments had been tried in Petrograd and Siberia. I took the matter up with the Foreign Minister, also with the Prime Minister, and also with the then Minister of War, Kerensky, the present Prime Minister. He is a genuine, a very magnetic man, of remarkable personality, a man who draws you, even though you do not understand Russian and he does not understand English, a man who in his person has been able to combine the divergent and warring parties of the Left, and who has carried that country through an almost impossible stage. I don't suppose he is a man who is equipped to do the building work that is required with the constituent assembly a few months later; but he is a man who ought to have our prayers, and may God help us to stand by him. I likewise interviewed the Chief of the General Staff, and also the members of the Soldiers' and Deputies' Committee. They have that impossible plan of trying to run an army with committees, and they are finding out its impossibility. Then, I had countless conversations with individual soldiers. Nowhere did I find opposition or indifference concerning this plan; but everywhere these men, high and low, said, "We want the United States to place at our disposal the message and means of the Young Men's Christian Association."

Since returning from Russia I have received a cablegram saying that permission is now given on all the Russian fronts, Baltic, Galician, Rumanian, Armenian, and Caucasus, for our work. They still have over 7,000,000 soldiers, and of that number over 2,000,000 are on the line in the front trenches, 1,000,000 more are in the depots or reserves, 1,000,000 are in charge of these communications and supplies, and 3,000,000 are back in training, or on leave, or otherwise occupied, so that they are not immediately available for military purposes; making an army larger than the English and American armies combined, and there it is, wide open to us.

This cablegram says: "We want you to send 300 American secretaries, and provide at least $3,000,000 for this work."

I began to move for that as soon as I got that message. I sent a number by boat as soon as I got back, and I am looking for all the men I am able to get. I want every man here to be a pair of eyes and a pair of ears in helping to discover some of the strongest men in America for this service. We cannot take weak men for this. These men must have resourcefulness, great patience, indescribable enthusiasm, and sometimes technical knowledge, and a knowledge of how to serve men. Is there a man in this room, or a man living in New England, to whom you are going to report, who would say that we should say "No" to a cause like this on the request of our great ally, Russia? Do I need to tell you what it means? My friends, I am not a military man, and I am subject to being checked up right here, but I have had conversations with some of the leading military authorities among the attaches of Petrograd, as well as Russian officers; and if we can hold the Russian army in being, even if it does not fight another battle, what does that do? That occupies on that front over 150 divisions of the German, Austrian, and Hungarian armies, with the vast supporting agencies of transportation and supply, which means the keeping from our western and southern fronts of that many men. I don't think that military authority was wrong when he said to me, "Mr. Mott, I think it means the saving of 1,000,000 lives on those two fronts." I have said it to myself in this crude way, that here is a giant pair of pincers, clasping the middle powers. If we let one side fall in helpfulness and uselessness, we necessitate the re-shaping of the strategy of this war, and we push it away back— possibly not as far as the autumn of 1919—but we put it very much farther back than we thought we should need to. Of course this has a bearing on every American home, and on our Allies, and on the splendid influence of the Russian revolution. And I don't understand the men and women of means in New England, if they do not give on a scale the like of which we have never witnessed, for an object like this. Now is the time to do this thing. There are some things we can do next year, and the year after, but not this.

Just as I was confronted with this great opportunity from Russia, they brought in this cablegram from France, from that wonderful man, Ned Carter, formerly secretary of the Association at Harvard, who was our leader in India, and now on our whole Western front. He said, "Will you forward an appeal to America to send 500 American workers to spread the Young Men's Christian Association among the great French army of 4,000,000 men?"

I had to decide that question right then and there, with the people standing around me. Perhaps you will say I decided right. I said, "America will do all and more than France ever asks us to do." I forwarded that message to America and sent that word back to France. After I got back to this country I took that matter up, and we are going forward with it.

Let me read one or two things more about Russia that I have here. After we got back to this country this cablegram came, from one of the greatest religious leaders of Russia. After thanking me for a service I had been able to render at Moscow he said: "IT WOULD BE A GREAT THING IF TO THE RUSSIAN YOUTH SHOULD BE OPENED THE ADVANTAGES AND TRAINING OF THE YOUNG MEN'S CHRISTIAN ASSOCIATION AS IT EXISTS IN AMERICA. SEND MORE SECRETARIES TO RUSSIA. MAY GOD BLESS YOUR WORK.

[SIGNED] ANATOLY, BISHOP OF TOMSK"

The sender of that message is one of the three most influential religious workers in Russia, and that is from another communion.

Then, let me read this message, that came from the American Ambassador at Petrograd: "PERMISSION GRANTED TO WORK ON ALL THE FRONTS. WE NEED 300 WORKERS AND SUPPLIES, AND AT LEAST $3,000,000 FOR THE YEAR. THE WAR MINISTER SAYS THE ASSOCIATION WOULD CONSTITUTE A BIG STEP FORWARD IN THE LIFE OF THE SOLDIERS, AND THAT IT IS NEEDED EVERYWHERE IN RUSSIA."

Then General Scott, our late Chief of Staff, wrote me a letter from Washington, the day he got back from Russia:

I hope you will push the plan of spreading the work of the Young Men's Christian Association throughout the Russian army. For years I have been intimately acquainted with the good, practical work done by the Young Men's Christian Association in the United States Army and Navy. I have seen its helpful activities in the Philippines, in Cuba, on our Mexican border, and elsewhere. We could not have done without it. It has been managed in such a broad-minded and wise way that it has been well received by officers and enlisted men, whose views on other questions have differed materially. I have just seen much of its work on the German, Austrian, and Rumanian fronts, and also in many garrison towns of Russia and Siberia, and am convinced that the Association work should be immediately organized in this great army, in order to assure the contentment and efficiency of the men, to raise their morale, and to help counteract the propaganda of intrigue which is doing so much to unsettle them,

The Rumanian situation must not be forgotten. It is of tremendous importance. I hear good reports about your work in the French army. I am not surprised that General Pershing wishes to have it rapidly extended.

I need not emphasize the importance of your choosing the best-qualified men to take charge of this work in the armies of our Allies. They could render no greater service to our country and our cause, even from a military point of view, than to help build up and save the power of these millions of men, on whom the great strain comes. Such a work requires the best men you can find.

And yet how few people in the United States see the importance of this work. I would that we could see it. When I think of those ten splendid divisions on the Rumanian front, saving the flank, and see behind them the wheat fields, and beyond those the oil fields, I think, what good will the submarine destruction be, if Germany can count on acquiring those lands. Germany can count the submarine out, if she gets through there. The time has come for us to do this thing.

Referring again to France, I want to read you this letter from that country. It came a few days ago from our trusted secretary, Mr. D. A. Davis, a graduate of one of our eastern universities.

Yesterday Carter, Sayre, Coffin, and I had the great privilege of dining with the French Commander-in-Chief at the French headquarters. Several of the most important members of the general staff of the French army were present. At the luncheon and afterward I had the opportunity of explaining something about the work that we are doing for the soldiers, and the general in charge approved our plans for doing the Association work on a large scale for the French army in the name of the Young Men's Christian Association. This is something that we have been hoping and praying for since the beginning of the war, and something which, until very recently, has seemed like an almost impossible thing; yet this is another evidence of the way in which God is making the impossible happen in these days. The French general headquarters is going to supply us with a list of the places, in their order of importance, where the Young Men's Christian Association work should be established for French troops before winter. Instead of the 100 centers which we had hoped to open, we shall in all probability be called upon to organize over 1,000. At the same time, the French army is granting us every facility in the way of transporting and getting material and men for carrying on the work. I think, without any exaggeration, and with a consciousness of the great things which have opened in the Association world up to the present time, that yesterday was one of the red letter days.

General Pershing sent us this telegram. I have known him since the Philippine days, and I have always trusted him, and he has never

misled me. He says: "THE GREATEST SERVICE AMERICA CAN IMME-
DIATELY RENDER FRANCE IS TO EXTEND THE WORK TO THE ENTIRE
FRENCH ARMY. CONFIDENTIAL. RAISING MORALE OF FRENCH TROOPS
IS VITAL INTERNATIONAL NECESSITY."

Notice, he does not say, "raising the courage of the French troops
is a vital international necessity." Notice, he does not say, "raising
the devotion of the French troops to the point where they will be
willing to die for America and the Allies is of vital international necessity"; but, "raising the morale." It reminds me of what Senator Root
said the other day when we were seeing the President. He said,
"Mr. President, I noticed in Europe that there is something about
this modern trench warfare that depresses the spirits of men." That
set me to thinking, and I don't suppose I could better define the work
of the Young Men's Christian Association to the armies of our Allies
than to put it in this language: It is to be a ministry to the spirit of
man. Speaking of France reminds me of that great military leader,
the greatest genius in this way that France ever gave the world,
Napoleon. He said: "Morale in war is to other factors as three to
one."

I could say that the work of the Young Men's Christian Association as it pertains to those armies is to deal almost exclusively with
morale. The French have not had the recreational sports that the
English and Canadian soldiers have had, and the French military
officials, seeing what we are doing among our own soldiers, and what
is being done in the Canadian and English armies by the Young Men's
Christian Association, and noticing how the recreational sports help
to bring up the morale and the spirit of the men—seeing our countless entertainments, and, above all, our refreshing ministry to the
spirit of man, and how it restores the spirit and prolongs the ability
to bear strain, recognize its need in their armies. There is a reason
for this, and it is doubly impressive to me that we have been led into
it by the civil and military leaders, and not by the religious propa-
gandists. You would think this was enough. But I received this letter
the other day from Italy, also, from this trusted man Davis—not the
one I read about Russia, but the one we had in the beginning of this
war in the French army. This letter I think will amaze every man
here.

At the time when our work for American soldiers in France was just
beginning, the Marquise de Tallyrand, a lady who has helped us very much
in our work here in France, brought Prince Borghese of Italy to a building
to see me. As perhaps you know, the Prince Borghese belongs to one of
the oldest and most respected of the titled families in Italy and has a very
strong influence in political, religious, and social circles. He is very well
regarded by the clerical party.

Prince Borghese was intensely interested in the work and program of the Y.M.C.A. and said that this was just the kind of work that should be carried on for the Italian army. He wanted to know if we would be able to help him, in case he could get an opening for our work in Italy. I explained to him in some detail the efforts we had already made; how we had offered our service to the Italian War Ministry, how we had seen many important people in Rome and other cities, and that apparently our offer had been refused because of the name of our society and the fear that there would be some kind of propaganda back of our work. He said that he believed that he could convince the clerical authorities of the need for our work and induce them to ask us to undertake it on behalf of the Italian soldiers. The Prince was so much interested that he came back a second time just before leaving for Italy and urged that we do all we could to back him up in case he secured the support which he expected he could get in Rome.

I immediately wrote to Rideout regarding the conference we had had and asked him to call on the Prince after his return. I have just received a letter from Mr. Rideout in which I find the two following paragraphs:

"You will be pleased to learn that I visited the Prince by especial invitation on July 24, and that word just comes from him that he will call at our office tomorrow at 11:30 A.M., with other parties interested in the development of this new project. If the outlook continues as favorable as at present, larger and more important conferences will follow as rapidly as they can be arranged. Our office secretary has been very busy with an extra amount of correspondence since my return to Rome, and as a result we were unable to get this report off on last night's mail. I am therefore able to give you more information about the conference just held here at our office with Prince Borghese and Father Genocchi. Both of these gentlemen have been studying the question of how our Association can co-operate most efficiently in the welfare work already being conducted for the Italian army under the direction of the head chaplain, Doctor Giovanni Menozzi.

"Father Genocchi informs me that they already have 140 Casa del Soldato, in which this welfare work is being conducted, but that Doctor Menozzi would most cordially welcome our co-operation (which would be equally favored by the Government officials interested). Two forms of aid are especially needed: First, a few experienced American or English secretaries who could assist Chaplain Menozzi in the supervision and development of this work for the Italian soldiers in the 140 centers now occupied, and the others which should be developed at the earliest possible moment; second, funds to meet the increasing needs.

"Chaplain Menozzi will probably write you shortly. Possibly Father Genocchi also."

From this it seems that Prince Borghese, immediately on getting to Rome, took the initiative in getting in touch with Catholic authorities, and then with Mr. Rideout. Father Genocchi, who came with Prince Borghese to Mr. Rideout's office, is a man whom I have met several times when I have been in Rome, and who is very sympathetic indeed. He is the man who has translated the four Gospels and the book of Acts into modern Italian and has superintended the distribution of millions of copies of the Gospels to the Italian soldiers. He, with two or three other priests, was exiled from Italy under a former Pope because of their liberalism. At the present time he stands very high in the counsels of the Church.

Doctor Giovanni Menozzi I have also met, and it was regarding him that I wrote to you at the time of my last visit to Italy. I knew at that time that Doctor Menozzi was appointed by the government to create the Casa del Soldato, and the fact that he has already created 140 gives evidence of his activity and devotion.

If the Prince Borghese, Father Genocchi, and Doctor Menozzi, agree in asking the Association to send experienced secretaries to help in the direction of the Casa del Soldato that they have already established, and to help in opening new ones, I think we ought, by all means, to respond favorably to this request. I see in it large possibilities.

I was not back in a white night in Russia at that time, but I was where I could call together the War Work Council, including some of the leading men of this nation; and when I read them this, they said, "We do not see the money, but we see the omnipotent hand of God, leading America into a great service for a great ally who needs that service; and, although we do not see the money to authorize you to send a favorable reply we approve of it." But, to make dead sure that we were being led on wise lines, a delegation was sent to Italy, with Mr. Sayre, son-in-law of the President, as chairman, and Bishop Wilson of the Methodist Episcopal Church, Professor Burkett of Cambridge University, and three others as members, who visited the Italian front, and who had long interviews with the civil, military, and ecclesiastical authorities; and when they got back to France I received this cablegram: "On return from Italy of our Association men headed by Sayre, intendant General Zacco has telegraphed Sayre as follows: 'Inform you, have communicated your program to the Commander-in-Chief, who accepts the maximum co-operation of your Association.' Sayre proceeded to London to confer with Yapp, who McCowen says desires to co-operate on big scale. From England Sayre will proceed to New York and confer with you. Meanwhile, suggest you recruit strongest possible Italian-speaking personnel for prompt action on Sayre's appeal."

Last Sunday night on the Fall River boat, I rode with Mr. Sayre, who had just returned from Europe, and for five hours he detailed to me that fascinating report. I hardly could take it in that I had lived to see the day that, with full knowledge of the conditions and spirit of the work here in America, these civil, military, and ecclesiastical authorities of Italy should say to the Young Men's Christian Association of the United States, "Send us 200 secretaries, and finance this work."

Gentlemen, we have come into a new day. Old things have passed away. All things may become new, not as the result of magic, not as a matter of chance, but because those of you who have come together here today, and men whom you will fire with your conviction, have the requisite leadership and spirit of sacrifice to enable America to do these things.

Time fails me to speak of those fragments of armies which we must also serve if they are to be served at all. I refer to the men of that Belgian army who have tinged the sand dunes of their coast with their lifeblood on our behalf, as well as their own. I refer to that army in Egypt, which went forth on what people have later called a forlorn hope. It can never be called that. Imperishable glory goes to those men who poured out their blood in Mesopotamia. I speak of that army which fought back the Germans in Serbia. I speak of that Rumanian army, which at one time received the brunt of the German attack. And I speak of other armies of our Allies. I would speak with fullest heart of the British, Australian, and Canadian armies, were it necessary; but they have found it possible, of their own resources, to spread the Young Men's Christian Association without our help, saving the loan of some of our leaders to all of their armies.

I must not forget the prisoners of war. Forget them, Mr. Chairman? I say the truth when I say that they are with me always. I visited many of these camps, where first I found 700,000 prisoners, on my next trip 3,400,000, on my next trip 4,500,000, and on the next trip over 6,000,000. They are there, in the midst of conditions that I do not attempt to describe. But I would remind you of what we are doing for those men. I see that graveyard identified by the crosses. I see that long row between the two armies, where for three miles on each side of the road are long, unbroken lines of graves. I see that marsh that I told some of you about—and these places are not all on one side of this war—where the men were forced through long months to build that railway, and where they worked in water up to their waists, and without the vegetables and acid for their food the scurvy broke out among them; and, as I look through there, I see their eyes sinking back, and their teeth falling out, and, strong men as they were, I see them crying like children. It has been almost bringing life into the dead to make these things physically possible by the work of our secretaries; and life from the dead, also, mentally.

A celebrated doctor said to me that we could do nothing better to prevent insanity in these camps—and the record has been a wonderful one—than to furnish music. I said, "I do not quite follow you. I think schools, colleges, and industries are better." But I have come later to see that he was more nearly right, although we are doing both of these things. We have planted a chain of schools and colleges all across Europe, with 300 to 5,000 men in each of them, with all the teachers furnished from among the prisoners themselves; and we are teaching them and training them; and we are also furnishing music, and where music has gone it has been like passing from darkness into day, and it has been life from the dead spiritually. I do not trust myself to say what I know in this respect. The question is this, my friends, shall America turn the prison life of Europe from a process of physical, mental, and moral deterioration into one of helpful physical recreation, growth in competency, increase in knowledge, welfare of our fellow men, and preparation for leadership when these men come home? These men of the Young Men's Christian Association in these camps are answering the question in the affirmative.

You say, "What will all this cost?" About $11,000,000 for work among the Americans here prior to next July; $12,000,000 for work among the Americans overseas prior to next July; over $3,000,000 for the 7,000,000 men of Russia in the Russian army and navy; nearly $3,000,000 for the 4,000,000 men in the French army; at least $1,000,000 for the 3,000,000 in the Italian army; and at least $1,000,000 by next July for the work in the prisoner-of-war camps. The budget amounted to a little over $31,000,000 that we submitted to our Budget Committee, made up of leading laymen of the United States, who met at the Bankers' Club in New York a few days ago. To my amazement—and yet I am glad I was amazed—as they faced up to these facts, one said, "I have only one criticism," after they had satisfied themselves, as those men only could do. And here was Mr. McCormick, the Chairman of the International Harvester Association; here was Mr. Mather, one of the greatest of the iron men; here were Mr. Dodge, and Arthur Curtis James, and William Fellowes Morgan, and William Sloane, and George W. Perkins, and others that I could name; and I have never seen such a strong committee to deal with a budget in my life; and they seemed to figure it down to a hair; and after they had done so, one man said, "You have not allowed for leeway, and I move that you make it $35,000,000." Mr. McCormick, in the chair, said, "I will not put that to a vote now, but I will ask each man to express himself orally. Three-fourths of them said, "Let us make it $35,000,000," and one-fourth said, "Let us hold it at $31,000,000." But when they had all expressed themselves, they said, "Let us make it unanimous"; and they brought it before the thirty-two cities represented at the general meeting, and after it had been expounded by men like Mr. Crossett, who had seen the work we were doing overseas, they approved unanimously the budget of $35,000,000, as the amount with which to serve those men, which makes an average of $1.50 each. And that is misleading, for I have told you that we plan to spend about $10 on each American. Of course we can do it, and of course we will do it.

My hope is that New England, in line with that splendid gift you made last spring, will provide at least $5,000,000 toward this $35,000,000. I recognize that it will call for a sacrificial effort. I recognize that it means that certain individuals, families, and firms may have to give as much as $250,000 for this great work. I fancy that was done for the Red Cross. Nobody in this room will speak more highly than I will of the Red Cross. I have seen too much of the life of the refugees in Europe—I have visited too many of the hospitals—not to speak on every fitting opportunity for the Red Cross.

But I remind you that here is a work that deals, like that, not only with the bodies of the men, but with the spirits of men and that is dealing with the morale of men; and I believe that the people who with great wisdom and generosity made capital gifts to the Red Cross will, because of similar conditions, make these great gifts here. But a large number who probably had thought of giving only $20,000 or $25,000, realizing what is at stake, for our own liberty and that of the world and the highest ideals handed down to us by our fathers, will extend their liberality to provide $100,000, and that, too, without pleading the fact that they have bought Liberty Loan Bonds.

And, by the way, let me say that anything that anyone can do to promote the flotation of this second great loan must be done, in season and out of season. We do not hasten this work that I am urging by failing on the Liberty Loan Bond work. Let there be no ambiguity on that matter. But, let no man say that, having invested in what is perhaps the safest form of investment in this country, therefore he should not put some of the money from that very investment in those bonds into this great work. And let him not say that on account of high taxation he has not the money available that he used to have; and let him not be afraid to cut into his principal, the way those men who have gone out there to put their lives at stake have cut into their principal, and their all. I am looking for men this year who are willing to cut into principal, and I am finding them in every city, and they are here in New England.

Mark my words, we shall not win the war unless we do cut into principal. And, that reminds me, that we must have not only money, but we must have life. I want more men like my good friend, Mr.

Crossett, who was living a busy life, concerned with large affairs, but who gave three months of his choicest time overseas, and Mr. Sloane, one of the busiest and wealthiest men of New York, who comes down to my office every morning and gives five-sixths of each day, and has done so now for five or six months, and more men like John Hoyt, and other businessmen who are placing their finest ability at our service in France, service that we could not hire with millions; and men like Judge Buffington, of the Federal Court at Pittsburgh, who gives us three months of recess, and Mr. Christy, one of the rising young lawyers of Pittsburgh, whom I have just sent to Russia. I am looking for busy men today, but men who are wondering if they cannot take on something else to help us in this work. I am looking for men like you, who can give us whole blocks of time between now and Thanksgiving. The only way we shall move New England, as it has never been moved before, is by sacrificial offering of money and life, and I am confident that New England will be true to those traditions that really made America, and will set an example for the other sections of the country to follow. New England has never failed, and this year she cannot fail.

LETTER FROM THEODORE ROOSEVELT

MY DEAR MR. MOTT: SAGAMORE HILL, November 6, 1917

It was a very real pleasure to see you. I most heartily wish you all success in your desire to get the amount of money indispensable if the Young Men's Christian Association is to do the work which it alone can do for the soldiers, and which it is vitally necessary to have done. I can speak from personal knowledge of this work. At the present time my daughter-in-law, Mrs. Theodore Roosevelt, Jr., is with the Association in Paris. I have myself seen, and benefited from, the canteens, the center of healthy enjoyment and of rest, provided by the Young Men's Christian Association for troops in the field. I know personally of its admirable work among railway men, which is in many respects closely akin to that which must be done among soldiers. In connection with the building of the Panama Canal I found that the Young Men's Christian Association played literally an invaluable part in providing healthy recreation, rest, and proper moral standards for the hard-working, vigorous northern men who under tropic skies were doing the kind of work which always before had meant a terrible death rate and frightful ravages by diseases, and widespread moral disintegration. Never before had such work been done with as low a death rate, as little disease, and as high a standard of clean and decent living, as in the case of the Panama Canal; and a large share in bringing about this result is attributable to the work of the Association on the Isthmus.

At this moment the work you are doing for our armies in France is of the utmost value to them; nothing else could take its place. Any failure to back it up would be a veritable calamity to the army. I trust that the American people, whose sons, brothers, kinsfolk, and fellow countrymen are at the front, will think of their needs and will aid them by responding to your appeal with the heartiest generosity.

Sincerely yours,

(Signed)   THEODORE ROOSEVELT

THE MORROW OF VICTORY IS MORE PERILOUS THAN ITS EVE

ARTICLE IN *Association Men*, JANUARY, 1918

To the members and friends of the Young Men's Christian Association today there come with peculiar timeliness and force the words of faithful warning spoken to his countrymen a generation ago by Mazzini, the great Italian patriot—"The morrow of victory is more perilous than its eve." The Association has had its days, yes, and its long years of adversity, of comparative unpopularity, and of meager success, but time has shown that these periods of discipline and testing and of humble working in obscurity have often proved to be among the most productive in the life of the Movement.

In the midst of great efforts also when it has been necessary for the entire Association and its constituency in a given community to put forth their full strength, or perchance when the whole brotherhood has become absorbed in a vast undertaking, as during the memorable November days of the recent campaign, men forget themselves and lose themselves in an unselfish cause, lower motives are submerged, latent energies are liberated, factional spirit and divisive tendencies give place to triumphant unity, and men are impelled to seek and to rely upon Divine guidance and power.

Such hours and experiences while not without their serious risks and trials are not the periods of gravest danger. At the climax of a great battle when the result trembles in the balance, on the threshold or eve of what proves later to be that of victory, men are putting forth all and the best that is in them, and then, if ever, they cry out for any help beyond and greater than themselves. But when the evening or it may be the long dark night of doubtful struggle is over and the morrow or new day of victory breaks, then comes a period of very real danger.

Such a time has come for our Association and we do well to recognize it that we may score an even greater victory—the victory over our own spirits, which is greater than that of capturing any fields external to ourselves. There is nothing whatever to be gained by ignoring or minimizing the reality or gravity of our perils.

First of all, there is the tendency after any great or prolonged strain to let down our powers. While it may be necessary and desirable for men to relax and refresh their physical and nervous energies after a period of great effort, they should redouble their vigilance with reference to guarding their spiritual standards and attitude. A man may wisely let his body or his brain take a vacation, but he cannot intermit for one hour the governing of his life by the highest ethical and spiritual principles.

This suggests another subtle danger which at times has manifested itself even with reference to the management and use of funds for altruistic purposes. Committees and others responsible for the care and disposition of benevolent funds have been known to juggle with their consciences and to justify to themselves the use of a part of the money for purposes foreign to those clearly set forth on the pledge form used or in the appeal which influenced the gifts. Any withholding or diverting of the money contributed by the rich or by associated poverty from the purpose for which it is given in this time of so great need and suffering would be visited with the most severe condemnation of God and man. It is believed that this peril is so clearly recognized that the great trust recently committed to the Association will be administered with such conscientiousness and scrupulous care that it will constitute an example in the realm of Christian philanthropy.

Enormous expectations have been created by the conduct and outcome of the recent campaign and there is danger lest we fall far short of fulfilling them. Here again to be forewarned is to be forearmed. The enlisted men of our army and navy and of the Allied armies and of the prisoner-of-war camps knowing of the large sum committed on their behalf to our charge will reasonably expect from us an enlarged and increasingly efficient ministry. The churches whose members have so largely contributed to the fund and whose leaders look to us to function for the churches laically, as the chaplains do clerically, will justly expect us to render a much greater service. The government and the military and naval authorities who have given us official status and exceptional facilities at home and overseas look to us to make good. The parents, relatives, and friends of the boys who have given with unexampled generosity and sacrifice and with a trust and expectancy which are deeply impressive have no other thought than that we will so help these boys that they will some day come home stronger and better men, and not blasted and weakened in character. Ten pairs of eyes are watching us today (the morrow of victory) to where there was one before the end of the recent campaign (the eve of victory). Thus the increase in our ability to serve has increased our obligation and our peril.

As we seek to render this larger service which is properly expected from us we must jealously guard against any tendency to extravagance or wastefulness. When a vast sum is poured out and made suddenly available it would not be strange were there a temptation in some quarters to spend money too easily, that is, without the most exacting and painstaking scrutiny. Much if not most of this money has been bought at a great price. Every ten dollars represents a certain number of hours of someone's labor. It constitutes, therefore, so much stored-up personality. It should be used as a priceless possession. Moreover, at a time of unparalleled want and suffering, when multitudes are starving and dying for want of the barest necessities, it is doubly incumbent upon us to make every dollar reach as far as possible.

We must resist, as we would the devil, any temptation to pride or boastfulness. The fact that millions of Americans have entrusted such a large sum of money to our care and to our use should not serve to elate or inflate us, but rather to solemnize and truly humble us. We should frequently remind ourselves of the warning of the Jewish rabbi: "Hear three things and thou shalt eschew transgression—the All-seeing eye and the All-hearing ear, and that all thy actions are written in a book." We should likewise heed the warning of our Lord to beware when all men speak well of us.

The very fact that the Association today is regarded with so much favor by all classes carries with it one of the most serious and alarming perils and that is that we obscure or compromise our most distinctive principles and character. We do well to remind ourselves that this is essentially and pre-eminently a Christian Movement. Were we to allow it to crumble down to the prevailing level of our day and to blend with the world we should destroy its distinctive character and rob it of its largest power of helpfulness. If we permit the world to invade the Association, the Association will lose world-conquering power. By an almost infinite process of exclusion this war is showing that all else is insufficient but that Christ was never so unique, never so necessary, never more sufficient. This is not the statement of narrow dogmatism, but of actual experience. It is highly significant that the nearer men get to the trenches the more central this point becomes.

All our perils may be summed up in one—that the leaders and members and supporters of this Movement may permit themselves to rely upon human wisdom and power rather than upon the Superhuman. A great religious thinker has pointed out that with Christ God was everything and the world nothing. We, His followers, should let this be the dominating principle and fact in our lives. Then we shall be sensitive to recognize and quick and strong to resist the many dangers which beset us and our Movement in this the day of immeasurably its most inspiring opportunity, its greatest responsibility, and its gravest peril. Thus viewed our dangers constitute an added attraction. They become not stumbling blocks, but stepping-stones leading us up into the mountain of highest attainment and highest achievement.

THE UNITED WAR WORK CAMPAIGN

LETTER OF PRESIDENT WILSON

THE WHITE HOUSE, WASHINGTON
September 3, 1918

MY DEAR MR. FOSDICK:

May I not call your attention to a matter which has been recently engaging my thought not a little?

The War Department has recognized the Young Men's Christian Association, the Young Women's Christian Association, the National Catholic War Council (Knights of Columbus), the Jewish Welfare Board, the War Camp Community Service, the American Library Association, and the Salvation Army as accepted instrumentalities through which the men in the ranks are to be assisted in many essential matters of recreation and morale.

It was evident from the first, and has become increasingly evident, that the services rendered by these agencies to our army and to our allies are essentially one and all of a kind and must of necessity, if well rendered, be rendered in the closest co-operation. It is my judgment, therefore, that we shall secure the best results in the matter of the support of these agencies, if these seven societies will unite their forthcoming appeals for funds, in order that the spirit of the country in this matter may be expressed without distinction of race or religious opinion in support of what is in reality a common service.

This point of view is sustained by the necessity, which the war has forced upon us, of limiting our appeals for funds in such a way that two or three comprehensive campaigns shall take the place of a series of independent calls upon the generosity of the country.

Will you not, therefore, as Chairman of the Commission on Training Camp Activities, be good enough to request the societies in question to combine their approaching appeals for funds in a single campaign, preferably during the week of November 11, so that in their solicitation of funds as well as in their work in the field, they may act in as complete co-operation and fellowship as possible?

In inviting these organizations to give this new evidence of their patriotic co-operation, I wish it distinctly understood that their compliance with this request will not in any sense imply the surrender on the part of any of them of its distinctive character and autonomy, because I fully recognize the fact that each of them has its own traditions, principles, and relationships which it properly prizes and which, if preserved and strengthened, make possible the largest service.

At the same time, I would be obliged if you would convey to them from me a very warm expression of the government's appreciation of the splendid service they have rendered in ministering to the troops at home and overseas in their leisure time. Through their agencies the moral and spiritual resources of the nation have been mobilized behind our forces and used in the finest way, and they are contributing directly and effectively to the winning of the war.

It has been gratifying to find such a fine spirit of co-operation among all the leaders of the organizations I have mentioned. This spirit and the patriotism of all the members and friends of these agencies, give me confidence to believe that the United War Work Campaign will be crowned with abundant success.

Cordially and sincerely yours,

WOODROW WILSON

MEMORANDUM OF AGREEMENT BETWEEN THE CO-OPERATING ORGANIZATIONS

(Adopted September 4, 1918)

It is agreed by the National War Work Council of the Young Men's Christian Associations, the War Work Council of the National Board of the Young Women's Christian Associations, the National Catholic War Council (Knights of Columbus), the Jewish Welfare Board, the War Camp Community Service, the American Library Association, and the Salvation Army:

1. That there shall be a joint campaign for funds during the week beginning November 11, 1918.

2. That by joint campaign we mean, so far as it can be brought about, a campaign undertaken through the agency of consolidated committees rather than seven separate campaigns in the same week.

3. That each society will adopt a joint pledge card.

4. That the committee organization now installed throughout the country for the collection of funds be disturbed as little as possible, and that the policy of addition rather than elimination be advised.

5. That in so far as the campaign has a name it shall be called the "United War Work Campaign" followed by the names of the seven organizations participating.

6. That Mr. Cleveland H. Dodge be the national treasurer and that the moneys collected in the United States be paid to him for proper distribution among the societies.

7. That all funds collected be distributed on a pro rata basis among the seven societies participating in the campaign; that is, the funds received shall be divided among the participating organizations in such proportion as the total budget of each organization bears to the sum total of the combined budgets. The budget estimates and percentages are as follows:

National War Work Council of the Young Men's Christian Associations	$100,000,000	58.65%
War Work Council of the National Board of the Young Women's Christian Associations	$15,000,000	8.80%
National Catholic War Council (Knights of Columbus)	$30,000,000	17.60%
Jewish Welfare Board	$3,500,000	2.05%
War Camp Community Service	$15,000,000	8.80%
American Library Association	$3,500,000	2.05%
Salvation Army	$3,500,000	2.05%

8. That specified or restricted subscriptions shall not be asked for, but if given, shall be credited to the particular association, such amount to be a part of the total and not an addition to it.

9. That the advertising which each organization has planned for itself proceed as planned but that some advertising be advised in the name of the United War Work Campaign.

10. That the expenses incurred in joint work in connection with the drive be paid on a pro rata basis.

11. That Mr. George W. Perkins and Dr. John R. Mott for the Young Men's Christian Association; Mrs. Henry P. Davison for the Young Women's Christian Association; Mr. John G. Agar and Mr. James J. Phelan for the National Catholic War Council (Knights of Columbus); Mr. Mortimer L. Schiff for the Jewish Welfare Board; Honorable Myron T. Herrick for the War Camp Community Service; Mr. Frank A. Vanderlip for the American Library Association;

Mr. George Gordon Battle for the Salvation Army; and Mr. John D. Rockefeller, Jr., Chairman of the Great Union Drive for New York City, and Mr. Cleveland H. Dodge as Treasurer ex officio, act together under the chairmanship of Mr. Raymond B. Fosdick of the Commission on Training Camp Activities of the War Department, or their alternates, in settling any questions between the seven organizations participating in this agreement or in handling any arrangements which have to be dealt with jointly, and, at the invitation of the Secretary of War, to discuss and adjust matters relating to the work of the several organizations which might involve duplication in the expenditure of money and effort at home and abroad.

WHY WE NEED MORE THAN $170,500,000

ADDRESS DELIVERED BY JOHN R. MOTT IN WISCONSIN, NOVEMBER, 1918

We have come here this afternoon, not in the interest of any one organization or of any seven organizations, but solely in the interest of those men and boys who make up the United States Army and Navy. And yet it is a most happy and significant circumstance that those seven great patriotic societies, the Young Men's Christian Association, the Young Women's Christian Association, the National Catholic War Council (working especially through the Knights of Columbus), the Jewish Welfare Board, the War Camp Community Service, the American Library Association, and the Salvation Army have blended their plans, their purposes, their sacrifices in the national interest and for the great cause that embraces the best of the world today.

When our President, that one who sees both sides of the shield with steadier eye than any other man living, that one who realizes, certainly as no other American, the situation as it is today, that one who has on his mind and heart every waking hour—and those hours are many each day—the vital interest of the Republic, that one whose heart interest, as I can testify from many a conversation, is with each one of these seven societies, when that great leader of ours, and the one I think of in a unique sense as the leader of the world, said to us, "The difficulties of your going forward with seven separate appeals are far greater than any difficulties that might attend your blending your efforts and going forward together"—that, so far as my knowledge goes, settled the matter once for all with every leader, member, and loyal friend of any one of these organizations. We trust our President. The American people have never parted company with him in this war in any one of his proclamations or requests, and the last one in connection with which they would part company with his leadership would be this one which seeks to unite all the forces of righteousness and unselfishness on behalf of the manhood and the boyhood of the nation who are seeking to bear the impossible strain of this greatest struggle. Certainly we will follow our leader to the end.

Therefore, within a few hours after the President had indicated his desire, the responsible leaders of all these seven societies came together and adopted that splendid Memorandum of Agreement that will go down through the years because of its breadth, its solidity, and its guiding principles. We appointed a committee of thirty-five known as the General Committee, composed of five men and women of each of the seven co-operating societies. A small Executive Committee was then appointed of one from each of the seven together with the chairman of the General Committee. I was asked to assume the burden of serving as chairman of these two committees and as director general, and consented to do so on one condition and that was that from that moment it be clearly understood I disassociate myself from any one of these societies and be regarded during this campaign as the servant of all. My condition was not only accepted, but every one of the thirty-five said, "We wish to be in the same catalogue in the interest of our boys and men and in the national interest."

There are manifest advantages in this co-operative arrangement of which we do well to remind ourselves in order that we may carry every man, woman, and child of the counties of this state with heart and conviction into this campaign and that there may be no mental reservation or pausing of will, but intelligent, open-minded, and hearty allegiance and co-operation. I need not linger to say that one advantage is that the co-operative arrangement will make possible large economies. A plan that brings all together in one campaign from the nature of the case means a great saving over seven successive drives conducted within the short period from the end of the Liberty Loan until the middle of January as was contemplated. It will mean not only a great saving of money, but even more the conservation of the time and the energy of many thousands of the busiest and most intelligent business and professional men of the country who give their time to every great patriotic endeavor of this kind no matter what its leadership. And even more the fact that we have now come together will in my judgment, if this war lasts, mean the saving of tens of millions of dollars by co-operative arrangements that do not involve any compromise of principles, but prevent unnecessary duplication in the expenditure of effort and money. Anything in a time like this, when we must curtail, which leads us to deny ourselves and husband our resources and make them all count, and which will save tens of millions is not without its marked advantage.

This co-operative plan will make for higher efficiency on the part of every one of the seven societies. It stands to reason that a plan that calls upon us to pool all our experiences will result in finer efficiency in each one of the societies because each one of these organizations has a splendid history; it has traditions of which it is properly proud, it has principles for which it would stand and fight, it has a philosophy and methods which have made possible great achievements. That leads me to remark that this plan of co-operation makes it easily possible for the strongest of these societies to help those who might not call themselves so strong. Some organizations that may not in the popular view be called so large, or so experienced, in the light of the teaching of the history of the world often are among the most useful societies. Take the nations, how true it is that some of the smallest and even some of the more obscure nations have lighted the way for the larger nations. A nation is not to be judged primarily by the number of its people, or the extent of its geographical area, or the magnitude of its industrial establishment, or the number of its millionaires, but by the character, the genius, the spirit of the people. By this abiding test any organization which is characterized by reality, by open-mindedness, by serviceableness, will be helpful to any other organization no matter how old or experienced that society may be. The advantage of this co-operative plan is that it makes possible the helping of the weaker organizations by the stronger. No man or organization was ever made weaker by being called upon to assume added burdens, and the weakest of organizations will gather momentum and courage from association with the others.

The bringing together in common action as well as the common plan of all these societies is bound to promote better feeling all over the United States of America. Say what we may as to the fine co-operative spirit which I have found existing in every one of these organizations, the fact remains that with the best of intentions we have all been living more or less in separate compartments, each one by himself, because we are all intense, we are all busy, we have all got more than we can do, and it follows that we do not see as much of each other as we might otherwise, and therefore, there has been quite a large zone of ignorance and that has resulted in prejudice and misunderstanding and at times even bitterness. Our new fellowship with one another is going to generate an atmosphere in which we shall all come to loathe to differ and to determine to understand. It is one thing to develop an atmosphere in which we come to differ with one another, but it is quite another thing to generate an atmosphere in which we come to resolve—that is come to make up our minds—that we will take the initiative in trying to understand those people with whom we differ, it may be, quite sharply. That will be a good thing for the nation.

Moreover, this plan of associating all of us together is going to promote religious unity at a time in the world when this means more than will appear on the surface. This arrangement stands not for undenominationalism, but for interdenominationalism. There is all the difference in the world. Undenominationalism, in which we would try to reduce ourselves to the lowest common denominator, says, "I will obscure, I will hide, I will minimize, I will apologize for that which is most distinctive to myself and my creed." Interdenominationalism says the very opposite of that. It says, "We will hold fast to that which is most distinctive to us." One of the finest things in that splendid letter of the President which summoned us to co-operate is the sentence which I think I can give exactly. With his usual felicitous phrase and with his finest penetration he says:

"In inviting you to enter into this patriotic co-operative endeavor I wish to have it distinctly understood that compliance with my request does not imply any surrender of the distinctive character or autonomy of any one of these organizations, because" he continues, "I well recognize that each of these organizations has traditions, principles, and relationships which it properly prizes and which, if maintained and strengthened, make possible the truest service."

What a splendid principle! In other words, the President says that such an arrangement is not one that causes that which you most value about yourself to disappear, but something that will strengthen and preserve it. The reason I value so highly so many of my Hebrew friends is that they hold on with such tenacity to that which is most distinctive to them, and those members of the Roman Catholic Church whom I number among my friends are those who never apologize for that which they most value. This likewise has been true of Protestantism, that it has not hesitated to proclaim its convictions. Thank God we have lived to a day like this and have got an arrangement that preserves everything that is good in every one of us.

This co-operative plan will promote the solidarity of the nation. I have made five visits to the warring countries since the war began, and I think I realize what is involved in this struggle. We are far from the end of it. Well may our hearts stand still this afternoon as an American people when we remind ourselves of the price to be paid by our country before a military victory is achieved, before which there can be no foundation for treaties of peace on a basis of justice, which we must have for the maintenance of our ideals and principles. Anything, therefore, which will lead this cosmopolitan nation, this land of many races and of many religions to find its unity, its deep solidarity and extend it, is in the national interest and in the interest of the cause for which our boys are laying down their lives.

Were I to mention another advantage of this plan and of its practice it is this, that it opens up boundless opportunities for all of us— opportunities for largeness of soul—how the people will expand under this conception; opportunities for illustrating genuine catholicity of spirit—how rare it is in the world after all; opportunities for exercising the finest leadership in the sense of that sentence in the Bible. "He who would be greatest among you shall be the servant of all"; boundless opportunities likewise to forget ourselves and to magnify others and to serve. What vistas open up on every hand to expand us and our nation. So I say when the people back home remind you that there are some things that may have caused mental reservations or some difficulties they see in the United War Work Campaign, remind them that difficulties are an added attraction and not without their great advantages.

We have a real difficulty and that is to get *at least* $170,500,000. I emphasize those words *at least* advisedly. I want to give some reasons why we must have more than $170,500,000, and when I remind myself who you are and whom you represent and what you have got to do before November 11, I am anxious to carry every man and woman with me. I am going to give reasons which I believe will convince every open-minded person that we cannot get along with merely $170,500,000. My first reason is the great expansion of the American army since the time that three or four of the largest of these seven societies assembled the data underlying their budgets, which budgets were approved by the War Department as part of this $170,500,000. I was one of those parties. I was on my fifth visit overseas back in March, April, and early May. General Pershing and our other leaders over there said, "We shall not have more than 1,000,000 American boys over here by March 1." We shall have almost exactly 2,000,000 by November 1. And when I got back here and talked with our military authorities, not one of them believed and expressed himself that by the middle of next summer we should have more than 3,500,000 men under arms or more than 2,000,000 overseas, and yet within a week I had a conversation with General Crowder in Washington. I said, "General, you will not be calling men up over thirty-six before summer?" He replied, "I shall be calling men over thirty-six before the end of January. We must have 4,800,000 men before the end of next summer." In other words, we must scrap that budget because we must do for the 4,800,000 the same as we are now doing for the 2,000,000 overseas and the 1,000,000 at home, or the opportunity will be taken out of our hands and we shall have to give way to other agencies that can do this work.

That leads me to a second reason why we must have more than $170,500,000—the most incredible growth of the United States Navy. We had 70,000 men in the navy at the time America entered the war and now we have over 500,000 men and boys, nearly all of them volunteers. When we entered the war the British navy was, of course, the great navy as it still is. Our navy is now larger than the British navy was then. When we joined the struggle we had 200 ships in action; by Christmas we shall have 2,000. We talk about the dangers of the boys in the trenches, but I would remind you that all of our boys over there in our navy—and we have more than many people fancy—all of our boys in the navy are in the front-line trenches. They are in the mine-strewn fields with the lurking submarines on every hand. They are taking their lives in their hands and by their ceaseless vigilance in the presence of death they are making it possible for our army to get over there with its remarkable record and for our army to be supplied. I am ashamed to say that the plans of none of our seven organizations at the time did justice to the United States Navy, and our consciences will not rest until we have included those boys. Therefore we have got to surpass the $170,500,000.

This war, unlike previous wars, is not a war of armies and navies, but a war of entire peoples, and that involves in a very unique sense the great industrial part of our nation and the allied nations. It is a war of machines, and in this plan we should be derelict, we should be lacking in perception if we did not make some provision to serve the men in the navy yards, in the arsenals, and in other militarized industries. I wonder we were so shortsighted, I wonder we did not see we were undercutting the men in the army and navy not to be serving likewise the morale of the men in the industries, and, therefore, I am glad to see these organizations desire to see us sweep past the goal in order that we may do our duty to these men.

Speaking of this being a war of entire peoples leads me to say it is essentially, more than any other war—and this has been in some measure true of every war—a war of women. Not in the sense we could have said that of any war, but in that larger sense that women are called to take the place of men in the ordinary vocations that men filled, also in the fact that millions of women are making munitions, therefore releasing men, and then to hark back to the original reason, just because this war is more deadly, more awful—unbelievably awful

—women have got to bear the larger part of the burden incident to the millions of graves of men, and the tens of millions of lame and crippled and the impossible burdens of taxation which will affect the women of more than one generation. Therefore, anything that God will let the Young Women's Christian Association or the Women's Section of the Catholic War Council and the Hebrew Welfare Board do to serve the women of our nation and of France and of other Allies, to help their morale, is in the national interest and in the international interest. That necessitates a much larger provision in the budget than you will find there.

Then there is another very strong reason why we have got to have more than $170,500,000 and that is that the center of gravity has, within several months, shifted from this side of the Atlantic to the other side of the Atlantic. I should like to change that. Within a few months the center of the heart interest of the American people has shifted from this to the other side of the Atlantic Ocean. It has been my lot within the last few weeks to visit thirty-one of the United States. My journeys have taken me to the rural districts. It has been deeply moving to me to see in the windows all through the country those little flags with one star, two stars, or more. The same is true among the houses of the workmen in all our cities. The other night an Irishman in New York came to see me. He had to work all day and he had to come to see me with the chance of not finding me in. I had met his son Over There; he was in the regiment with my son, the 165th New York or the old "Fighting 69th" of the old Civil War days, a regiment made up of 85 per cent of Irish Catholics; so my son, who is a Protestant if there ever was one, has had a Catholic chaplain, Chaplain Duffy. I met a number of my son's comrades and my son said to me when I was going, "I wish you would just call up over the telephone the fathers and mothers of those boys you have met so far as you can and write others and tell them you have seen the boys." I sent a letter to this Irish laborer and he came in to thank me. He had three boys over there. He had lost one of them and he said, "I wish I had another boy to give to take his place." And also among the wealthy you find distributed these service flags. We are proud of our country, rich and poor. You can go behind any of those windows and you will find there hearts that are beating with special reference to what is now taking place or is soon to take place over there. This has a financial aspect which shows why we must have much more money because these few societies which we represent are, through military necessity, the only organizations permitted to work among our men overseas. This necessarily puts a larger burden on these societies for they have got to do, in addition to their own work, all that thirty or more denominational, welfare, and patriotic societies are doing for the soldiers and sailors here.

Then again the army over there is broken into many parts. You will not find them as we do in great cantonments at home, save where the men may be massed in front-line trenches or immediately behind in the rest camps or reserves. You will find there an American regiment of say 26,000 men scattered as I did the other day in thirty-five or more villages. I found 170 in this village, 252 in that, and so on, in different numbers billeted in those villages. Let me take you to just one of those villages. I went into a haymow that had chinks in the sides which let in the snow and rain. I found seventy men sleeping there, and down below them that night they had taken hay and scattered it in a thin layer over the ground and 100 were to sleep there. Some were to sleep in the chicken house and others in warehouses. I found still others in some of the less desirable rooms that the officers had not commandeered or on back galleries and porches where the rain and snow drifted in. I did not find in one of those villages a club or a town library or an Association building, nor did I find a saloon where there would be warmth. You might go to a wine shop and buy wine to take home with you to drink, but there was no place where the boys could congregate. Just think what it costs to plant the work of one of these societies like the Young Men's Christian Association or the Knights of Columbus in places like that contrasted with one large cantonment here where there are forty to fifty thousand men. Some may say, "Go with your work only into villages that have 1,000 boys or more." If you had gone to the village where I found my boy and possibly 200 other boys, if you found your boy where I found my boy you would have said, "If necessary I will mortgage my farm in order that these organizations may have money enough to enable my boy to have a place where he can get warm and a place light enough to enable him to see to write his letters home."

The expense is also increased by the fact that the United States Army is being constantly shifted, except in the front--line trenches. I have a little chart in my hotel which shows how one division of the army was moved five times in six months. The divisional secretary of the Young Men's Christian Association, said to me, "I have had to open up thirty-five Association huts five times, making 175 in six months." That is fearfully expensive. Someone might say, "Just open them up the first time so the men will have a splendid example and an inspiring memory." The American people will not stand for anything except that these organizations follow the boys through to the end.

It costs more also because the French railroads have been worn out or overworked by the war demands and pressure. The fact is they are not able to get supplies to build new equipment. Therefore the Young Men's Christian Association, following the lead of the Red Cross, have developed or are developing their own motor transport, and the Knights of Columbus and the Salvation Army have to do the same, but let me say to you that is a most expensive process; but we must do it because we must have the personnel and the supplies where the men are.

That reminds me of another reason and that is that everything costs so much overseas, and the prices are sure to continue to mount.

Still another reason why we must go beyond our goal of $170,500,000 is the continuity of this service. I think, as I look over this audience and remember where we have been, that most of you are familiar with the first stages of this continuity. For example, the troop trains that bear the boys from the villages to the camps have tested workers from some one of these societies to give out the magazines and writing paper and to answer a hundred and one questions for the boys in the midst of their strangeness and that first bit of lonesomeness. Moreover, I think you have visited these camps and seen how the Young Men's Christian Association, the Knights of Columbus, the Jewish Welfare Board, and the Library Association have spread what I will call the network of their friendliness and helpfulness among these tens of thousands of boys. You have seen at the gateway of the camps those splendid hostess houses of the Young Women's Christian Associations and the fine work of the War Camp Community Service outside the camps. Most of you know when the summons comes for those long trains to bear the boys to the ports, and on all these we seek to serve them. At the ports of embarkation we have our agents working day and night helping them. There these societies mass their efforts of unselfishness in order that the last touch—and many thousands will never tread American soil again—that last touch, whether it is to be temporary or permanent, shall be one of abounding cheer and good will and unmistakable assurance that the entire American people go with them as they launch out on the great adventure.

Up to a few months ago, notwithstanding the efforts we put forth, the War Department would not allow one of our representatives to cross with the men, but now on every transport you will find representatives of one or more of our societies as well as the government chaplains. In those days the men on board had no library, no magazines, no movies, no lectures, no sports, no religious services. You will now find all these things on every transport.

You then come to the ports of debarkation. I stood the other day at the foot of the gangplank of one transport and saw 3,600 men come across it. As one of them said to me one day, they expect to face everything over there. As they stream into that port you would find at least twenty branches or buildings of the Young Men's Christian Association and of the Knights of Columbus. There have been as many as 160,000 American soldiers and sailors helped at one time by these societies at that port.

The Red Cross, that great sister society with whom we consider it an honor to be associated, furnishes the canteen privileges for the men while in transit. Our agencies again get in touch with them and serve them in the camps in the intermediate areas where the final edge is to be put on these men for the great work that awaits them. Up into the zone of repose or combat you will find representatives of the Young Men's Christian Association and some of the other agencies right back of the front-line trenches and even in those trenches you will find this ministry going forward. The other night about midnight I went into one of those centers of service near the trenches, an old wine cellar sixty feet long, twenty feet wide, and a little deeper than I am tall, and there I found 100 of our American soldiers who had been on sentry duty or were to go on such duty that night. The Association secretary told me that since late afternoon he had served 1,100 cups of cocoa and chocolate and he said, "At intervals in the night I am going to send out pails of coffee and chocolate to the men in the trenches." You will find similar service rendered by the Salvation Army and the Knights of Columbus. I went out with my guide into the front-line trenches and into no man's land and picked my way to another hut. There we had to wake up the secretary; he had gone to sleep he was so worn out. That day the commanding officer had said, "You cannot have more than seven men at a time in your dugout" because the Germans had located and shelled it. Still there are people who tell you this is a bulletproof job. It is reported that the Young Men's Christian Association has lost as large a proportion of its workers, men and women, from shellfire, as our army has lost. They are constantly sharing the sacrifices and dangers of the men themselves.

Follow this work back into the hospitals. The Red Cross says to these organizations, "We want you to come in and provide your activities, such as the recreational sports, the movies, the religious services." You may have to follow some of the men into a German prison camp. I shall not forget them. Some of you know that from the beginning of the war until America went into it, I spent considerable time serving the "Allied prisoners," as we call them today, and the enemy prisoners in the various belligerent countries. That took

me to Germany and Austria three times, in 1914, 1915, and 1916.
I know these camps today where there are languishing, or in working
parties, three or four million Allied prisoners. I know their lot, it
is indescribable. I am glad one of our men has been permitted to
stay there—Hoffman. Germany has permitted him, although he is
an American of the Americans, to stay there and guide all our work.
We have had to withdraw the other American workers; but we have
sent in Norwegians, Danes, Swedes, Dutch, Swiss, to take their places.
The Red Cross supplies our prisoners with food and clothing but our
Association furnishes them libraries, schools, lectures, movies, music,
and recreation, and this prevents men from going insane and keeps
them from moral deterioration and physical collapse.

At a port in France the other day I had checked off the entire list
of places which I was to visit but the secretary said there was one
place I had not visited. Then he took me out to the cemetery. There
I found a few scores of new American graves for soldiers and sailors.
He told me that up to a few days before he had had to bury all the
dead, but that recently a Catholic priest has come to help him. He
said that he had to write to the families of the boys who lie here.
Then he told me this very beautiful thing—he had gone to the French
mothers in that town to enlist them as godmothers of these American boys. A godmother is a French woman who will keep flowers on
that American's grave until the close of the war. The last person
to visit the cemetery before we arrived was one of those lonely
French women who had lost her husband in Picardy a few days before. She came in with her little children. She placed them between
the graves of the two Americans for whom she had promised to be
godmother and tried to explain to her little children why those two
American boys had come over 4,000 miles (for they were from our
Middle West) and laid down their lives to make forever secure the
liberties of France and the world.

Thus these societies accompany and serve the boy from his home
to the camp, during his training at the camp, to the port of embarkation, and while waiting there, also on the high seas, at the port of
debarkation, through the further training period in France, into the
trenches, at the hospitals and leave resorts, in the lonely prison
camps, and then through the long dangerous period of demobilization and all the way homeward until you go to meet him at your own
station, or in Chicago, or on the Atlantic seaboard. In a word—from
home back to home, and during all the intervening spaces of time these
organizations will be home for the boy. When the men, women, and
children of your state understand this they will say, "Let us forget

the goal of $170,500,000, and let us give these societies enough money to do this work properly."

I will mention in brief another reason why we must exceed $170,500,000 and that is the comprehensiveness of this ministry. These societies are to be the American home to every boy. That is enough on which to stake the whole argument. They also must be the American school and the American college. To this end we have just started the American university in khaki. We must likewise be the American club at its best for all these boys and the American library, and the American stage at its best, and the American churches and synagogues. In a sentence, we seek to reproduce for our soldiers and sailors all that is best in American life. This is costly, but none too costly. Why, $170,500,000 will mean about ten cents a day for each American soldier, and that does not include the navy, or the women affected by war conditions. That does not include our Allies. We ought to increase the average amount for the soliders and sailors alone to at least fifteen cents a day, and of course the American people will do it when they understand.

We must not forget our Allies—those who for three long years before we saw our duty and acted upon it, and for our sakes as well as theirs, were bled almost white. We must expand our work on behalf of the French army of 4,000,000 through the agency which we have been financing, the Foyer du Soldat. It is now established at 1,000 centers as a result of our help and we have been asked to assist in planting it in 1,000 more places. In the same way we must enlarge our co-operation with the Casa del Soldato, which with our aid in men and money are working among the 3,000,000 Italian soldiers. Likewise we must do more for the Belgian army, for the Portuguese, and for the Allied armies in the Balkans, in Egypt, in Palestine, and in Mesopotamia. And we must not abridge but augment what we have begun to do for the labor battalions of Chinese, Indians, Africans, and West Indians behind the fighting lines in France, all emphatically in the interest of saving the American boys and of winning the war. I am proud of the fact that at least $25,000,000 of these consolidated budgets goes toward these Allied armies and the prisoners of war; it ought to be $50,000,000 or more.

I mention one other reason why you must get the people of your own and of the other states to forget the goal of $170,500,000. How do you forget anything? Do you forget yourself by saying, "I will now forget myself?" Is that how you forget yourself? The only way a man ever forgot himself was by losing himself in a great cause. The only way this state and the other states can forget themselves is by becoming lost in a cause so tremendously great and necessary that they will forget money just as the boys have forgotten their lives. That is what the work over there means, it is to get over the top. We do not want to stop at any goal.

I want to mention this other reason—and there are a great many more—and that is that these societies may be in a position to meet emergencies and crises. After all that is what war consists of. If you cut out of war the unexpected, the emergencies, the calamities, and the crises, you do away with war. I am free to say that these societies have not included in their budgets enough to meet emergencies. One of these organizations, the Young Men's Christian Association, as you know, made a drive last year for $35,000,000. You can always trust the heart of the American people. They knew better and they subscribed $54,000,000. Notice what that made possible in this one respect. I left America March 21. Do you remember what that day was? The day the Germans' great offensive of this year began. I had found England serious on other occasions; this time I found her suffering. I found she had lost eighty-nine of her Association huts. I said—I did not have time to cable—"There are people in America who would like to give $500,000 to replace them." On my return to America my Committee criticized me for one thing and that was that I did not promise $1,000,000 instead of $500,000. We cast that bread upon the water; it came back not after many days but after a very few days because, within three weeks after I promised the $500,000, the United States War Department and our President decided to brigade American troops with those of our Allies. Within two days two divisions of the American soldiers were sent across the Channel and they were put in the very sector where we had arranged to replace the English huts. That reminds me of another illustration. I left Europe for home about the time when the Germans had begun their push to the Marne. When I reached New York I saw they had actually reached the Marne. I took out my map of the French Foyers du Soldat, which correspond to the Young Men's Christian Association in our army—they had nearly 1,000 huts—and I said, "I am afraid the Germans have got about ninety of those huts." A cablegram came within a few days stating that they had lost over 100. We had a reserve fund to permit us immediately to send money for equipment. That is the sector around which the American name has become imperishable, that is where we pushed the enemy back and where we defeated the Prussian Guard for the first time in any battle in this war. There again we installed these facilities in time to serve the American boys as well as the French soldiers. At the time the Austrians pushed the Italians down beyond the river to the plains we learned in New York that Father Menozzi, the head Catholic chaplain of the Italian army, one of my friends, lost 140 of his Case del Soldato and our organization—a Protestant society—cabled to him, "We will replace them all." Since that time it has been my pleasure to visit that whole line and I saw where these huts had been restored. At his invitation and with his co-operation we have 200 American workers carrying on their activities and working with perfect accord. Examples like this, showing the value and necessity of our having money with which to meet emergencies, we might multiply. But the point I want you to carry and give effect to is that this logically means we must have more than $170,500,000.

Now to sum up, in view of what this will mean for the American soldiers and sailors during this coming winter, which is going to be a terrible winter; in view of what it is going to mean for the millions of homes from which these boys have come and from which they are going to come; and in view of what it would mean to the enemy if we were to fail—we will not fail, but we will lose ourselves in our great cause and therefore find ourselves way beyond the goal.

TELEGRAMS TO UNITED WAR WORK CAMPAIGN DIRECTORS

MESSAGE SENT AS DAY OR NIGHT LETTER TO ALL STATE CAMPAIGN DIRECTORS, NOVEMBER 9, 1918

ON BEHALF OF UNITED WAR WORK CAMPAIGN COMMITTEE REQUEST YOU PROMPTLY RELAY TONIGHT TO EACH DISTRICT COUNTY AND IMPORTANT LOCAL CHAIRMAN OR DIRECTOR OUR UNITED CONCLUSION THAT NO MATTER HOW NEAR OR HOW DISTANT PERMANENT PEACE MAY BE THE LONG PERIOD OF DEMOBILIZATION AND THE PERIOD WHICH WILL PRECEDE DEMOBILIZATION WILL PRESENT GREATER NEED THAN EVER FOR THE SERVICE OF THE SEVEN CO-OPERATING ORGANIZATIONS AND THEREFORE THAT THE REQUESTED OVERSUBSCRIPTION OF FIFTY PER CENT IS MOST NECESSARY. OUR ADVISERS OF THE AMERICAN ARMY AND NAVY CONCUR IN THIS JUDGMENT. I HAVE CONFERRED ON THE SUBJECT WITH WAR DEPARTMENT AND PRESIDENT WILSON AND THEY STRONGLY EMPHASIZE NEED AND IMPORTANCE OF THIS WORK FOR THE PERIOD TO FOLLOW CESSATION OF HOSTILITIES. LETTER FROM PRESIDENT WILSON WILL APPEAR WITHIN TWO DAYS EXPRESSING HIS SATISFACTION THAT OUR PLANS HAVE BEEN ENLARGED TO RENDER THIS GREAT PATRIOTIC SERVICE. THE MONTHS FOLLOWING VICTORIOUS ENDING OF WAR WILL BE ACCOMPANIED WITH SPECIAL DANGERS. WE NEED NOT BE SOLICITOUS FOR OUR SOLDIERS AND SAILORS WHEN THEY ARE DRILLING AND FIGHTING AND CONFRONTING THE GREAT ADVENTURE OF LIFE AND DEATH BUT RATHER WHEN THIS GREAT INCITEMENT IS WITHDRAWN AND DISCIPLINE RELAXED AND HOURS OF LEISURE MULTIPLIED AND TEMPTATIONS ARE INCREASED. THE SEVEN ORGANIZATIONS WILL THEN BE MORE NEEDED THAN EVER TO PREVENT PERIOD OF DEMOBILIZATION BECOMING PERIOD OF DEMORALIZATION. IT TOOK OVER TWO YEARS TO COMPLETE DEMOBILIZATION AFTER THE FRANCO

PRUSSIAN WAR EIGHTEEN MONTHS AFTER TURCO RUSSIAN WAR TEN MONTHS AFTER SOUTH AFRICAN WAR THIRTEEN MONTHS AFTER RUSSO JAPANESE WAR. ALL WITH WHOM WE HAVE CONSULTED AGREE THAT IT WILL REQUIRE MORE THAN ONE YEAR TO DEMOBILIZE AMERICAN FORCES. FOR THIS PERIOD OF GRAVEST DANGER OUR ORGANIZATIONS ARE PLANNING TO ENLARGE GREATLY OUR PHYSICAL AND SOCIAL PRO-GAM BY PRESENTING SUCH HELPFUL COUNTER-ATTRACTIONS AS TO KEEP MEN FROM WRONG ASSOCIATIONS AND PRACTICES. WE ARE ALSO EXTENDING GREAT EDUCATIONAL PROGRAM INVOLVING USING OF THOUSANDS OF TEACHERS AND SPENDING MILLIONS OF DOLLARS ON TEXT BOOKS AND REFERENCE BOOKS. REMARKABLE RELIGIOUS PROGRAM WILL BE CONDUCTED INCLUDING USING OF LEADING RELIGIOUS PREACH-ERS AND TEACHERS OF AMERICA. TO OCCUPY ALL OF THE TIME OF OUR MEN IN THESE USEFUL WAYS WILL COST MUCH MORE THAN TO HELP THEM DURING FRAGMENTS OF THEIR TIME. WE THEREFORE CALL UPON ENTIRE AMERICAN PEOPLE TO SUBSCRIBE GENEROUSLY IN GRATEFUL RECOGNITION OF THE MARVELOUS SERVICE RENDERED BY OUR MEN AND WITH THE THE FIRM PURPOSE TO MAKE THE PERIOD OF DEMOBILIZA-TION NOT A PERIOD OF PHYSICAL MENTAL AND MORAL DETERIORATION OR WEAKENING BUT RATHER A PERIOD OF CHARACTER BUILDING OF GROWTH IN USEFUL KNOWLEDGE AND WORKING EFFICIENCY AND OF PREPARATION FOR ASSUMING LARGER RESPONSIBILITIES AS CITIZENS ON THEIR RETURN HOME. PLEASE GIVE THIS MESSAGE IMMEDIATELY TO PRESS.

JOHN R. MOTT

NIGHT LETTER SENT NOVEMBER 15, 1918, TO ALL STATE DIRECTORS
OF THE UNITED WAR WORK CAMPAIGN

PRESIDENT WILSON HAS JUST SENT IMPORTANT TELEGRAM ADDRESSED CONJOINTLY TO ME AS DIRECTOR GENERAL AND CLEVELAND DODGE AS TREASURER UNITED WAR WORK CAMPAIGN READING AS FOLLOWS:

QUOTE. WHITE HOUSE, WASHINGTON, NOVEMBER 15, 1918. I AM SURE THAT THE ENTIRE AMERICAN PEOPLE ARE FOLLOWING WITH EAGER AND RESPONSIVE INTEREST THE PROGRESS OF THE UNITED WAR WORK CAMPAIGN. NOW THAT THE CESSATION OF HOSTILITIES HAS COME WE HAVE ENTERED UPON A PERIOD IN WHICH THE WORK OF OUR SEVEN WELFARE AGENCIES ASSUMES IF POSSIBLE AN ADDED IMPORTANCE. THE INCITEMENT UNDER WHICH OUR SOLDIERS AND SAILORS HAVE BEEN WORKING IS WITHDRAWN, THEIR HOURS OF LEISURE ARE MUCH MORE NUMEROUS, THEIR TEMPTATIONS ARE GREATLY MULTIPLIED AND INTENSIFIED. IT IS CLEAR THAT TO MIN-ISTER TO THEM FOR ALL OF THEIR TIME IS GOING TO REQUIRE A LARGER FINANCIAL OUTLAY THAN WHEN THEY WERE BEING SERVED FOR BUT A SMALL FRACTION OF THEIR TIME. ONLY TWO DAYS RE-MAIN BEFORE THE CAMPAIGN CLOSES AND VERY MUCH MORE MONEY WILL BE NEEDED BEFORE THE DESIRED LARGE OVERSUBSCRIPTION IS SECURED. I CANNOT BUT BELIEVE THAT OUR PEOPLE FROM ONE END OF THE COUNTRY TO THE OTHER WILL RALLY IN GENEROUS AND SACRIFICIAL GIVING TO COMPLETE THIS FUND AND TO GIVE OUR MEN THIS FRESH AND UNMISTAKABLE EVIDENCE THAT WE ARE ALL STILL BEHIND THEM AND WITH THEM DURING THEIR PATIENT AND LONG VIGIL IN OUR BEHALF AND IN THE SOLE INTEREST OF COM-PLETING THE HIGH PATRIOTIC DUTY ON WHICH WE SENT THEM FORTH. UNQUOTE.

JOHN R. MOTT

The Influenza and the United War Work Campaign

report of november, 1918

In some quarters the question has been raised, Will the campaign be deferred because of the widespread epidemic of influenza? The General Committee, composed of five leaders of each of the seven organizations which have united for the coming campaign, have decided, after careful consideration and after wide consultation to adhere to the original date and to conduct the drive as planned, November 11 to 18. It is recognized that the epidemic constitutes a handicap but the disadvantages of putting off the campaign outweigh any apparent advantages of such delay. It will be necessary for the leaders and workers everywhere to put forth added energy and to exercise their best judgment and ingenuity in adapting plans to meet the changed conditions. The following considerations and recommendations may be suggestive:

1. The Fourth Liberty Loan Campaign, by far the most stupendous undertaking of its kind in the history of the world, has been carried through to a successful issue in the midst of the same epidemic and also in a time of unsettling peace rumors.

2. The fact that many public meetings are not permitted may not be without its advantages. It leaves people more time to read, to think, and to decide. Time is required to face up to large opportunities and to devise liberal things.

3. More effective use should be made of the printed page to help offset the lack of big meetings. Local publicity committees and campaign workers in general should plan with this definitely in mind. Let them not depend alone or chiefly on national, department, and state headquarters for printed matter, but make larger use of local space and local talent.

4. Study how to effect a great increase in the amount of personal solicitation. Whether there is an epidemic or not, this is the method of securing the largest subscriptions and the largest number of subscribers. This was the secret of rolling up in these recent influenza days the phenomenal list of over 20,000,000 subscribers. It explains the even greater number of subscribers in the Second Red Cross Campaign a few months ago. It is not without its encouragement to remember that the very prevalence of the epidemic means that many people can more readily be found at home than under normal conditions, also that many will have more time to give to personal solicitation.

5. Moreover, because of the handicap occasioned by the epidemic, many a man who had planned to give one-third of his time to promoting the campaign will now be willing to devote two-thirds of his time to this patriotic object rather than to see it fail. Men will see that their unselfish and generous co-operation is absolutely essential.

6. While state and municipal health regulations may prevent the holding of mass meetings or public gatherings of any kind, they will not interfere with countless little groups of from two to seven or eight coming together at all hours of day or night to consider the claims of this important national and international object. There is not a town large or small in which influential citizens cannot invite a few men to luncheon or dinner in their homes, or to their offices and there appeal to them for generous subscriptions. Experience shows that these small informal groups yield many of the largest gifts. If the epidemic leads us to rely less on great mass meetings and more on spreading a veritable network of these face-to-face and heart-to-heart conferences of from two to five or ten men each, it will result in larger financial returns than might have been secured under normal conditions.

7. As the people cannot come together on Sundays or other days for religious services, this leaves much valuable time free. Wise planning will result in pre-empting much of it for the informal little group meetings indicated above, and for very profitable personal solicitation.

8. Much of the time that would ordinarily be spent in working up and attending great meetings may be spent to splendid advantage in thinking out and giving effect to plans to secure large gifts from firms, companies, and corporations. It takes thought to determine the lines along which influence can best be exerted and to bring that influence to bear. One successful solicitation of this kind may be the equivalent of 100 popular subscriptions secured as the result of a big meeting.

9. Chief thought and effort and the greatest influences should be concentrated on reaching the comparatively small proportion of the people in the community who give by far the largest part in every popular subscription. In a recent campaign in a small city about 13,000 subscribers gave over $500,000, but 92 per cent of the whole amount came from fewer than 1,300 persons. A study of many canvasses in cities large and small has revealed the fact that fully seven-eighths of the money secured came in each case from about one-eighth of the subscribers. It might be added that those who subscribe the largest amounts are not, as a rule, reached by public meetings. Nothing

in this statement should be construed as minimizing the necessity and importance of securing in every community as large a number as possible of small subscriptions from those who are unable to give more.

10. In some communities where weather conditions are favorable it will be possible to hold meetings in the open air. This plan was frequently employed in the recent Liberty Loan Campaign.

11. In a time like this when so much of the work will have to be done by personal solicitation, larger use than ever should be made of automobiles. Iowa is a rural state and has learned the value of this method. No matter how much the epidemic may spread in that state, the Ford will carry its people over their goal for a large oversubscription.

The Largest Voluntary Offering in History

In the history of mankind the largest sum ever provided through voluntary offerings for an altruistic cause was the great fund given in November, 1918, in the United War Work Campaign. In the period beginning November 11, a day forever memorable as the one on which hostilities ceased in the Great World War, the entire American people—the rich and the poor, the members of all parties, races, and religious faiths—united their gifts and sacrifices in rolling up the vast sum of over $190,000,000. This fact alone would give the campaign unique distinction.

When the unfavorable circumstances which attended this great effort are borne in mind, it becomes all the more remarkable. If the success of an enterprise or the greatness of a victory are determined by the number and extent of the difficulties and obstacles overcome, then the triumph achieved by the multitude of workers who carried through to a successful issue this patriotic endeavor was indeed notable and truly great. In the history of financial campaigns, when was there ever one conducted in the face of so many difficulties?

To begin with, the time for preparation was all too brief, having been confined to only two months, because of the long delays and uncertainty occasioned by the series of merger discussions and negotiations, involving, as they did for certain of the organizations, a threefold scrapping of the machinery, reorganization of the forces, and changing of the publicity program. No great campaign was ever preceded by such a brief preparation. Even the scant two months left for this purpose was cut into for three weeks by the Fourth Liberty Loan and, near the threshold of the campaign itself, by a general congressional election.

More serious still was the nationwide spread of the deadly influenza epidemic, which has had a death toll of twice as many lives as America has laid down in the war. The speaking program had virtually to be abandoned. Literally tens of thousands of speakers who had prepared themselves to help in the campaign could not be used. In some states not a single meeting could be held. All their churches, schools, and theaters were entirely closed. No meetings or luncheons or parades or community singing were permitted. In one state which has gone over the top, 40 per cent of the members of teams and committees were confined to their beds by the epidemic during the week of the campaign itself.

The false peace report which set the entire land ablaze came on the day when thousands of communities had planned to have their preparatory dinners or meetings for the final coaching of their working staff and for striking the keynote of the campaign; and the genuine peace report, which even more thrilled and absolutely absorbed the minds and hearts of the people, claimed the initial day of the campaign with its spontaneous celebrations in every city and hamlet of the land. In addition, certain states devoted the following day to a peace holiday. The confused or conflicting statements regarding the policy of demobilization as given out near the close of the campaign undoubtedly constituted another handicap, notwithstanding the clear and satisfying deliverances on the subject which were made by the War Department. Almost every community experienced real difficulty in connection with its publicity. The greatest world news of modern times, coming right in the very week of the campaign, necessarily commanded the first pages and often the entire space of the papers.

Moreover, there is no doubt that the high taxation prevented as large participation on the part of the wealthy and well-to-do classes in this campaign as in previous war drives. With few exceptions, they were not able to give so much relatively as they gave, for example, in the Red Cross and Association campaigns, notwithstanding the fact that they were equally interested. It was also undoubtedly true that because of the merger arrangement, none of the seven organizations was able to set forth the claims of its work with the same freedom, fulness, and compelling force which have naturally characterized it in its previous individual financial drives. This was inevitable and from the best of motives, because the leaders of all the co-operating societies were anxious not to do anything which might seem to the others like exploiting their particular agencies. It must be admitted also in fairness that in every community there have been some who were unable to favor the joint campaign and who therefore could not conscientiously devote to it their time and resources.

In the face of all these and other very real difficulties and handicaps, the fact that the leaders and friends of the co-operating agencies have been able to carry the campaign through with such signal success and favor is nothing less than marvelous and constitutes an event truly worthy of the great days in which we are living and of the great cause for which men have been dying and for which we have all been working in the effort to secure this much-needed and most important fund.

This generous and sacrificial offering puts all the seven co-operating organizations in a position to render a larger and better service to the men of the American army and navy and of the forces of our Allies and to other men as well as women seriously affected by war conditions. This is most providential, because the history of all wars shows that the period following the cessation of hostilities is the period of greatest danger. Our men are now face to face with the three gravest tests—the test of victory, the test of demobilization, and the test of readjustment. The timely generosity of the American people makes possible the meeting successfully of these trying experiences and causing them to yield priceless values. We can prevent the period of demobilization becoming one of demoralization. We can make sure that the coming months, with their great vacant spaces, shall be months not of physical, mental, and moral weakening of our men, but months of character building, of growth in useful knowledge, of increase in working efficiency, and of preparation for assuming the larger responsibilities of citizenship which await them on their return to their home communities. Of all the vast sums raised and expended in connection with the World War, and it has been announced by financial experts within the past few days that the war itself has cost the belligerent nations $200,000,000,000, what fund has been so potential for good or so highly multiplying in possibilities as this one which is to be devoted so largely to maintaining the ideals, strengthening the purposes, and releasing and guiding for the great constructive and reconstructive tasks of the world the latent energies of the flower of the manhood of America and her Allies?

The United War Work Campaign has furnished the most impressive example thus far afforded of religious unity and co-operation. When before have the leaders and the many millions of followers of the Protestant, Roman Catholic, and Jewish religious bodies of a great nation joined forces for the accomplishment of a common unselfish object? In doing this no one of them has obscured, minimized, or apologized for that which is most distinctive in its life and work. The campaign has been an illustration of interdenominationalism rather than of undenominationalism. It might have been regarded as wonderful had these bodies come together on a platform of putting aside their differences and all that is most characteristic of them; but it has been far more wonderful that they have been able to come together and work together and speak together just as they are, each being true to its own best self. The campaign has generated in many a community in atmosphere of truer understanding—an atmosphere in which, as has been pointed out, men come to loathe to differ and to determine to understand. It is a great thing for any people when, without weakening or sacrificing any vital principle, they make up their minds or resolve that they will seek to understand those with whom they may conscientiously differ.

The campaign has been a great experience for all of the seven co-operating organizations. It has afforded each a boundless opportunity to serve the others through placing at their disposal its experience, its organization, and its working force. No organization, just as no individual, was ever made one whit weaker by seeking unselfishly to help others. The campaign has given each agency literally thousands of new contacts in every section and one might almost say in every state. We have thus been ushered into countless new friendships and into a wider and richer fellowship. Thus our opportunity to bear witness to that which we most value has been greatly widened. The spirit of true tolerance and of sympathetic appreciation has been developed and men's souls have been expanded. What man is there who has thrown himself into the activities of these recent weeks who has not come forth a larger man?

The great triumph of these memorable days is due to the large-minded and large-hearted co-operation of all elements in our national life. It would be difficult, yes, impossible, to name all to whom we are indebted. President Wilson, through his two messages, one at the beginning and one near the close of the campaign, insured the responsive confidence of the entire nation. The Secretary of War, the Secretary of the Navy, the Secretary of the Interior, the Director General of Railroads, the Secretary of Agriculture, the Secretary of Commerce and Labor, the Comptroller of the Currency, and other leaders of the government gave the weight of their influence and the force of their influential advocacy to the campaign. The telegrams of endorsement from General Pershing, Marshal Foch, and other great commanders did much to stimulate the gifts of the people. The Army and Navy Commissions on Training Camp Activities, the Committee on Public Information, the Council of National Defense, and the corresponding bodies in the various states and in thousands of communities placed themselves solidly behind the drive, as did also the governors of virtually all the states. Mr. Roosevelt, Mr. Taft, and many of our other statesmen and political leaders by addresses and articles rendered invaluable co-operation. The great sister organization, the American Red Cross, called upon all its workers and chapters to do all in their power to insure the success of the campaign. The Protestant pastors, the hierarchy of the Roman Catholic Church, and the rabbis in all parts of the land mobilized their religious forces in the interest of this notable effort on behalf of our soldiers and sailors. One cannot speak too highly of the devoted and most efficient service of the committee members and executive staff of the national, departmental, state, county, and local campaign organizations. There has been nothing like it in the history of campaigns, and this is saying a great deal.

The remarkable co-operation of other countries should also be borne in mind. As the opening date of the campaign drew near, cablegrams were sent to several nations primarily with the thought of enlisting the interest of Americans resident in those lands. By the time the campaign closed over $2,000,000 had been subscribed in these neighboring and distant countries, the natives of the countries as well as the Americans and other nationals joining in the giving. Porto Rico subscribed over $100,000, although their offering came right on the heels of the disastrous earthquake. In Cuba $275,000 was subscribed, $100,000 being given by the national government and the President of the Republic serving as honorary chairman of the Campaign Committee. In the various larger cities of Mexico all nationalities united under the leadership of the American ambassador in providing over $100,000 for the fund. The citizens of Hawaii gave the sum of $330,000, thus establishing a new record. The cablegram to the Philippines suggested that they raise $100,000 for the cause, but they replied that they would give $250,000. In Japan the Foreign Minister organized a committee with Prince Tokugawa as its chairman, and the sum of $360,000 was raised as an expression of sympathy for America in the war. In China the governments in the North and in the South vied with each other in generous offerings to the fund. The meeting launching this co-operative effort was held in the Winter Palace and was attended by the members of the Cabinet, the leading members of Parliament, and the foreign ambassadors. The Chihli Provincial Assembly subscribed $100,000. Each of six cities gave $100,000, or more. In all, China gave over $1,000,000. The Russian merchants in Harbin contributed 1,200,000 rubles.

Never before have foundations, corporations, companies, banks, industries, and the rural population of America participated so generally and so generously in a great popular subscription. Through all the coming years the gifts and sacrifices of many millions, from the richest to the poorest and from the youngest to the oldest, in every corner of our country and from neighboring as well as distant lands will be held in grateful memory. Many a time in the future the American people will be called upon to give, but never will they be summoned to associate themselves in furthering a greater cause in the midst of greater days.

Above all, as we remind ourselves of the difficulties, humanly speaking insuperable, which have attended this great undertaking and as we recall the wonderful miracle which has been wrought in ushering in the world-wide and, as we trust, enduring peace which synchronized with the launching of the campaign, let us reverently and gratefully acknowledge Almighty God as the great and only efficient Cause of this great victory of peace, as He was of the great victory of the war.

LETTERS OF TWO WAR PRESIDENTS

After receiving the following letter of President Wilson my attention was called to a communication of President Lincoln evoked by a cause similar to the one which in these days is so near the very heart of the American people—the welfare of our soldiers and sailors. The two letters are reproduced in the hope that the spirit and heart interest which they manifest may be communicated and be expressed in generous and sacrificial giving toward the United War Work Campaign.

JOHN R. MOTT

I

EXECUTIVE MANSION, WASHINGTON.
February 22, 1863.

REV. ALEXANDER REED:

MY DEAR SIR:

Your note by which you, as General Superintendent of the U. S. Christian Commission, invite me to preside at a meeting to be held this day at the Hall of the House of Representatives, in this city, is received.

While, for reasons which I deem sufficient, I must decline to preside, I can not withhold my approval of the meeting, and its worthy objects. Whatever shall be sincerely, and in God's name, devised for the good of the soldier and seaman, in their hard spheres of duty, can scarcely fail to be blessed. And whatever shall tend to turn our thoughts from the unreasoning and uncharitable passions, prejudices, and jealousies incident to a great national trouble, such as ours, and to fix them upon the vast and long enduring consequences, for weal or for woe, which are to result from the struggle, and especially to strengthen our reliance on the Supreme Being for the final triumph of the right, can not but be well for us all.

The birthday of Washington and the Christian Sabbath, coinciding this year and suggesting together, the highest interests of this life, and of that to come, is most propitious for the meeting proposed.

Your obt. Servt.

A. LINCOLN.

II

THE WHITE HOUSE, WASHINGTON,
November 8, 1918

MY DEAR DR. MOTT:

I am sure the people throughout the country will understand why it is that I am unable to fulfill the desire of my heart to make a public address at this time in the interest of the approaching campaign.

It has been with sincere gratification that I have observed the wholehearted co-operation of the Young Men's Christian Association, the Young Women's Christian Association, the National Catholic War Council, the Jewish Welfare Board, the War Camp Community Service, the American Library Association, and the Salvation Army in response to my request that they combine their respective financial drives in one United War Work Campaign, November 11-18, to secure the sum of at least $170,500,000 for their invaluable work. The wise economy of money and effort, the increased efficiency which will result from a blending of experience, the creation of an atmosphere of truer understanding, the unmistakable evidence of a growing unity of spirit and the influence of all this in strengthening the national solidarity is reassuring in the extreme.

As you now stand on the threshold of presenting your appeal to the entire American people, I wish to renew the expression of my conviction that the service rendered by these welfare agencies is indispensable, and my earnest hope for the abundant success of the campaign. The inevitable growth of the army and navy, and the multiplying demands for our help from France, Italy, and Russia, make it clear that a generous oversubscription is highly desirable. No matter how distant the day of peace may prove to be, it will be followed by a long period of demobilization, during which the opportunity and need for the constructive work of these organizations will be quite as great as in wartime, and I am glad to note that your plans contemplate serving the soldiers and sailors in this critically important period. I am particularly pleased to know of the comprehensive program of education to be carried out during the coming months.

Gifts that provide the service which this campaign makes possible are not so much gifts to organizations as gifts—invaluable gifts—to our soldiers, sailors, and marines and constitute an appropriate expression of our gratitude for their patriotic and unselfish devotion. The whole plan of the United War Work Campaign is inspiring and is most emphatically in the interest of the nation and of all the lands with which we are associated in these momentous days.

Cordially and sincerely yours,

WOODROW WILSON

CRITICISMS OF THE WAR WORK ANSWERED

ARMY Y.M.C.A. AUTHORIZED TO OPERATE CANTEEN

After several conferences at General Pershing's Headquarters during the summer of 1917, it was agreed that the army "Y" should take full charge of the canteen service, including the purchase of stock in America, in Great Britain, in France, and in the neutral countries of Europe.

Bulletin No. 33, issued by General Pershing's Chief of Staff, stated that all goods were to be sold at "Y" centers at purchase cost price, plus cost of transportation, with a slight margin added to cover goods lost in transit. The order also provided that the canteens were to be operated by the "Y" as an agent acting under the general direction of the respective army officers and the plan was designed to release enlisted men for direct military service. The colossal task of operating the canteen was undertaken by the army Y.M.C.A. with full knowledge of the inevitable criticism which would follow.

STATEMENT BY JOHN R. MOTT, GENERAL SECRETARY, NATIONAL WAR WORK COUNCIL, Y.M.C.A.

So much criticism of army Y.M.C.A. methods has been heard in the last few weeks that I have decided that the one thing to do in fairness to the millions who have subscribed to its fund, and in fairness to the Association itself, is to discuss in detail each criticism which has been raised. We have caused an investigation to be made and we are giving our conclusions. It may be that there will be further criticism. It is our judgment that this should be frankly and fearlessly faced. If we were to evade criticism, we should be false to our trust. As we recognize whatever of truth it contains, we shall be able to profit by it and to amend our methods in such a manner as to give the maximum of service. There is another aspect. Much of the criticism is utterly unfounded, but only by challenging such criticism can the public have a clear conception of the facts in the case.

It is the history of every great effort that mistakes are made and no one, no matter how exalted his person or how unimpeachable his integrity, can escape. Other important organizations have passed through a similar experience. Much of the adverse comment is due to misconception or to partial knowledge. Among the criticisms most frequently heard concerning the army Y.M.C.A. are the following:

Operation of Canteens

Question No. 1. Is it true that the army Y.M.C.A. has been profiting by the operation of the canteens overseas?

It is not true that the army Y.M.C.A. profited by the operation of canteens overseas. In the terms of Bulletin No. 33 from General Pershing's Headquarters, it was provided that if there were any profit derived from the canteens, the army Y.M.C.A. would use it exclusively for the benefit of the men in the army. The discrepancy between the quartermaster prices and army Y.M.C.A. prices was investigated by the War Department. The investigation proved they had lost thousands of dollars and that no profit was made.

Statement of Third Assistant Secretary of War F. P. Keppel

Matter of prices asked by army Young Men's Christian Association for its articles sold in canteen overseas already investigated by War Department and conditions being remedied. Army Y.M.C.A. originally asked by General Pershing to run canteen for army on cost basis. To do this had to reckon in price fixing such overhead charges as transportation charges and marine insurance so that prices were much higher than in this country. Army Young Men's Christian Association made no profit but lost thousands of dollars. Arrangements now made will enable them to obtain supplies from sources that will reduce overhead charges and keep prices down.

Statement of Raymond B. Fosdick, Chairman of War Department
Commission on Training Camp Activities

Raymond B. Fosdick, Chairman of the Commission on Training
Camp Activities, upon returning from an investigation of auxiliary
agencies in Europe, as quoted by the New York *Times* as saying:

"I should like to take this opportunity to remove a misapprehen-
sion about the army Y.M.C.A. which has gained considerable ground
not only with our fellows abroad, but with the people back home, and
that is that the army Y.M.C.A. is making money out of the canteens
which it is operating for the forces. At General Pershing's request I
went into this matter thoroughly and the report is absolutely without
foundation. I mention this matter only because the widespread rumor
is most unfair to an organization which is doing heroic service."

Prices Now Same as Charged by the Quartermaster

"All goods on sale to the A.E.F. in army Y.M.C.A. canteens in
France after November 1 will be sold at the same prices charged by
the Quartermaster's Stores." This announcement was made following
the receipt of a cable from Paris stating that this arrangement, which
the army Y.M.C.A. has been trying for several months to make with
the army authorities, had been granted by General Pershing.

General Pershing also has arranged that the canteen be extended
to the huts of the Salvation Army and the Knights of Columbus. Thus
all three organizations will become in a sense agents of the Quartermaster's Department, which will supply the goods to be sold, keep
prices uniform, and arrange for part, at least, of the transportation.
—From New York *Sun*, October 27, 1918.

How "Gift Tobacco" Was Sold

*Question No. 2. Is it true that gift tobacco was sold at army
Y.M.C.A. canteens overseas?*

It is true that in a few cases gift tobacco was sold at army
Y.M.C.A. canteens, and the circumstances are these: The New York
Sun, the Chicago *Tribune,* and possibly other parties, shipped to-
bacco to France in care of the Quartermaster, with the intention of
having it distributed free to soldiers. Some portions of this tobacco,
because cases were not sufficiently marked, were sold to the army
Y.M.C.A. by the Quartermaster and retailed in certain army
Y.M.C.A. canteens to soldiers at the price paid the Quartermaster.
Later, when soldiers came to open these parcels, they found in them

evidence that they had been intended for free distribution. In every case where these were returned to the army Y.M.C.A. it furnished free an equivalent amount of tobacco from its own supplies. The New York *Sun* had investigated several stories of this kind and found the facts to be as stated above. The Quartermaster concerned has also investigated the matter and fully exonerates the army Y.M.C.A.

History of an incident in which army Y.M.C.A. sold gift tobacco.

On October 14, W. E. Stewart, Acting Divisional Secretary, purchased Piedmont cigarettes "16" from the Third Division Sales Commissary. On opening these it was found that each carton contained a post card addressed by some individual or firm in the States indicating that the particular carton was a gift for the person to whom addressed and apparently intended for free distribution. The cases containing these cigarettes bore no marks to indicate the nature of the contents. Mr. Stewart reported the matter to the Third Division Sales Commissary and to the Y.M.C.A. of the Fifth Region. In response to this report Mr. Stewart received the following letter:

FROM: C.O., Sales Commissary Unit No. 4, A.P.O. 740, A.E.F.
TO: Y.M.C.A., 3rd Division, A.P.O. 740, A.E.F.
SUBJECT: Gift Cigarettes

1. Through an error of the Supply Depot at Gievres, this commissary received several cases of Piedmont cigarettes, each carton of which contained a return post card stating that these cigarettes were a gift from "The New York *Sun* Tobacco Fund."

2. These cigarettes were sold you in case lots before this was discovered, there being no marks on the cases to indicate that this was gift tobacco. This matter has been taken up by this commissary with the Supply Depot at Gievres, and in all probability these cigarettes will be replaced.

(signed) C. P. HAFFLEY,
1ST LT., *Q.M.C.U.S.A.*,

October 23, 1918.   *Quartermaster.*

FURNISHES FREE SUPPLIES

Question No. 3. Is it true that the army Y.M.C.A. furnishes free nothing more than writing paper to men overseas?

It has been the policy of the army Y.M.C.A. to give free service and not primarily free supplies. This policy has from the beginning commanded the approval of the army authorities. Nevertheless the army Y.M.C.A. service, without charges to the soldiers, sailors, and marines included in the war zone more than 1,900 huts, tents, and buildings of various designs that served as home, church, club, and theater; free entertainments by noted musical and theatrical stars, miles of motion pictures, postal and money transfer service; thousands of dollars' worth of athletic equipment and athletics directed by world-famous athletes; social, religious, and educational activities. During one month in the latter part of 1918 the army Y.M.C.A. distributed free to soldiers in the front lines more than $75,000 worth of supplies.

This is directly in line with action taken by the committee of eleven officially representing the seven welfare agencies recognized by the U. S. government overseas as follows: "Except in the actual fighting areas there shall be no free distribution of supplies except where a permanent work is maintained by the organizations concerned."

AVOIDED DUPLICATION OF EFFORT

Question No. 4. Is it true that the army Y.M.C.A. has failed to keep in touch with the wounded and ill?

In order to prevent any duplication of effort overseas, an agreement was reached between the American Red Cross and the army Y.M.C.A. This provided that the American Red Cross should concern itself with the care of the wounded and ill; the army Y.M.C.A. and kindred organizations, with the well. Therefore under the agreement opportunities for service to the wounded and sick were limited.

RELEASED ALL MEN OF DRAFT AGE

Question No. 5. Were men chosen for army Y.M.C.A. work who were of draft age and fit for army service?

During the first months of the war, some men who were physically fit but had not yet been called for service were sent to France. Within a few months most of these men had volunteered for military service. The comparatively small number who remained as late as August of the present calendar year, were then notified that they must either enlist or leave the service of the army Y.M.C.A. Practically all of these were divinity students and thereby exempted.

NO "BOMBPROOF" JOBS FOR ARMY "Y" WORKERS

Question No. 6. Is it true that the army "Y" workers overseas did not go to the front lines but persistently dodged danger?

The best answer to this question is that since the army "Y" went overseas to serve the American Expeditionary Force, nine of its workers have been killed by shellfire while on duty and twenty-nine were seriously gassed or wounded. In addition to this, thirty-one have died in the service, chiefly as a result of exposure and overwork. It might also be of interest to add that ten have been cited for bravery or decorated. In the Argonne fight there were 700 "Y" secretaries, fifty of whom were women canteen workers, attached to the different fighting units. All of these workers remained in the danger zone and frequently under shellfire during the entire offensive.

RELIGIOUS ATTITUDE OF ARMY "Y" WORKERS

Question No. 7. Is it true that the typical attitude of the army Y.M.C.A. workers has been that of holier-than-thou persons?

This question is of special interest because we have recently been taken to task for the very opposite of that implied in this question. The charge has been earnestly pressed by not a few that the army Y.M.C.A. has been untrue to its religious tradition and has not sufficiently set forth the claims of religion upon the soldiers. When an organization is criticized with equal strength by critics holding conflicting and directly opposing views, one comes to the conclusion that after all it must be holding a fairly straight course between extremes.

UNSYMPATHETIC WORKERS REPRIMANDED

Question No. 8. Is it true that some of the overseas secretaries have been impatient in their dealings with the soldiers?

Considering the fact that many army Y.M.C.A. workers continued at their posts for eighteen hours at a stretch, sometimes without meals, it would be but natural that a few might have lost their self-control and have manifested a wrong disposition; but we are glad to believe, in the light of the great mass of testimony, that this has not been the characteristic attitude of the vast majority of the workers. I have heard the complaint made by a few soldiers that certain of the army Y.M.C.A. workers have been prone to pay more attention to the officers than to the enlisted men and that they have at times treated men who have come into the canteens in an unsympathetic and inhospitable manner. Wherever our supervisory secretaries have learned of these complaints, they have acted promptly and, to my knowledge, where the charges have been substantiated, have reprimanded the workers concerned and when it was felt a reprimand was not sufficient the workers were recalled and sent home.

CAREFUL IN SELECTION OF PERSONNEL

Question No. 9. Is it true that the army Y.M.C.A. has sent overseas men utterly unfit for the tasks they were called upon to perform?

It is not true in any sense that the army Y.M.C.A. has given little thought to its selection of men for overseas service. It must be remembered that when the army Y.M.C.A. began erecting the structure upon which to build its great work, it faced the condition where the young and physically fit man would necessarily look to the army and navy. The army Y.M.C.A. had the choice of the physically unfit and the men beyond the draft age. It made the best possible selections from the available material. It erred in some instances. It was impossible for it to do otherwise. The men were needed instantly. But where the army Y.M.C.A. detected any error or mistakes of judgment, it recalled the men it had selected. One instance of this shows that a man never even set his foot in France. The decision to recall him was made before his transport had tied up to the pier. Every possible effort was made to prevent the enrollment of men whose only conception of their mission was that of a junket. In this connection it will be interesting to note that the army Y.M.C.A. has already sent over 7,000 men and 1,500 women, of whom full 5,000 are still there at work. When this large number is borne in mind, it should not be surprising that here and there, under the trying experiences of the work, there should be found men who are disqualified. It is our fixed practice to recall all such cases. Less than 200 cases from among the more than 8,500 men and women sent overseas have been returned for moral lapses, discourtesies, inadaptability, or other reasons.

WAR DEPARTMENT APPROVES CURB ON RECRUITING

Question No. 10. Is it true that the army Y.M.C.A. has caused scores of men to be taken from gainful occupations and, after promising overseas service, turned them back without occupations?

It is true in certain cases. It is equally true of the government of the United States, and other civilian organizations. And where the army Y.M.C.A. has called scores, the army has called thousands to give up their gainful occupations. The army Y.M.C.A. expended its energy in bringing men to New York City to embark for overseas service when the war came to an end; and it was still expected by the army Y.M.C.A. that these men who had been called from gainful occupations would serve the troops in France. The War Department indicated strong preference that men should not be sent from this side but wherever possible should be taken from the army overseas. It has recently announced that it will release officers and enlisted men, who are especially qualified to assist in the educational program and other activities of the organization. This will mean that soldiers in France can enter army Y.M.C.A. service immediately. Of course, it involves a large saving in transportation but affects and embarrasses those men who were ready for overseas service. These men are in exactly the same position as officers and enlisted men discharged because the period of emergency, or the need for their services no longer exist. It is unfortunate and the sympathy of the army Y.M.C.A. goes out to those. Their plight is one for which the army Y.M.C.A. is in no way responsible and one which it cannot remedy. Approval of the "Y" course in restricting its secretaries bound overseas to educational, entertainment, and physical work is expressed in the following letter from Secretary of War Baker:

Secretary Baker's letter to Dr. Mott

MY DEAR DR. MOTT:

The War Department is in thorough agreement with the plan being followed by the National War Work Council of the Young Men's Christian Association and other organizations in refraining from sending overseas any further workers except those who are now absolutely essential.

As soon as the armistice was signed the War Department felt that with the exception of a few highly trained experts, who were needed immediately to fill vacancies in specified positions, no additional men should be sent abroad, not even where men were already under appointment and waiting to sail.

These men, who had been recruited for overseas work and were at the last moment disappointed, are worthy of praise, not only for their willingness to undergo arduous service, but also for their quick readjustment of plans when the sudden ending of hostilities prevented the consummation of their cherished hopes.

The action of these organizations in withholding overseas recruits should be understood as in direct accord with the wishes of the War Department and should not be the occasion of criticism.

Cordially yours,

(Signed) NEWTON D. BAKER,
Secretary of War

WASHINGTON, December 23, 1918.

THE "Y" HUT—A HOME FOR NEARLY THREE MILLION SOLDIER BOYS

The "Y" has provided more than 1,900 huts, tents, and buildings of various designs in the war zone and nearly 600 in the army and navy camps in the United States.

The "Y" hut is the soldiers' and sailors' church. No effort is made to force religion on any man, because no effort is necessary. The boys have welcomed the services and have been eager to accept millions of Scriptures and booklets provided.

Clubs, hotels, restaurants, and rest areas have been provided. Entertainment facilities at leave resorts have been provided for more than 70,000 men every week in France.

Libraries are maintained in nearly all the army Y.M.C.A. huts in co-operation with the American Library Association.

Writing material is furnished free to the fighting forces wherever they may happen to be.

Athletics under the direction of the world's noted athletes, are provided for the men when off duty. Equipment is furnished free.

Hundreds of tons of supplies have been shipped from this country for the boys over there. In one month—December, 1918—900,000 packages of biscuits, 1,650,000 pounds of chocolate, 90,000 cakes of soap, 3,000,000 cigars, 70,000,000 cigarettes and 50,000 pounds of cocoa to be sold at Quartermaster's prices were provided in the "Y" canteens. Other necessities in like proportion were provided during the same month. In the last three months of 1918 sales at less than cost in "Y" canteens exceeded $5,000,000 a month. The deficit sustained by the "Y" on these sales since August 1, 1918, is at the rate of between two and three million dollars, annually. This deficit will be paid out of the contributions to the army Y.M.C.A.

Fighting men overseas send home more than $3,000,000 each month through the "Y" banking and postoffice department. Service is free.

The world's leading educators are assisting the "Y" in setting up an extensive educational program that will fit the men for return to the duties of civil life.

The "Y" is co-operating with the government in activities incident to demobilization and reconstruction.

Miles of motion pictures and theatrical entertainments by famous stage stars are provided under the direction of the "Y." In a single month, October, the "Y" was giving 6,088 shows abroad.

The long arm of the army Y.M.C.A. reaches all of the way with the boy—from the time he leaves home until he returns. On the troop trains, in the training camps, at the port of embarkation, on the transports right up to the front-line trenches and back again you will find a "Big Brother" of the "Y" always on the job and willing to serve. Wherever you find a soldier or sailor you will find evidence of the loving care of the folks back home expressed through the army Y.M.C.A.

CRITICISM OF THE WAR WORK OF THE YOUNG MEN'S CHRISTIAN ASSOCIATION

ADDRESS DELIVERED FEBRUARY 8, 1919, IN CARNEGIE HALL BEFORE THE LEAGUE FOR POLITICAL EDUCATION

Naturally more of the complaints concerning the war work of the Y.M.C.A. come to me as General Secretary of the National War Work Council than to any other one person. It will interest you and I think surprise some of you when I say that the chief impression made upon me by reviewing all these criticisms is this: What a vast area of this work is untouched by these complaints and what a comparatively small part is touched at all by them! How many complaints have we heard, in a time when we might have expected to hear more than usual, concerning the regular work of the Young Men's Christian Association that existed before the war and that has gone on right in the teeth of this war; that work of thousands of Association branches in North America, with their 5,000 executive officers, with more than $100,000,000 in buildings have been working ceaselessly night as well as day, for the physical, social, mental, moral, and spiritual betterment of all classes of men and boys? It seems to me that there never has been a period since I have known the Association (and I have known it for over thirty years) when I have heard so little criticism concerning this work of the Associations on behalf of young men in American cities and rural communities, young men in industries, on railways, in colleges, and elsewhere, as in this war period! I would remind you that from this established and well-known work have come largely the real leaders, the effective methods and the spirit of the war work of the Y.M.C.A. That is, they are all of a piece. There has not been raised up for serving the soldiers and sailors a new Movement that has taken over some new traditions, ideas, and leaders or that is animated by a new spirit.

How many criticisms have you heard about what this organization did for soldiers and sailors before this war? I have not heard, at a time when the law of association would have called it up, if at any time, any criticism by veterans of the Civil War concerning what the Y.M.C.A. did under the name of the Christian Commission which, as every well-informed man here knows, was the Y.M.C.A. working for our soldiers in that struggle, furnishing the workers, the money, the plans. Nor have you heard, I venture, any serious criticism regarding what was done in the Spanish-American war. Not long before his death I had a conversation there on his porch at Oyster Bay with Roosevelt and he harked back to the splendid service rendered by the Y.M.C.A. in Cuba, in Texas, and in other parts of the South, and from that he went on to say, "Anything I can do to help you men in this present time, I am going to do." "Oh, for the touch of a vanished hand and the sound of a voice that is still!"

Nor have we heard any complaint whatever concerning what the American Y.M.C.A. did on the plains of Manchuria and in the ports of embarkation of the Japanese Islands in the Russo-Japanese war when, in union with the Japanese Association workers, it was permitted to minister to 700,000 Japanese soldiers in the midst of very difficult conditions—a work so well-done, notwithstanding the meager resources at the disposal of the Association, that the ruler of Japan, a non-Christian ruler, was so profoundly impressed that he made his first gift to Christianity, a gift of $5,000 toward the army work under American Y.M.C.A. leadership.

Come now to our work in Mexico and on the Mexican border, how insufficiently that work was done, and yet how little complaint about it we have heard at a time when, if ever, I repeat, men would be recalling weaknesses and pointing to flaws. Only last April when I was having luncheon with General Pershing at his Headquarters in France, he spoke with deep appreciation of the way the American Y.M.C.A. had served along the border during that trying, irksome period and how this organization had gone with him into the area of occupation and stood by when it was most needed. I remind you again, the character of the organization has not changed, its ideals have not been abandoned, the original spirit has not departed.

Now take the war work that we have been doing on this side of the Atlantic since America entered the war. Have you been keeping a record as has been done in my office? If so, you will find there have been next to no complaints about what we have done in the great cantonments and other large camps and in countless small detachments from sea to sea and along our coasts in serving the American army and navy. To my mind it is highly significant that working in nearly 1,000 buildings, tents, and other structures, with a staff of over 4,000 secretaries conducting their varied, helpful activities before the very eyes of the people who could criticize, were there ground for criticism, the Association has been commended for doing a very good piece of work and by none has it been more praised than by the men who are being served and also by leaders of the sister organizations with which we were glad to co-operate in the recent campaign.

Now look beyond the United States in this war. What complaints have you heard about our work on behalf of the Italian army of 3,000,000 men? In Italy we have been working under more difficult conditions than in certain other parts of the war zone. The Supreme Command of the Italian army had an inspection made of what the American Y.M.C.A. was doing for the A.E.F. and on the strength of that investigation said, "We must have a similar work in the Italian army." They invited us to furnish secretaries and to back the work financially. When I was in Italy a few months ago I visited this work of ours, from the sun-baked plains of Venetia, away up to the icy heights of the Trentino, where in the midst of the granite crags I found what we call the huts, or abodes of the Casa del Soldato under the leadership of the American Y.M.C.A. This was 6,000 feet above sea level on the snow line, where the Association workers as well as the soldiers suffered more than at any other point unless it be the men who suffered so much from heat on the plains of Mesopotamia. The King of Italy sent for me to visit him in his villa near the front lines. He kept me an hour questioning me about our methods and our work. I was wearing the Association uniform, as was the custom in the military zone. His Majesty, observing the triangle on the sleeve, asked me to tell its significance. This afforded me a good opportunity to explain the distinctive principles of our work. He became especially interested as I expounded the physical, mental, and spiritual building up of men. At the end of the interview he said, "Tell the American Y.M.C.A. to spread its work to the maximum in our army." We now have nearly 300 workers there under the leadership of Dr. Nollen, President of Lake Forest University.

What have you heard in the way of adverse criticism concerning the activities of the Y.M.C.A. throughout the vast areas of Russia? When I was there as a member of the Root Mission in 1917 I was much impressed by the opportunity to serve the then dissolving Russian army and loyal elements among the Russian peoples, and it interested me to see that every member of the Mission came to the conclusion that the American Y.M.C.A. should be extended to Russia in that hour of grave national need.

With such encouragement as the President and others gave we established the work and now have a staff of nearly 100 men in Vladivostok and scattered across Siberia almost to the Urals, also in the region of the northern ports. Before the more ominous stage of the Revolution we had our workers in the heart of ancient or Holy Russia and along the disintegrating Western front. We have had an extensive correspondence with those workers and have had interviews with Russians of various parties, but I do not recall a single adverse criticism made with reference to that work. I wish you could have heard Dr. Masaryk, the President of the new Czechoslovak Republic, comment upon it with the greatest appreciation. Some of you heard Mr. Colton quote the Czechoslovaks as saying that they look upon the American Y.M.C.A. as the uncle of the Czechoslovak Movement, having in mind the way in which we befriended them in the darkest hour and the practical manner in which the Association has served them all through their remarkable Russian experiences from the time they were imprisoned until they had fought their way to the Pacific. In a very true sense the American Y.M.C.A. helped them to become the rallying center around which gathered other stable elements. Later, when the Allies went in we were permitted to serve the American, the Canadian, the British, the French, the Japanese, as well as the Czechoslovak troops and the loyal Russians. General Graves, the highest American military commander now on Russian soil, has recently said that in his judgment the American Y.M.C.A. has done more to stabilize Russia than any other influence, and that it has been the best interpreter of the spirit of the American people to all parties in Russia.

Think also of what we have been permitted to do in hand with our British brothers, all through the war, in serving the men that have guarded the Suez Canal, that great Allied key position; and how we have been permitted with the Australian, the New Zealand, and the British secretaries to go with Allenby all through the wonderful Palestine campaign; and how, with the British and Indians, with whom it has been an honor to be associated, we were able to work and to suffer on the plains of Mesopotamia until splendid victory was achieved; and how we have been able to blend the sacrifices of the American people, as well as the Association experience in those never-to-be-forgotten days of helping to nerve the men to impossible tasks on the Gallipoli Peninsula, where undying glory gathered round the heads of the men who survived as well as of those who perished; and how in Macedonia, where the great bloody wedge was driven in that took Bulgaria out of the war and stabilized Greece, the American Y.M.C.A. was not found wanting.

Nor do I need to remind you of what we have done for the great French army to whom we owe the liberty of the world more than to any other army—that army of 4,000,000 men. In that army of double the size of the A.E.F. all the Y.M.C.A. work has from the beginning been financed by America and many of the leaders for this ever-expanding ministry of practical helpfulness have come from America. When I was over there in the autumn of 1914, before we had a War

Work Council, I left $2,500 in the hands of a Frenchman and said, "Get an opportunity for the American Y.M.C.A. to serve the French army." He tried in vain for months. After failing with the War Ministry, he finally got permission from one French general to open up what they called the Foyer du Soldat, or to use the full title, Foyer du Soldat Franco-Americaine Y.M.C.A. This general said, "Try it out in one place." The experiment was so successful that he then permitted them to spread it throughout his entire army. Then the general of the neighboring division wanted it; then the general on the other side; and then others, until it spread rapidly through a large part of the army. When I was over there last April, Clemenceau, in speaking to me of the seven or eight hundred Foyers already established, said that they had been one of the principal factors in maintaining the morale of the French army.

Some weeks after that we received in America the cablegram stating that in the Verdun fortress the one thousandth Foyer had been dedicated. The French War Ministry, which at first had turned a deaf ear to this work, sent a deputation to New York and laid before the National War Work Council of the Y.M.C.A. the request of the French government that we spread our work to 2,000 points, thus making possible covering the entire French army. You do not deceive the French. Face to face with what the Association was doing in our own army and recognizing its real merit, they said, "We want to entrust this great enterprise of serving our troops to the American Y.M.C.A." The other day at our last meeting at the Biltmore Hotel, some of you were present, and heard that splendid telegram from M. de Billy of the French High Commission in Washington. I do not see how he could have spoken more generously or more intelligently of what we have been doing than he did in that message.

Nor have you heard, I venture to say, a well-authenticated criticism concerning what the American Y.M.C.A. has done for the four or five million prisoners of war. The American people should be reminded that the American Y.M.C.A. alone has been permitted to serve the prisoners of war on both sides of the struggle from almost the beginning of the war. I know I am well within bounds when I say that this agency was the means directly and indirectly of saving the lives of tens of thousands of prisoners; and the sanity of thousands more; and its spiritual ministry was literally life from the dead for multitudes. It is one of the most fascinating and wonderful chapters in the entire history of war service. "I was in prison and ye came unto me," was one of Christ's supreme tests of men.

We now come to the A.E.F. and if there is any part of this work of which I am more proud than of another it is the work of the American Y.M.C.A. in the A.E.F. You have heard some criticisms of it. I want to tell you some things now that you have not heard criticized.

You have not heard anybody, enemy or friend, criticize the fact that the Y.M.C.A. have had in operation in the A.E.F. 1,500 huts, rented buildings and tents, the free use of which is given to every man in the American or Allied uniform. Last winter men did not criticize the fact that we paid between $60 and $70 a ton for coal in order that in hundreds of villages and other places where our men were billeted there might be one place, and often it was the only place during those bitterly cold days and nights, where our boys who had been drilling on the sodden ground and had wet feet or in the drifting sleet and rain and had wet clothing could come to dry themselves and get some warmth, and also have light, where they could write their home letters and read the magazines. You have not heard that criticized. If you did, you know what you thought of the thoughtless ingratitude which prompted it.

How many within your hearing have criticized the fact that we have sent overseas hundreds of athletic directors above draft age and that we have already spent between $1,000,000 and $2,000,000 on athletic supplies for the free use of American soldiers and sailors that, as Mr. Perkins put it, the men, as they come from the strain of trench life or out of the awful scenes of warfare, might through recreational sports have a chance to clear their minds, and that the men in the midst of the tedium of camp life might revive their tired spirits.

Have you heard criticism concerning the fact that we are maintaining overseas 100 entertainment troupes selected by some of the leading members of the theatrical profession and that their entertainments are provided free for the A.E.F. in France and England?

Have men complained to you (they used to do so over a year ago before we had the service well-organized) that we are showing over 4,000,000 feet of films each month in our Y.M.C.A. huts and tents to a nightly attendance of nearly 300,000?

Have men complained in your hearing of the hundreds of thousands of dollars that we have spent in free musical instruments and in sending musicians and musical companies? Included in their number is the daughter of the President to whom I would pay a tribute for her democracy and her splendid spirit of service.

Who has complained to you about our giving away over 10,000,000 sheets of writing paper each week and the envelopes? Some did complain about the poor quality of the paper, but they forgot that we were then under government restriction with reference to the use of paper.

Have men found fault with the fact that we have supplied each year hundreds of thousands of dollars' worth of American magazines and other periodicals free of cost to the men?

Have you heard any people criticize the fact that we have sent over some of the most distinguished, brilliant, and popular lecturers to the men—and the number of those lecturers is increasing—that they may help the soldiers to become re-oriented and readjusted to the new demands of their own country to which they are so soon to return?

Have men complained to you that we have afforded facilities for the fellows who had to leave high school, college, and night school to take up their studies and that they may thus come home more highly efficient and better-prepared to cope with their problems in the days of keen competition that lie ahead?

Have men complained that we have just ordered about $2,000,000 worth of textbooks and school materials that are to be given away absolutely free to the soldiers, and that the American Library Association has joined hands with us and have said they will give $1,000,000 for books of reference that the men could carry on their private studies or class work? A message has reached us indicating that the government itself may reimburse the Y.M.C.A. and the Library Association for what they are expending for these quantities of books.

Have men complained to you about the plan we are now carrying out of sending over the leading preachers of the United States of America? I use that word advisedly, it is a wonderful list. I make bold to say that in all history helpful messages will never have been preached with greater adequacy and power to bodies of men of any nation than with the A.E.F. this season.

Have men complained to you that we obeyed Pershing when he said "I want the American Y.M.C.A. to take charge of the leave resorts?" First at Aix-les-Bains, then seven or eight others, now the number has passed a dozen, and I heard recently they want us to take four more. If you have heard people complain let them come to my office and see the letters that have been written by the soldiers to our women canteen workers and our men secretaries to the effect that they had been given the best vacation of their lives there in the midst of inspiring and uplifting associations.

Have men complained to you that we change their money at more favorable rates than others do? Has there been objection that we have sent free of cost from the boys themselves to the members of their families over 275,000 remittances aggregating over $16,000,-

000? Nearly 2,000 of those 275,000 remittances have not yet been delivered. The other day in New York I heard the reason why one had not yet reached its destination. We had tried several avenues, at last we learned that all six members of the family had been blotted out by the influenza. With the help of the postmasters and other agencies we are hoping that the comparatively small number of undelivered remittances may ultimately reach their true destinations.

Have men complained in your hearing that for months and up to within a week ago the only worker on any transport was a Y.M.C.A. worker? Now there is an arrangement by which the Morale Division of the War Department takes charge of the welfare service on transports and the Y.M.C.A., the Knights of Columbus, the Jewish Welfare Board, and the Red Cross unite in manning adequately the great transports and so far as possible the smaller ones.

Do men complain that the hundreds of American city Young Men's Christian Associations in league with our work over there in the A.E.F. give regular membership privileges free for at least three months to all men in uniform, and that in addition to all this we have made one of the major points of our policy the helping of men in the matter of re-employment? It is said that the employment bureaus of the Association are the most effective of all agencies for this purpose because of their many years of successful experience in rendering this particular kind of service.

Now I come to some things concerning which there has been complaint. As I do so, I ask you in view of all that I have just stated in barest outline, Is it fair that the attention of the American people should be riveted on what is relatively but a very small fraction, to the exclusion of this great volume of unselfish, patriotic service that makes up the vast, vast majority of the activities and the constructive work of the Y.M.C.A. overseas as well as at home? You say, "Certainly not!" And the American people when they understand will say "Certainly not!" They will not be hoodwinked. Their sense of justice and fair play may be absolutely depended upon. The Y.M.C.A. has its mistakes and limitations in common with all human organizations. The criticisms that have come to us have been chiefly with reference to the canteen. It is not necessary that I remind this particular company that Pershing was glad to have the Y.M.C.A. take charge of the canteen in order, as he said, that there might be released for combat that many more fighting men. By having our women workers and our men above draft age take on this service the desired end was accomplished. He well knew as we do what a thankless task it is, made especially so by an impossible situation, namely, that the government in those days did not buy or ship supplies for us, although we earnestly desired to have them do so. I went to the government myself and said, "We are in an impossible position. You still have Quartermaster's Stores in the army that as a rule can buy goods lower than any other organization can buy them in this country and you do not have to pay tonnage or insurance charges as we do. You have these Stores in the army, and now you encourage us to conduct the canteen or post exchange and we have to pay higher prices for the goods, we have to pay shipping and insurance charges and overhead expenses that do not enter into your Quartermaster's charges. It looks to me," I said, "as though we must either hand this back or else we have got to have matters equalized." The government agreed with me. It took a long time to bring about the desired change but I am glad to say that at last we have the arrangement by which we now buy our canteen supplies from the Quartermaster and by which he fixes the prices. So we have the same prices as the Quartermaster Stores. Therefore, the criticism that we sell at higher prices than the government ought to be counted as a matter of the past.

Growing out of the complaint that the Y.M.C.A. had charged higher prices in its canteens than had to be paid at the Quartermaster's Stores, for reasons which have just been stated but which apparently were at times not understood by the men, is the charge that the Association has been profiteering. This charge has been investigated on two occasions by the War Department, and each time it pronounced the charge to be groundless. Were all the expenses charged against the canteen which properly should be charged against it, such as the salaries of the thousands of men and women canteen workers, it would be seen that the canteen has been operated at a loss. Even had there been a profit or should there later be any profit, there has been an agreement with General Pershing from the beginning, which is stated in one of his General Orders and which is clearly understood by all concerned, that such profit is to be expended by the Association in connection with the various services which it is rendering the soldiers through its countless recreational, social, educational, and other activities. The Association has not only operated the canteen at a loss, but has also given away millions of dollars' worth of free supplies in its front-line trench work, or while the men were going into action or coming out of action or under other circumstances of special strain. Apart from the most generous provision made by the Red Cross for soldiers and sailors in transit, I know of no agency which has expended so much money on free supplies. It will be interesting to point out that, contrary to the popular impression, a uniform policy is being worked out by the various welfare agencies overseas with reference to the giving away of supplies.

The criticism that the Y.M.C.A. sold gift tobacco and certain other gift articles has been explained so many times to the satisfaction of all who have looked into the matter that it is not necessary to reiterate the explanation. The New York *Sun,* which no one would call a special pleader, made its own independent investigation of this complaint and completely exonerated the Y.M.C.A. Its statement can be examined by anyone in the leaflet entitled "Criticisms and Answers" to be obtained of the Y.M.C.A. at 347 Madison Avenue, New York.

Complaints have been made with reference to certain members of the personnel of the Y.M.C.A., as to lapses in character, as to inefficiency, and as to wrong manners, attitude, and spirit. Wherever such charges have been made with sufficient definiteness to make it possible to deal with them they have been investigated promptly and any necessary action has been taken with equal promptness. The Y.M.C.A. could surely have no object in overlooking such complaints, for its one desire is to make its service of the army and navy as efficient as possible. It is an impressive fact that among all the criticisms of this kind which have been made in this period of criticism, charges thus far have been made against only between thirty and forty different persons, and all of these have by no means been substantiated. This is a remarkable showing when it is recalled that the Y.M.C.A. now has a staff of nearly 12,000 men and women, the large majority of whom are overseas—a staff numbering possibly over seven times as many as the combined staffs of the other welfare agencies working at the same points and in the same areas.

Some have made criticisms with reference to the administration. It would be strange were this not the case. The Association was called upon suddenly to deal with a vast situation involving many new and difficult conditions and, because of the Draft Law, necessitating the use of a vast number of untrained workers. The wonder of people most familiar with the facts is that the administration has proved to be as efficient as it is. Nevertheless, we have not been unmindful of its weaknesses and shortcomings, and you will be glad to know that valuable constructive measures have been taken to strengthen the administration both at home and overseas. For example, in France, we have recently sent some of the ablest members of the War Work Council to have immediate supervision of the work and workers. When I state that such men as George W. Perkins and Mortimer L. Schiff are members of this committee, it will give instant confidence.

Again and again the complaint is made that the Y.M.C.A. does not help the wounded. Those who voice this complaint are evidently ignorant of the understanding entered into between the Red Cross and the Y.M.C.A. by which the Red Cross are regarded as responsible for serving the sick and the wounded in the hospital areas. The Y.M.C.A. is not at liberty to work in these areas, save on the invitation of the Red Cross.

Now and then one still hears the complaint that the Y.M.C.A. did not work at the front and in the real danger zones. The facts, however, as reported by the military authorities and others in touch with the situation have shown how absolutely untrue is such a charge. Only the other day it was pointed out that ten Y.M.C.A. workers in France were killed by shellfire or by gas, at least forty others were seriously gassed or wounded, thirty-nine more died as a result of wounds or accidents or as a result of disease occasioned by exposure or overwork in front-line service, and that many had been cited or decorated for special bravery in their work in most dangerous positions. During the fighting in the Argonne, 700 Y.M.C.A. workers, fifty of whom were women canteen workers, were attached to the different fighting units, with which they remained in the danger zone and frequently under shellfire. There were also over 200 helping the men under similar conditions in the Chateau-Thierry and St. Mihiel drives.

The attitude of the Y.M.C.A. with reference to criticisms is to welcome all honest and constructive criticisms, no matter from what quarter. We judge of the honesty of critics in two ways: first, Is the person who makes the criticism ready to give us the name, date, and place? He should at least be willing to do so in strict confidence. I need not add that we carefully guard any such confidence, but it is impossible to deal adequately with criticisms unless the critic is willing to be thus definite. If he is unwilling to afford you a handle of which you can take hold, is it unfair to assume that there is something ulterior or unfair behind his criticism? The second way by which we judge the honesty of a critic is his attitude and action after he has shared with you the information on which his criticism is based. If, after he has given you the definite facts and his best personal advice and you have assured him that you will give the matter prompt and thorough attention, he goes behind your back and continues to knock and to spread distrust, you can make up your mind that he is not playing the game and that there is something sinister back of it all.

Our request of all sincere critics, and by that I mean all those who really desire to have the grounds of criticism removed for the good of the service on behalf of the men in the army and navy, is fourfold: in the first place, be definite. Secondly, be constructive. No critic should be content with dealing simply in negatives. If he is a true patriot, he surely desires to have every American institution become stronger and more efficient. Thirdly, play the game; that is, when assurance has been given that the complaint will be investigated and that it will be dealt with conscientiously, give the organization the benefit of the doubt. Fourthly, let him tell all the good things he knows about the Association. A lady was talking with a wounded soldier in a hospital the other day, and in answer to her question about the Y.M.C.A. he replied, "It is no good. It is a bunch of grafters." She asked him to give his proofs and she jotted down in writing what he had to say. After he had told all the unfavorable facts which he had to give regarding the Association she asked, "Is there any good thing about the Y.M.C.A. work overseas which you can mention?"

He was puzzled a little at first, and then said (and, I repeat, he had called the Association workers "a bunch of grafters"). "Yes. In that port where I spent so much time they gave us the best meals at the lowest prices we had anywhere."

She inquired, "Was there anything else good about the Y.M.C.A.?"

"Yes. They changed my money there at satisfactory rates. We fellows had been greatly fleeced by others before."

"Was there anything else?" she pressed.

"Yes. The Y.M.C.A. had the place where we fellows used to meet; it was a bright, warm place, in fact the only place of that kind open to us. No, no, let me correct myself. I belong to the army, but I will say that the Y.M.C.A. did a great thing for the navy in that town. They had just dedicated a navy hut, one of the finest I had seen anywhere in France, and it was awfully popular with the men of the navy."

"Did you see anything else good?"

"Yes. They had the American magazines and writing paper and other things that the men wanted."

"Were all these things supplied free?"

"Yes. I don't remember that they charged us for any of them. By the way," he continued, "do you know that great preacher to young men?" He could not tell the name and she could not make out from his remarks who it was, but I have learned since that it was Dr. Truett, of Texas, one of the greatest preachers to men in the United States. "I am not much on religion, but that man got me and got me on the day I ought to be got." And so he went on, she told me, until before he finished he had mentioned a dozen or more things in praise of the Y.M.C.A., in contrast with the two or three minor matters to which he had called attention at the beginning of the conversation.

We do not expect to escape criticism. One day our chief secretary in France went to General Pershing, when there were quite a number of criticisms because we were not getting supplies overseas fast enough and were not getting them up to the front as quickly as desired, for the simple reason that the government itself could not give us the necessary tonnage because of military necessities and the fact that they had been obliged to take over a number of our motor trucks for pressing military needs, and said to the General, "We are having many criticisms, General." Pershing replied, "The Y.M.C.A. are not in this to avoid criticism, are they, but to render as much service as possible to the men under the limitations under which we are all working in this war." To my mind, that sentence puts the whole business in a nutshell. It would be difficult, I fancy impossible, to mention an organization or to name a department of our own government or of any other government which has not during the war and during the postwar period had its shortcomings, weaknesses, and grounds for complaint. In the long run, no organization and no individual will suffer from criticism, provided it has the right attitude toward criticism, and that attitude, I need not point out again, is to welcome all honest, constructive criticism and to deal as promptly and thoroughly as possible with it at its sources. Lincoln was criticized right up to the time of his death. At one time a friend came to him and said that Stanton, one of the strongest members of his Cabinet, had spoken about him as "that stupid old fool." When the friend reported this to Lincoln, Lincoln replied, "Stanton is a levelheaded man. There must be something in his charge. I will speak to him about it." Jesus Christ was criticized all through His public ministry. You will remember how His good was evil spoken of and how His enemies traced the greatest things He wrought to an evil spirit. May we, like Him, meet such charges with humility, unselfishness, and courage. Then we can be trusted with larger things. If men lose their desire to profit by experience and to improve; if they lose their confidence in the truth and its ability to prevail no matter what may be done to cloud the issues; if they lose their genuine optimism, then they suffer; but if, on the other hand, they meet their criticisms with open and responsive minds and deal with them positively, constructively, and hopefully, they and the cause they represent will come forth stronger and more serviceable than ever.

CLOSING UP OF THE WAR WORK

LETTER OF DR. MOTT TO THE LEADERS OF THE YOUNG MEN'S CHRISTIAN ASSOCIATIONS OF NORTH AMERICA

347 MADISON AVENUE, NEW YORK CITY
October 20, 1920

DEAR COLLEAGUES:

There are a number of important matters on which I wish to communicate with you in an informal and intimate way.

1. The chief burden with which I have returned from my recent journey overseas, and concerning which I have written in the forthcoming number of *Association Men,* is that we must do everything in our power to augment the spiritual vitality of America and in particular, of our Association Movement. While there is much to encourage us in the growth and activity of the Associations and in the work being accomplished by their supervisory and training agencies, the fact stands out vividly against the black background of the world's need, both at home and abroad, that the vast work which the Association Movement of North America is undertaking is wholly beyond its present spiritual resources. We are doomed to disappointment unless with new meaning, undiscourageable purpose, and self-sacrificing unity we avail ourselves more largely of the limitless resources of God. The wider our outreach, the more necessary it is that we give attention to the cultivation of the inner life of ourselves and of our members. Undoubtedly our principal need is that of a deeper experience of the Living Christ. For twenty-five years I have spent a part of each year in the foreign fields of our work, but I feel this burden so much that I plan to spend the present working year in the home field. Moreover, I have, after holding the position for twenty-five years, laid down the general secretaryship of the World's Student Christian Federation which has taken months of each year and have also resigned certain other positions in order that I might concentrate more largely on Association problems and opportunities. I am glad that in these ways and also through the relaxing of the pressure of war and postwar conditions I am able to identify myself with you more fully than ever in helping to place this vital emphasis.

2. The International Convention at Detroit authorized the appointment of certain commissions. The one on the colored work was created several months ago and at its first meeting worked out a policy for dealing with new and critical conditions in the work and

relationships of the colored Associations. The Commission on the Army and Navy Work held its initial meeting in April and is to hold its second meeting November 12. The Commission on Convention Representation and Rules has only recently been appointed. The other commissions will soon be appointed and at work.

3. The Detroit Convention asked the International Committee to make a fresh study of its own organization. The Chairman has appointed the following group to form a special commission for this purpose: Messrs. E. L. Shuey, L. A. Crossett, W. W. Fry, R. W. Harbison, E. W. Hazen, W. D. Murray, and L. T. Warner. This commission will carry forward the study began by the Fry and Crossett Commissions, holding such hearings and conducting such investigations as may be required. I speak not only for the commission but also for myself, my associates, and the International Committee and its staff as a whole when I request that all who have criticisms and constructive suggestions which in their judgment will tend to improve the organization and work of this agency of the Associations will kindly write to any member of the commission or to myself on the points in question. And here let me again express my personal gratitude to those members of the brotherhood who have performed that highest office of friendship, namely, the coming to me frankly, directly, and promptly with any criticism or counsel which they thought was calculated to enable me or those associated with me to render better service.

4. With reference to the regional organization called for by the action taken at Detroit, let me report that thus far in the central region only has the plan been launched. This was done in the representative and helpful meeting held in Chicago last March. At the meeting of the International Committee held in Atlantic City in September steps were taken preparatory to calling at an early date similar gatherings in the other regions to perfect the simple organization involved in the new plan. I assume that it is well understood that the aim is not to build up a new agency of supervision or an executive body. The chief functions of these regional committees will be those of reviewing and recommending. Their interpreting and mediating service will also be of great value. They will help greatly to co-ordinate the varied work of the International Committee in a given region and will likewise facilitate preserving right relations between the International and state committees. It is thought by some that this plan will further a larger decentralization of the International Committee work. All this will result in a finer service to the local Associations whose servants these agencies are. We covet the con-

tinued best thought of all Association workers in this formative stage of the working out of the Regional Plan.

5. We need your help with reference to the finances of the International Committee. In common with other Association agencies and with all denominational and interdenominational bodies the Committee is in a critical position financially. The home work budget for the year 1920 calls for $867,317. Economies are being effected which will reduce this to $814,250. Toward this there had been raised in cash by October 16, $311,384, and there were estimated reliable pledges, probable renewals, and additional income from endowment aggregating $165,000, leaving a balance to be secured in new gifts by December 31 of at least $337,876. The revised foreign work budget for the year 1920 calls for $1,535,728.98. Toward this there had been received in cash by October 18, $591,371.70, and there were estimated reliable unpaid pledges aggregating $378,934.89, leaving a balance to be secured in new gifts by December 31 of at least $565,422.39. This constitutes by far the greatest financial need which the Committee has ever been obliged to bring to the attention of the brotherhood. Both budgets have been carefully considered and approved by the Budget Reviewing Committee authorized at the Detroit Convention. Besides this the home work budget has had the benefit of thorough examination by a special committee of the city general secretaries' Association and the foreign work has had the benefit of similar work on the part of the Messer Commission. All our accounts and records are open for inspection to any accredited representative of the Associations and we are most anxious to have brought quickly to our attention any point on which further information may be desired in order that any real friend of the work may be able both to support and to advocate the support of the International Committee with sincere and strong conviction. Knowing what I do about the burdens which some of you are carrying in your own work, I find it impossible to express adequately my sense of heartfelt gratitude for your generous attitude and co-operation. If the International Committee, which is the national servant of the Associations, suffers at this critical time in the life of the Movement, all the Associations will suffer with it. It is my belief that as a result of the larger loyalty and unity of the brotherhood asserting themselves, this most difficult situation will be met.

6. Brief reference should be made to a few appointments. Mr. E. L. Hamilton has been made senior secretary of the Transportation Department, with Mr. H. O. Williams as his associate, since Mr. John F. Moore was called to become an associate general secretary

for the Home Work Division of the International Committee. Mr. F. A. McCarl has been appointed senior secretary of the Army and Navy Department to succeed Mr. J. S. Tichenor who has become associate general secretary for the General Service Division. Mr. W. F. Hirsch has become senior secretary of the reorganized Educational Department, that Mr. Orr may concentrate on the expert counseling and editorial work of this rapidly enlarging work (after a visit to Europe where he goes to place the North American experience at the disposal of the Associations in the different countries). In the absence of Mr. E. M. Robinson from the country to further the plans of the World Outlook Commission, Mr. Arthur N. Cotton will serve as acting senior secretary of the Boys' Department. We hope to be able to announce in the near future the successor to Mr. Bilheimer as regional executive secretary for the western region, Mr. Bilheimer having resigned the position to become an associate general secretary for the Home Work Division. Mr. E. C. Carter of the foreign work has, at the request of the English National Council, been allocated to serve as an associate national secretary of that Council.

7. The meeting of the Executive Committee of the National War Work Council held in New York on October 13 was one of unusual importance. The following paragraphs are reprinted from a report of this meeting which was prepared for the November number of *Association Men:*

> Most of the time of the meeting was spent in the capacity of a session of the Budget Committee with Mr. Cyrus H. McCormick of Chicago presiding. The financial transactions, commitments, and position of the Council were carefully reviewed. Final allocations were made under recommendation of the Budget Committee: (1) For work for the American Army and Navy at home; (2) for the American Army and Navy abroad, including a small appropriation for the service of the American marine; (3) for the educational service of ex-service men, including a limited appropriation for the interracial work; (4) for work for Allied armies and prisoners of war. The appropriations under the last two headings were made as final appropriations within which these pieces of work must be completed so far as their support by Council funds is concerned.
>
> After making the allocations for the foregoing objects there remained a balance of $7,461,009. In accordance with the report of the Committee of Three, adopted by the Executive and Finance Committees on January 20, 1920, and confirmed by the War Work Council at its last meeting on April 13, 1920, this balance will be devoted to the erection, enlargement, and maintenance of permanent Y.M.C.A. buildings for American soldiers and sailors and to a reserve fund to be held "for rendering Y.M.C.A. service in

any grave national emergency." This, thus, finally disposes of the entire war work fund. The following important resolutions were also unanimously adopted:

Resolved, That the chairman of the Executive Committee appoint a Committee of Five and that the International Committee be requested to appoint a Committee of Five, these two committees to confer and to report, if possible, at the next regular meeting of the Executive Committee: (1) A suggested division of the unallocated funds between permanent army and navy buildings and a reserve fund, in accordance with the report of the Committee of Three as adopted at the meeting of the War Work Council at the Yale Club, April 13, 1920; (2) a plan for the custody or trusteeship of these funds; (3) a plan for the dissolution of the War Work Council by December 31, 1920, if feasible; (4) a plan for the supervision and carrying out of the budget expenditures authorized at this meeting of the Executive Committee.

Resolved, That the joint committee be requested to prepare and submit to the members of the Executive Committee in advance of their next meeting a summary of its recommendations and that its report should include, if practicable, a suggested list of needed permanent buildings for the army and navy.

Resolved, That the request of the Washington Association, which has been under the consideration of the Budget Committee, be referred to this joint committee for its consideration and report.

Resolved, That the allocation of the funds made at this meeting is made with the understanding that while for the most part the appropriations are based on the needs for the year 1921, they may be expended during a shorter or longer period of time, according to the needs and conditions affecting their wisest and most helpful use. Furthermore, it is understood that, if any portion of the funds allocated to either of the two main divisions of the budget (namely, work for the American Army and Navy at home and abroad, and work for Allied armies and prisoners of war) be not eventually required for the main division to which it is allocated in the budget, such portion shall revert to the reserve fund, but permission is implied for adjustments between subsidiary items under the main divisions referred to.

Every effort is being made, in accordance with the universal sentiment of its members, to hasten the closing up of the work of the National War Work Council as soon as this can be wisely done. A new and complete financial statement will be published as soon as practicable after the next meeting of the Executive Committee by which time the Budget Reviewing Committee will have completed its report. In this connection it should be stated that the United War Work Campaign plans to issue a full official statement as soon as all of the state audits are completed.

Mr. Sloane, Chairman of the War Work Council, has appointed Messrs. C. H. McCormick, John J. Eagan, Harold I. Pratt, L. T.

Warner, and Roger H. Williams to represent the War Work Council on the committee mentioned in the first resolution above, and Mr. Marling, Chairman of the International Committee, has appointed Messrs. William Sloane, L. A. Crossett, Robert Garrett, W. H. Crosby, and A. E. Marling to represent the International Committee.

8.   We stand near the threshold of another year's observance of the Week of Prayer for Young Men. In the official Call which was posted to you last week Mr. Marling and I tried to voice what we believe is the conviction of all of us. In closing I would venture by repeating to call particular attention to the last two paragraphs of this Call:

"The conscientious observance of the Week of Prayer for Young Men is a most significant event. It is a clear recognition of our belief that our God is a living God, a present God, an almighty God, a loving God, and, therefore a God interested in His children, and responsive to their deepest needs and highest aspirations. It is a clear proof that there are bodies of men all over our own and other lands who believe in the reality and efficacy of intercession.

"If here and there Association leaders find themselves uninterested or unresponsive and practically decided not to observe the coming Week of Prayer, they should become alarmed; because it is an indication of loss of perspective or of the failure to estimate relative values rightly, and it is a sure sign of growing dependence upon human wisdom and energy. The ground of our chief solicitude should be not the forces of evil which oppose us but rather the weakness of our own lives. Whatever we do, therefore, to widen, deepen, and lend reality to the days of united prayer in November will be striking at the heart of our gravest problem and will be unveiling the hiding of our power."

It is not essential that we live so many years, or that we perform so many actions in a given year, but it is absolutely essential that we truly represent Christ and that we become more and more like Him. And is it not true that if we are to become like Him manward we must become more like Him Godward?

Faithfully yours,

JOHN R. MOTT

DISSOLUTION OF THE NATIONAL WAR WORK COUNCIL

Preamble and Resolutions as adopted by The National War Work Council of the Young Men's Christian Associations, December 29, 1920.

These were ratified, confirmed, and approved by the International Committee at its meeting February 10, 1921, and the Council was finally dissolved March 8, 1921.

PREAMBLE

In view of the fact that immediately after the United States entered the World War the International Committee of Young Men's Christian Associations, on the recommendation of leaders in Association work—local, state, and international—created the National War Work Council of the Young Men's Christian Associations of the United States and committed to it responsibility for the general direction of the war work of the American Associations wherever carried on, and in view of the fact that the World War is now almost universally regarded as over and that the time has come to place all remaining work for soldiers and sailors and other classes which have been served by the War Work Council on a peacetime basis, and, therefore, to relate such work, as far as possible, to the regular permanent agencies of the Association Movement, the Executive Committee of the National War Work Council considers that the time has come when the Council should relinquish further responsibility for the supervision and conduct of war work and be dissolved as an organization, and therefore recommends the adoption by the National War Work Council of the following plan:

SECTION I

1. That the unallocated balance of National War Work Council funds (now estimated as $7,461,009) be placed in the hands of a Board of ten Trustees, the personnel of which shall be as follows:

William Sloane	Alfred E. Marling
Harold I. Pratt	Lewis A. Crossett
Robert Garrett	Cyrus H. McCormick
John L. Severance	James Logan
Charles J. Rhoads	John R. Mott

2. This Board shall be known as the Trustees of the War Fund of the Young Men's Christian Associations of the United States of America, hereinafter called the Trustees. The Trustees shall serve until they shall have carried out the provisions of this report. Four of their number shall constitute a quorum. They shall have power to fill vacancies in their number due to death or other causes. The Trustees are empowered to make rules for the conduct of their business. Provision shall be made for taking a vote by mail when it is not considered necessary or expedient to call the Trustees together.

3. The Trustees shall report to the International Conventions of the Young Men's Christian Associations of North America and in the interim annually to the International Committee of Young Men's Christian Associations of North America, hereinafter called the International Committee.

4. The Trustees shall make investments suitable for trustees' funds and

shall place the funds in charge of one or more trust companies or other qualified banking institutions for custody and will advise with one or more said institutions as to investments.

5. The International Committee, through its Army and Navy Department, shall make a study of the field, and from time to time recommend to the Trustees where buildings should be erected and the probable cost thereof; whereupon, if the recommendations are accepted by the Trustees, an appropriation shall be made by them and paid over to the International Committee or to the metropolitan Association by which the title is to be held in the manner to be agreed upon by the Trustees and the officers of the International Committee or the metropolitan Association, as the case may be.

6. Money allocated by the Trustees for the erection and maintenance of permanent Y.M.C.A. buildings for the American Army and Navy shall be paid to the International Committee or to the metropolitan Association which is to hold title to the property, approximately as is required for the purpose of acquiring such property or erecting such buildings.

7. The Trustees shall at their discretion insert in their agreements with the International Committee and the metropolitan Associations such clauses as may be thought necessary to safeguard permanently the funds appropriated.

8. If, in the judgment of the Trustees named in subdivision 1, the incorporation of the Trustees shall be hereafter desirable, the said Trustees by action of a majority of them, are authorized at any time to incorporate under the membership laws of the State of New York, in such manner as they may be advised by counsel, with the understanding that the said corporation shall assume all the duties and obligations which were prescribed for the said Trustees, and shall bear the same relation to the International Committee of Young Men's Christian Associations with reference to the whole situation as the Trustees would have in case the incorporation had not been had, and in case of such an incorporation the said Trustees are authorized to make, transfer, and set over to the said corporation any and all money, securities, and property in their hands, and the receipt of the duly accredited officers of such corporation shall release the said Trustees as to any and all property thus turned over, and the said Trustees shall, after such conveyance, be relieved from any further obligation or responsibility in connection with the aforesaid trust.

9. The Trustees may fill any vacancies in the Liquidation Committee caused by death, accident, ill-health, or otherwise.

SECTION II

1. That the unallocated balance of funds of the National War Work Council of the Young Men's Christian Associations (now estimated as $7,461,009) be divided as follows: one-half to be devoted to the erection, equipment, maintenance, and/or endowment of permanent Y.M.C.A. buildings for the use of the men in the American Army and Navy, and one-half to be devoted to a reserve fund to be held for meeting needs of soldiers and sailors at home or abroad created by any national emergency.

2. The income from the reserve fund and also from any temporarily unemployed part of the building fund shall be used for the erection, equipment, maintenance, and/or endowment of permanent Y.M.C.A. buildings for the American Army and Navy, or for such other purposes in the army and navy work of the American Young Men's Christian Associations as the Trustees may consider will best fulfill the intent of the donors. If it should be found later that the War Work Council had underestimated its liabilities, or that the sums appropriated by it for the specific purpose of the approved budget were insufficient, the Trustees may make appropriations to meet the situation.

3. If, after three years (that is, after January 1, 1924) all or any part of the reserve fund shall not have been required for meeting national emergencies, such remaining sum shall be devoted to the erection, equipment, maintenance, and/or endowment of the permanent Y.M.C.A. buildings for the American Army and Navy, or for the support of the regular work for soldiers, sailors, or marines of the United States in accordance with provisions of Section I. If, by January 1, 1928, any portion of the fund remains in the hands of the Trustees unallocated, it shall be turned over to the International Committee to be used in accordance with the terms of this report.

4. If, in the opinion of the Trustees, before January 1, 1928, or of the International Committee after that date, any unexpended portion of this fund cannot reasonably be used for the purposes mentioned in this report, then the use of such unexpended portion of the fund shall be referred to the next ensuing International Convention, which, upon such reference, shall have full power to dispose of such unexpended portion of the fund.

SECTION III

1. The responsibility for the budget expenditures which have been authorized by the Executive Committee of the National War Work Council of the Young Men's Christian Associations shall be intrusted to a Liquidation Committee of five members of the present Executive Committee, viz., Messrs. Lucien T. Warner, Roger H. Williams, William H. Crosby, John Sherman Hoyt, and Charles W. McAlpin, which Committee shall be responsible to the Trustees of the War Fund and shall work in close conjunction with the Army and Navy Department of the International Committee in reference to expenditures for the American Army and Navy and with the Committee on Allied Armies and Prisoners of War, in reference to expenditures related to that Committee.

2. The funds for these budget expenditures shall be held by the Trustees and shall be paid over from month to month to the Liquidation Committee in amounts approximately as needed on the basis of the adopted budgets and commitments for both 1920 and 1921 as approved. The Liquidation Committee shall also be empowered to carry out contracts with workers and others to complete pieces of work for which specific appropriations have been made or reserves set aside and to adjust and settle claims.

3. Funds in the hands of the disbursing officers of the present War Work Council will be transferred by book entry and placed to the credit

of the Trustees on the books of the Liquidation Committee, these amounts to be verified by the cash audit of Messrs. Price, Waterhouse & Company.

4. Resolved that the Liquidation Committee of the Trustees of the War Fund of the Young Men's Christian Associations of the United States be and hereby are authorized to open an account in the Equitable Trust Company, New York, and that authority to sign checks against this account be granted to Charles H. Burr, Treasurer, and B. B. Baldwin, Deputy Treasurer, or either of them when countersigned by any one member of the Liquidation Committee composed of Messrs. Lucien T. Warner, Roger H. Williams, William H. Crosby, John Sherman Hoyt, and Charles W. McAlpin, or to any two members of the above named Liquidation Committee, and be it further resolved that the Equitable Trust Company be and hereby is authorized to accept the signature of any one of the above names on checks of $250 or less.

5. Any funds not eventually required for the completion of work, or for the fulfillment of other objects for which appropriations have been made or reserves set aside, shall be turned back by the Liquidation Committee to the Trustees to be used by the latter for any of the purposes set forth in Sections I, II, and III.

6. It is intended that the Liquidation Committee, by working in close co-operation with the Army and Navy Committee and the Committee on Allied Armies and Prisoners of War of the International Committee, shall make it possible for these two committees to be so thoroughly in touch with the whole operation that by December 31, 1921, when the Liquidation Committee shall automatically go out of existence, these two permanent committees may take over any remaining work with the least possible adjustment and change.

7. The Liquidation Committee shall, as soon as possible after the close of its work on December 31, 1921, render to the Trustees final accounting and an audited statement of its transactions in fulfillment of the provisions of this Section.

8. Be it further resolved that this action be submitted forthwith to the International Committee of Young Men's Christian Associations and, that the International Committee of Young Men's Christian Associations be requested to ratify, confirm, and approve the action taken, and to take such action as is necessary to dissolve the National War Work Council in accordance with these resolutions.

FINAL REPORT OF THE NATIONAL WAR WORK COUNCIL

347 MADISON AVENUE, NEW YORK
May 10, 1921

*To the Donors and Friends of the National War Work
Council of Young Men's Christian Associations:*

In sending out this final audited financial statement on behalf of the National War Work Council of Young Men's Christian Associations of the United States, let me reiterate on their behalf the expression of deep and abiding gratitude to the many thousands of workers who carried to a markedly successful issue the three successive War Work Campaigns, and also to the millions of donors, large and small, who in every community of the land gave so cheerfully, generously, and sacrificially toward the great patriotic and Christian undertaking to which we had all set our hands.

It will be recalled that in the First Campaign conducted soon after America entered the war, our goal was $3,000,000 and approximately $5,000,000 was secured; that in the Second Campaign conducted in the autumn of 1917 we asked for $35,000,000, and eventually $54,000,000 was contributed; and that in the Third or United War Work Campaign the share of the Association in the sum of $170,-500,000, set as the goal, was $100,000,000 and the Association has received over $108,000,000 as its share of $190,000,000 collected. Thus the American people committed to the National War Work Council of the Associations the vast sum of over $167,000,000. The magnitude of this offering may be more fully realized when we remind ourselves that this is a greater sum than is today invested in Young Men's Christian Association buildings and other property in all the world after seventy-five years of Association history.

The Associations can ever point with pride and satisfaction to the able and conscientious administration of this trust. The National War Work Council, composed of over 200 leading laymen from all parts of the country, under the able chairmanship of Mr. William Sloane, took their responsibility seriously from the beginning of their work in April, 1917, until the dissolution of the Council on March 8, 1921. Meetings of the full Council were held, as a rule, semi-annually for formulating main policies and for determining or revising budgets. A Budget Committee composed of twenty or more leading business men of the nation served under the leadership of Mr. Cyrus H. McCormick with rare devotion throughout the entire life of the Council. A very representative Executive Committee held unhurried and largely-attended meetings every two or three weeks during the war. The able Finance Committee with Mr. George W. Perkins as chairman had weekly meetings and for much of the time met twice a week. It may be questioned whether any of the great war trusts had the benefit so continuously of the personal supervision and direction of such a large company of men of outstanding and successful financial and business experience.

A tribute should also be paid to the 25,000 men and women workers in the training camps at home and in the areas overseas, as well as on the staff of the various headquarters, national and regional.

Without their extreme devotion this vast, comprehensive, and, on the whole, highly efficient ministry could never have been accomplished.

In retrospect, the enormous volume and the almost infinite variety of the war work of the Associations become more apparent. The facts are effectively and interestingly set forth in the booklet, *Summary of World War Work of the American Y.M.C.A.*

The full and wonderful story of this patriotic endeavor on behalf of the 4,800,000 men in the American Army and Navy and of 19,000,000 men of the Allied forces as well as of the 6,000,000 prisoners of war will be told in the several volumes of the permanent history now in preparation.

Above all, we would humbly acknowledge the manifestation of the guidance and power of Almighty God and of His overruling of human mistakes and shortcomings, also the wonderful triumphs achieved in His Name along the whole pathway of the service rendered our soldiers and sailors on behalf of the nation and of the Churches.

JOHN R. MOTT,
General Secretary of the
National War Work Council

DISPOSITION OF BALANCE

The net assets of the National War Work Council at the date of dissolution on March 8, 1921 were transferred to the Trustees of the War Fund in the amount of and are to be used in accordance with resolution adopted by the National War Work Council at its meeting held in Buffalo, New York, December 15, 1920, as follows:		$18,503,805.54
(a) For liquidation of all unpaid balances, growing out of operations prior to 1921, including unexpended portions of approved budgets for 1920 and carried forward to 1921	$1,468,157.00	
(b) For meeting calls on contingent items carried in "Reserves," the final outcome of which cannot be determined at this date	453,252.47	
(c) For the meeting of expenditures made under the approved budget for 1921 as per details in second column of the statement following	7,160,150.99	
Total apropriations (see details below)		9,081,560.46
BALANCE		$ 9,422,245.08

In accordance with resolutions adopted at the Buffalo meeting, one-half of the above balance or .... $ 4,711,122.54 has been placed in a special "Reserve Fund" to be held by the Trustees of the War Fund for a period of three years to meet any national emergency. The other one-half or .... $ 4,711,122.54 is to be used for the erection, maintenance or endowment of buildings, sites, their equipment and maintenance for the use of the men of the American Army and Navy.

STATEMENT OF RESERVES, LIABILITIES, AND ADOPTED BUDGET FOR 1921:

	Reserves and 1920 Budget Balances carried to 1921	Budget for 1921	
Overseas:			
For work with American Army of Occupation in Coblenz		$ 765,021.60	
For work with American Navy forces in Mediterranean		65,000.00	
For work with American Merchant Marine		150,000.00	
For work with Allied Armies and Prisoners of War in France, Italy, Poland, Czechoslovakia, the Balkans, Turkish areas, etc.	$ 600,769.00	1,866,000.00	
New York Headquarters Administration AFIG work		30,000.00	
		2,876,021.60	
United States and Territorial Possessions:			
Work with our Army and Navy on Military Reservations, in Port Cities, Service Men's Clubs and in co-operation with City Y.M.C.A.'s		1,458,070.23	
Educational Service for ex-soldiers and sailors, Americanization, Free Scholarships and Vocational Guidance	75,090.12	1,960,000.00	
Interracial work following demobilization in Southern States	46,117.56	150,000.00	
War Historical Bureau		66,287.28	
Headquarters Bureaus (Administration)		149,771.88	
Unpaid Special Appropriations	24,917.20		
Unpaid Appropriations for Army and Navy Y.M.C.A. buildings	675,000.00		
Special fund for contingencies		500,000.00	
CURRENT LIABILITIES:			
Accounts Payable	46,263.12		
RESERVES:			
For claims of returning secretaries	259,681.93		
For rehabilitation of leased properties	42,164.93		
For French Import Duty and other claims	30,893.12		
For account of motor trucks, supplies, and transportation—U. S., French, and British Governments	120,512.49		
Total 1920 and 1921 budgets unpaid, March 7, 1921	$1,921,409.47	$7,160,150.99	$9,081,560.46

NATIONAL WAR WORK COUNCIL OF THE
YOUNG MEN'S CHRISTIAN ASSOCIATIONS OF THE UNITED STATES

FINANCIAL STATEMENT

March 7, 1921

RECEIPTS

Contributions:

First campaign	$ 5,114,183.09	
Second campaign	53,337,767.53	
Third campaign (United War Work Campaign)	108,509,500.00	
Third campaign (Direct contributions)	51,667.51	
Overseas	105,063.13	
		$167,118,181.26
Miscellaneous donations		446,492.78
Interest on bank balances		1,543,109.28
Interest on securities		1,315,706.97
Miscellaneous income		250,423.87
Total receipts		$170,673,914.16

EXPENDITURES

United States (For details see Exhibit A)		
Construction and equipment of buildings, etc.	$ 8,460,169.09	
Operating expenses of camps and other activities	28,144,094.89	
Appropriations to affiliated organizations for services furnished to soldiers and sailors	2,983,975.10	
Expenses at the headquarters of the six military departments	2,047,312.58	
	$41,635,551.66	
LESS—Net income from salvage operations	739,303.54	
		$ 40,896,248.12
Overseas (For details see Exhibit B):		
Construction and equipment of buildings, etc.	$12,158,597.57	
Field operations and other activities	46,644,760.67	
Paris, London, Coblenz, and Divisional Headquarters expenses	2,589,736.78	
	$61,393,095.02	
LESS—Net income from salvage operations	2,948,993.09	
		58,444,101.93

Loss on operations—Post Exchanges and canteens (For details see Exhibit C):

Trading profit		$ 339,747.38	
DEDUCT—Amount paid on account of appropriation to American Legion of profit before adjustment of exchange		500,000.00	
		$ 160,252.62	
ADD—Loss on liquidation of Post Exchange merchandise and other Post Exchange assets incidental to conversion of proceeds of sales Francs 110,395,767 into United States currency during period of and subsequent to fall in French exchange from normal to present levels		5,658,629.52	
			5,818,882.14
Loss on exchange on surplus funds. Francs 10,235,500 returned to United States			827,680.00
Expenditures for work with Allied armies and prisoners of war disbursed through the International Committee (for details see Exhibit D)			29,674,192.95
Appropriations to the United States Army and Navy for recreation work			2,776,500.00
Educational service and interracial work expenses and advances			4,941,887.27
Provision for claims of returning secretaries			350,000.00
New York Headquarters expenses:			
Administrative and general activities (For details see Exhibit E)	$ 3,571,373.34		
Campaign and publicity expenses	1,563,670.93		
			5,135,044.27
Selecting, recruiting, and training secretaries, including travel and sustenance expense			3,305,571.94
Total expenditures			152,170,108.62
Balance			$ 18,503,805.54

NEW YORK, May 10, 1921.   WILLIAM SLOANE, *Chairman, Executive Committee*
CLEVELAND H. DODGE, *Treasurer*
R. P. BRAINARD, *Comptroller*

ASSETS AND LIABILITIES

Current assets:

Accounts receivable	$	317,768.78
Inventories, canteen, etc.		54,826.19

United States Liberty Bonds and certificates of indebtedness (par value)........		16,308,650.00
Cash in banks, on hand, and in transit:		
United States	$ 690,322.94	
Overseas	1,606,877.34	
		2,297,200.28
		$18,978,445.25

LESS—Current liabiilties:

United States:			
Accounts payable		$ 39,471.11	
Overseas:			
Accounts payable	$ 6,792.01		
United States, French, and British governments for motor trucks, supplies, rail transportation, etc.	104,397.42		
		111,189.43	
Reserves:			
For claims of returning secretaries	$ 259,681.93		
For rehabilitation of leased properties and contingencies...................	64,297.24		
		323,979.17	
			474,639.71

Transferred to Trustees of the War Fund of the Young Men's Christian Associations of the United States	$18,503,805.54

EXHIBIT A

EXPENDITURES IN UNITED STATES
FROM APRIL 26, 1917, TO MARCH 7, 1921

Construction and equipment of buildings, etc.:

Northeastern Department—51 buildings...................		$ 553,110.70	
Eastern	" 228 "	2,561,947.84	
Southeastern	" 205 "	1,245,794.01	
Southern	" 219 "	1,054,788.92	
Central	" 176 "	1,812,331.17	
Western	" 75 "	1,024,830.41	
Troop transportation department and miscellaneous equipment		207,366.04	
			$ 8,460,169.09

Operating expenses of camps and other activities:

Operation and maintenance of service buildings.............	$ 5,267,294.01	
Uniforms and equipment of secretaries...................	790,460.43	
Religious literature, meetings, Bible classes, salaries of religious secretaries and musical directors.............	2,770,985.66	
Educational literature, lectures, French instruction, and library service	1,527,499.74	
Concerts, vaudeville, and other entertainments, including services and incidental expenses of talent and salaries of social secretaries...................	1,526,185.90	
Motion picture exhibitions, rent and purchase of films, etc.	2,913,073.64	
Athletic supplies and salaries of physical directors..........	1,818,479.87	

Lincoln Christian College

Writing materials, camp newspapers, and publications, etc.	1,021,397.08
Railroad fares and incidental expenses of secretaries accompanying troops on trains and ocean transports, etc., including necessary equipment and free supplies	3,901,282.42
Administrative expenses at camp headquarters	1,581,679.34
Automobile equipment, maintenance, and supplies	843,707.33
Office supplies and expenses, telephone, telegraph, postage, stationery, etc.	664,942.10
Sex hygiene education, literature, etc.	91,807.47
Expenditures for territorial work, Canal Zone, Porto Rico, Philippines, etc.	1,011,243.19
Work in war industries—spruce logging camps, munition plants, etc.	521,084.05
Students' Army Training Corps expense	563,680.14
Miscellaneous losses and expenses, including loss on realization of securities and sale of merchandise, etc.	1,329,292.52

28,144,094.89

Appropriations:

To local Y.M.C.A.'s for services and entertainment furnished to service men and demobilized troops	$ 1,686,094.84
To local Y.M.C.A.'s for work among soldiers and sailors in cities near large camps and ports	674,207.01
To Army and Navy Y.M.C.A. branches for services furnished to soldiers and sailors	543,873.25
To Federal Council of Churches for their war work	79,800.00

2,983,975.10

Expenses at the headquarters of the six military departments:

Salaries	$ 998,519.74
Traveling expenses of staff	398,227.57
Furniture, fixtures, and equipment	146,464.76
Office rent, supplies, telephone, telegraph, postage, etc.	504,100.51

2,047,312.58

$41,635,551.66

LESS—Net income from salvage operations	739,303.54

$40,896,248.12

EXHIBIT B

EXPENDITURES OVERSEAS
FROM COMMENCEMENT OF OPERATIONS IN 1917 TO MARCH 7, 1921

Construction and equipment of buildings, etc.;

Huts and tents	$ 5,883,557.43
Furniture, equipment, and motion picture outfits	3,603,289.15
Motor transport and miscellaneous equipment	2,671,750.99

$12,158,597.57

Field operations and other activities:

Free canteen service	$ 2,878,736.41
Christmas gifts and entertainments	695,512.06
Gift boxes distributed at debarkation ports in U.S.A. to returning soldiers	436,158.06
Writing materials, free newspapers, etc.	3,399,906.04

Operation of leave resorts	1,199,330.99
Operation of hotels	871,018.19
Motion picture expenses	1,914,879.14
Concerts and entertainments	1,669,744.37
Athletic and physical training expenses	2,479,732.73
Salaries and living allowances of secretaries and workers	16,433,599.36
Uniforms and equipment for secretaries	3,353,916.97
Ocean, rail, and other transportation, insurance, and miscellaneous expenses of secretaries and workers	4,602,389.86
Operating expenses of huts and field units	1,520,440.28
Operating expenses of motor transport	1,982,687.96
Religious work expenses	633,326.30
Educational work and library expenses	760,956.36
Other association service	638,932.00
Direct expenses and losses incidental to banking service (A.E.F. remittance orders, cashing checks, changing foreign currency, etc.)	345,280.96
Miscellaneous losses and expenses	132,118.08
Provision for rehabilitation of leased hotels, leave resorts, theaters and other properties	696,094.55

46,644,760.67

Paris, London, Coblenz, and Divisional Headquarters administrative expenses:

Administrative salaries and expenses	$ 2,104,228.39
Rent, heat, light, etc.	419,069.83
Publicity expenses	66,438.56

2,589,736.78

$61,393,095.02

LESS—Net income from salvage operations   2,948,993.09

$58,444,101.93

STATEMENT OF OPERATIONS OF POST EXCHANGES AND CANTEENS
TO MARCH 7, 1921

EXHIBIT C

Operations in France and Great Britain:
Subsequent to May 1, 1918:

Sales		$39,369,463.60
LESS:		
Cost of merchandise sold	$37,682,952.69	
Expenses of motor transport assigned to canteens and warehouse expense	2,502,412.50	
		40,185,365.19

Net loss $ 815,901.59
Prior to April 30, 1918:
Profit on operations   11,676.33

Loss on operations in France and Great Britain $ 804,225.26

Loss on operations in Italy..............................   10,452.68
Loss on operations in Germany..................   3,620.55

      Total loss on operations.................... $ 818,298.49

ADD:
   Profit on raw materials shipped
     to manufacturers for conversion $ 923,581.70
   Profit on purchases and sales to
     Quartermaster's Corps 190,419.33
   Miscellaneous profits and earn-
     ings 44,044.84
                                                1,158,045.87

     Trading profit before charging
      living allowances and travel-
      ing expenses of canteen work-
      ers, rent of huts, or any
      proportion of the Paris Head-
      quarters expenses .... $ 339,747.38

DEDUCT—Amount paid on account
   of appropriation to the American
   Legion of profit before applying
   loss on conversion of Post Ex-
   change assets into U. S. currency...   500,000.00
                                                $ 160,252.62

ADD—Loss on liquidation of Post
   Exchange merchandise and other
   Post Exchange assets incidental to
   conversion of proceeds of sales,
   Francs 110,395,767, into U. S. currency during period of and subsequent to fall in French exchange
   from normal to present levels...........   5,658,629.52

      Net loss   .... $ 5,818,882.14

EXHIBIT D

EXPENDITURES FOR WORK WITH ALLIED ARMIES AND PRISONERS OF WAR
(Disbursed Through the International Committee Y.M.C.A.)
FROM COMMENCEMENT OF OPERATIONS IN 1917 TO MARCH 7, 1921

Allied Armies:

France	$8,866,912.41
Great Britain	1,580,323.75
Italy	3,840,988.18
Russia (including A.E.F. in Siberia)................	7,932,210.97
Poland	1,366,826.44
Czechoslovakia	1,159,808.18
Other countries	3,242,895.32
	$27,989,965.25

Prisoners of War:

In Germany	$ 487,908.42	
In Austria-Hungary	247,447.23	
In France	223,000.77	
In Great Britain	211,351.23	
In Russia	254,404.32	
In Switzerland	265,200.42	
In other countries	408,547.67	
		2,097,860.06

American Soldiers and Sailors:

Adriatic—Levant	$ 88,597.23	
Merchant Marine	96,495.49	
Miscellaneous	40,786.28	
		225,879.00

Administration:

New York	$ 557,170.92	
Overseas	434,769.90	
		991,940.82
		$31,305,645.13

DEDUCT — Contributions received from outside sources, less cash and other sundry items on hand March 7, 1921 .... 1,631,452.18

Net amount advanced by National War Work Council $29,674,192.95

EXHIBIT E

ADMINISTRATIVE AND GENERAL ACTIVITIES EXPENSES AT GENERAL HEADQUARTERS IN NEW YORK
FROM COMMENCEMENT OF OPERATIONS IN 1917 TO MARCH 7, 1921

Office expenses, rent, light, etc.	$ 611,079.28
Comptroller's Department expenses, including traveling auditors	213,140.15
Purchasing and stores division salaries and expenses	156,225.56
Furniture and office equipment (less income from salvage)	91,387.65
Religious Bureau expenses	130,947.18
Construction Department expenses	32,367.75
Treasurer's Department, including expenses of disbursing remittances from soldiers overseas	140,104.09
Interest on borrowed money	137,811.98
Insurance premiums—fire, fidelity, and casualty	87,852.76
Legal expenses	62,501.06
General administrative and executive expenses	664,877.43
Intelligence Department expenses	20,396.30
Educational Bureau expenses	39,923.51
Expenses of purchasing and accounting bureaus in connection with overseas work	301,975.10
Other bureau expenses (Physical, music, sex hygiene, transportation, etc.)	533,077.75
Miscellaneous unclassified expenses prior to April 1, 1918	347,705.79
	$3,571,373.34

CERTIFICATE OF INDEPENDENT AUDITORS

PRICE, WATERHOUSE & CO.
54 WILLIAM STREET
NEW YORK

April 27, 1921

Trustees of the War Fund of the
Young Men's Christian Associations of the United States,
347 Madison Avenue, New York City

We have audited the books and accounts of the National War Work Council of the Young Men's Christian Associations of the United States at its headquarters in New York, Paris, and London, and at the six military headquarters at New York, Boston, Chicago, San Francisco, and Atlanta, from the commencement of its operations on April 26, 1917, to March 7, 1921, and have been furnished with statements of the overseas accounts at Coblenz prepared by the overseas Comptroller, and we find that the foregoing financial statements have been correctly prepared therefrom.

The contributions represent those actually received at the headquarters at New York, Paris, and London on or before March 7, 1921, but do not include the Council's proportion of the undistributed resources of the United War Work Campaign at that date. We made a thorough test of the expenditures and found that they had been made under sufficient instruction and were properly vouched. The securities owned, which represent donations by contributors and actual investments, and the cash on hand were verified and found in order. All ascertainable liabilities have been included in the financial statements.

WE CERTIFY that, in our opinion, the foregoing statements are properly drawn up so as to show correctly the transactions of the National War Work Council of the Young Men's Christian Associations of the United States, from the commencement of its operations on April 26, 1917, to March 7, 1921, the date when its assets and liabilities were transferred to the Trustees of the War Fund of the Young Men's Christian Associations of the United States.

PRICE, WATERHOUSE & CO.

RECOGNITION OF THE ASSOCIATION'S WIDE SERVICE

FROM *Association Men*, JULY, 1919

The United States, France, and China recently paid appreciative honors to the Association by decorating Dr. John R. Mott, General Secretary of the International Committee and of the War Work Council.

The Distinguished Service Medal was awarded him by General Peyton C. March, "for especially meritorious and conspicuous service." This was presented by Secretary of War Newton D. Baker, on the Capitol steps at Washington.

The title of Chevalier de la Légion d'Honneur was conferred "on behalf of the grateful French Government for the work of the Y.M.C.A. in the Foyers du Soldat, Union Franco-Americaine." The ribbon was presented by M. Casanave, High Commissioner in the

United States at the last meeting of the War Work Council in New York City.

Silk flags of the Allied nations which flew in Shanghai during the United States War Work Campaign were presented on behalf of the Chinese National Council by David Z. T. Yui.

WAR WORK ADDRESSES

Dinner of the International Committee of Young Men's Christian Associations, held in Honor of General Pershing, New York City, May 10, 1921

INTRODUCTORY ADDRESS BY JOHN R. MOTT

Mr. Chairman, Ladies and Gentlemen:

The Young Men's Christian Association has called out and mobilized the greatest and most beneficent among the lay movements of all the Christian centuries. You will recall that Gibbon pointed out as the first among the causes for the early and rapid spread of Christianity that each individual Christian looked upon it as his most sacred and solemn duty to spread among his companions the inestimable blessings which he had received. Therefore, the merchant presented Christ to the members of his guild, the soldier to the others in his legion, the scholar to those gathered around the same teacher. It was the constant collision of souls inspired by the great Christ that explained the thorough as well as rapid spread of the Christian religion.

The Young Men's Christian Association in this country alone is working at over 2,000 centers and has a membership of nearly 1,000,000 men and boys, not to speak of the successive millions who in other days have been impressed by its program and caught its spirit and translated into business, professional, and civic life the principles and spirit of Jesus Christ. It has thus become a great power in permeating the life of the nation with its vitalizing principles and with its spirit of service. The Young Men's Christian Association has also consolidated the scattered lay forces of our all too divided Protestant Christendom and enabled them to present a united front to a united inertia, to a united indifference, to a united sinfulness, and to a united unbelief; and as a result has pushed forward constantly and triumphantly the limits of Christ's Kingdom.

The Young Men's Christian Association has emphasized, illustrated, and done much to realize the highest ideal of manhood. I was talking with one of the outstanding leaders of the British Churches not many months ago. He said to me that he regarded the most original contribution of the Young Men's Christian Association, and in some ways its most highly multiplying contribution to our civilization, was the working out of what we symbolize by the Red Triangle, which stands for the symmetrical development of manhood. It was said of Lorenzo dei Medici, the brilliant Italian, that he was cultured but corrupt, wise yet cruel, spending the morning in writing a sonnet in praise of virtue and spending the night in vice. I care not how well educated a man may be or how splendid his physique, if he comes out into the world corrupt in heart, with loose ideals, he is a menace to society and to the life of the nation. The Association, therefore, by influencing increasingly the sport life of our nation with that which is wholesome and fair and sportsmanlike; by leading a great educational program that tonight has enrolled in its classes more young men than all the colleges of the seventy Protestant denominations of the United States and Canada; above all, by waging an unwearying campaign of confronting men of inquiring minds with the Living Christ and His challenging program—by these and other practical and vital means the Association is developing symmetrical manhood and buttressing at every point the life of the nation.

This organization also, in uniting class or group to work on behalf of class or group, is in a very secure way anchoring sound principles among these various groupings of the national life. Its departments working in the cities, in the rural communities, in the universities, along the railways, in the merchant marine, in the standing army and navy, among colored men, Oriental men, and men of many other nationalities woven into the texture of our national life, are along the various lines of cleavage directing power where it can be most widely and most advantageously distributed, and thus impressing the life of the nation.

The Young Men's Christian Association of America, for some reason that never fails to move me with awe, has had the unique honor of transplanting to many other nations of the world its dynamic and vitalizing principles and its effective adaptations of applied Christianity, so that from the American base have gone out influences spreading the modern idea of the Association now to nearly thirty nations, the most progressive nations of Asia, the most forward-looking countries of Latin America, the groping new nations of Europe, the beginnings of nationalities on the African continent. It is a great trust to be permitted to help fashion the ideals and practices of the coming leaders of these nations. I need not remind you that the Association in seeking to win these nations for Christ and His Church lays its hand upon the three or four most influential classes, the educated classes, the moneyed classes, the ruling classes, and the great and surging tides of democracy. Along these four great lines it proceeds from triumph to triumph in spreading the principles that mean so much to us here in our American life.

It was a great honor to be permitted to have any part as an organization in serving the incomparable army under the American colors. General Pershing, I believe that you led and inspired the cleanest army, the most united army, and, I hope it does not seem boastful or invidious to say the most idealistic army. What do we not owe to the note you struck in the early days! We esteem it a high privilege that we were permitted to work under your leadership over there and among your colleagues in the camps here at home; to do our part along with the other welfare societies in ministering to that splendid body of 4,800,000 men who made up the American army and navy. We shall never cease to be grateful. I would be true to my heart tonight and pay a tribute to those men who made this so largely possible, and even more to the women—those 25,000 men and women who served at home and overseas—and behind them to those millions of men and women of America, rich and poor, who associated their gifts and sacrifices that this patriotic and Christian service might be rendered. We sometimes overlook the fact that we of all these welfare societies were permitted to serve 19,000,000 Allied soldiers and nearly 6,000,000 prisoners of war both in the Allied and enemy countries. In my recent journeys I found that that unselfish service has opened up doors across the breadth of the world for that which this organization stands for in time of peace as well as in days of war.

Think also of the great unifying power of the Young Men's Christian Association. It is dealing with the three greatest problems of our day. One of those is the social problem, especially in the industrial area, another is the racial, and the third, the international. The social problem in the industrial area. By breaking down the barriers between man and man and fusing together all right-thinking and forward-looking men, no matter to what group they belong, by working not only in what we call the zone of agreement but likewise under the power of Christ and in following His principles ever widening that zone of agreement, this organization is fitted to render unique service. The racial problem. I was in the South last week and saw, under the splendid leadership of such white men as John Eagan of Atlanta and Dr. Dillard, and of such colored men as Major Moton and Bishop Jones, the most remarkable service being rendered by the Association in promoting right relations between the races. It impressed me as one of the greatest contributions being made on any continent for the solution of what is a world-wide problem—this racial problem. The international problem. The American Ambassador in Paris once said to me that in his judgment this Movement was doing more to unite the nations than are arbitration treaties, peace conferences, and military alliances. Later when I had the honor of being received by His Majesty, the King of England, and quoted this remark, the King quickly said, "The Ambassador is right because this Movement is uniting the hearts of the coming leaders of nations." Most aptly did he express what we see in progress in the international contacts among the rising generation. It will be more true of the boys who are coming on, because the present is the most remarkable generation of boys that ever lived. By the way, General Pershing (addressing the General), a few days ago on my way East from California, I was much pleased to hear a fellow passenger say that your boy is one of the most active and beloved of the boys in the Young Men's Christian Association in Lincoln, Nebraska.

The Young Men's Christian Association is today at the fork in the road. We have come as an organization to one of those points of decision at which now and then each individual stands, when it becomes necessary not only to give play to our feelings and to exercise our brains but also to use our wills. You ask, What is this fork in the road for the Young Men's Christian Association? It is a choice between contraction and expansion. Are we going to minister to millions of men and boys or only to hundreds of thousands? Are we going to enter those thousands of doors recently opened across the world, or are we going to let them close before our eyes? It is a choice not only between contraction and expansion, but also to use the military phrase, between guiding on the past and guiding on the future. Surely the men or women who are in this room tonight do not wish us to guide on the prewar past. Surely you do not wish us to guide upon the confused days when the world was in convulsion. We must regulate our plans not so much by the inadequate plans and standards of the past and by our visible resources as by the beckoning hand of Christ; His beckoning hand is a pierced hand, and that hand never pointed an organization save to great need and to boundless opportunity. It is a choice between following and leading. What is needed in the world today is organizations that are not so much influenced by example as they are concerned with setting precedents. We are waking up to the fact that we have come into a new day and that the old categories, the old methods, and old achievements will not suffice. Only such prophetic and heroic leadership will command the following and call forth the devotion of the present alert, inquiring, and forward-looking generation. It is a choice between smallness and greatness. You and I all saw in the last four years some men and women in our communities expand from little men and women into true greatness. I am sorry to add that in recent months we have seen some we thought had risen into greatness shrivel up into littleness and pettiness. God forbid that we should come out from the spell of those great days when we saw a land of large dimensions, when we looked down through never ending vistas, when above us there were lifted heavens, and when we mingled with great spirits.

Under the noble and exalted leadership of our great guest and friend, millions of our best youth went to the war. In those crucial days when hearts stood still, tens of thousands of them laid down their lives. Many did so with smiling faces. Why? Because they believed in their souls that their cause was righteous, and secondly, because they believed that you and I would rear on the foundation laid by their lives a worthy superstructure. I sometimes fancy that I hear them marching—"the chariots of Israel and the horsemen thereof." May a double portion of their spirit come upon us and may we ever, with intense and self-forgetful lives and with the use of our time, our money and our influence, prove ourselves worthy of them and worthy of the coming day.

ADDRESS BY GENERAL JOHN J. PERSHING

I am particularly happy to have this opportunity of meeting with the representatives of this great Christian organization. In the last three-quarters of a century the influence of the Young Men's Christian Association has been extended practically to every corner of the globe. My own personal acquaintance with its endeavors has covered many years and many lands.

It was during the earlier period of our occupation of the Philippine Islands that I first met Dr. Mott, who even then had become a world figure, whose able direction and foresight gave impulse to others, and who because of his leadership, stands foremost today among thousands of able devotees to Young Men's Christian Association ideals. It was at a banquet in Manila on a very warm evening when Dr. Mott, speaking of the future of the Young Men's Christian Association, aroused his audience to a warmth that far surpassed that of the climate, with the result that there were eventually erected three splendid Young Men's Christian Association buildings—one for young Americans and two for the Filipinos themselves.

In the Island of Mindanao as early as 1903, a Young Men's Christian Association secretary followed the troops into the interior, and came to my headquarters with his tent and his newspapers and phonograph. Friendly Moros made frequent visits to my camp and on one occasion this secretary appeared among them with his phonograph, and permitted several datos to talk into the machine. Then with something of the air of the magician, he would wave the crowd back and grind out the words spoken by the Moro. Upon hearing their own voices reproduced, they were mystified and stood aghast as much as to say "There ain't no such darned thing." The Young Men's Christian Association secretary became very popular and freely went from place to place among these warlike people quite unmolested.

In China and Japan the influence for good has been immeasurably great. Under the direction of their wide-awake secretaries there has grown up a remarkable enthusiasm for physical development. The principal centers of Young Men's Christian Association control are alive with activity, and teams in the various sports meet as frequently as possible to compete internationally for honors. The result has been an extension of Young Men's Christian Association prestige that must have a marked effect not only upon the future of the individuals concerned, but upon the relations that the people whom they represent shall bear to each other. It all must lead to a better understanding and draw them and us closer and closer together in friendly intercourse as time goes on. This work richly deserves the unstinted support of all farseeing Americans.

The early appearance of the Young Men's Christian Association with the army was in the days when the soldier was rarely in the minds of our people. Luxury was unknown and none was expected, pay was meager and the isolation at times became very irksome, so the Young Men's Christian Association worker was a welcome companion and his comfort gratefully received.

On the border and in Mexico, the Association realized more than ever the opportunity to aid in affording the men of the service clean recreations. It provided reading rooms, clubs, games, lectures, movies, all of which served to keep them from the temptations that constantly follow in the wake of an army, or are found indigenous to the locality where the soldier's lot is so frequently cast.

The extension of Young Men's Christian Association work here in America has been very gratifying. There lies in the heart of every man a desire to live honorably among one's fellows, but humanity is not yet able to rise much higher than its environment. Where ennobling surroundings are absent those of another sort are found and in spite of the better instincts evil influences prevail. But we must not forget that the difficulties of reform are much greater than those of guidance. There are yet some 2,000 cities of over 5,000 inhabitants each in our own country which have not yet been reached by this Association. When we look around and see the wreck of nations, it makes us, or should make us, stop and consider our own condition, and I believe that there is no other organization quite so well-fitted to meet the needs of our young men in America as the Young Men's Christian Association. As a power in the development of good citizens not only among our native-born but among the foreign-born there is no agency that surpasses the Young Men's Christian Association. Here there opens up a large field of endeavor, wherein many of our own people need not only the spirit of Christianity but the spirit of patriotism as well, which is, in fact much the same thing. Instead of 1,000,000 members of this Association in America there ought to be 10,000,000.

It was in the World War that we came in closest touch with the organization. Your representatives were already in the field when our advance troops reached France. They were ready and anxious to be of every possible service. Supported by your patriotic membership here at home and under the leadership of that able administrator, Mr. Carter, the organization began to expand at once to meet our needs. We all had our hands very full in those trying days. The army had to be organized, and a great general staff had to be built up to handle the multitude of details as to plans of operations, supply, and transportation. It was in the midst of these preparations that I called up Mr. Carter and asked the Young Men's Christian Association to take charge of the army canteens to follow our troops; he responded promptly and entered upon the work as a duty.

This placed the Young Men's Christian Association on a business basis, involving direct responsibility to the A.E.F. for an immense undertaking. They had to buy and sell without profit just as the army would have done. At first Mr. Carter's request for a certain allowance of tonnage was granted, but as time went on and our limited shipping became less and less able to carry our actual needs in war material, his quota of monthly tonnage was very much reduced even in the face of increasing demands. So through lack of transportation facilities, he was unable to provide the canteens with all they required. Furthermore, the personnel of the Young Men's Christian Association had to be expanded in almost the same proportion as the army, had to be organized to conduct this large business, which was only one of its numerous activities, with such untrained personnel as could be hastily mustered here at home.

All these things were a tremendous handicap, and when its work came to be compared with that of other welfare organizations operating with far less responsibility and covering only special areas, there arose some unjust criticism of which other organizations too often took advantage. But as a matter of fact this feature of the work of the Young Men's Christian Association deserves great praise, and I should like to express here in this presence my deep appreciation of the results obtained.

In the field of education, athletics, and recreation after the Armistice the Young Men's Christian Association took the lead, without any question, and as a matter of fact about nine-tenths of the welfare work that was carried on in the A.E.F. was carried on under the direction and guidance of the Young Men's Christian Association. Due largely to its efforts, our men were given opportunities for improvement, travel, and entertainment that aided us materially in upholding the high standards of conduct always maintained in our forces abroad.

Finally, I wish to express the belief that this Association will continue to grow in usefulness to humanity, and will early become a universally recognized force in our national life against which the powers of evil may not prevail.

THE WORK OF THE AMERICAN YOUNG MEN'S CHRISTIAN ASSOCIATIONS ON BEHALF OF THE ALLIED ARMIES AND PRISONERS OF WAR

ADDRESS BY JOHN R. MOTT AT DINNER IN HONOR OF MARSHAL FOCH, NOVEMBER 21, 1921

Representatives of the Young Men's Christian Associations of America have assembled here tonight from all parts of the nation to pay tribute to our distinguished guest, the greatest military commander of modern times, the greatest leader of men of all time, and a Christian of simplicity and reality. We represent the 1,000,000 members of 2,000 Associations scattered through all our forty-eight states. We would humbly and with our whole hearts not only pay our tribute of honor and of undying gratitude for your triumphant leadership of the militant forces of justice and righteousness during the recent fateful and tragic years, but would likewise present to you as our Supreme Commander a brief report of our stewardship in the service we were called upon to render to the vast bodies of men under your direction.

The very day that America recognized her duty and joined the Allies, the American Young Men's Christian Association placed itself at the service of President Wilson and the Army and Navy Departments of our government. This organization had already won the complete confidence of the nation because of its splendid services in the Northern and Southern armies in the great Civil War a generation ago, and more especially because of its later indispensable service in the Spanish-American, South African, and Russo-Japanese Wars. In the light of the valuable experience thus acquired, the Association work expanded by leaps and bounds with the growth of the American army and navy until at the time of the signing of the Armistice we were ministering to 4,000,000 American soldiers and to 800,000 American sailors. Although as General Pershing pointed out in a recent address in New York, the Young Men's Christian Association performed nine-tenths of all the welfare work in the American army and navy overseas, we would recall gratefully the splendid service accomplished by the other welfare societies in the more limited areas where they elected to serve. The Association has also been assigned major responsibility for such work among the American forces on the Rhine. On the American army and navy alone, this Association has expended during and since the war approximately $125,000,000.

Great as has been the work accomplished for the American troops, many consider that an even greater contribution of the American Association was that made to our Allies. Apart from the Red Cross, which performs an entirely different function, this was the only one of the American welfare societies which during the war and since the war served the Allied armies. Even before the United States recognized her duty and joined in the world struggle, the American people, through this agency, had begun to manifest their heartfelt sympathy with the soldiers of the other armies and had begun to establish among them practical and helpful agencies. First of all, we secured permission to serve the prisoners of war of all armies. This unique and greatly needed effort, which we began in the prisoner-of-war camps of Germany and Austria-Hungary, expanded until by the end of the war our Association workers had identified themselves with the hard lot of between five and six million prisoners of war in nearly every country engaged in the struggle. It would be difficult to exaggerate the helpful character of this work in the lonely camps in the way of meeting the severe physical necessities of the prisoners, of providing them with recreation, useful mental occupation, and religious ministries, in every case according to their own faith. To its great value the different governments have borne emphatic testimony.

The French army was the first army to which the American Young Men's Christian Association extended its co-operation. This took place in connection with my first visit to the warring countries in the late autumn of 1914 when I met with Mr. Emmanuel Sautter, later known as the highly efficient Chief Director of the Foyer du Soldat Franco-Americaine Y.M.C.A. We guaranteed to provide from American sources the money necessary to launch and conduct this work, on condition that he secure permission of the French military authorities. This happily was soon accomplished, and the first, or model Foyer was established. Its success was so apparent that similar Foyers were rapidly established through the same division. The commanders of other divisions requested similar help. From this time on it became impossible to keep up with the demand for the spread of this agency, the proved helpfulness of which was so quickly and generously recognized by the French military authorities, and by none more than by our honored guest. By the time of the signing of the peace, over 1,500 Foyers were at work in all parts of the French army, near and far. The American Association has counted it a great privilege to continue to provide almost entirely the money necessary for the conduct of this work. From the beginning down to the present time, they have furnished for this purpose very nearly $9,000,000 gold, and in the whole range of American beneficence there has been no contribution of the Association which the American people have been more glad to make. Besides the money, we have been delighted to place under the direction of Mr. Sautter hundreds of our best American men and women workers who, in collaboration with their French colleagues, have made possible this great patriotic and international undertaking. Possibly there could be no better evidence of the indispensable value of the work accomplished in the war than the fact that since the war closed the French military authorities have insisted on the continuation of the Foyer work, so that now throughout the French army in France, in Germany, and in the Near East, the Foyer is still working at full strength. Moreover, its success in the army has led to its extension throughout the French navy, and still more striking is the fact that in the devastated areas and in other parts of France the soldiers who experienced the benefit of the Foyer in war time have helped to establish civilian Foyers to serve the young men and boys of France in peacetime.

Besides this notable work in the French army, the American Association has served nearly every other Allied army. It co-operated with the British Young Men's Christian Association in furnishing men and money for work among the British and Canadian forces in France and likewise among the British and Indian troops in Egypt, in the Gallipoli Peninsula, in Mesopotamia, in Palestine, in East Africa, and in India. Called to Russia at a late stage, it conducted its activities for a time with the crumbling Russian army, and since

then has sought to do all in its power to help the young men of the
loyal elements of the true Russia among the millions of Russian
refugees in France, in Poland, in various parts of the Near East, and
in faraway Siberia. Next in magnitude and importance to the work
in the French and British armies was that which the American Association was called upon by the Italian military authorities to do
among their forces—a work accomplished through what was known
as the Casa del Soldato, where we worked in closest co-operation with
an Italian Roman Catholic society; and it is interesting to add that at
the time when virtually all the huts and the buildings of this society
were destroyed, the American Young Men's Christian Association
provided the money to restore them. Still later, a similar work was
established in the armies of Portugal, Rumania, and Greece, but two
of the most highly efficient parts of the work were those conducted
by the American secretaries in the armies of Poland and Czechoslovakia. Within the past year or two we have ministered to over
1,000,000 men in the Polish army with the highest expressions of
appreciation from both Polish and French military leaders. The interesting and fruitful work of the Association on behalf of the
Chinese labor battalions behind the French and British forces in
France, likewise the work on behalf of the Japanese army in Siberia
should not be overlooked in any comprehensive survey.

To summarize, the American Association conducted its work
during the war not only throughout the American army and navy,
along with other American welfare societies, but also as the only
American welfare society in Allied armies numbering nearly if not
quite 20,000,000 men, and likewise among not less than 5,000,000
prisoners of war. For the accomplishment of this service it furnished
nearly 26,000 American men and women workers and secured from
the American people for this great program about $170,000,000.
Its work continues today among between two and three million Allied
soldiers, chiefly the French and Poles.

What is the significance of a work like this? First and foremost,
military authorities insist upon its military value in helping to maintain and strengthen the morale of the men. The Allied Supreme Commander has repeatedly emphasized, as has possibly no other military
commander in modern times, the transcendent value of morale, or, as
he has better expressed it, the spirit of the soldier. It would be difficult to overstate the importance of a work like that of the Foyer in the
different armies in counteracting the influences of war-tiredness, loneliness, idleness, doubt, and propaganda, which tend to weaken or
destroy morale. Its constructive program of providing physical com-
forts, of promoting the contentment and peace of mind of the soldiers,

of insuring a wise use of their leisure hours, of preoccupying their minds with uplifting influences, of helping to preserve home ties and to remind the men that the people of their own and Allied nations stand behind them with their heart interest and generous gifts, of deepening the conviction as to the righteousness of the cause for which they are fighting, and, where necessary, of affording facilities for the priests and chaplains to provide the uplifting ministries of religion— in these and other ways such work as that of the Foyer maintains, refreshes, and strengthens the spirit of the men in the midst of loneliness and strain.

In the second place, as we look back over the years of the war and the trying years which have since elapsed, we clearly recognize the great good accomplished by this work in promoting friendly and co-operative relations between the nations who made common cause in the great struggle. This has been particularly noticeable and impressive in the relations thus maintained between France and America. The countless contacts established in the Foyers during these never-to-be-forgotten years have served to knit together with enduring bonds of friendship the leaders of tomorrow in these two great sister republics.

In the third place, such a work, bringing together, as it has done, men of different religious communions, Protestant, Roman Catholic, Greek Catholic, and Hebrew, has developed among them all a larger tolerance and has generated a new and most helpful atmosphere—an atmosphere in which men loathe to differ and determine to understand. This desirable result is accomplished without proselytizing and without the weakening of the religious affiliations of any. On the contrary, there has been a strengthening of religious ties.

Above all, this unselfish undertaking has furnished a most helpful preparation for a great, constructive, and permanent peacetime work on behalf of the young men of all our nations. We of America wish to congratulate our brothers in France that the Foyer is an indigenous institution. Judged by our experience with the Association here in America, the Foyer in France has a great future. What work could be more important in the coming day than to influence the ideals, character, and spirit of the young men and boys, because the destiny of any nation is determined by the opinions and ambitions of its young men and boys.

In giving this brief report of the co-operative work of the American Association in all the armies under the leadership of the Allied Supreme Commander, we would renew our expression of profound and undying gratitude and our purpose in time of peace as well as war to do all in our power to safeguard the priceless results achieved in the great struggle.

RESPONSE OF MARSHAL FOCH TO GREETINGS EXTENDED BY THE YOUNG
MEN'S CHRISTIAN ASSOCIATION AT A DINNER IN HIS HONOR
AT WASHINGTON, D. C., NOVEMBER 21, 1921

There is no greater eulogy to be made of your Young Men's
Christian Association work on behalf of the Allied armies than to
enumerate in figures, the services that were rendered. There are no
words that speak better than these figures; I cannot better them. But
I must say here, in my capacity as Chief of the French armies, how
greatly we have appreciated the services that you were able to render
us. In 1914, led by the great principle of unselfish service, you started
to aid, to relieve the prisoners of war; and shortly after we asked
you: "Come and help us to uplift our soldiers."

The French soldier, it is known, is brave, full of initiative; he is
full of impulse, he is full of that spirit which is called the "French
fury," but will it last? The world doubts it. Will it hold out? Will
he be steadfast? Will he last in a long war? All the world asks that
question.

Well! Yes! To the great astonishment of the whole world this
soldier was seen to endure, to hold out during battles lasting more
than twenty days, under continuous fire, persistent, without any
shelter, having very often for cover only the bodies of his comrades
who had fallen; during four winters he was seen maintaining his
trench warfare, a war in the flood land, having for sky but the sky
of winter, with its clouds and its rigors, and his only shelter a hole in
the ground.

In this effort, all moral supports seemed sure to break under a
bombardment which never ceased. What man was there whose nerves
were sufficiently strong to endure for entire years? Above all, the
loneliness, the reaction, the depression, the melancholy, that which
was recently and very judiciously called the "blues," invaded the
minds and seemed as if they must turn the soldiers away from facing
the enemy.

Well! This morale we have been able to sustain, thanks to your
powerful help, thanks to the Foyer du Soldat Union Franco-American
Y.M.C.A., into which the tired soldier came for new strength, and
to find a touch of that family life, or at least that familiar contact
which seemed to him an infinite comfort. This was the means by
which resistance was maintained, and when we wished to advance, we
found energies much better revitalized and much better prepared because these soldiers who had felt and proved in themselves the contact
of this good will, placed entirely at their disposal, believed themselves
obliged to pay still once more with their lifeblood and advance.

When we definitely launched our final offensive, they were driven forward by the inspiration of the forces behind, and the soldiers marched ahead with resolute step determined and conscience-bound to go to the very limit.

From this direction came that magnificent blast which, driving our sails and our flags, carried them forward in an irresistible assault, to that moment on November 11, when the enemy cried "Halt! Enough!" Yes! Our flags blending with each other, we forged resolutely ahead, driven by that impulse, not only of soldiers who felt themselves supported by the organization behind them, but above all, by their faith, their religious belief, and their absolute self-sacrifice.

Then, let me, gentlemen, attribute a great part of our success to you, as much in the defensive as in the offensive by that support which you gave us, and because you sheltered all that work in the shadow of the finest of ideals, the principle of unselfish service.

I would never conclude, gentlemen, if I attempted to tell you all the sentiments that inspire me in the presence of such results, but I must tender to you the greatest "Thank you!" that I find in the depths of my heart, for all the work you have undertaken and realized.

LETTER REGARDING THE CRITICAL SITUATION IN EUROPE, AUGUST, 1916

Some time I hope to have opportunity to tell in a more intimate way of the vivid experiences through which I have just passed and of the exceptional exposure which I have had to the leaders as well as the peoples in connection with my visit to the principal countries now at war—England, France, Germany, Austria-Hungary, and Russia. Although the journey has occupied less than two months and has been most intense and absorbing, it has seemed like an age, and has taxed to the limit every power of mind and heart. There has not been a day which has not been attended with real perils but these have been lost sight of in the midst of boundless opportunity to serve and to sympathize with men.

An outstanding impression has been that of the vast range and depth of human suffering occasioned by the war. Overpowering as were the facts presented by the millions of wounded and maimed men and boys, one's soul was even more profoundly moved by the silent suffering of the anxious and the bereaved. I do not recall visiting a home which had not suffered affliction, nor did I meet a person across whose life shadows had not fallen. Even here at sea on the Atlantic Ocean we find ourselves still under the heavy spell of these indescribable sorrows.

No end of the awful struggle is in sight. While there are signs that lead one at times to think that the war is now approaching its real climax, it would be a mistake to assume that this means its speedy conclusion. In each country I found the people tired of the war but no nation gave evidence of being exhausted and in no land were the leaders ready to take the initiative in moving in the direction of peace. We may as well adjust ourselves to the unwelcome and tragic fact that all these lands must suffer far more before there can be an enduring peace.

In contrast with my visit to these countries in the early stages of the war, I was impressed this time by the alarming development of distrust, bitterness, and hatred. Equally striking was the increased sensitiveness of all the peoples. As a result of the terrific tension of the two long years, the war has got on the nerves of everybody. The feeling toward America has completely changed. One of the best indications that we as a nation have been truly neutral is the fact that both sides in the present struggle regard our actions and policy with so much dissatisfaction and displeasure. Be that as it may, the present is not the time to argue with Europe, still less to criticize any of the nations now engaged in the war, or to make peace proposals to them. Difficult though it may be, the best attitude for Americans, for the time being, is to be willing to be misunderstood, to keep quiet, and to serve.

Another impression, which helped to counteract the awfully depressing facts and circumstances to which I have referred, was that of the volume of unselfish activity and service to be found in every part of Europe, both in the belligerent and in the neutral countries. I question whether in the history of the human race there has ever been a time when so many people have forgotten themselves in the service of their own and of other peoples. While here and there improvements might be suggested in the methods of philanthropy and in the practical means of helpfulness, the spirit everywhere manifested is beyond all praise and is preparing the way for a new Europe.

My chief solicitude, which I am free to say is stronger even than when I left America, is lest the American people, because of our being at such long range and because of our lack of imagination and credence, fail to enter sufficiently into fellowship with the sufferings of the hundreds of millions of our brothers and sisters in Europe.

Against the black background of deadly strife and cruelty, of indescribable misery and suffering, the most inspiring and hopeful sight is that practical ministry on behalf of the millions of men and boys in the training camps, in the trenches, and in the prisoner-of-war camps, which the Association Movement has made possible. Premier Asquith has recently spoken of this as the greatest thing in Europe. I found this view shared by the leading men of all the nations as well as by the soldiers themselves and the members of their families. As you know, the object of my journey was to study how we might most wisely conduct and enlarge this work in each country, and to prepare even now for the conservation of results after the war. As a result of studying conditions on the spot and of conferring with our own workers and with trusted leaders in the different countries, we have been able to work out plans which I trust will enable us to meet this opportunity—the like of which we shall never again confront. If ever money was placed where it brought, as it were, life from the dead and beneficent results out of all proportion to the sum invested, it has most surely been in the case of the money given toward this particular undertaking.

In the light of what I have seen, I fear that during the coming autumn and winter we shall witness immeasurably greater suffering than in either of the preceding years. It is essential that we not only continue to do all in our power to carry forward this practical and truly Christlike ministry to the bodies and souls of suffering men (of whom there are not less than 5,000,000 in the prison camps alone), but that we give ourselves more to prayer that God Himself may bring an end in His own way to a situation that has become impossible for men to control or for the world to bear. In a conversation with me a royal personage of wide international influence—one who made as deep an impression on me as anyone whom I have met this year —made the remark, "We must pray that God may work a miracle." The more I have pondered her words the more I have seen in them. Surely God can end this war as suddenly as it began; and only a great manifestation of His wisdom, of His spirit of brotherhood and justice, of His power, will insure the ushering in of that day for which the nations long and suffer. In some way men of reality, who actually believe in God, must be led through prayer to concern themselves more than at present with the discovery of His mind and the doing of His will.

JOHN R. MOTT

JOHN R. MOTT IN POLAND, APRIL, 1924

A LETTER TO ASSOCIATION FRIENDS BY PAUL SUPER, NATIONAL SECRETARY OF THE YOUNG MEN'S CHRISTIAN ASSOCIATION IN POLAND

The names of three Americans, said different Polish speakers at banquets in honor of Dr. Mott, will long live in the memory of Poles because of their great and helpful services to the new Poland during the trying months following the rebirth of the nation at the end of the Great War: the names of Wilson, Hoover, and Mott. This state-

ment, spontaneous in widely separated cities, is the key to an understanding of the wonderful reception given Dr. Mott during his recent
visit to Kraków, Warsaw, and Lodz. Leaders in civilian and military
life vied with each other in showing him special honors, and in honoring the Movement he represents.

Kraków, the ecclesiastical, cultural, and historical capital of
Poland, lies near the southern border. It is a proud and dignified
center of learning and Polish tradition. Here one of Europe's oldest
universities is located, founded in 1364. Here Copernicus was a
student and teacher. Here the great Tartar invasion of 1241 met its
first serious obstacle and was checked. Here lie buried the great of
Poland, kings, patriots, poets, archbishops. Here the ancient Catholic
Church is rich and powerful, owning perhaps a third of the real estate
of the old walled city.

Major General Listowski, William Rose, and I met Dr. Mott and
his party at the frontier and escorted them to Kraków in a private
railroad car. At the depot a notable reception committee had gathered, composed of representatives of the government, the army, the
university, and the Young Men's Christian Association. Count
Puslowski, a friend of Dr. Mott's during his 1920 visit, was there as
interpreter. The army band played "The Star Spangled Banner,"
brief words of welcome were spoken, and the party was off to the
Wawel, the historic citadel, castle, and cathedral in the heart of the
city, and indeed, of Poland. A visit to this shrine, sacred to every
Pole, is the proper salute to the country. The pages of history are
turned back a thousand years, and the deeds of great leaders of the
spirit of man are brought to knowledge or renewed in memory.

The noonday event was a dinner in the Grand Hotel, the old
Czartoryski Palace, and it was a gathering worthy of the elegance
of these impressive rooms. Though corps maneuvers were in progress the Minister of War telegraphed to the highest generals to be
present at the dinner to honor the Movement and the man who had
done so much for the Polish soldiers and prisoners of war. Five
generals were, therefore, on hand, a lieutenant general, three major
generals, and a brigadier general. It was a distinguished gathering,
including the governor of the province, the president of the Polish
Academy of Science, the president of the Academy of Art, the pro-
rector and an ex-rector of the university, the vice-mayor of the city,
well-known professors, members of the old nobility and aristocracy,
and representative business men. Kraków outdid itself. So much so,
indeed, that an ultramontane paper protested against such honors
being given a private citizen.

Later in the afternoon Dr. Mott addressed a notable gathering of 250 leading men and women in the council hall of the city, the presiding officer being the Lord Mayor. This was followed by a dinner with directors of the Association for an intimate discussion of the Association's problems. The directors are a strong, energetic, and highly respected group, at least half of whom are widely known in Poland.

A night's ride northward brought the party to Warsaw, a city of 1,000,000 population, the geographical center both of Poland and of Europe. Here also Dr. Mott was met by a reception committee of prominent men including the general commanding the troops about Warsaw, the head of the American Department of the Ministry of Foreign Affairs, the President of the Polish-American Chamber of Commerce, the President of the Young Men's Christian Association and others. The day was spent in inspection of the Association plant, in necessary official calls, and in conferences.

At night, with the famous General Sikorski, Minister of War, as the presiding officer, there was a dinner to Dr. Mott in the Hotel Europe, with a large number of distinguished guests. Among them were cabinet ministers and ex-ministers, several senators, professors, representatives of foreign governments, editors, prominent business men, and Association leaders. After coffee General Sikorski rose, and, in a speech of deep gratitude and appreciation of the Young Men's Christian Association as both a war and a peace organization for the building of character, decorated Dr. Mott with the star order of "Polonia Restituta" (The Restitution of Poland). We are informed that it is the highest decoration given any foreigner except a king or a president.

General Sikorski spoke with deep feeling as, describing the terrific Russian invasion of 1920 he said, "Even then, when the cordon of the Bolshevik army was tightening around our group from Polesia (General Sikorski's army)—when we were hopelessly severed from food supplies, it was then that the Young Men's Christian Association train arrived with a staff of untiring workers under the American flag. Your valiant workers spared no effort in keeping up the courage of thousands of our soldiers and officers, who were sacrificing everything for their beloved country and for western civilization." Passing from the war to the peace work of the Association he continued, "Today the Young Men's Christian Association stands out before us as a model of organized service." In presenting the decoration he said, "It is my great pleasure to present to you in the name of the President of the Republic of Poland, this modest expression of our deepest gratitude. The most beautiful monument in Poland would fail to express fittingly our indebtedness to you."

Another night's ride brought the party to Lodz, "the city of a thousand smokestacks" as Ebersole calls it. This is Poland's great textile city, with a population of 500,000, and here the Young Men's Christian Association has its strongest and most highly developed Association. Here again Dr. Mott was met at the depot by high military and civilian officials and Association leaders, the educators of other cities giving way here to men in industry. The band, instead of soldiers, were city police. The Lord Mayor gave an address of welcome to which Dr. Mott responded. Then began a full day, including special exercises in the largest public school, a dinner in the beautiful home of the president of the Young Men's Christian Association to meet a group of textile men and bankers, a gymnasium exhibition by 100 boys of the Boys' Department, a meeting of active members, and a banquet in the evening with 130 of the leading men of the city, the governor presiding and the general commanding the Lodz district at Dr. Mott's side.

The whole tour was a remarkable and impressive demonstration. In both Kraków and Lodz the invitation to the chief function went out over the name of the governor of the province. Interest was added to the day in Warsaw by the fact that on that day the new gold standard currency was issued and the era of debased currency came to an end. Dr. Mott was deeply impressed with the extraordinary courtesy of the Polish people. Details were attended to with a grace, courtliness, and finish quite beyond the custom in less idealistic nations. We were proud not only of Dr. Mott, but of the Poles. They do know how to do things, and no attention is too much trouble.

The value of the visit is clear and large:

1. It renewed in the mind of the Poles the memory of the great service of the Young Men's Christian Association in war days.
2. To our newer members it brought a vivid sense of the Association as a world Movement, and a new revelation of its strength and standing.
3. It brought new and valuable friends to our side.
4. It gave us a large amount of favorable newspaper and magazine comment, some of it from pens formerly against us.
5. It was a big public demonstration of the fact that the Young Men's Christian Association is very much alive in Poland.
6. It greatly heartened our small and hard-working staff of Polish Association secretaries.
7. It led General Sikorski to come out clear and strong for the Association. He is one of the great men of Poland. Though only forty-two he is Minister of War and has been Prime

Minister. His belief in our work will strengthen many a weak heart in time of difficulty.

8. Dr. Mott was able to call to the attention of the leaders in each Association the condition that particular Association must fulfil to qualify it for continued growth and lasting service. In so doing he carried each Association definitely forward.

9. Dr. Mott's stirring addresses, full of testimony to the place and power of Christ, profoundly moved the leaders of Poland, where such words from the lips of a layman are rare. Thus our Movement is not only pushed forward but lifted and given added spiritual tone.

10. Finally, the visit gives me this opportunity, which I value highly, of showing you the esteem in which the Young Men's Christian Association is held in Poland, and of urging that our American leaders continue to father the promising young Polish Movement until this country, bound to us by many ties of blood and sentiment, be thoroughly on its feet, and the Young Men's Christian Association permanently rooted in its life.

We made careful preparation in work and prayer. Our hearts are filled with thanksgiving.

Constructive and Destructive World Forces

Address at Pittsburgh, Pennsylvania, December 5, 1919

It has been my pleasure and duty for well-nigh thirty-one years to travel over a very considerable portion of this world again and again on various errands related to the plans of Christianity. These journeys have taken me to almost every corner of the earth, to not fewer than forty-six or forty-seven different nations, and to most of them again and again. I make this personal reference merely as a background for the statement that there is a certain advantage in going over the world at intervals from time to time in that it enables one to observe tendencies and to get a line, as it were, on the entire world situation; and to observe contrasts.

Of the six journeys that I made during the war period, three took me into the nations on both sides of the war, and three of them, on account of America having entered the World War, were confined to the Allied nations. I have returned from these more recent journeys overwhelmed with the impression that we are now called upon to deal with an entirely new world. I need not tell anyone here that it is a shaken world. Those foundations that we called foundations a few years ago, we have discovered were but shifting sand. Pillar after pillar of our civilization to which we have pointed with pride and confidence throughout all the years of our lives has crumbled at our feet. Gradually the gaze of the world has been withdrawn from these other supports that failed us and has been riveted upon the one foundation and the one pillar that stands, the Lord Jesus Christ. I sometimes feel that this great World War might almost be characterized as an almost infinite process of exclusion, eliminating one after another other grounds of confidence and fixing the eyes of the world on the One Who is the same yesterday, today, and forever.

Nor do I need to tell you that it is an impoverished and over-burdened world. The war has cost the world over $260,000,000,000. We, in this country, in the first session of Congress after America entered the war, appropriated for military and naval purposes more money than had been spent by all the Congresses from the time of the foundation of the Republic up to the Congress to which I refer, for all purposes combined. Mark my words, the curfew is going to ring late among the nations. The hours of leisure and pleasure are going to be few for scores of millions of people. The backs of entire peoples are going to be bent low not only in this generation, but in innocent generations yet unborn.

It is also an exhausted and overwrought world. I noticed this very much on my last journey, although it was taken some months after the signing of the Armistice. Wherever I went I found the people irritable, impatient, extremely critical. I would say that the world is on its nerve, and that the nerves in large parts of the world are worn threadbare; it is a rent and embittered world. Here I have in mind not simply the obvious, the fact that the two groups of nations that were but yesterday at each other's throats are today feeling the deepest emotions of bitterness and are in the midst of grave misunderstanding. Nor do I have in mind that which is more serious, that in each one of those groups of nations recently at war there has been a falling out; that there have come multiplied misunderstandings and jealousies and a recrudescence of national and racial prejudices, a working at cross-purposes. I have something in mind still more serious and that is that across the world, in every nation recently at war and in nations which did not enter the war, there has been cast a great chasm between classes.

Some of us who were members of the Root Mission sent by the President to Russia in the summer of 1917, shortly after the beginning of the Russian revolution, saw the beginning of that fell disease called Bolshevism. We were conscious of its serious character, but little did we believe that shortly it would eat like some rapid cancerous disease through the tissues of the less vital nations and on into some others of the most abounding vitality. It spread all over Russia, then over that fringe of lands from Finland to the Mediterranean and the middle countries, and on into Western and Southern Europe. In Rome the other day machine guns appeared on the streets to combat the Bolshevist uprising. In Bologna they have named a street Lenin. The leaders of the French Republic are burdened with solicitude because of the serious menace of the same disease. In England, the Foreign Office counted in one week not less than 500 meetings. We have it in our midst, often under other names. Lenin, I sometimes think, was the most sinister and formidable figure raised up in this World War, a man of strong mentality and strong will power. He has known exactly where he wanted to go and he has not deviated a hair's breadth from that path. While the Allies have been unable to agree three days together what they will do with Bolshevism, Lenin has hewed to the line. His aim has been not to divide the world along vertical lines of nationality, but along horizontal lines of class, with the engendering of bitter hatreds, and fanning the flames increasingly. I say it is a rent and embittered world.

Nor do I need to remind you that it is a sorrowing and a suffering world. I see the 11,000,000 graves that were filled by the military and naval operations of the war or what was immediately incident thereto. I never seem to be out of sight of them, and I don't suppose I ever shall be. I have spent a great deal of my time on these six journeys during the war period in the homes of the people, high and low. I think I am accurate when I say I did not visit a home in any of these lands across which the dark shadow had not been cast at least once with great distinctness as a result of the war.

They are sorrowing, I think, more today than yesterday because they have had time to count their losses, they are free from preoccupation, the tragedy of it all has broken in on them, the chair is vacant, the familiar form is not to come back through the garden gate. And it is not merely the mental anguish, but physical suffering such as we have never known. On other occasions I have met groups of Pittsburgh citizens and shared with them what I learned of the sufferings in the hospitals and in the prisoner-of-war camps. I see right now that great hospital with 352 wards, every one filled with fifty beds and every bed with a shattered body. I see that receiving hospital at Moscow right now, where I went with my son; that day, twenty-six trains had come in filled with wounded from one sector of the Galician front alone.

And yet I would remind you that more people will die as a result of this war, this winter, than in any year of the war from the battle wounds or diseases occasioned by the war. If you had been with me not very many months ago with Hoover, with his maps on the wall showing his wonderful work of helpfulness, vessels crossing the world to the places of need from the places of plenty, you would have been reminded vividly of the ameliorating influence he was wielding. A personal friend whom I met in Rome told me that in the buffer States alone, tens of millions are on the very edge of starvation. It is going to be an awful winter. The world has known nothing quite like it, and I do not except last winter or the winter before.

And it is a confused and bewildered world. I am speaking quite frankly tonight. I have found mighty few people who know the way, and I have been thrown with what are known as the leaders of the nations. I have found them, as I got near their hearts, greatly troubled and in confusion. It is a mighty serious moment when we have blind leadership.

Thank God I can pass quickly on to say that it is a plastic world.

The titanic forces of this world war have made the world molten. It is soon to be cast into new molds. Shall they be the old molds that held back the progress and vitality of the world, or shall they be molds that shall liberate, emancipate, and vitalize mankind through the centuries.

Thank God I may also say it is an humbled world. That is something new, surely. All my other journeys have led me to see nations arrogant and self-satisfied, thanking God that they were not as other nations are. But not so today. It is a very encouraging sign to find the greatest nations of the world bowed in humility.

And thank God it is a teachable world. Everywhere, among the high and the lowly I have found people asking three questions if I talked long enough with them: "How did we miss the way?" "What is the way out?" "How long, O God, how long?" Everywhere they are asking these questions. It reminded me of the Old Testament saying, "When Thy judgments are in the earth, the inhabitants of the world learn righteousness." What a teacher! What lessons! What scholars! It is a most hopeful sign.

And I say with prayer and gratitude, it is a comparatively unselfish world. Not as unselfish as it was a year ago. Let your memory travel back a year. Almost anything you asked of the American people then, they did with a glad heart, with boundless gratitude. And we are by war not as unselfish as we were two years ago. Let your memory lead you back to those days when the outcome of the war was not a foretold matter. We were girding ourselves to great sacrifice. Again I say, no appeal could be made to us in connection with which the people did not leap beyond the goal. But compared with what we were and the other nations were before the war, it is still a most unselfish world. I was talking one day to our recent Ambassador to London, Mr. Page, and I asked his advice as to whether I should approach two men, who were strangers to me, regarding a certain matter. "Would it not be presumptuous in me to make such a request of them?" I asked. "Oh, no," Mr. Page replied, "you will not find a selfish man in Europe." I was surprised, but I did not find a man or a woman who gave the impression of thinking of self.

It is an expectant world. The eyes of the world are turned largely in one direction. One is humbled at the thought that notwithstanding the shortcomings, notwithstanding the mistakes, notwithstanding the bitter disappointments, and I cannot overstate this, the eyes of the world are largely turned to the United States of America. May we not ultimately disappoint them? They are disappointed now, but ultimately may we not disappoint them in their aspirations, in their reaching out for sympathy, guidance, and relief.

It is a new world, and it brings a summons tonight that is irresistible. We are summoned to unite ourselves with all other large-minded, large-hearted, forward-looking American people to counteract the great perils which are besetting our nation. One great danger is lest we should lean on our past, our recent past, and become proud and self-satisfied. That has ever been the undoing of nations and peoples. Another danger that is imminent is that we shall relax discipline, effort, and sacrifice. It is startling to find, as I have had occasion to do recently in my trip through thirty-two States, evidences of a falling back into ways of luxury and extravagance, of seeking ease and of working along the lines of least resistance and softness. It is startling; and how incongruous it is in view of the accumulated responsibilities!

Another danger; our people are coming down from the mountains of idealism. Another danger is that we are drifting back into zones of selfishness, and find ourselves defending positions of which we should have been ashamed eighteen months ago. We could not then have looked our boys in the face under such circumstances.

Another danger is that of divided counsels. When we stood together as we did stand together, nothing could stand against us. Another danger is that of inadequate leadership in the sense that Christ meant when He said, "He who would be greatest among you, shall be the servant of all." Nothing less than a getting together and seeing things in true perspective and becoming alarmed in time, and not taking off the edge of our alarm, will save us from drifting back into smallness from greatness. We are summoned to avert these dangers.

We are summoned likewise to help realize the aims for which we fought the war. It is well to be reminded of them tonight. One of these was in order that nations might be liberated. We partially liberated some of these. It is not enough to have the shackles broken and fall clanging at our feet. We learned after our Civil War that that was but the beginning of the process. Some of the so-called free nations are far from free, today.

What did we fight that war for? May I use a word that was coined in the World War and that has brought both hope and despair —self-determination; we fought the war that all peoples might have adequate opportunity to determine for themselves their development. Think of the Valley of the Nile tonight under the old conditions, of the old Levant, and of the newly created States and the enlarged States, the States fringing Russia. Shall the dead have died in vain?

In the third place, we fought that World War, in the words of our President, to make the world safe for democracy; or in other words of the corollary, that democracy might be made safe for the world. What an idle word it is to say that Russia might have been made safe for the world following the Russian revolution. I have reminded you that it made possible the removing of a disease that is eating its way through the tissues of the world. Somebody asked my solution of the Russian problem. My answer was "If the Allies will agree for six months on anything for Russia, Russia will be stabilized."

I am reminded of a letter I once received from Theodore Roosevelt. He was then President. The letter contained this sentence that I have thought of a great deal since: "No land more than Russia holds the fate of the coming years." That land stretching from Pacific to Atlantic, blending the strongest strains of Europe and Asia, having the three most powerful religions, Greek, Catholic, and Protestant Christianity, Judaism, and Mohammedanism, with the strongest racial traits with the possible exception of the Chinese. They hold the fate of the coming years. How important it is that we make that new democracy not as it is today, a menace against which we declare a blockade, even against its ideas, but to make it a source of vitality and hope to unnumbered millions. Surely we didn't go into that war to start and then quit!

And, in the fourth place, we fought that war in order that wars might end. I remind you that there are twenty-three wars now being fought. Be our views what they may in reference to the League of Nations, I don't suppose that there is a person here who does not believe in our eventually working out some international arrangement that will minimize and perhaps some day make impossible a recurrence of this awful calamity. Let us not make the mistake of a century ago such as the Holy Alliance. I sometimes think that there has been a high Providence at work in delaying the realization of our hopes in that what is wanted is not to come in any easy way, that the nations must count the cost, and, I would say, Christian nations especially. I have no confidence in any arrangements that may be made unless there has been breathed into them something that will affect men internally; their motives, their attitudes, their disposition, their spirit. It is an idle dream to think that we can hold this world together by military force or except by releasing great spiritual forces from within.

I have summed it up to myself in this way. It is one of two things; we must either have such a colossal military and naval establishment, one so colossal that it would break down the world to maintain it, as it is breaking down Japan today, or (notice my language closely) the spread of Christianity in its purest form. That is one choice, not only to relieve these impending perils, but also those which will come hereafter; and, to this end, we are summoned to the world-wide spread of Christianity in its purest form.

It is an idle dream to think of America sending out enough missionaries to do that. Even if we could get the men and the money, they could not accomplish the task. It would be resisted and resented by those nations and races rising in their independence and self-determination. And even if they did not resent and resist it, it would not be good for them in the light of the history of civilization. It took a German to lead the German Reformation. It took John Knox to stir Scotland to its depths and make it a power for Christian truth. It took Joseph Neesima to commend Christianity to the masses of Japan. Americans have always most forcefully moved Americans. So it will ever be. It is the sons and daughters of the soil who make Christianity vital and conquering and of compelling power. Therefore, you see the logic of what I am leading up to. We must concentrate on that which alone will make possible the permeating of those lands with the Christian spirit. In other words we must use strategy. What is strategy? Strategy is that science which enables a nation or a man, it may be with comparatively small resources, to achieve great results and perchance to overcome forces far greater apparently—or actually. Therein lies the significance of the American University at Cairo. It says the only way to dominate a backward civilization is to make sure of a proper leadership tomorrow by influencing the ideals, the character, the practices, and the relationships of those who are now the youth. As a well established proverb puts it, "What you would put into the life of a nation, put into its schools."

When, five years ago in Pittsburgh, I spoke in the interest of the launching of this project, I reminded you that there were six places that Christianity should dominate. I would not be concerned by the millions of peoples that lie back of those places. They were Tokyo, Peking, Shanghai, Calcutta, Constantinople, and Cairo, and I maintained then that the most neglected of the six was, and, I regret to say, still, because of the war, is Cairo.

You ask me would I change this list. I would not omit any of this list. Constantinople has a relatively smaller interest, Cairo a greater. I would probably add Moscow and I would add one more in what I call the tinderbox of the world, either in the Balkans or in one of the newly created States, such as Czechoslovakia and Poland.

Today I would put a great underline beneath everything which was said, five years ago, regarding Cairo. Why is it that this great world power of 200,000,000 Mohammedans have seized on Cairo as their brain center and have held it for centuries? Why was it that Germany forced her principal penetration into the Near East and thus brought on this war? Why is it that Great Britain has placed her leading diplomats and administrators in this fringe of the Mediterranean and the Nile Valley? Why is it that the Allies almost risked losing the war in the only place it could be won, on the Western front, and distributed their meager forces in the Near East? Why did the Young Men's Christian Association, not simply of the United States, but of England, Canada, and New Zealand, concentrate in the Nile Valley as at few other places on the world map? Why was it? Because they studied what the French call grand strategy. What is grand strategy? Grand strategy is that which takes in the whole map. The reason why Germany held the lead in this war for four years was that she regulated her plans by the whole map. It was not until well on in that period that the Allies asserted their unity of purpose and made possible one mind looking at one map and coordinating all their forces.

This is pre-eminently the lesson for Protestant Christianity to learn. We deserve to be humbled in the eyes of the world if in days like this we cannot find our unity and assert it in the way that has been suggested tonight. It was grand strategy that led all eyes to focus on the Near East and Cairo, and I fancy it was that which led the large-minded men and women here five years ago to see and seize the unique opportunity presented by the Cairo University project and make the first notable gifts toward launching it.

I sometimes wonder whom I envy the most. Sometimes I think I envy my friend Watson, that he is permitted to enter into the heritage of the fifty years of tears, efforts, sacrifices, and the holy living of his sainted father who gave his life to that Nile Valley, to enter into the sowing and watering of these two generations, to be permitted to be the first president of an institution that through all time will be pointed to as one of the great lighthouses of the world.

And yet, I sometimes wonder whether I wouldn't envy more the man who would perhaps give a quarter of a million dollars, or the family that would give a hundred or two hundred thousand dollars, to build in quickly this vision while the world is plastic, while all things are possible. What mighty power is that of consecrated wealth —whether that wealth be great or small! It stirs me to the depths to reflect on what would be accomplished if twenty or thirty individuals or families as a result of generous devising and real sacrifice were each to devote $10,000 or more to this great undertaking.

Then I think of the limitless power of associated poverty and trust that those in charge of the plan will perfect an arrangement which will enable a great many men and women of limited financial resources but whose hearts and prayers are rich toward God and His program to give out of their poverty to the cause we here have so much at heart.

I remember one time after one of my trips to the warring countries, when I was reporting to the President in the White House. He said to me, "Mr. Mott, give me your dominant impression." And I replied, "If you let me put it in the language of the Scriptures, 'As your faith, so be it unto you.'" And so I say to the American people "As your faith." What is faith? It is the giving of substance to things hoped for, the filling in of things not seen. My friends, it is a sacred privilege to rekindle the fires once lighted by the Christian Apostles. Such is Egypt. What more highly multiplying thing is there that a man can do than to set gushing the living waters over great areas across which there has been coursing for centuries the curse of death —for Mohammedanism is a curse; it darkens, it blights, it degrades, it deadens, it disintegrates—across those vast areas over which have coursed the curse of death, to set gushing a great living fountain that shall turn desert places into blossoming rose buds. And what greater honor could man have, than to help make Cairo a great generating and propagating center for a leadership that will influence three continents, Africa, Asia, and the danger zone of Europe?

OUR MAJOR OPPORTUNITY

It has been my lot to visit the warring countries five times since this struggle begun. In the first place in the autumn and early winter of 1914, when I went to both sides of the war. A year later I visited not only the western front, but made the equivalent of two extended journeys through the middle countries or powers. My third visit took me back among these middle nations, also to the western countries and over on the eastern front of Russia. A year ago I was sent with another group of citizens on a special mission to Russia when I had the opportunity of traveling the whole breadth of Russia, and twice visited not only the new or Siberian Russia, but the old Russia also.

I have returned within the last few days from my fifth journey. This last journey has been confined to the western and southern fronts. I went that whole length, from an unnamed port on the English Channel, along that vast bridge of steel and human blood, across France and Italy, and on to Venetia, in the heart of the Trentino. These successive journeys have given me an opportunity to study the armies that make up this colossal conflict. I have mingled with the soldiers and sailors of all these countries with the exception of Turkey and parts of the Balkan States, but of all these armies and navies, there is none like that of America.

This is not a matter simply of personal pride, although I do have great pride in this army and navy. The provost marshal in one of our ports said to me that among all the 8,000 soldiers who had landed the previous week and passed through that city, which is one of the greatest of temptations, I think, he had only gathered in three bottles, in contrast to the experience of a similar official who had had to deal with another army which came into that port under similar circumstances, and who had assembled at least a wagonload. In all those crowded weeks I spent on this recent journey, I did not see one drunken American soldier or sailor.

I was talking one day with one of our leading generals right at the front, one who has had the most fierce combats of any of our generals. He said to me that one of his Roman Catholic chaplains had remarked the day before that in the previous week he had received 2,000 confessions, but he added, "Only two or three of those told of having stained their garments."

Right after that I was having luncheon with General Pershing, when he volunteered this statement with great eagerness: "I venture to say that there has never been an army with higher average in spirit, character, and efficiency, going forth on a more important errand, and animated by more unselfish spirit and high ideals."

General Edmonds, head of one of our important divisions, said while I was in his office, that he had learned over the telephone of a part of his division having been caught between the barrage of the enemy and that of our own side, and having therefore been fearfully punished. He pointed out on the map where they had received their first baptism of fire. I asked: "How do you account for the fact that these young boys, going into this veritable hell of fire and blood, stand like veterans?" He said: "Mr. Mott, it is due to the tradition of the American mother."

Now gentlemen, your Chairman was right when he said that no more important object could have brought us busy men together from all these important states than the cause you see right now. We have met to consider how to conserve and hold in permanence the tradition of the American mother, because to the Young Men's Christian Association chiefly has been entrusted, on behalf of the American people, this great responsibility. And that leads me to remark that the people in this country are through the Young Men's Christian Association confronting their greatest opportunity over there. I think I know opportunities. John Wanamaker has said that he looked upon me as an expert upon opportunity. It would be something strange if I had spent thirty years cruising over this world, doing nothing but studying, if I did not come to recognize opportunity. With that as a background, let me say that I have never faced an opportunity for the American people like the one which confronts us through this particular constructive ministry of the Young Men's Christian Association for our army and navy overseas.

I emphasize not only the army, but equally the navy, because we have got a wonderful navy. When America entered this war the navy numbered only 70,000 men; now it numbers over 450,000. By the end of this year it will number over 500,000. It is already larger than the British navy was when America entered the war. When we entered the struggle we had less than 200 ships; we shall have 1,900 by Christmas. What do we not already owe to our navy? We talk about the dangers of the front-line trenches. I would remind you today that every American of our navy in those waters of Europe is literally in the front-line trenches; there amid the mine-strewn fields and the lurking submarines, they are taking their lives in their hands every waking hour, and are making possible this phenomenal record of our army overseas, supplying it adequately and preparing it for what may be the final tasks of this great struggle. In all our thinking together let us blend the blue with the khaki; let us have in mind these two great parts of America's contribution to the struggle.

You say: "How is it that our greatest opportunity is 'over there' rather than somewhere else?" I can convince you in one sentence —that is, that the war is to be decided over there, not in America, not in Asia, nor Africa, nor Australia. Therefore, the center of strain for America is there, the prices are to be paid there, the issue will be determined there.

Since my fourth visit I found that the center of gravity, I use that word advisedly, of America's interest has shifted from this side of the Atlantic to the other side of the Atlantic; the heart interest of the American people is now centered overseas.

In this journey that Mr. Perkins and I have been taking all over the United States, having met already representatives of twenty-eight states, and we are to meet with others in a few days, we have been out on lonely roads at times, either singly or together. I have been out on such roads recently in the Northeast, the Middle West, the Rocky Mountain region in the Far West, the Southwest, and now here—how many times was I reminded of this yesterday, as I went around this beautiful city—everywhere we seemed to see in the windows the service flags; here one star, there two stars, there perchance three or more stars. What more appropriate emblem? I have said to myself, and I wish to keep saying to myself, "Every father and mother behind those windows, and the little brothers and sisters, have their heart-strings now, for the boy or boys that have gone overseas, drawn out taut in intensity to that part of the world." Already, when they pick up the morning papers, the heart stands still or beats with reference to what is happening and is to happen there. I maintain, therefore, and not one thoughtful man will contradict me, that the center of heart interest is "over there"—our greatest opportunity, potentially in the sense of what those men represent, a cross-section of the flower of the manhood and boyhood of the American people, intensively in the sense that they are to stand the great strain—how many times did I find when I talked, on this visit with the Allies, the pathetic eagerness, the confidence with which they looked to the coming of our men to make the final decisive action, and I say our greatest opportunity extensively is there.

Sixty thousand men landed in the ten days before I left the other side. They are landing today at the rate of about a regiment a boat. Before we finish our round here we shall have our first million there; we shall have our second million there before the snow breaks up.

The comprehensiveness of this mission of the Young Men's Christian Association to our soldiers and sailors must impress every man in this great assembly. We are over there, as I have implied, not chiefly to represent the Young Men's Christian Association; in fact, that has been long ago forgotten. We have become lost in a great cause along with the whole American nationality. We are over there to reproduce the Young Men's Christian Association—and it is still worth reproducing and we are there to reproduce what is needed of the American school, the American college, the American library. We are there to reproduce all the best features of American club life and of the American stage. We are there to reproduce on a far larger scale than I had fancied we should be obliged to do, the life and activities of American churches, because only recently, as you know, was the new chaplain's bill adopted, which will shortly give us three chaplains per regiment, or one for every 1,200 men. I would remind you that we had very few chaplains compared with the number that are now authorized. Bishop Brent charged me to do everything I could to speed up the getting of the required number of chaplains. In this long intervening and critical period, the Young Men's Christian Association has been obliged to speak for the American churches, and we have not been ashamed of its voice. Among the nearly 3,000 workers we have, I assume that about one-fifth are clergymen, pastors of our various American churches, who have felt it an honor to put on the Association uniform and work with the lay brethren in bringing pure religion to the multitudes of American soldiers and sailors.

We are over there to reproduce all that is best in American life. It is a tremendous responsibility, and one that may well command the devotion and the earnest backing of every influential delegate, who has come here today.

You are all familiar, I fancy, at least with the early stages, of what I would call the continuity of the work of the Young Men's Christian Association in the army and navy. Our Chairman has reminded us of the first stages of that continuity. You all know how the Young Men's Christian Associations are permitted to place a secretary on each troop train which carries the men of the new draft into the cantonments or camps, and there help the men to adjust themselves to the new conditions and purposes. How many of us have not gone out to Camp Gordon, or to similar camps, where we have seen this splendid network of unselfishness, of kindness, of practical helpfulness let down over these tens of thousands of the flower of manhood and boyhood. Any man who has gone and has noticed this practical work of the Young Men's Christian Association, Knights of Columbus, Red Cross, War Camp Community Service, must have gone away with a heart beating with satisfaction that God had provided something better in this war than in any preceding struggle for the maintenance of the morale of our soldiers and sailors.

Then some of you know that on each of the great troop trains that are stealing away almost secretly nowadays, taking our men to the ports of embarkation, the War Department has permitted one or more secretaries on each of these trains to minister to them in countless practical ways that mean so much to these men.

The last thing Mr. Perkins and I did before we left New York was to vote on the largest appropriation we have ever made for a Y.M.C.A. hut for a certain port from which go most of the American soldiers. We said to ourselves "The last touch these men have with their native land, let it be our most adequate touch, let it be one of great friendliness, of complete helpfulness, one that can assure them that the people are behind them to the end."

The War Department, for a few months, has permitted the Young Men's Christian Association to place two secretaries on each transport. Before that was done our men needed tremendously something of this kind. They did not have writing paper, books, magazines, religious services, because the chaplains were so few, and in many cases there were none present. Now you find all these helpful influences and agencies placed at the disposal of every contingent of American soldiers.

The other day I was made a guest of the navy. I went back with a sense of appreciation of the great strain under which these men are working. I saw the practical work, even on the homeward voyage, of the Young Men's Christian Association. There they minister to the gun crew, and a goodly number of invalid American officers and men, and I said, "Just imagine all these influences cut out." The man does not live in America who would stand for it.

I have been allowed by General Pershing and other military authorities, including the French and some in England, to bring out certain maps and charts that I might show them in a personal way to the War Work Council and its friends. There (pointing to the map) is an unnamed port, you will see a number of dots. Every one of these represents an army Y.M.C.A. Away up here where my finger is you will see a cluster of ten of those dots, one of Napoleon's old camps, where there are 12,000 soldiers. I have seen as high as 28,000 there, having their rest. The blue dots represent aviation huts; these dots represent hotels—here is a five story hotel which is always crowded; three or four Y.M.C.A. restaurants where the men can get wholesome food without being fleeced; garages, warehouses, baseball diamonds, football fields—ministering to 100,000 American soldiers there, not including some of the Allied armies.

One of the women canteen workers said, "We have ministered in this one hut in the preceding twelve months to 1,100,000 different soldiers." You and I have heard of or seen cathedrals or clusters of university buildings that have cost from one to three million dollars, but I venture to say that in a much longer period of time, not one of them has been able to minister to so many different people. This hut idea is going to live long after this war. We are learning that we can do a lot of things with much less money than we thought we had to have.

Right in here is a section where tens and hundreds of thousands of these men are halted and massed for further training, not only men,

but officers. The most splendid officers' training ground I have ever
seen in all my journeys, is one for the American officers, where, under
the guidance of French, Italian, English, Belgian, and American
officers, they have the finishing touch put on their training.

We then passed up into the advance section, or as the French
would say, the zone of combat. There men's hearts begin to stand
still. That is the great focus, as this map will show you. This map
was corrected up to the hour that I left Paris. Up to the night I left
Paris there were 606 dots representing Y.M.C.A. huts for soldiers—
huts, dugouts, cafés, canteens, run in the interests of the American
army and navy. We now have over 700 places where this particular
industry is going forward.

When you study that map closely you will notice that about one-
third of those dots, about one-third of those Y.M.C.A.'s are under
shellfire. One of the leading men of this country, if you would call a
man a "leading man" who would say such a thing, spoke of this work
of the Young Men's Christian Association as a shellproof job. Let
me read you a few cablegrams that have come within the last few
weeks:

PARIS, FORSEC, N. Y.   JUNE 25, 1918

AMEX TROOPS ASSURED REGULAR AMERICAN FOURTH BY Y.M.C.A.
PROGRAM WILL TOUCH ENTIRE ARMY INCLUDING THOSE IN FRONT
LINE. ATHLETICS, DRAMATIC, AND MUSICAL ENTERTAINMENTS,
ORATORY. SPECIAL PATRIOTIC PAMPHLET TO BE DISTRIBUTED
TO EVERY SOLDIER. PAMPHLET CONTAINS EXTRACTS FROM PRES-
IDENT WILSON'S SPEECHES, APPROPRIATE POEMS, OTHER INSPIR-
ING MATERIAL HANDSOMELY PRINTED AND ILLUSTRATED. ENTER-
TAINMENT INCLUDES EVERYTHING FROM JAZZ BAND TO GRAND
OPERA WITH ALL STANDARD VAUDEVILLE STUNTS. PATRIOTIC
SPEAKERS WILL BE SENT TO FIFTEEN CAMPS TO DELIVER ORATIONS.
THEY AND DRAMATIC AND CONCERT TROUPES WILL APPEAR TWO OR
THREE TIMES DURING FOURTH. FIELD DAYS HELD EVERYWHERE.
ONE OF THE ONE HUNDRED AND FIFTY "Y" ATHLETIC DIRECTORS
LOCATED BASEBALL WHEREVER FIELD CAN BE HAD. BIG FIELD DAY
AND BALL GAME IN PARIS AREA WILL ATTRACT THOUSANDS OF
SPECTATORS. ESTIMATED TWO HUNDRED THOUSAND AMERICAN
SOLDIERS WILL COMPETE FOURTH SPORTS IN FRANCE UNDER AUS-
PICES OF Y.M.C.A. ATHLETIC MEETS WILL BE HELD WITHIN RANGE
OF GERMAN GUNS IN SEVERAL SECTORS. FRENCH PEOPLE WILL GET
THEIR FIRST REAL IDEA OF HOW AMERICA CELEBRATES INDEPEND-
ENCE DAY.

CHARLES B. KEELAND

LONDON, FORSEC, N. Y.   JUNE 28, 1918

FOURTH OF JULY PROGRAM LONDON: SECRETARIES MEET MEN ARRIV-
ING STATIONS. CONDUCT SIGHT-SEEING TOUR, GUESTS OF ASSOCIA-
TION. ARMY AND NAVY BALL GAME. KING ATTENDING, PITCHING
FIRST BALL. GARDEN PARTY OFFICERS. INN LIVERPOOL OPENS. ASSO-
CIATION PROGRAM IN EVERY AMERICAN STATION.

EWING

Do you wonder that I say that the zone of combat is the focus of interest? One-sixth of our workers over there are women, the finest women we have been able to choose. They beg me to use any influence I might have to let them work in these first-line sectors. This spirit, the making ourselves one with the risks, the suffering, and the dangers of the soldiers, has made us to be regarded as indispensable by officers and men.

We go right up into the front-line trenches. I can just see one of those dugouts, out where I was the other night, between 11 and 2, in a wine cellar. I had to stoop to go down into the cellar; there was no ventilation except the door. I found over 100 American soldiers packed in there. The Y.M.C.A. canteen secretary told me he had been working sixteen hours, that he had made over 100 cups of chocolate, sending them out to the men in the front-line trenches. I came to another wine cellar under a front-line trench, in a village which had received 4,000 German shells that day—largely gas shells. The secretary said one of the shells had fallen into the front end, and another at the other end, the Germans had evidently located it. The officer said, "You must not ever let more than twelve soldiers in at once, thus reducing the risk." I could tell you of scores of Y.M.C.A. men who are in the front lines.

Then we follow the men back to the hospitals, and there we join hands with that association we are ever proud to be associated with, the Red Cross. Anything which God will ever let me do for the Red Cross, having seen what I have of its work, I will gladly do. Mr. Davidson, the president of the American Red Cross, at luncheon with Mr. Perkins and myself the other day, hit off what Mr. Perkins and I called the best demarkation of the work of these two splendid sister societies that we have ever heard. Mr. Davidson said: "My idea of the Red Cross is that its work is for the sick and the wounded and the refugees; and that the Y.M.C.A. work is for the well and even for the men when they are convalescent—going to get well." We said, "That strikes us as a splendid epitome of the facts, showing how they fit together."

Now, the Red Cross, in charge of the hospitals, recognizes that the Y.M.C.A. has specialized for seventy years on what we call the activities—that is, the physical, social, educational, moral, and re-ligious activities—the building up of the young men and boys. And they wisely say to us, "That's not our business, we invite you to bring your workers into our hospital buildings or enclosures and place these facilities not only at the disposal of our hospital staff of workers and orderlies, but at the disposal of the convalescent soldiers"; and you would call us blameworthy if we refused to answer an appeal like that. So that we have gone with the men into the hospitals by this invitation. We follow the men also into the leave resorts. You know, every American soldier over there is entitled to seven days' leave at the end of every four months. It is my understanding that this leave does not accumulate; therefore, the men will not be able to make the journey back to America, the way the British and Canadians go over to England. Most of them will take their leave in France—and I am afraid we are over there for a good long time.

Now, General Pershing joined with the Y.M.C.A. in working out a plan that I think is the best ever devised. He said, "I don't want these men to go to the great centers of population." So we went down and got one of the leading resorts and rented all the buildings there. The Y.M.C.A. in addition to that, rented the second greatest gambling place in the world (laughter and applause), and are getting ready for business (applause). We put in fifty to sixty of the best American men and women that we could pick out of all our staff of nearly 3,000. Gentlemen, I don't suppose Americans or the men of any nation have ever had such leaves as our men get there; and we give them the leading theatrical attractions of the world, the best entertainers— because we have a committee of the leading actors of America that are picking these entertainers—the best lecturers we can find, the best preachers of all denominations in America. The men get crowded into those seven days what they can't and don't get elsewhere. You ought to read the letters I get from those men.

By the way, this continuity goes beyond where I have indicated. It goes to the men even into the prison camps of Germany—because, as you have noticed, we have now got our American prisoners in Germany and their number is destined to increase. I will not forget the prisoners, no danger of that. My three extended visits to the prison camps in the middle countries has seared upon my memory for all of my living days, the sad lot of these 4,000,000 or the 6,000,000 prisoners of war who are today languishing in the prisoner-of-war camps of the middle countries, or driven in those galling, grinding working parties.

My brothers, don't forget what I am now saying, that the more successful we are as allies—and we are going to succeed—(Applause) the more successful we are, the more suffering will be the lot of the prisoners of those allies unless we keep these indirect doors open. I say "indirect," for up to the time America entered the war, we were allowed to have American secretaries all over those middle countries. They accomplished marvels. I think, when the history of the war is written, it will stand as one of the bright pictures. Naturally, when we entered the war we had to withdraw our last men. Our last secretary, who strangely has been permitted to stay in Germany, will leave there this month, July, and thus we shall have no American left, instead of 100 that we had, approximately.

You say, What can we do? We have replaced our Americans by Danes, Swedes, Norwegians, Dutch, and Swiss, and are working through neutral agencies, but America will continue to the end, as she has done from the beginning, to finance that whole proposition. (Great applause.) While the Red Cross will provide the food packets and where necessary, the clothing, for the American prisoners, we shall have to reproduce this entire Association activity program.

Mark my word, what you need more there than elsewhere is useful occupation, because the great danger in the prison camps is insanity. You will hardly believe it when I tell you what I have seen and heard, oh, you'll wonder with me, but if you had only been with me in those camps! By giving useful occupation to those men, we promote sanity, and that's life from the death—we must keep it up.

In a French community the other day—it was a port—the Y.M.C.A. secretary said, "Mr. Mott, you have finished your inspection?" I said, "Yes, every place is checked off." He paused and said, "No, there's one place I haven't taken you that we are concerned in as the Y.M.C.A." He then took me out to the cemetery, there I saw scores of new graves, American graves. He, a layman, told me that he had been obliged, up to within a few days, to bury all the dead, Protestant, Roman Catholic, Hebrew, and agnostic. He said, within a few days he had received the help of one Roman Catholic Priest, a Frenchman, and said he himself had had to write the letters to all the families back at home, telling of the last hours and hopes and wishes, and send on those little mementoes that will be forever prized by the old and the young in those families. Then he told me the most beautiful thing I heard on this last journey, because in the midst of the tragedy there is a great deal that is beautiful; how he had conceived the idea of going to certain French mothers in that city and asking them to become godmothers of those dead American soldiers and sailors. This French mother will say, "I will keep that grave strewn with flowers until this war is over." The keeper of the cemetery said to me that, "the last person in here before you arrived was a French widow who lost her husband within a week or two of the drive in Picardy. She came in with six little children, stood them up before two American soldiers' graves she had promised to be godmother for; and he said she tried to explain to the youngest of those children that these two American boys had come from their homes, over 3,000 miles away, to lay down their lives with the French soldiers' to make secure the liberties of the world. (Great applause.)

Thus you see, gentlemen, what I mean by continuity. We follow the men to the cantonments, we are with them there, to the port where they say good-bye, on the high seas, at the port of debarkation, in the intermediate area, in the zone of battle, in the front-line trenches, joining hands with the Red Cross in the hospitals, in the midst of the joy of their life, in the midst of their loneliness in the prison camps, by the grave, in the last offices, and, thank God, we shall follow them back home, where the other day, Mr. Perkins and I saw a mother lift her child into the arms of its father, who had been allowed to go back home. We shall follow them from home and be with them in town. (Great applause.) That is the mission of the Y.M.C.A. and the man, woman, and child doesn't live in these states who, when they understand it, regardless of their party or religious affiliation, will not say we must have a hand in this great undertaking. (Applause.)

I have spoken of this, Mr. Chairman, as a national board. I would remind you that it is also the greatest cosmopolitan board in the world. Some of you may prick up your ears when I say that because you have heard me at your gatherings in the South before speak of world boards, and I mean precisely what I say—I am ashamed of myself that I didn't say this earlier. And as my last tour drew to a close, I said to our chief secretary, "Oh, that we might gain twenty-four hours, that I might conduct an Allied conference in Paris"; and by pushing up the night, as we have a habit of doing, we gained twenty-four hours, called an Allied conference in one of the hotels in Paris. Notice who were present: leaders of the Y.M.C.A. work in the English army—I don't like to use that word "English," I mean English, Scottish, Welsh, and Irish (Applause); of the Canadian army—by the way, they are a mighty close second to us; of the Australian and New Zealand army; the South African army; the American, the French, the Italian—because I found three divisions of Italians blending their blood with the rest of us; the Portuguese army; the Indian cavalry; the Russian—by the way, the division that has suffered most in this recent offensive, relatively, has been that Russian division—that has fought a good fight. (Applause.) We are not through with Russia yet. (Great applause.) There is no more masterly or ominous piece of German propaganda than that which is seeking to spread distrust, discord, impatience, neglect, among the Allies with reference to that former, and I maintain present, ally that already has laid down 3,500,000 lives, has had 2,000,000 of its sons and daughters mutilated so that they will never fight again; that, notwithstanding the so-called treaty of Brest-Litovsk, still has in the enemy's hands 2,000,000 and more Russian prisoners. I maintain that we shall not let the German propaganda, preying on 2 per cent of Russia's 180,000,000 population, keep from our side that land which, more than any other, I believe with Colonel Roosevelt, holds the fate of the coming years. (Applause.) We stand, therefore, with our President, with his fine gift of intuition, who with correct intuition has gripped the heart of the Russian people, and he well knows that that does not belong to Germany. Now, besides those nations that day in that room in Paris, I had present with me leaders in the work among the Chinese laborers and the Chinese, who had come all the way from China, who came to work under constant shellfire; there we had the labor battalions of America, of Madagascar, of New Caledonia, of the West Indies, of Indo-China—gentlemen, I venture to say that never since Christ came among men have there been gathered within four walls leaders of so many great bodies of men, who had come together in one battlefield to unite under one great object, to make secure for time and eternity the liberties of the human race. (Great applause.) Therefore, the Y.M.C.A. has not only seen opportunity, but seized opportunity. American is financing exclusively that marvelous work in the French army. (Applause.)

When I was over there in the late autumn of 1914, I left $2,500 by faith with one man. I said, "Get permission from the French government to serve the French army." It took four months to get the door open, but finally one general said, "You can try it out there in our army"; then the neighboring general had it reproduced. By that time the War Ministry began to take notice and said we could do this at 500 places. When I came back from Russia, the word awaited me that the French government wanted us to spread this work not to fifty but to 1,300 places. And the other day, some of you heard the words of the War Ministry, saying that the War Ministry of France, on military grounds, wished the American Y.M.C.A. to spread this work on to 2,000 places, covering the whole French army of 5,000,000. (Applause.)

The same thing is true of the Italian army of 3,000,000. The other day, the King of Italy, when I was down there on the southern front, sent for me and received me in audience in his little villa, right up there under shellfire, in a little room, I should say, twelve feet square, with one simple iron bed and a little dresser and two hard chairs, and a few war maps on the wall. He had been cross-examining me, and saw the Red Triangle on my arm, and said, "What does that mean?" Well, gentlemen, I then had my opportunity literally to "preach Christ in Caesar's house." (Great applause.) When I had finished and explained what we are after—now notice this—he said, "Mr. Mott, I wish you would tell the American people to spread this work to the maximum in the entire Italian army." (Applause.)

A Roman Catholic friend said the other day, "Can I consistently give anything to the Y.M.C.A.?" I said, "If you can give to a movement as popular as the Y.M.C.A., and if you can give to the army of 3,000,000 of whom less than 5,000 are Protestant, surely you can give to the Y.M.C.A. because you must stand by your fellow religionists." And I might have said the same thing to him about the French army and the prisoners of war. There is no doubt that the Roman Catholics will stand with the Protestant and the Hebrew and every loyal citizen in making possible this program. (Applause.)

Now, we have got to have a great deal. We must have by the end of September over 4,000 of the best men and women that America can produce, to send overseas. And I call upon you, gentlemen, before God—I say it reverently, because I realize the weight of this thing, it's on me heavy—I call upon you, before God and in the name of our boys, every man of you to be a pair of ears and a pair of eyes and a voice in helping us to discover, not the second best, but the best men and women of your section, to go into this most important work. I say no man here, as I have said it in other parts of our nation, no man is too important or too busy to drop anything he is doing unless it is an indispensable part of the winning of this war, to enter this service, which is the most vital factor in the accomplishment of our great purpose. (Applause.) We are not doing the fair thing.

I found this letter last night, if I haven't misplaced it, from our chief secretary, Mr. Carter, in which he touched my conscience. I hope it will touch some of you: "We are in gloom over the gassing of Cooper and Smith. There seems to be pretty good evidence that Cooper would not have been gassed if understaffing of the Y.M.C.A. hadn't resulted in his overwork. For days he had been going twenty-four hours a day because no help had been sent him. In his exhausted condition, he became careless about his gas mask and probably, when the alert came, did not have sufficient reaction to get his mask on." This touches me, because one of my sons is in that division, and all the Y.M.C.A. secretaries are under terrific strain because of the result of understaffing. I visited one division of our army, 27,000 men, with only one Y.M.C.A. secretary. Two other divisions from America landed while I was there and were locked in with the British, and we had to fall back on the British women, who never fail us, because we didn't have American men and women enough to serve our own men. So don't let this slip off your mind and memory today; let it work on the conscience until some of the best men here today may offer themselves for service over the seas. Don't take men that are indispensable. We want the indispensable men.

Now, we must have not only men, but money, we need at the least $112,000,000, at least that. Mr. Perkins will enlarge on that story, but I just want to mention, as an eye-witness, some of the reasons why we have to have so much money overseas.

In our last budget, in which you stood with us, we spent about two-thirds of the sum on this side of the Atlantic. In this next budget we must spend about four-fifths on the other side of the Atlantic. You say, Why do we need so much money, such a large sum as $112,000,-000? Well, because overseas we are asked to do what is divided up at home between thirty and forty other organizations, between thirty and forty denominational, interdenominational, and secular societies, inside and outside of the camps, in America; that is, under their exclusive authority—I mean in addition to what the Knights of Columbus, the Hebrew Welfare Board, and the American Library Association are doing—and the Y.M.C.A. has cabled that the Jewish Welfare Board will carry on its work as a part of the Y.M.C.A. in their huts. I am not at liberty to go into military matters here, or I could show you quite quickly why Pershing limits the number of societies, not through prejudice, not through lack of desire, but through military necessity, and he has wisely picked the Y.M.C.A., for, as one of our Presidents said at the time the Panama Canal was built, when he was complained to by a congressman for appropriating government money, "If you will show me another organization that will make these men more efficient, I will immediately transfer the appropriation from the Y.M.C.A. to that organization." (Applause.)

We must have much more money, in the second place, because each division of the American army is broken up there into many little detachments. In this country you would find the division at a cantonment where there are forty-five or fifty thousand men. Where did I find that division? In an area twenty miles long and thirty broad. In ten villages I found 500 to 1,000 American soldiers. In more than twenty other villages, I found fifty, 100, 200 American soldiers. I said, "Where are they living?" They took me up into a hayloft—bitterly cold winds swept through—eighty men had to sleep there. They took me down below, where I found my son sleeping, and on the ground with a little hay strewn about, there seventy were to sleep. I found others in dark, damp, gloomy places. Occasionally a French villager had been able to save a little more space than others, and had a place where they had been able to shield them from the driving snow. Now, any father or mother here, if he had been with me in one of those villages where there were 200 men, would have said, "Don't cut out that village." He would say, "We must have a Y.M.C.A. in each of these," because there is no library in any one of these villages, no club there, no open church, no saloon—in the sense we understand it in this country, a place where men could sit down and visit, buy a bottle, and go away. Not until the Y.M.C.A. came in was there a place where a man could sit down and get dry. How many soldiers visited me and have said to me after they had been drilling on the sodden ground, in the rain, that the only place they could sit down and get dry was the Y.M.C.A.—because coal is sixty to seventy dollars a ton there. The only place they could sit down or write a letter or read a paper was in this hut. What man will say, "We must cut the Y.M.C.A. out of this place?"

We must have a lot of money, further, because the soldiers over there are constantly moving. That represents the men of one division of our army (indicating on map); first here, then moved 160, then 100, then a few miles, then up to the front-line trenches, where I found out those 27,000 men moved from the first position five different times in six months. The Y.M.C.A. traveling secretary said to me, "Mott, I have had to open up over thirty Y.M.C.A.'s five times, that is 150 Y.M.C.A.'s I have had to establish in six months." What man of this city will say, "Establish the Y.M.C.A. at the first position, set a good example, a good memory, and then say good-bye to the men?" The men will not say it, but it costs a lot of money. (Applause.)

Another reason we must have money: The French railways were nearly broken down until America has restored them and put in some of our own lines. We would have failed to do what Pershing and the American fathers and mothers wanted us to do if we had not developed our own transport system of automobile and motor truck. It is frightfully, almost unbelievably, expensive.

Another reason we must have much money is that everything costs so much more over there than here, and the prices will continue to mount, we cannot escape it—it's war, and we have got to do this work where men need it most.

I would mention another reason why we have got to do it, and that is because we have got to be ready to meet crises—that's what war is, it is made up of crises.

Let me show you this map. I saw this on the wall in Paris a night or two before I left there, and I said, "I wish I had a map like that," and to my surprise, they brought it down to my train. Every one of these red spots represents what the French call a Foyer du Soldat. You see, on this map they are all numbered in the order in which they were established. As I said a few minutes ago, they have all been given by America. The other day—I was so busy during the second day of the offensive I didn't look at the map—I took it down to my office. Here's ————— and here's —————and here's ————— here's —————. Then came that cablegram that I read to you, that ninety-three of those huts had been destroyed or captured by the enemy. Since then we have had cables saying the number is 102. That is a crisis, but thank God, we have an organization that can instantly provide the means to substitute those huts. (Great applause.)

I landed in England ten days after this year's western offensive began. I found England serious before, but not suffering until this time. They were not talking, they were quietly suffering. They seemed to be stretched on the cross. While I was there, I learned they had lost eighty-nine of their huts in Flanders in the first eleven days of the offensive. I learned indirectly that those were valued at $500,000. I didn't have time to cable to America and get a reply, but I learned it by intuition—I said I knew the American people. Then I called together a group of the leading British citizens, and I said America will wish to replace all of these huts. (Great applause.) When I reported it to the War Work Council, they said, "We want to criticize you, Mott, for one thing, that is that you didn't offer them $1,000,000, instead of $500,000. (Applause.)

We cast our bread on the waters that day. You notice, we didn't think of anything but the British. Within two weeks before I left France, we had had two American divisions brought in from England and brigaded with the British at the very places where we were replacing these huts. We cast our bread on the water and it came back to us, not after many days, but in fourteen days. And you have heard of that disaster in Italy. That concerned only one of the six armies at the front—and by the way, it wasn't the Allies that stopped that disaster, it was the army under the Grand Duke of Aosta, who pinned them there; but the Italians lost 106 of their huts. Our Council sent a cablegram within two days that we would gladly replace their huts, which we have done. (Applause.) We won their hearts, and the King said, "Come in and show us how to do this work." Again I say, Isn't it a great thing that you and I are not alone, that we have an agency in which our own citizens, studying the great strategy of this work, provide the principal factor, the morale making it vital? As I sit down, let me leave this thought with you—the sense of the urgency of this business.

I was talking with a friend of mine, a great athlete. I said, "How do you size up the military situation?" He said, "Mott, the ball is on the five yard line, and is in the enemy's hands." I said, "I don't agree with you, I put it much further back than five yards, but I said I am obliged to admit that at the present time, the initiative, that is, the ball, is with the enemy."

Before I left America to go to France this last time, a leading business man of this nation placed this wording over his desk at his office: "Germany is winning the war." I would change his wording entirely and have it read like this: "Germany is winning the war, but Germany is not going to win the war." (Great applause.) There is all the difference in the world, there is the difference between victory and defeat, the difference between liberty and slavery, the difference in making this world livable for our children and our children's children, or something for which we shall hang our heads in shame. But we have got to pay colossal prices. It must be a military victory, and it must be a political victory. While we shall have to pay prices that may well cause our hearts to pause in this moment, God grant, my friends, that when the end comes and these boys of ours come back on the troop trains and the troopships, and you go down to the train to meet them—to meet your boy, or maybe go all the way up to New York or to Newport News to meet him, and as they come down those gangplanks, as they leap out of those car windows as well as doors, then as some of them are brought out on stretchers, then as some are led out, who will not be able to see with their eyes that did once see us, we will see them, God grant that none of us then may be afraid or ashamed because we left anything undone that we might have done in that year 1918, the climax year of the war. (Great applause.)

CONSTRUCTIVE PLANS FOR MEETING THE CRITICAL RUSSIAN SITUATION

REPORT PREPARED FOR PRESIDENT WILSON

Germany has been and is waging an able propaganda in Russia to weaken and destroy the fighting spirit of the people. We found evidences that this effort is generously financed, that it is conducted on a large scale, and that it has been most effective. It can be counteracted and overcome only by means of an adequate campaign of education.

There is in operation in Russia today no really adequate plan designed to counteract the efforts put forth by Germany to poison opinion and to paralyze action. There are commendable efforts both on the part of individual Russians and of certain of the Allies, but none of these activities singly or all of them combined are capable of meeting the need.

There has been no time when co-operation in this sphere would count so much in Russia as the present. Owing to the prompt initiative of President Wilson in recognizing the Provisional Government and owing to the visit and the work accomplished by the Special Diplomatic Mission, America just now has most favorable access to Russia.

Russia is ready to listen to America, and is eager to learn from her. Moreover, the present is incomparably the most critical period from a military point of view. The liberties of Russia—all that the Russian Revolution has made possible—are endangered by Germany.

From the point of view of winning the war, it is vitally important that Russia be kept in the war, and, to this end, that her people shall be led to realize vividly what is at stake, and that they shall be inspired with hope in the successful outcome of the struggle. If, through our failure to keep alive the interest of the Russian people and to maintain among them a realizing sense of the significance of the sacrifices already made, Russia should lose heart and virtually be eliminated from the war, the consequences will be most serious.

Russia is possibly the most isolated nation among all the Allies. This is due to her geographical position and the very poor means of communication with the outside world. It takes a longer time to receive letters and periodicals in Russia from the other Allies than is the case with any other Allied country. Moreover, the Russian press has the most meager and unsatisfactory foreign cable service. Germany has so clouded the waters of the press in the Scandinavian countries that little light of the kind most needed comes from Russia's nearest and most accessible neighbors.

It is estimated that Germany has spent in her propaganda of intrigue in Russia since the Revolution 48,000,000 rubles, or $3,000,-000 a month. It is estimated that it costs the Allies $10,000,000 to keep one regiment one year at the front. The proposed campaign of education is directed to helping to develop a spirit which will hold on the eastern front 640 regiments of over 3,000 men each. The combined daily expenditures of the Allies have mounted to over $75,000,000. This vast outlay is devoted almost exclusively to providing for the material factors essential to the proper prosecution of the war. Is it not desirable to devote the relatively small sum suggested to insure the larger conservation and exercise of the moral factor in that area of the war where the situation is so critical?

If Russia can be helped to hold her armies in being and to keep her men in the trenches, it will make it necessary that the enemy countries maintain on the eastern front over 140 divisions of troops. This has a most direct bearing on the extent of the exertions and sacrifices of America in the war.

The Russian civil and military authorities have given assurance that they would welcome and give every facility to any efforts which America might put forth in the direction of wise educational effort.

There should be large use of effective pamphlets and leaflets. There is no land in the world where the thirst for literature dealing with current questions is greater today than it is in Russia. This is, of course, due to the Revolution. Among those who can read there is only one activity which is more in evidence, and that is talking. Large use should be made of pictures or illustrations in connection with the new printed matter. Arrangements should be made with the news kiosques throughout the country to slip these leaflets into all papers sold.

A well-managed film service would also accomplish in Russia more than in any other land. The experience of the British has pointed the way to a wide use of this means.

The most popular method for influencing Russian opinion is that of speech. Therefore, large use should be made of well-qualified speakers or teachers. Why should there not be a carefully selected body of hundreds of able Russians going as teachers about the towns and villages as well as among the millions of men under arms? These speakers or teachers could be brought together in large groups or companies for the purpose of preparation for their work and of unifying its impact.

Russia has called to the colors since the war began not less than 13,200,000 men. This constitutes the largest army assembled by any one nation in the history of the world. Of this vast number it is estimated that fully 2,000,000 have already been killed or have died as the result of wounds or diseases occasioned by the war. Another 2,000,000 are today prisoners of war in Germany, Austria-Hungary, Bulgaria, and Turkey. Another 2,000,000 may be classified as permanently ineffective, chiefly those who have been seriously mutilated in warfare or shattered by disease. This leaves 7,200,000 men as comprising the total strength of the Russian army of today. Some authorities whom we consulted give a somewhat lower figure, but more would place it even higher. Of this army of today probably 2,100,000 are to be found in the seventy corps on the European front and the five on the Asiatic front; 1,000,000 in the depots or reserves; 1,000,000 in connection with garrisons and communications—thus leaving a little over 3,000,000 in training, on leave or otherwise not immediately available for military operations, but potentially a most important asset. On this vast host of Russian men and boys rests the tremendous responsibility of maintaining and pressing the war on the long drawn out eastern front. The effectiveness and faithfulness with which they perform this critical duty will determine, far more largely than we in America have realized, the extent of the exertions and sacrifices, and the laying down of life and substance, of the American people in connection with the great struggle. Whatever can be done, therefore, to insure and develop the highest working efficiency and truly triumphant spirit of the Russian soldiers has a most direct, practical, and vital bearing on the destiny of America and the other Allies.

That there is imperative need of instituting measures for rendering practical service to the millions of Russian men and boys under arms or in uniform there can be no question in the mind of any one who has firsthand knowledge of conditions. This need existed before the Russian Revolution. A similar need had been recognized in all the other Allied armies, and with greater or less thoroughness was being met; but, notwithstanding the most helpful activities of such agencies as the zemstvo unions, there has been lacking in the Russian army from the beginning an agency to specialize on the physical, mental, social, and moral betterment of the men as has been done in so many of the other countries by the Young Men's Christian Association. The Russian Revolution has greatly accentuated the need. From the nature of the case the minds of multitudes of Russian soldiers have been more or less absorbed with the political and social issues thrust upon them by the Revolution. Moreover, the subtle, able forces of German intrigue have taken advantage of these unsettled conditions and have waged a really masterly propaganda among the large numbers of the troops in the garrisons, in the training camps, and, to a larger degree than might be thought possible, at the front. As one studies these troops wherever they are congregated throughout Russia or Siberia, at the front or at the base, one is impressed by the vast numbers who either are not occupied at all with activities related to the war or are devoting themselves to aimless and unprofitable political discussion. The practical problem, stated in a sentence, is: Shall these millions of young men and boys in garrisons, in reserve camps, and at the fighting front spend the five or more leisure hours which they have each day in idleness or in unprofitable or weakening agitation, or shall they devote these spare hours to healthful physical and social recreation, growth in knowledge and working efficiency, and unselfish service to their fellow men? This war has shown the supreme importance of morale. Napoleon went so far as to maintain that morale counts for an army as three to one. How important it is that everything possible be done during these coming months to improve the morale, to strengthen the discipline, and to raise the spirit of our comrades in Russia.

The marvelous success achieved by the Young Men's Christian Association in the British, Canadian, and Australasian armies not only on the western front, but also in Egypt, Mesopotamia, Salonika, and on the Gallipoli Peninsula, in the wonderful French army, as well as in the newly forming American army, has demonstrated the adaptability of this organization for meeting the situation in Russia. Some of the American Association secretaries, who have long been at work there in the prisoner-of-war camps, have become so impressed by the need and by the urgency of the situation that they, without knowledge of each other's action, have already inaugurated work among the Russian soldiers at a number of points as widely separated as Petrograd on the west, Tomsk and Irkutsk in Siberia, and Tashkend in Turkestan. These efforts have met with the instant and enthusiastic approval of both soldiers and officers. To promote recreation and the physical conditioning of the men, football, volleyball, track athletics, relay races, and aquatics have been introduced. The educational work included language schools, courses for other useful studies, libraries, reading rooms, lectures, and moving picture shows. Wise use was being made of high-grade theatrical plays. The musical features of the work were also most welcome. The moral life of the soldiers received sympathetic and careful attention. Wherever possible, the men were being enlisted in unselfish service among their fellows. Why is not this work reproducible throughout the entire Russian army?

In order to ascertain whether the Russians would welcome American co-operation through such an agency as the Association, I had interviews with a number of persons. I discussed the matter at length with Prince Lvov, the former Premier, and found him most intelligently sympathetic. Mr. Terestchenko, Minister of Foreign Affairs, responded heartily to the suggestion. I had but a short conference with the Minister of War and Marine, Mr. Kerensky (the present Premier), and arranged to go into the subject more fully with him at his leisure, but he had not yet returned from the front when I was obliged to start back to America. Other members of the War Ministry, however, have indicated to us their hearty approval. The Chief of the General Staff assured me that he and his colleagues would welcome the help of this American Association. Many of the Soldiers' Deputies, as well as other soldiers, were interviewed and brought together in groups for consultation.

Careful investigation has made it clear that the soldiers of Russia present to America possibly the largest single opportunity to help which has come to us during the war. Here is a field that stretches one-third of the way around the world. It involves literally millions of men and boys—nearly as many as today are serving in the combined armies of Britain, Canada, America, and France. It is wide open to our friendly approach. It is a most responsive field. At many points the Russian army reminded one quite as much of older boys as of mature men, and these hosts of boys, and the men too for that matter, can be led anywhere by workers of warm hearts, wise heads, and unselfish spirit. They are most responsive to kindness. Very many of them are eager for self-development and are truly idealistic. To deal in any worthy or adequate way with this boundless opportunity means that we must send over to Russia as soon as possible at least 200 of the best-qualified workers we can find. The difficulties which await these workers are so subtle and serious that we should send only men of established character, of rich experience, and of undiscourageable enthusiasm. It may be found wise and practicable to establish a language school where all these workers can spend at least a short period on arriving in Russia, although a man should begin his study of the Russian language the day he decides to enter this field. For every American secretary there should be two or more Russian workers.

It would be difficult to overstate the urgency of this extraordinary situation. The late autumn and the winter months will constitute the most critical testing period. If these men can be afforded pleasant and profitable occupation during this trying time it will insure conservation of probably the greatest single asset of the Allied cause; whereas, if through the influence of counterrevolutionary forces, of German intrigue, and of disintegrating habits of dissipation and idleness, the great Russian army should be permitted to dissolve or be riven with seams of weakness, the most disastrous consequences will follow. Just now America, as no other nation, holds the key to the situation. Her prompt recognition of the Revolutionary government and her genuine and expressed desire to do anything in her power to help Russia, make the Russian people peculiarly hospitable to American ideas and workers. It is well for us to keep reminding ourselves that the Russians have long been fighting our battles for us, and this at a terrific cost. Anything which we find it possible to do in the way of giving money to extend a great, practical, unselfish ministry of this kind, we should promptly do.

THE CHALLENGE TO THE YOUNG MEN'S CHRISTIAN ASSOCIATION AS THE FIRST WORLD WAR DRAWS TO A CLIMAX

ADDRESS AT A MEETING OF THE COMMITTEE ON WORK IN WAR INDUSTRIES, 25 MADISON AVENUE, NEW YORK, MARCH 5, 1918

I fancy that we shall spend few days during this period of greatest strain through which our nation will have passed—which time will prove to be of larger meaning to the successful waging of this great war and to a final triumph, than the hours that we spend here today and tomorrow.

The colossal dimensions of this trouble continue to impress themselves upon us. When I returned from my first journey through the warring countries, late in 1914, I estimated that there were not less than 17,000,000 men under arms. When I returned from my second and more extensive journey, over a year later, which took me to both sides of the struggle, I was obliged to report that the number of men under the colors of their respective nationalities was somewhere between twenty-six and twenty-seven millions.

Coming back from a third journey the following year, which was still more extensive and which took me much further along the fighting lines and among the reserves and the training camps of the nations on both sides of the war, I answered the questions as to how many men there were under arms by saying that in my judgment the number was well past 30,000,000.

Coming back from Russia last year I was pressed with the same questions, and while I had not had an opportunity to visit the western front on that journey, I had kept tolerably well in touch with the military statistics, and had come to the conclusion, before the dissolving of the Russian army, that we were called upon to reckon more nearly 37,000,000 men and boys under arms in all the belligerent countries that have been obliged to mobilize. The figure could not be less than 37,000,000.

Since then has come this dissolving and crumbling of the Russian army; although I would remind you that these men are still in uniform and have not yet returned to constructive work in their nation, and still have to be reckoned with in ways quite as baffling, and presenting quite as important an aspect from certain angles as before. When you remember that in no previous war have more than 2,000,000 men been lined up against each other at one time, and that now, even excluding Russia, we have probably fourteen to fifteen times as many men under the colors of their nations, in arms, under arms and arrayed against each other, the colossal dimensions of this struggle are apparent and are overpowering in their influence.

Now, the Young Men's Christian Association, early and late, recognized a call coming from those millions of men under arms, heeded that call, and has rendered a service of increasing value in its constructive character and in its moral and spiritual fruitfulness.

I would remind you, however, this morning, that there is another army, far more extensive than this one, which has made this war absolutely unique among the great wars of the world; and that is this vast number of men and boys, and last—I should not say last— women in industries, because I found in Germany the last time, that they have not less than 13,000,000 women and girls employed in what we would call industries and agricultural pursuits with special reference to prosecuting the war. It is not for me this morning to mass these statistics of the various nations now at war more than to say that the number in industry mounts far higher than the number of those under arms in these different nationalities.

This war is unique in that whole nations are now mobilized for war; not simply armies and navies, but whole nations; and in proportion to the extent and thoroughness of this industrial and agricultural mobilization will be the efficiency and the achieving power of the military and naval mobilization. This has not been recognized as fully by some of the Allied nations as by some of the Central Powers, notably Germany. I said, during times of peace, after my various visits to Germany, that that country impressed me as the most highly organized nation which I ever visited. Japan is a close second, and Belgium, before the war, stood very close to Germany in point of thoroughness of industrial organization.

This war now draws near to its great climax. The most solemn reflection that came to me the last time I was in Germany, during one of the four or five visits that I have made to that country since the war began, was that they had reduced the war to the normal; that is, war had become a natural function in every phase of the complex life of Germany.

I said, God forbid that it shall ever become that way in our other nations. I hope we may never have to say that war has become a normal and continuous function; that we have got the matter so organized and so natural to our national life that we can keep it up year after year. And yet I am obliged to say this morning that the Allies, and our country in particular, must more highly and thoroughly and comprehensively organize the industrial side of our life, and relate it to this great struggle. Happily we are able to do this. Fortunately the leaders of the nation, both those of the present government, and men who are not related to the present government, see with clear and steady eye what we have to do. Our forces are being mobilized as never before in the life of this nation, and related to this serious task of waging this war to as successful and speedy an issue as possible.

An imperative demand comes at a time like this to the Young Men's Christian Association to gear all its machinery, to augment its directive energy, and to relate itself to this larger army—far larger than our military and naval forces will ever be, even if we carry this draft to the very limits, as we may be called upon to do before this war reaches its conclusion—I say the Young Men's Christian Association is summoned to relate itself to these rising millions in industry and to make these unique contributions, which we are in a position to make.

We are called to do this by our government. This is an impressive letter which has been read by our chairman. I have similar statements by other members of the cabinet, and we are all familiar with the different utterances of our President, not only the speeches he has made, but some of his strongest written declarations. There is no ambiguity about the appeal that has come from our government to the Association to help speed up the war through the military and industrial forces of the nation.

Secondly, this demand comes from our Allies. I fancy there is no more appealing word which has come to the nations that have made common cause with us, than the word of appeal that has come within the past eight or ten months from them to busy ourselves, especially with these industrial processes; and of those many messages that have been borne to us by cable or letter or voice, none to my mind was more deeply moving than the one brought to us by his Grace, the Archbishop of York, last Sunday.

His apt text was, "They summoned their partners in the other boat to come over and help them." He appealed to the American nation. He did not expect we would get the military establishment over there large enough to turn the scale in this great critical period of the war, but by speeding up our shipbuilding industries and our munition production and our food conservation activities, we might be able to render the greatest possible services to the Allies in this period of principal strain.

So I say, the demand comes from each one of our principal Allies that we throw ourselves with our great unspent energies, with our boundless latent resources, into these industrial processes, these constructive processes, these buttressing processes, which will help steady and sustain the great military operations of our Allies until our own military and naval forces may be sufficiently augmented for us to render enough service to turn the tide of war!

The demand also comes from the men in the army and navy. When you get right down to the bottom of this war—say what we may about other wars—of what value is sacrifice over there in the trenches and in the mine-strewn fields unless we have shipping sufficient to send over food and munitions for every man?

And of what value are sacrifices over there, unless we have so augmented our production in industries and in agriculture that when we have shipping, we have also supplies to send in a steady and increasing stream?

The demand, I say, comes from our brothers under arms, in their lonely vigil along those coasts and as they are now being pushed up towards the trenches, as well as their comrades in the Allied lines, who have so long stood the strain and paid such an incredible price to hold back the enemy until the time that we could get ready.

In the fourth place, the demand comes from the industrial workers themselves. They are patriots, if this country has patriots anywhere. I find myself very much out of patience with insinuations to the contrary. I have found both employer and employee ringing true and marked by a spirit of patriotism and devotion to serve the enlisted men.

Considering their salaries, it was nothing less than magnificent the way the workingmen responded when we raised our $50,000,000. I do not know whether to speak more strongly of the laboring men giving out of their earnings, or corporations that this year had the courage, and what I call the patriotism, to cut through red tape, and to make us, as never before, large contributions from corporation funds towards those great war objects.

So I say, I bitterly resent statements that I sometimes read and hear to the effect that the industrial plants of this nation are not so much committed in point of patriotism, devotion, and sympathies as any other groups of people of the country.

The demand comes from these industries that the Young Men's Christian Association do for them what it is doing for the enlisted men in the army and navy. They say, and they properly say, that "if the enlisted men, who up to this time have had far more done for them in the way of insuring their physical comfort and their highest working efficiency, still need agencies like the Young Men's Christian Association"—and they concede it as shown by their gifts—"surely *we* stand in need of this constructive and co-operative agency!"

Then if I might mention still another quarter from which the demand comes, I would say it comes from the religion which you and I have professed, the religion which is primarily and distinctively a religion of unselfishness, which is primarily a religion of service. It is a religion which says, "To whomsoever much has been given, of him shall much be required." You and I cannot profess this religion without hypocrisy and not place its agencies, such as the Young Men's Christian Association, at the disposal of any body of men who have subjected themselves to great strain and responsibilities. The guiding principles of our faith accentuate the willingness of the services that the Association can render.

The Association in this war is in a class by itself in certain respects.

In the first place, it is the only agency which ministers to every side of the man, and in times of greatest strain such ministry is indispensable. You cannot, with wisdom, omit touching any side of a man in times likes these. In these days men need every function and power at its best. The Young Men's Christian Association, in seeking to minister to a man's physical efficiency and to his intellectual outlook and interests, and working up to his higher responsiveness, to his spirit of co-operation, to his moral ideals, and to his spiritual impulses and nature, is doing on both sides of the ocean what no other organization with which I am familiar is doing.

In the second place, the Association is unique among all these agencies, in that it is under the impulses of the great religion of brotherhood. As you study the other religions of the world, and as you study non-Christian agencies, how distinctly, how vividly, how appealingly stand out the Association and other agencies that bear the name of Christ.

This, I say, is the great agency for promoting brotherhood and understanding, or I might use an entirely different phrase and say it is the great agency for promoting unity; and in time of war, if ever, we need unity!

We need unity between employers and employees. The Association, not by discussing it, but by relating itself in many patriotic tasks, furnishes the atmosphere and the disposition which make possible understanding, and therefore true unity. Not only so, it is promoting unity between the arms of the service.

In Germany there is the closest co-operation between army and navy, and industry. We have got to see it in our own country. The Association, so far as I know, is the only comprehensive agency that is serving both the enlisted men of the army and the navy, on the one hand and then, on the other hand, reaching out to serve the various classes of industry.

It will do more than any other agency, therefore, in the process of its unity campaign, to co-ordinate, to weld together in good unity those classes which are to make a united nation, not only employers and employed, but also what I will persist in calling the various arms of the service.

The Young Men's Christian Association is unifying the various forces of the different Allied nations. I do not recall any organization which is touching the armies and the industries of our own country, and all of the railways that have made common cause with us, as has this Association.

You are familiar with the widespread extent of the organization, not only in the British army but also in the British industries. I think most of you in this room are familiar with the fact that we have been called upon to extend the Association work to the larger Italian army. We have had there nearly fifty secretaries who have gone in within the last few weeks.

You are familiar with the fact that we have had possibly the greatest opportunity opened to us in this war in connection with the French army. The government over there has sent us a cablegram within the last ten days, in the name of the premier and the commander-in-chief of the French army, asking us to open up work at ten new points each day in the French army for an indefinite period—that is, for months; and they are asking us to send twenty-five American secretaries each week for a long period.

I do not recall in the history of the Association, or in the history of any Christian organization, that such a generous task has ever come to any other nation to spring to its co-operation.

Then I could go through the other Allied nations, and personally I still put Russia in this list. She has been shattered and has been obliged to withdraw from the fighting lines for reasons that I think are fully understood in this room. How can a nation remain in the fighting lines when its army has no ammunition and no railroads to bring up food? Certainly they have today more difficulties than they have ever had. Their armies are pushed back to the middle of their territory.

We have 119 secretaries over there, scattered all over Russia, from whom we are hearing as rapidly as may be; we have our government means of communication; and I have not discovered anything from my visits to Russia, from the responses of our secretaries, or from the communications to our government, that leads me to believe that the great mass of the people is pro-German. We make the mistake of the ages if we hand over 180,000,000 people to the Germans, without protest, and without an effort to prevent it, after the great price they have paid during the war. I have telegraphed our men to busy themselves with these things, with these millions of men in the great cities, to try to get them occupied, to open up day and night industrial schools, and to do everything that they possibly can to show that America has not forgotten this great, suffering Russia. We will not be so ungrateful as to forget that they have already sacrificed over 3,000,000 men for the ideals that have made us enter the war; and we recall with sympathy the men on the streets, their struggles, their sacrifices, and their wounds. Because some men have got possession of the country and handed it over to anarchy and misrule, we will not abandon this great nation to the enemy.

What I am saying is predicated upon the theory that the Allied

nations are going to win. If you have any thought that the Allies are
not going to win, forget what I have said. But let us remember that
if the Allies do not win, that means that the pendulum swings back
for generations in the progress of civilization.

Shall we in these days be so shortsighted as to make impossible
our dealing with Russia? Shall we hand her over to the enemy?
Certainly not!

So I could go to the other nations that have at one time or another been related to us, and show you how the Young Men's Christian Association is on the spot, is seeking to deal with industrial as
well as with naval and military forces; and that it is the only organization, I repeat, that is asserting this great unifying influence between
all the nations now associated with us.

Now, for reasons like this, I view with great satisfaction this
conference called by the Industrial Committee; and I believe the
work that will eventuate from the discussions of this conference, and
the work of the committees, will give a leadership, a direction, a valuable constructive program, and a inspiration at a critical moment in
this war.

If I were not drawn in so many directions, my heart and my
judgment would draw me very much in this direction, and, were I
free, nothing would please me more than to associate myself in some
executive way with you in helping to work out this program.

May God help us, not only to see the opportunity, but to seize
it! There is all the difference in the world between men. There are
some men who sit in a meeting and listen when you point them to
the open door; then, because of their busy lives or their preoccupa-
tions, or their lack of will power, or the spirit of sacrifice, they pass by
this open door, and live to see what we are seeing in Russia and other
places, where doors did open to which attention was called, but people
did not enter. Therefore we are paying the price, and the war prolongs. May that not some time be said of the United States of
America!

PART FIVE

THE NATIONAL COUNCIL OF THE YOUNG MEN'S CHRISTIAN ASSOCIATIONS OF THE UNITED STATES OF AMERICA

THE NATIONAL COUNCIL OF THE YOUNG MEN'S CHRISTIAN ASSOCIATIONS OF THE UNITED STATES OF AMERICA

✸✸

IN PREPARATION FOR THE CONSTITUTIONAL CONVENTION

A REPORT OF THE FIRST MEETING OF THE COMMITTEE OF THIRTY-THREE IN *Association Forum*, JANUARY, 1923

O F IMMEDIATE AND GROWING INTEREST to every leader and member of the brotherhood is the forthcoming Constitutional Convention. The members of the representative gathering at Atlantic City were of one mind that such a Convention be held and with gratifying unanimity decided on its general plan and basis. A Committee of Thirty-Three was elected to whom were committed the determination of the date and place of the meeting and all general arrangements.

The Committee of Thirty-Three held its first meeting on December 16 at the Hotel Sinton in Cincinnati. It was attended by twenty-six members and one alternate. This included all but two of the twelve members from the eastern region, all of the nine members from the central region, all but one of the five members from the southern region, one of the three members and one alternate from the western region. Neither of the two members or their alternates from the Pacific region was present. The one member from Canada was present, also the one representing the colored men's Associations. Seldom has a large and widely representative Committee so quickly found itself and settled down to united, constructive work as did the group in Cincinnati. It was evident from the very start that the spirit which pervaded the Atlantic City Convention animated the members as they addressed themselves to their important task. The following organization of the Committee was effected: Chairman, Judge Adrian Lyon of Perth Amboy, New Jersey; Vice Chairman, Mr. H. M. Beardsley of Kansas City, Missouri; Treasurer, Mr. F. W. Ramsey of Cleveland, Ohio; Executive Secretary, Dr. John R. Mott, New York; Associate Secretaries, Mr. F. B. Shipp of Pittsburgh, Pennsylvania;

and Mr. Philo C. Dix of Louisville, Kentucky. These six officers together with Mr. Charles W. Bishop of Toronto, Canada, were constituted the Executive Committee of the Committee of Thirty-Three. A Finance Committee was appointed consisting of the Treasurer, Mr. Ramsey as Chairman, together with Mr. Burke Baker, Mr. William Francis, Mr. J. G. Rosebush, and Mr. F. Louis Slade.

After prolonged and careful consideration it was decided to hold the Constitutional Convention at the Hotel Cleveland in the city of Cleveland, Ohio. Several other places in the central region as well as in the eastern and southern regions were considered but the final decision was unanimous. The determining consideration was the fact that Cleveland is practically the geographical center of the Association brotherhood of North America. (See note on page 359 of the 1922 Yearbook.) It was more difficult to arrive at a united decision concerning the date but the Committee finally agreed, after weighing again and again the arguments pro and con, on October 17-26, 1923, with the understanding that the Convention would continue in session longer should this be found necessary. A number of the businessmen on the Committee expressed strongly their conviction that to insure the presence of leading laymen throughout the entire Convention, it should, if at all possible, be brought within the limits of practically one week, and all present deemed it of the utmost importance that all delegates to the Convention should be chosen and should accept with the understanding that they will be present throughout the entire period.

The Committee passed upon a draft for the official call of the Convention and this has already been sent to the president and general secretary of every Association in North America and likewise to all the General Agencies.

The matter of financing the Convention received a great deal of attention not only of the Finance Committee but also of the Committee of Thirty-Three. After debating different plans with various modifications, it was finally decided that all expenses be pooled, that is, the traveling and hotel bills (not to exceed $5 per day) of all delegates elected by state and interstate conventions and by the Canadian National Council, traveling and hotel expenses of the Committee of Thirty-Three and of the number of delegates not to exceed sixty to be appointed by the Committee of Thirty-Three, and all general expenses of the Committee of Thirty-Three in connection with its various meetings and the work of its subcommittees, and that each state and interstate group of Associations and also the Canadian group bear its pro rata share of the total expenses on the basis of the number of delegates to which it is entitled. The total budget has not yet been finally determined but it will probably exceed $50,000. It will be drawn up in detail as soon as a more exact calculation of traveling expenses is made. This cannot be completed until the number of delegates to be elected is determined and this in turn depends on a revision of the membership statistics in the case of certain Associations which in reporting for the 1922 Yearbook failed to indicate the number of active members. These facts will probably be known by the middle of January. This pooling plan for meeting the expenses seems to meet with general approval. It is thought to be the most democratic arrangement. No more will have to be paid on account of the delegate coming from the furthermost point in North America than for a delegate from Ohio. The fact of a man's financial ability will in no case be a determining factor in his appointment.

The Committee of Thirty-Three considers that one of its main functions is that of assembling and arranging necessary information and placing this at the disposal of the delegates, and so far as practicable, of the entire brotherhood. This is essential in order to conserve time and to insure the most intelligent, prompt, and orderly discharge of the business of the Convention. To facilitate this end, nine fact-finding committees were appointed at the meeting in Cincinnati, the names and members of which are as follows:

1. Raising of General Agency and Missionary Funds
       H. M. Beardsley, Chairman
       H. D. Dickson
       E. W. Grice

2. Interrelationship of General Agencies and Local Associations
       Judson G. Rosebush, Chairman
       Philo C. Dix
       C. W. Bishop

3. Convention and Conference Practice
       Adrian Lyon, Chairman
       C. L. Hibbard
       W. T. Diack

4. Occupation of the Home Field
       F. M. Hansen, Chairman
       F. Louis Slade
       R. R. Moton

5. Association Foreign Work
       Wilfred W. Fry, Chairman
       Cleveland E. Dodge
       W. S. Stallings

6. Publications

> E. L. Shuey, Chairman
> William Francis
> W. Knowles Cooper

7. Training Agencies and Personnel

> O. E. Brown, Chairman
> C. W. Bishop
> R. W. Cooke

8. Property Titles and Trust Funds

> Alexander S. Lyman, Chairman
> Alfred E. Marling
> F. B. Shipp

9. Basis of Association Active Membership and Control

> J. C. Baker, Chairman
> A. J. Holden
> H. W. Stone

The matter of most urgent concern as well as of greatest importance is the selection by the various state and interstate groups either at their regular conventions or at conventions specially called for the purpose, and by the Canadian National Council, of the delegates and alternates to which they are entitled. It is desired that all these conventions be held before April 15, 1923. Already the Associations of Iowa have held their convention and appointed their delegates and alternates. The Committee of Thirty-Three in their recent meeting, in line with the action of the Atlantic City Convention, emphasized the importance of having the delegation in each state as representative as possible of the different groups or types of Associations. The Committee doubt not that the brotherhood will give themselves to prayer that men may be chosen because of their knowledge, constructive ability, co-operative spirit, and unselfish desire to see the Association organization and policy made as acceptable as possible for accomplishing the purpose of Christ and of His Church on behalf of the young men and boys of North America and of the wide world. The Committee of Thirty-Three wish sincerely to discharge the great trust committed to them of serving in every way in their power the Constitutional Convention by facilitating the work of the delegates. They are sincerely seeking to interpret the mind of the brotherhood and at every stage of their work will welcome all constructive suggestions and counsel.

ADDRESSES AT THE CONSTITUTIONAL CONVENTION OF
THE YOUNG MEN'S CHRISTIAN ASSOCIATION,
CLEVELAND, OHIO, OCTOBER, 1923

REMARKS IN THE AFTERNOON SESSION OF THE OPENING DAY
OF THE CONVENTION

I do not believe it is the will of God that we should leave this place until something creative has been done that will stand through all the ages. If you were to ask me what that is, I should say I do not know, but never have I had more unshakable belief than I have this day, as I look into the faces of my brothers from all the American states and from the Canadian provinces, that we have been brought here by God Himself, and not in vain, but to do something forward-looking, truly prophetic, therefore courageous, constructive, and enduring. I hope that we shall not adjourn and that not one delegate will leave until something has been done that will issue in at least the following things:

First of all, that we may have a mandate given as to what the principals, that is, the local Associations as represented here by their leading laymen and secretaries, desire that their agents, the so-called General Agencies, shall do in the realm of service and how they had best do it. We want a fresh mandate that will be unmistakable as to what the Associations desire their General Agencies to be and to do, and a plan that will make these agencies much more responsive in the discovery and doing of that will than they have been in the past. Whatever has been unsatisfactory in this respect in the past has not been due to intention, or to lack of intention, but to want of clearness in definition and of a definite allocating of responsibility. We must not adjourn, therefore, until something has been done that will give us this desired result.

In the second place, we should not leave until something has been done that will issue in greater economy. I do not mean that we shall necessarily spend less money. We shall spend vastly more than we have ever dreamed of spending if we are to do the will of God! This country and Canada are not suffering from lack of money. But it is contrary to the will of God that we should waste one dollar. It is not so much the amount of money as it is the widespread conviction that through unnecessary duplication, overlapping, friction, misunderstanding, and what not, we are not spending the money to the very best advantage. I find that the rich men and the poor men are not resenting the spending of their money, if it is in line with the wisest economy and if every dollar is made to count to the maximum.

In the third place, I hope that we may not adjourn until plans have been launched and processes have been inaugurated, that will result in higher efficiency. My brothers, we need to gear up our organization and program to the modern age, and to its overwhelming requirements at home and abroad. We need to be more nearly in line with the last word of scientific thought and human experience as applied to the religious and social realm. Of all organizations, we who have had the honor of leading the way among altruistic societies, should not lag behind in this day of progress.

Again, it is my deep conviction, and I think it is shared by everybody here, that we should not adjourn until something has been done that will set us all free—free under specific instructions. Do not misunderstand me. I repeat—that will set us all free under specific instructions. Where the Spirit of the Lord is, there is liberty, there is large freedom. No organization, as no individual, can express itself in the largest and most beautiful and helpful way in the realm of service unless it has the liberty of the Spirit. We want freedom from uncertainty, freedom from suspicion, freedom from working at cross-purposes.

My brothers, let us get into deeper places. We have come together for something vastly more important than tinkering with machinery and drafting resolutions. We have come to find, if it be possible, more fully the mind of our Lord. "He made known His ways unto Moses; His acts unto the Children of Israel." We want to get beyond the knowledge of the acts. We want to know His ways of large liberty, of large freedom in the deepest things of God.

My last word I say with still deeper conviction and feeling. Let us not go out of this Convention—surely it is the will of God!—until there has taken place that wonderwork which results in unity. I admit this is a wonderwork. Not of men lest any man should boast; it is the gift of God. I do not find this unity in any other religion save that of Jesus Christ our Lord.

Thank God, Mr. Chairman, we have been called to something that is too hard for us! Not collectively, still less singly, not in partisan strife, shall we arrive at this great wonderwork. But as in humility we prostrate ourselves in our rooms, before we come into the sessions, and then exhibit that love that thinketh no evil and that doth not behave itself unseemly, there will be generated here that atmosphere in which all great creative works take place.

REMARKS IN THE CLOSING HOUR OF THE CONVENTION

My friends, I know I interpret what lies in the mind and heart of every one here when I say that this has been one of the great days of our lives. In all my years of Association service, beginning thirty-five years ago last month, I can think of no one day which to my mind has had quite so large significance. This has indeed been a creative hour. The vitalizing, the germinating work of the Living Christ has been here in these acts in which we have united in His name.

I have been profoundly impressed, as I am sure all of us have, by the high level on which this gathering has moved. We have had here during these intense days an exhibition of the control and support of God and a manifestation of that fine courtesy, that downright frankness, that ability to work together, even when we differed, that wondrous generosity, which are the marks of His Spirit. We take it not to ourselves.

Moreover, we must have felt—I know we hardly had time to think of it—the atmosphere in which men come to loathe to differ and to determine to understand each other at any cost; and we have paid prices. I suppose there is not a man here who has not paid the price, but we have gloried in it because in the pathway of sacrifice has ever been the large fruitage of the expanding Kingdom.

Yes, these have been creative hours. While there are divisive influences at work all over the world, possibly never more deadly than at the present time, and while we have been conscious at times of powers that would bring their disintegrating influence to bear upon us, even in the midst of the holy associations and activities of this Christian assemblage, thank God that through our corporate faith and the working of three great unifying factors, these have been transcended, have been surmounted.

We have been drawn together here by a common loyalty. Jesus Christ Himself, our Lord, has been in our midst. As we have reminded ourselves of Him in prayer and in song, and even in discussion, we found ourselves nearer one another.

We have been drawn together likewise by a common obligation. I suppose this work of the Young Men's Christian Association has seemed to you, as it has to me, never quite to difficult as it is now— and yet that is the glory of it all. This common obligation to make Christ known and recognized not only in our lives but in all the brotherhood and through all human relationships has placed upon us a colossal load. We have been reminded of other difficulties not only in the sessions of the Convention, but in informal gatherings. I think of that one, for example, last Sunday afternoon, when we confronted afresh our great trust on behalf of the hundreds of millions of men and boys of less favored lands and races. As we then saw our overwhelming responsibility, we were drawn together, as is the case in every great struggle or stupendous undertaking.

We have been drawn together, not only by a common loyalty, —and the man is not here, I fancy, who would not lay down his life for his Lord—and by the common obligation of a world need and tragedy; but also by a common experience. We men shall never forget these days and we shall never forget these nights—perhaps I should add also the mornings.

Some of you who were members of a committee in which I counted it a great honor to blend my best thought and experience with that of my colleagues, will remember that in an hour of greatest difficulty, when it seemed hopeless to think of our ever coming to see eye to eye, I called attention to these words: "Until we all come in the unity of the faith and the knowledge of the Son of God, to a perfect man, to the measure of the stature of the fulness of Christ." How wonderfully this truth has been illustrated in the days that have elapsed since I tried to gather up in that word what I looked upon as the process which alone would bring us together.

Now, Mr. Chairman, with thoughts and emotions like these surging in our minds and hearts, are we not agreed that our preamble is hardly adequate? In the early morning hour I tried to formulate in a few words what would serve in some measure as an ascription of praise, as a confession of faith, and as an act of dedication as well as an expression of the great purposes for the realization of which we here enter into covenant. I would venture to suggest the following as a substitute for the proposed preamble:

"We, the representatives of the Young Men's Christian Associations of the United States and Canada, in Constitutional Convention assembled, reverently and joyfully confessing our faith in Jesus Christ our Lord and only Savior, and our unswerving allegiance to His Church, recognizing humbly the creative hand of God along the pathway of three-quarters of a century of corporate experience, and dedicating ourselves afresh to our great mission of bringing under the sway of His Kingdom the young manhood and boyhood of North America and of the other lands served by our Associations, and with the desire of conserving all the values of our past and likewise of unifying and strengthening our work so as to enable the North American Associations to meet the requirements of the modern age and of the coming day, hereby adopt the following Constitution of The National Council of the Young Men's Christian Associations of the United States of America."

In moving this substitute or amendment, I think I need not add that my whole mind, that is, my best judgment, and my whole heart, are behind every part of this report; not only so, but my will is there and I stand ready to do anything in my power to facilitate our extending up and down the brotherhood this atmosphere and this spirit and these convictions that we all now share, notwithstanding our recent divisions. In fact, I have gone ahead of instructions. We have made provision in the Constitution for a National Secretarial Cabinet composed of leading national secretaries and all the senior state secretaries. I have just said to some of my friends among the state secretaries that I plan to call together this new body the moment the Convention adjourns, to begin at once, without waiting for the referendum, our united fellowship, our united planning, and our united action —thus demonstrating our new, and as I believe, our triumphant solidarity.

THE FIRST MEETING OF THE NEW NATIONAL COUNCIL, JUNE, 1924

A meeting of the Committee of Thirty-Three was held in the Association Building in Washington, on June 3, 1924. The meeting was devoted to matters pertaining to the setting up of the new National Council. It also dealt with the preparations for the first meeting of the Council to be held in Buffalo, December 3-6, 1924.

A report was rendered indicating that 1,482 Associations had become member Associations of the new National Council by April 30, the date on which was closed the list of Associations which are to participate in the creation of the electoral districts.

It was also reported that eight state or interstate groups of member Associations had already dealt with the matter of the creation of their respective electoral districts and that in all the remaining state and interstate areas this step would be taken by November 1.

Considerable work was done on the preparation of a suggested agenda for the first meeting of the Council. This will be perfected at the next meeting of the Committee of Thirty-Three and then sent out to the elected members of the Council.

The subject of the financing of the Buffalo meeting of the Council was carefully considered. The decision of a previous meeting to follow the pooling plan, which was used in connection with the Constitutional Convention in Cleveland, was confirmed. In due time a letter will be sent by Treasurer Ramsey to the various state and interstate organizations giving the particulars of the plan.

The following three important committees were agreed upon and appointed:

(1) Committee on National Council Organization: E. L. Shuey, Chairman; Alexander Lyman, W. W. Fry, W. K. Cooper, J. G. Rosebush, F. M. Hansen, F. B. Shipp, Adrian Lyon, and J. R. Mott, ex officio.

(2) Committee on National Council Program and Budget: F. W. Ramsey, Chairman; A. E. Marling, C. L. Hibbard, J. C. Baker, R. W. Cooke, F. L. Slade, and Adrian Lyon, and J. R. Mott, ex officio.

(3) Committee on Methods of Financing the General Agencies: Cleveland E. Dodge, Chairman; W. T. Diack, William Francis, H. D. Dickson, P. C. Dix, Burke Baker, and Adrian Lyon, and J. R. Mott, ex officio.

REPORT OF THE INTERNATIONAL COMMITTEE, 1924

To The National Council of the Young Men's Christian Associations of the United States of America:

The Constitutional Convention of the Young Men's Christian Associations of North America, held at Cleveland, Ohio, October 17-23, 1923, in addition to adopting a constitution for the National Council of the Young Men's Christian Associations of the United States of America, which was submitted to the Associations of the United States for their referendum vote and was approved by a large majority, also adopted the following resolutions:

> *Resolved,* That the Young Men's Christian Associations of North America do hereby approve and adopt the following findings:
>
> 1. If and when the findings of the Constitutional Convention are approved by majority vote of the Young Men's Christian Associations of the United States, such changes as may be involved in such findings regarding the organic relations between the Associations of Canada and of the United States be and hereby are approved.
>
> 2. That pending the next International Convention, the International Committee of Young Men's Christian Associations, in consultation and agreement both with the National Council of Canada and the National Council of the United States, be, and hereby is authorized and instructed to make such transfer of its duties, funds, or properties as may be required by the adoption of the findings of the Constitutional Convention.
>
> 3. The next ensuing International Convention shall make such redefinition as may be necessary of the functions of itself and of its agent, the International Committee, and such changes in its composition and rules as may be required by the adoption of the findings of the Constitutional Convention.

These resolutions were submitted to the Associations of the United States and Canada for their referendum vote as Proposal Number Two and were approved by a vote of 1682 for to 13 against.

In view of the adoption of the constitution for the National Council of the United States and the approval of the foregoing resolutions, the International Committee hereby reports that in accordance with the provisions of the new constitution and of these resolutions, and after consultation and in agreement with representatives of the National Council of the Young Men's Christian Associations of Canada, it, the International Committee, is prepared to transfer to the National Council of the Young Men's Christian Associations of the United States of America such of its duties, funds, and properties as the National Council may find it possible and desirable to take over.

By way of preparation for such transfer the International Committee herewith submits a report of the work for which it has been responsible. In this report effort has been made to give the information that will enable the new National Council best to carry on the duties for which it will be responsible.

The International Committee has also ventured to make certain recommendations concerning the continuance of the work.

BEGINNINGS, COMPOSITION, AND ORGANIZATION OF THE INTERNATIONAL COMMITTEE

At the first convention of the Young Men's Christian Assoications of the United States and Canada, held at Buffalo, New York, June 6-7, 1854, there was appointed a Central Executive Committee of what was known for nine years as "The Confederation of the Young Men's Christian Associations of the United States and British Provinces." This committee, merged later into the International Committee, has continued in existence for seventy years.

At the eighth convention held June 4-6, 1863, in Chicago, the Confederation was reorganized into its present form and became known as the Convention of the Young Men's Christian Associations of the United States and British Provinces.

The twenty-third convention, held at Baltimore in 1879, changed the name of the convention to the International Convention of the Young Men's Christian Associations of North America, and designated its executive agent as "The International Committee of Young Men's Christian Associations of North America."

The convention of June 1-5, 1866, held at Albany, placed the headquarters of the Committee in New York City, where it has ever since remained. Before that date, the Committee had for a period of twelve years been located successively in Washington, Cincinnati, Richmond, Charleston, Philadelphia, and Boston. Since 1866, or for fifty-eight years, it has had its headquarters in New York City. The number of influential laymen identified with it has steadily grown, increasing from five in 1866, all resident in New York City, to nearly 200 at the present time, from all parts of the United States and Canada. The growth in financial resources has been very great. The total expenditure for the fiscal year, 1866-7, was $1,100; the total for all operating expenses in the year 1923 was $4,484,748.

The Executive Committee

The Executive Committee is composed of fifteen members, including the chairmen of the Regional Committees and of the Canadian National Council who serve in an ex officio capacity as members of the Executive Committee. The committee meets monthly, except during July and August, and also on call. Fifteen meetings were held during the past year.

The Executive Committee represents the International Committee ad interim and has general oversight of all its work, with specific responsibility for the budgets of the several divisions of the International Committee. It is also responsible for making recommendations concerning the more important matters which require action by the International Committee.

The General Secretary's Office

Five secretaries are related directly to this office, namely: the general secretary, the associate general secretary, the consulting general secretary, and two assistant secretaries. The general secretary is the executive officer of the International Committee and its Executive Committee. He is assisted in the discharge of his duties by the other secretaries related to his office and by the several associate general secretaries who are also assigned specific responsibility for the divisions to which they are related.

In accordance with the special arrangement made when the present general secretary assumed office, he devotes a portion of his time to the work of other related organizations. His duties require extensive field visitation at home and abroad.

The Cabinet

To facilitate the work of the employed staff of the International Committee, there were formed in 1920 four cabinets, as follows:

1. The United Cabinet, which is composed of the general secretary, the associate general secretaries, the regional executive secretaries, the consulting general secretary, the senior secretary of each department and bureau of the Home and General Service Divisions, and the senior secretary of each major subdivision of the Foreign and Overseas Divisions. The United Cabinet meets monthly, except during July and August, and on call.

Its functions are to insure the unity and efficiency of the secretarial forces of the Committee through the processes of conference, interchange of experience and opinion, and personal fellowship and to confer with and advise the general secretary of the International Committee on all matters affecting the interests of the Committee.

2. The Home Cabinet, which is composed of the general secretary, the associate general secretary, the consulting general secretary, the associate general secretaries assigned to the Home and General Service Divisions, the regional executive secretaries, and the senior secretaries of each department and bureau of the Home and General Service Divisions. The Home Cabinet meets monthly, except during July and August, and on call.

Its work for the Home Division is similar to that of the United Cabinet for the Committee as a whole.

3. The Foreign Cabinet, which is composed of the general secretary, the associate general secretary, the consulting general secretary, the associate general secretaries assigned to the Foreign Division, and the senior secretary of each principal subdivision of the Foreign Division. The Foreign Cabinet meets monthly, except during July and August, and on call.

Its work for the Foreign Division is similar to that of the United Cabinet for the Committee as a whole.

4. The Overseas Cabinet, which is composed of the general secretary, the associate general secretary, the consulting general secretary, the associate general secretaries assigned to the overseas Division, and the senior secretary of each principal subdivision of the Overseas Division. The Overseas Cabinet meets monthly, except during July and August, and on call.

Its work for the Overseas Division is similar to that of the United Cabinet for the Committee as a whole.

The Staff Meeting

A meeting of the secretarial staff or of those members of the staff who may be at the headquarters office is held each month, except during July and August, and on call of the general secretary. These meetings are intended to provide opportunity for the interchange of information, experience, and opinion about the work and varied interests of the International Committee as a whole.

The Annual Conference

For a number of years the International Committee and its entire staff have followed the practice of holding in the early autumn a conference, usually extending over three days. These annual conferences have been the occasion of greatest value for discussion of many aspects of the work of the International Committee, for meetings of sub-committees and the staffs attached to each, for inspirational purposes, and for maintaining the unity and solidarity of the complex and world-wide work. They have abounded in most helpful fellowship for the laymen and secretaries engaged in promoting the program of the International Committee.

THE ROCKEFELLER REPORT

Special attention is called to the survey of the home work of the International Committee made during the past two years under the auspices of John D. Rockefeller, Jr. Probably in the case of no other organization in the history of religious and philanthropic agencies has such a thorough survey and exhaustive study been made of its organization and financial problems as was made by Raymond B. Fosdick, Mark M. Jones, and other representatives of Mr. Rockefeller.

Because of the great importance of this study to the work of the International Committee, reference is here made to it and to the suggestions in the report which will undoubtedly be of large significance to the new National Council. The study was begun early in 1922 and extended over a period of more than eighteen months. The final printed report was given to the International Committee early in 1924.

The International Committee has already responded to scores of the recommendations of the report. Some were adopted while the study was yet in progress; others after its completion; and others have been under consideration since the report was received. Because of the anticipated early transfer of most of its organization and work to the National Council and pending the opening of a new fiscal year, the International Committee has, however, necessarily deferred final action on many of the recommendations of the report.

The International Committee most heartily commends to the National Council early and thorough study of this survey and report in the belief that it has suggestions of great helpfulness for the Council and for the Association Movement as a whole.

The International Committee also takes this opportunity to give public expression to its appreciation of the thoughtful generosity of John D. Rockefeller, Jr., in making the report possible. Above the considerable monetary expense involved in making this survey and issuing this report, the service thus rendered by Mr. Rockefeller and his able group of investigators and advisors has a value beyond computation.

GOVERNING PRINCIPLES FOR THE ASSOCIATION MOVEMENT[1]

FROM THE REPORT OF THE INTERNATIONAL COMMITTEE OF THE YOUNG MEN'S CHRISTIAN ASSOCIATIONS OF NORTH AMERICA, TO THE NATIONAL COUNCIL OF THE YOUNG MEN'S CHRISTIAN ASSOCIATIONS OF THE UNITED STATES OF AMERICA, 1924

In the course of over half a century of experience the Associations of North America have evolved certain governing principles for their national corporate action. These may well be considered by the National Council as it assumes its new responsibilities and proceeds to lay down its policies. These principles, which have hitherto not misled the brotherhood, may afford trustworthy guidance for the coming day.

1. The dominating and pervading purpose of the North American Movement is that of relating young men and boys to Jesus Christ, to His Church, and to the program of His Kingdom. This principle among all others holds the primacy. The largest and most vital and enduring results have been achieved where it has been given right of way, where it has governed all policies and plans, and where all the complex and multiform activities of the Association have been motivated and shot through with such spiritual meaning and passion. Herein lies the secret of mastering one of our admittedly most baffling problems, that of dominating and utilizing most beneficently our vast and ever-growing material equipment and resources.

2. The distinctive mission of the Association is to liberate, enlist, train, and wield a great lay force for the cause of righteousness and unselfishness. Discerning leaders of the Church have borne appreciative testimony to the greatness of this contribution. In view of the fact that the life of the world is so much more highly organized now than in the past, this characteristic service of the Association will be more needed than ever. The only hope of permeating and controlling all departments of modern life with the spirit of Christ is through getting men to recognize and accept their responsibility to give expression to their religious faith and convictions within the sphere of their daily calling and in all their human relationships.

3. The idea symbolized by the Red Triangle should continue to be held in proper prominence in working out and applying the Association program. This principle might well be bracketed with the one just stated, regarding the lay aspect of the Movement, as one of the two most unique gifts of the Association to present-day Christianity.

---

[1] These principles were formulated by John R. Mott.

This insistence on the threefold, or symmetrical development of man, this recognition of the unity of man's personality—body, mind, and spirit—is basic in the Association structure. May it never become common in our thought or treatment, but rather evoke a deepening sense of reverence, as suggesting the idea of the central Fact of our religion, the Incarnation—Christ taking on Himself the form of man and continuing to clothe Himself with men.

4. The Association was called into being to strengthen the hands of the Church. The Young Men's Christian Association is not a Church; it cannot perform the functions of the Church; it cannot substitute the Church; it is not a rival of the Church. It is the servant of the Church. It exists to strengthen, and in no sense to weaken the Church. The Church afforded the conditions which made the Association possible. The Association was called into being through loyal members of the Christian Church. It is recognized by the Church. Its support—material, moral, and spiritual—has come largely from the Church. As well might the child disparage the parent, or the parent the child, as for the Association to regard lightly or with indifference the Church, or the Church the Association. That the Association may realize its providential purpose with reference to the Church, there must be the closest collaboration on the part of both Association and Church leaders in all matters of major policy.

5. The Association stands for, and should increasingly illustrate, the interdenominational and interconfessional principle. At times the Association is superficially called an undenominational organization. There is a very wide difference between undenominationalism and interdenominationalism. Undenominationalism would reduce the members of the various Churches to the lowest common denominator. In drawing into its fellowship and activities the members of the different Church bodies, the Association emphasizes that it wishes them to be true to their respective mother Churches. It thus seeks to illustrate, not the oneness of uniformity, but unity in diversity. Its teaching, fellowship, and action exhibit vastly more power and richness than vague, weak, colorless undenominationalism. In the outreach of the program of the North American Associations to lands of other great Christian Communions this point assumes added significance. Without compromising its other guiding principles, and without forfeiting its original spirit, it is thus permitted to make a great contribution to the young manhood and boyhood of all historic bodies of Christendom.

6. The democratic character of the Association—local, state, and national—must be maintained. The history of many brotherhoods and men's guilds throughout the centuries shows clearly that to ac-

complish this desired end involves a fight for life. The drift or tendency in an organization, as it grows in size and wealth, is for its management and control to gravitate more and more into the hands of the few. The democratizing of the American Association Movement nationally by setting up a National Council, composed of men elected directly by members of groups of Associations in 115 electoral districts, is a splendid safeguard against this peril, because the plan is sure to keep the national body quickly responsive to the expressed will of the brotherhood. Measures must now be taken to insure a corresponding democratic control of the Associations themselves. The examples are alarmingly numerous of boards of directors and other supervisory managing committees which are in no sense democratically constituted, and which are largely out of touch with the membership which they seek to serve. The generation-long danger of the form of professionalism, known as secretarialism, has not abated, and calls for the exercise of vigilance, self-effacement, and the hardest kind (and yet the most rewarding kind) of work of distributing responsibility, if this peril is not to continue to threaten the truest democracy in this lay Movement.

7. From the earliest beginnings of the Movement, the independence and autonomy of the local Association has been recognized as a fundamental principle. The individual local Association is the unit in the Association Movement. It is the principal; the various General Agencies of the Movement have all been created by it and are its agents. The discussions of recent years, while clarifying and strengthening this position, have also made it plain that the local Association, the individual unit, in becoming a member of the national organization voluntarily delegates in a measure, its autonomy, that is, in so far as this is necessary to insure giving effect to the instructions issued by the official representatives of the Associations in convention. Some have held that the autonomy of the local Association is to be held so absolute and inviolable that even the local Association itself may not federate its efforts with those of similar Associations to authorize corporate action. It is possibly true that a body ceases to have absolute autonomy when it unites with another body in any common task, just as no citizen of a free country can claim to be absolutely free; but, on the other hand, it is equally true that a body which cannot yield for specified ends and for definite periods a share of its authority, cannot claim autonomy. If an Association cannot give up authority it is not free and therefore not autonomous. Even if it is true that originally the individual Associations may have been organized on the principle of absolute independence and autonomy, does not any fair interpretation of our history show that the Asso-

ciations by participating in the international, national, and state Conventions, and by creating General Agencies and endowing these General Agencies with certain functions, have themselves in so doing incurred responsibilities and obligations as absolute and inviolable as are their own independence and autonomy?

8. A highly efficient national organization is essential in order that the services needed and desired by the Associations may be rendered, and in order that the Associations in their united, corporate capacity may meet great national and international needs and opportunities. It is a mistake to assume that the Associations desire to be weak in corporate action. While wisely they have sought to keep their agents responsive to their will, they have shown in every important test their recognition of the need of a national agency able to further strongly and worthily a comprehensive and rich national and international program. Moreover, in extending the Association to other lands they have invariably pursued the same statesmanlike policy. They have always, at home and abroad, been responsive to national and racial aspirations, and have encouraged the finest national solidarity. This, in turn, explains why their policy has commanded the confidence of national governments of so many lands, and the heart devotion and following of the peoples of these lands. In a Movement so highly departmentalized or specialized as that of the American Association it has been most important, through an effective national body, to further desirable co-ordination, co-operation, and unity. It has been gratifying to observe the growing recognition of the interdependence of all parts and aspects of this extensive and complex enterprise.

9. While maintaining in the national organization an adequate central oversight, direction, and control, it is desirable that there be a policy of wide and wise decentralization, or devaluation, of responsibility for the administration and conduct of the work itself. Every growing movement is called upon from time to time to reorganize its work and redistribute burdens. The Rockefeller Survey and Study of the Home Work of the International Committee revealed the need of relieving congestion in the general administration; and pointed the way, followed later by the Constitutional Convention, of assigning to a series of service committees a very large measure of responsibility for the actual management of the program of activities. This should result in an improved service through accelerating processes of clearance and decision, and through enlisting the larger initiative and wider participation of members of the brotherhood. Moreover, in accordance with this guiding principle continued emphasis will be laid on transferring to the state organizations, as rapidly as practicable,

responsibility for much of the field work, except in certain clearly defined national and highly specialized aspects of the enterprise.

10. The Associations of the United States and Canada should continue to sustain the closest fraternal and official relations to each other. From the time this organization was established in the two countries the most intimate co-operation and unity have been maintained. Marked advantages have been realized from this constant interchange of experience, and from international fellowship in thought, prayer, and work. The providential relation of the two countries, as to geographical position, intermingling of peoples, and common Church problems and responsibilities, accentuates the desirability of the policy and practice of co-operation. Moreover, there is the inevitable reaction of the two nations upon each other on the lower levels, and the consequent need of helping each other to safeguard the highest ideals. Add to all this the great and unique responsibility of the English-speaking countries in world service, and there can be no question as to the wisdom of devising ways and means by which these two strong and independent national Movements may continue to move forward together in most helpful relation to each other.

11. The American Associations need ever to preserve a realizing sense of the fact that they are a part of the world brotherhood, and seek to discharge the responsibilities thus involved. From the time that they, as a charter member, performed their high function of joining with other national and international groups of Associations in establishing the World's Alliance of Young Men's Christian Associations, they have been at the very heart of this world expression of the Movement. The launching and wonderful development of their foreign work program has served as a constant reminder of their obligation to serve other nations and races, and to co-operate with them in the world-wide extension of the Association. Now that the world has found itself as one body, with the result that the nations and races are acting and reacting upon one another with such directness and power, and, at times, also, with such possibilities of danger and conflict, it is of the utmost importance that the American Associations, through their relation to the World's Committee, as well as in the outreach of their own foreign work, recognize more fully and discharge more adequately their responsibilities as members of a world brotherhood.

12. It has ever been a governing principle with the American Association Movement to try to meet national and international crises through placing their services at the disposal of great bodies of young men in need. Possibly the most conspicuous example in all our history was the one which led to the overseas work. Through

the guidance of an overruling Providence we were permitted in their most trying hour to minister to not less than 19,000,000 men in Allied armies, and, in addition, to 6,000,000 prisoners of war of both sides of the great struggle. As a result of becoming absorbed and losing ourselves in this Christlike service, 10,000 new doors have been opened to the Association across the breadth of the world. The practical helpfulness of the work in the war and postwar periods has led to an irresistible demand from governments, from religious leaders, from discerning and trusted American observers, and, above all, from the young men themselves, for our continued assistance in establishing this work on a civilian basis. Because of the exhaustion of war work funds, which had been raised for the specific purposes for which they have been so carefully expended, it has been necessary to contract the overseas program at a rapid rate. This has greatly stimulated self-support. The present is a most critical moment. If the American Associations will extend a helping hand for but a few years more, this vital, and in some ways most highly multiplying piece of work to which they have ever been related, will become domesticated in genuinely indigenous national Association Movements.

13. The Association Movement on this continent has reached a stage in its evolution where there is need of emphasizing, as never before, its intensive development. This calls for the larger employment of the scientific method. What has been well called the "engineering function," as contrasted with the work of promotion, should now be held in greater prominence. In particular, more of the leading minds in the national organization, as well as locally, should be occupied with making surveys, conducting original research, and evolving programs. Without doubt, the Association, as an organization, has, in recent years, been producing Christian work or activity more rapidly than it has been drawing, with scientific thoroughness, lessons from its experience to guide it into a far more efficient and fruitful ministry for the period immediately before us. It must be frankly admitted that much of our present organization and policy is inadequate to meet the exacting requirements, the stern challenges, and the inspiring opportunities of the coming day.

14. At all costs the Movement, both nationally and locally, must preserve its power of growth. Too many are prone to think of the Young Men's Christian Association organization as a machine. Its leaders and members need constantly to remind themselves that it is a living organism. Nothing, therefore, can be more important than the maintaining of its vitality. To this end, there should be the greatest encouragement of the creative processes. The spirit of adventure, discovery, and invention should never be repressed but welcomed on

every hand. Visions and plans of timely and wise expansion, both in the partially occupied and in the totally unoccupied fields, should receive sympathetic and reverent consideration, for they are usually born in an atmosphere of unselfishness, and in the pathway of a seeking to extend the reign of Christ. Well might we become alarmed if the Association organization were to become static. Then the word Movement applied to it would be a misnomer. The signs would begin to multiply that our mission as a great and growing unselfish brotherhood had begun to contract, and that we must give way to other organizations and uprisings of men possessing more courage and sacrifice to meet opportunities. It hardly needs to be pointed out that the power or capacity of growth carries with it the maintenance of intellectual open-mindedness and genuine spirituality in the eager search to know and heed every true and authentic word of reverent and thorough scholarship in the realm of biblical research, religious education, Christian sociology, and other departments of learning bearing upon the development of reasonable and vital faith and of Christian character.

15. The Young Men's Christian Association must retain and emphasize its youth movement character. To this end the processes should constantly be furthered which result in keeping tides of youth not only pouring into the organization, but also into its lay and secretarial leadership. As a movement grows in years, there are certain tendencies to throw its control into the hands of the old. This is the inevitable outcome of the acquisition of large property interests and of the evolution of a vast and highly complicated organization calling for extended experience and maturity of judgment for their proper management. This necessary and reasonable requirement but accentuates the necessity, therefore, of utilizing every other opportunity and means of enlisting and pressing forward into paths of ever-enlarging responsibility the ambitious and resourceful youth. We know not what will be true of coming generations, but we do know that the new generation, which so largely constitutes the present membership, and which outside our membership is surging about us so largely untouched by our program and influence, holds in its hands the destiny of the coming day. Wherever else we fail, we must not fail in winning them. To this end, we must present to them heroic challenges, and afford them adequate outlet for the expression of their aspirations and sacrificial devotion. Moreover, recognizing that it takes like to reach like, we must more and more thrust forward the youth into positions of leadership and trust.

16. In the Association, as in every other Christian and unselfish enterprise, the largest results of its work and influence lie outside its

own immediate organization. President Wilson once remarked that what impressed him most about the Young Men's Christian Association was the fact that its leaders and members so little appreciated its power and its possibilities of influence. In recent years, in the development of its community-wide emphasis, and its nationwide and world-wide programs, one could recognize indications that the leaders were beginning to realize the obligation of the Association to extend its service beyond its own borders. It will be a great day for Christ's Kingdom when we all more generally recognize the limitless possibilities of placing more largely at the disposal of the Churches and other organizations the Association ideas, experience, methods, and leadership. Whatever concerns the welfare of a young man or boy anywhere and at any time, concerns the Young Men's Christian Association. Our attitude and spirit should not be that of guarding jealously what we consider to be our own field and prerogatives, but rather that of eagerly seeking to discover the best ways, both directly and indirectly, of influencing aright the maximum number of young men and boys. It should be pointed out, and especially emphasized in this connection, that if the Association is to become a propagating base from which this high and unselfish ministry will be communicated to other movements in a position to influence for good the successive generations of youth, the best life of the Association itself must be most generously safeguarded and developed that it may have truly generating, and therefore propagating power. No lack of conviction, leadership, sacrifice, or effort should cause us to forfeit a field or work to which we have become providentially related, and for the cultivation of which the Christian Church holds us responsible.

17. No organization maintains itself at a higher level than that occupied by its leaders. The Young Men's Christian Association is no exception to this rule. It is of cardinal importance, therefore, that more men of strength of personality, of recognized gifts of leadership, of the most thorough intellectual training, of genuine personal experience of Christ, and of a sense of Divine mission, come into the leadership of the Association in all departments and aspects of its work. The securing of men who are absolutely first-class from every point of view will help to scale up the ideals, standards, efficiency, and attractive power of the secretarial vocation. Moreover, the Association will fall down before the great demands made upon it unless it insures a better-trained leadership. This is necessary in order that the Movement as a whole may be ushered into a more advanced stage of development and usefulness. All our plans need rethinking. Our program must be restudied and restated in the light of the new outlook in the realm of thought and of human relations. We are called

upon to meet new and unexampled opportunities and unknown experiences. Our leaders must possess the mental background and the habits of mind which make possible grappling successfully with the large unsolved problems before the Association—problems involved in modern religious education, problems of a comprehensive vocational educational program, problems of the discovery and training of workers, problems of the right acquisition and use of money, problems of the social mission of the Association, problems of assimilating men of different political and religious antecedents and ideals, problems of inflamed race relationships. Moreover, if the Association is to command more largely the interest, confidence, and co-operation of men of education and culture, it must have a better-furnished and better-educated leadership.

If the religious and social-service program of the Association is to present a more winning and convincing apologetic to thoughtful and inquiring young men, we must have leaders with a scientific and spiritually-minded understanding of the eternal foundations of our faith. In order to achieve a closer and more efficient correlation of the Association with other constructive agencies and forces, especially the Churches, men of larger comprehension are essential. Men of greater caliber and of ampler preparation are likewise essential, if our leaders are to stand and work on a common platform of research, discussion, intellectual fellowship, and service with the leaders of the Churches, and of other altruistic and idealistic forces of the community and of the nation.

RECOMMENDATIONS OF THE INTERNATIONAL COMMITTEE TO THE NATIONAL COUNCIL

1. That the Council, on the threshold of its life, give priority in its corporate thinking, planning, and action to strengthening the leadership of the religious forces of the Association Movement in order that a clear and authentic lead may be afforded the new generation in the realm of faith and conduct; and, to this end, that the collaboration of the best-equipped minds, the most deeply taught spiritual guides, and the most prophetic voices of our day be enlisted by the Council as speakers, teachers, and writers.

2. That, in view of the fact that the effective key to the solution of virtually all the problems confronting the Association, the Church, and the nation lies in influencing aright the ideals and habits of the youth, and that, therefore, in reality, the destiny of the Association

Movement will be largely determined by the relation it sustains to the new generation, the Council should see that the comprehensive findings of the recent Pörtschach Conference are held in prominence in its boys' work program, and that the brotherhood, through the coming Third General Assembly, to be held at Estes Park in the interest of Association service with boys, study and suggest how these findings may best be applied in the American field.

3. That, in view of the fact that the Young Men's Christian Association stands at the fork in the road as to whether or not it will maintain its position of helpfulness as the one interdenominational, voluntary society at work among the young men in the universities, colleges, and schools, the brotherhood, as a brotherhood, recognize that the time has come to concern itself with the problem thus presented. The issue at stake concerns profoundly every part of the work of the Movement. The Council, therefore, should put itself solidly behind the advance program of the Student Movement; and recognizing that this will, in the near future, call for very large sacrificial co-operation, it should give particular attention to the financial requirements of this critical situation.

4. That the Association membership and leadership be called upon by the Council to heed the heroic challenge, which comes with unique appeal to an organization made up of young men and boys, confronted with the present unprecedented industrial, international, and interracial situation throughout the world. As a preparation for meeting this exacting demand, the Council through its several divisions should lend full co-operation to the inquiry recently projected by the World's Committee. In connection with this inquiry groups of young men in all lands are to give themselves, under wise and experienced guidance, to the study of the facts, to the discovery of the mind of Christ with reference to meeting the facts, and to resolute application of them. Moreover, in order that these groups may be characterized by reality, their members should be governed by the principles and spirit of Christ within the sphere of their daily relationships.

5. That adequate provision be made by the Council in the new organization from the very beginning for developing the research and the survey functions, in order to insure the highest efficiency of the organization, and its most economical and fruitful operation.

6. That the Council, in setting up its new organization, follow the policy of appointing committees to carry through specific tasks within a specified time, rather than that of establishing many permanent standing committees. In constituting committees, while due regard should be paid to insuring a proportionate geographical representation, chief emphasis should be placed on the securing of a

personnel thoroughly qualified for dealing with the questions involved. A special effort should also be put forth to weave into the newly formed committees a larger proportion of young men than at the present time generally obtains throughout the brotherhood.

7. That the Council adopt the plan of having written commissions given to all divisions, departments, bureaus, and committees, and specific written charges or instructions to each member of the secretarial staff.

8. That the Council encourage the plan of democratic assemblies, councils, and conferences of representatives of the Associations interested in various specialized aspects of the work of the Association, for example, the educational, physical, religious, boys', transportation, colored, student, personnel, for the purpose of generating the most helpful ideas, initiating forward movements, and evolving new plans and methods; with the understanding that these bodies will be articulated with the regular organization of the Council, and that their activities will be subject to the supervision and approval of the Council.

9. That the following commissions, appointed or authorized by the International Convention at Atlantic City in 1922, be requested to make the results of their work available to the National Council through the appropriate channels:

The Permanent Committee on the Association Vocation;
The National Board on Certification;
The Commission on the Occupation of the Field;
The Commission on Methods and Materials for the Development of an All-round Program for Men;
The Commission on Advance Program among Student Associations;
The Commission on Town and Country Fields;
The Commission on Membership Problems;
The General Counseling Commission of the Churches.

10. That, in view of the large and growing importance of Washington as a national capital and as a center not only of nation-wide but also of international influence, in view of the recognition of this fact by so many leading national bodies—commercial, industrial, educational, fraternal, and religious—and in view of the significance of all this to the Association Movement, the Council take over the committee recently appointed by the International Committee for the purpose of making a study of the plans and requirements of the Washington Association, and that the work of this special committee be carried forward with expedition and thoroughness.

11. That the Council appoint commissioners to meet with similar representatives of the Canadian National Council and of the International Committee for the purpose of drafting a plan defining the relationships which should exist between the two Councils and between them and the International Convention, which plan shall be reported to the various bodies concerned for their consideration and action.

12. That, in determining the time and place of the next meeting of the National Council, the Council confer with the International Committee, with a view to arranging, if practicable, that the meeting of the International Convention and that of the National Council be held in juxtaposition to each other.

13. That the Council recommend to the next International Convention that such changes be made in its rules as will make them harmonize with the new relationships resulting from the creation of the National Council of the United States.

14. That, in view of the great importance of developing intimate working relations with the Churches, and in view of the recent establishment by many of the larger communions of standing committees on the young Men's Christian Associations, and in view of the appointment of a General Counseling Commission of the Churches, the Council takes steps through the General Board to articulate the General Counseling Commission of the Churches with its own organization and work.

15. That, in view of the extension of the Young Men's Christian Association in recent years to countries where the Eastern Church predominates and in view of the remarkable welcome which has been accorded by its leaders and members to our representatives, and the wide opportunity which has thus been opened to the Association, the Council, through the outreach of its foreign program, seek in every way in its power to place at the disposal of this historic communion the benefits of its experience in work for young men and boys in all parts of the world.

16. That, in view of the long-established and markedly successful policy of the North American Associations in the countries of Latin America, the Council, in extending its ministry to the young men and boys of other lands predominantly Roman Catholic, continue to follow the principles and methods which have hitherto met with such general acceptance.

17. That the Council welcome the proposal of the recent National Convention of the Young Women's Christian Associations of the United States, suggesting an exploration of the possibilities of closer co-operation between that organization and our own organi-

zation; and that the Council, through its General Board, facilitate in every way the realization of the end in view.

18. That the Council endorse the project-budget plan, as illustrated in the budget brought before it at the present meeting through the Committee of Thirty-Three, and adopt this plan for the future, together with the measures necessary to realize from it the full benefits of wise standardization and consequent economy and efficiency.

19. That, in view of the rapid growth of community chests and financial federations, and of the direct bearing they have on the income of the entire Association Movement, including local Associations and all General Agencies, the Council appoint a commission to study the questions involved in the participation of the Associations and their General Agencies in community chests or other financial federations, and that such commission be requested to transmit its findings to the Associations.

20. That the National Council have one office for all financial approaches to the Associations and to individuals; and that the Council adopt the plan of having one full-time salaried treasurer and also one full-time salaried controller.

21. That, because the present endowment funds provide less than 3 per cent of the total income required for the proposed budgets of the Council for 1925, and because of the heavy burden placed on the Association Movement in being obliged to raise from contributions more than 72 per cent of the total required annual income, the Council make a thorough study of the advisability of largely augmenting its permanent and special endowment funds.

22. That, in the interest of more efficient and economical management of such services as Association Press, *Association Men,* and the Building Bureau, whose business operations require the maintenance of large stocks and the carrying of large amounts in current accounts, the Council study the question whether these forms of service shall be continued, and, if their decision is in the affirmative, whether it might be well to secure a capital fund to help stabilize and maintain them.

23. That, since at the call of the International Committee there has recently been held at Lake Placid a conference of senior secretaries of the International Committee related to the Foreign and Overseas Divisions, together with the general secretaries of the various national committees, at which for a fortnight, united and constructive study was given to the problems in connection with the outreach of the North American Associations to other lands, the findings of this conference be given thorough consideration by the National Council.

24. That the Council seek to conserve the unparalleled results which have come to the American Association Movement in the pathway of its war and postwar work in Europe and the Near East through merging this work with the Foreign Division, in accordance with the action taken at the Atlantic City Convention, and through domesticating the budget of this part of the work in the heart and sacrificial devotion of the brotherhood.

25. That, in considering the proposed budget for 1925 submitted through the Committee of Thirty-Three, the Council examine with care each project of the work now being carried on at home and abroad with a view to effecting further economies, and where necessary, to the enlarging of the present services.

26. That, in view of the recent exhaustive study of the organization and administration of the work of the International Committee on the home field by representatives of John D. Rockefeller, Jr., and of the great value of the many suggestions made by these able and expert examiners, the Council and its General Board give thorough consideration to their report, particularly the following sections:

  a. Instruments for Co-ordination;
  b. Financial Suggestions;
  c. Programs and Services;
  d. Headquarters Office Matters;
  e. Organization Problems.

27. That the transfer of the operations and the operating accounts of the International Committee to the National Council be made as of January 1, 1925.

28. That the Council and its various subdivisions make an early and careful study of this report of the International Committee, of the proposed project budget, and of the supporting documents and papers mentioned in the report, with special reference to understanding and carrying out existing commitments, maintaining all important relationships, preventing loss of momentum, and meeting pressing opportunities.

ON BEHALF OF THE INTERNATIONAL COMMITTEE,

JAMES M. SPEERS, *Chairman*

JOHN R. MOTT, *General Secretary*

NEW YORK CITY, November 20, 1924

RESPONSE OF JOHN R. MOTT TO THE CALL OF THE NATIONAL COUNCIL

EXTRACT FROM MINUTES OF THE MEETING OF THE NATIONAL COUNCIL OF THE YOUNG MEN'S CHRISTIAN ASSOCIATIONS OF THE UNITED STATES OF AMERICA, HELD IN BUFFALO, DECEMBER 3-6, 1924

I know you do not want to make it more difficult for me, but you certainly have. Your call has not come suddenly, and yet I find myself with no prepared words. How can I find myself? Never have I passed through such a period of uncertainty as during the past few months—uncertainty which has continued to this very day. The International Committee has had a provision by which its secretaries retire at the age of sixty. I have never had any other thought or purpose than that I should comply with this regulation. I could not imagine myself, nor could you, permitting an exception to be made in my case. Then all of you are familiar with my spoken and printed messages in which during recent years I have voiced as one of my deepest convictions that we who have been carrying the chief responsibilities for the Movement must give way to the oncoming generation, that we must transfer our burdens to younger shoulders, that we must pass on the great torch to the more ardent hands of youth. This conviction is stronger today than it ever was, and it adds to the difficulty of the position in which you place me.

You should all know, what not a few present already know, that in recent years there have been pressed upon me most important and urgent appeals from trusted leaders of the Churches, both at home and overseas, calling upon me to place my experience at their service in some of the larger constructive plans of the Kingdom. I have been looking forward to the day when I might make to them some worthy response. It has been these facts and considerations which have made my position so impossible and have kept mind and heart in such a state of unrest as your letters and your personal interviews have multiplied, all appealing to me to stand by, at least through the transitional period from the old to the new regime. Do not misunderstand me. While life lasts I shall treasure these letters, and I shall leave them to my children.

Three times was I called to the general secretaryship of the International Committee. The first time I declined the call, although Mr. Morse insisted that I keep it before me two years, that is, during the period of my first world journey. The call was renewed about ten years later and was promptly declined. Nearly a decade later it was pressed upon me again by my friends Wilfred Fry and Fred Shipp. It was not the arguments about the importance of the work, or about the greatness of the opportunity, through which God spoke to me, but the presentation of fact showing that I was absolutely needed. My friends, the experience of these recent days, and, in particular, of these last hours, has been similar to that through which my wife and I passed in 1915 in the spacious areas of the Pacific Coast. Your insistent, united appeal has become cumulative. It seems to be a case where I must distrust myself and trust you. It seems to be a time when I must follow my heart rather than my reasoning. Through the experiences of these difficult days I see something else—that Hand, which hitherto I have found to be an unerring Hand. It has been a loving Hand. It has carried me over continents and seas through countless perils, and has overshadowed and protected my wife and children. And, as I have tried to tell sinful and tempted men of all nations, it is a pierced Hand. It has often pointed to lonely, difficult places but it has never misled. Did I not believe that it was His Hand beckoning me to identify myself with you for what you call a necessary, but in my hope still a limited, period, I should not feel that I could go forward.

And now, as I consent to go with you another stage in our journey of united service on behalf of the young manhood and boyhood of the nations, I want to tell you what my understanding is of the conditions on which I accept your generous and deeply moving call, for, if I am wrong, it is not too late for you to stop me. My understanding is that you are calling me (your spokesman said to lead) to serve a united Movement. I say quite frankly, I should not hear the call of God if there were un-Christian divisions among us, and if we were entering upon a period of misunderstanding, suspicion, and controversy. I interpret it rather to mean that you ask me to go with you in a united brotherhood, in an ever-deepening fellowship in which no rifts can be found.

It is my understanding also that we are committed to a forward and, at the same time, an intensive Movement at home and abroad. Here again you will correct me if I am wrong. If God has spoken any word to this Council and to our brotherhood it has been an unmistakable summons to spread the healing and protecting branches of our Movement far more widely as well as to sink its life-giving roots much more deeply. We are to press onward, not to mark time, nor to recede. If I have mistaken your wish and purpose, I must heed other voices of the Church which summon me to identify myself with her onward and intensive movements.

This reminds me that in calling me to stand by and carry on, you are not asking me to sever my official relationship to those other interdenominational and international movements which I have been serving. Would that I could have served them better! They evidently need me more now than ever. If such continued service is not possible, I must ask the General Board to reconsider this action. Happily the Church is not divided against itself and these different services in her name are mutually supporting. I would hope that I could clear matters so that, with the exception of a few weeks, I might give the next twelve months almost without interruption to the great tasks now in hand right here in our own native land. I could not, however, delay beyond that responding to certain appeals involving our own work as well as other interests of the Christian Church beyond the seas. It is due you all that I should thus share with you the essential facts in my situation.

It is my clear understanding, moreover, that we are all committed to one of the great guiding principles of the Cleveland Constitutional Convention—that of the decentralization, devolution, or distribution of the burdens of administration or management of the work. This is to apply not only to the home field, which has been chiefly in our discussions during the past few years, but also and equally to the work of the foreign field. You are calling me to help work out with you this process of decentralization with the belief that it will insure a more widely distributed, and a more efficient service to the young men at home and abroad.

And am I not right, that you do not call me to stand alone? The genius and spirit of this Council is that we are to bear one another's burdens. This very afternoon we are to have a test, that is, when we face up to the budget for the first year of the life of the Council. If we, the members of the Council, assume this as a united burden, as I understand we mean to do, we shall lift it in a way that no other fund has ever been raised in this brotherhood, and set a fresh example to organized Christianity. I repeat, you do not mean to call me to a lonely post. But, if you were to ask me to describe the chief emotion which, prior to this hour, has been sweeping over my heart ever since I came to Buffalo, even in the midst of the terribly busy hours we have been spending here as well as in some of the wakeful hours of the watches of the night, it has been the feeling of loneliness. How strange it should be so in such a fellowship, and in the midst of such unselfish activities! And yet I am glad to say that emotion has given way before the explosive power of another, namely, the emotion of joy because of the deepening consciousness of our spiritual unity in a common sacrificial service. With a sense of unworthiness I accept your call. God sparing my life, I will serve you and with you to the very limit of my powers, even though it be for a restricted period. And I shall welcome the day (not that I want to leave this wonderful fellowship), when you say to me, "We can now let you go to respond to some of the other calls of the Church founded by our Lord and Savior and purchased by His precious blood."

PRESIDENT LYON: I am sure I speak the language of each heart here, when I say that we enter into the spirit of what Dr. Mott has said, and assent not only to the letter but to the spirit of the conditions upon which he continues to serve with us in this great cause. And may God help us, every one, to bear the burdens that come to us mutually in the service of this great brotherhood.

PROPOSED DRAFT OF AGREEMENT*

BETWEEN THE INTERNATIONAL COMMITTEE OF YOUNG MEN'S CHRISTIAN ASSOCIATIONS, THE NATIONAL COUNCIL OF THE YOUNG MEN'S CHRISTIAN ASSOCIATIONS OF THE UNITED STATES OF AMERICA, AND THE NATIONAL COUNCIL OF THE YOUNG MEN'S CHRISTIAN ASSOCIATIONS OF CANADA, REGARDING FUTURE RELATIONSHIPS BETWEEN THE YOUNG MEN'S CHRISTIAN ASSOCIATIONS OF THE UNITED STATES AND CANADA

For over half a century the Young Men's Christian Associations of the United States and Canada have been bound together in fellowship and service. Marked advantages have been realized through these years from the constant interchange of experience and from international fellowship in thought, prayer, and work. The providential relation of the two countries, as to geographical position, intermingling of peoples, and common Church problems and responsibilities, accentuates the desirability of the policy and practice of co-operation. Moreover, there is the inevitable reaction of the two nations upon each other on the lower levels, and the consequent need of helping each other to safeguard the highest ideals. Add to all this the great and unique responsibility of the English-speaking countries in world service, and there can be no question as to the wisdom of adopting a policy which will enable these two strong and independent national Movements to continue to move forward together in most helpful relation to each other. Therefore be it

    I. *Resolved,* That the International Committee of Young Men's Christian Associations be continued for the purpose of holding and safeguarding the property interests already committed to it, or which may hereafter be committed to it, and in which the Associations of the United States and Canada have a common interest.

    II. *Resolved,* That the Associations of the two countries unite from time to time in a common International Convention. The National Coun-

---

* *National Council Bulletin Supplement,* June, 1925.

cils of the Associations of the two countries shall appoint a joint committee which shall be responsible for the calling and conducting of each such convention. The functions of these conventions will be as follows:

1. To help preserve the historic unity in spirit, purpose, and program of the Associations of the United States and Canada;
2. To provide for representatives of the Associations of the United States and Canada opportunities for interchange of experience and opinion concerning all Association interests;
3. To provide stated occasions for a general inspirational assembly in which every Association of the United States and Canada may have direct representation;
4. To consider and to act jointly on matters affecting the basis of membership of the Associations of the United States and Canada.
5. To make recommendations to the National Council of the Young Men's Christian Associations of the United States, and to the National Council of the Young Men's Christian Associations of Canada, concerning any other matters affecting both Movements.

III. *Resolved,* That the National Councils of the United States and Canada continue the policy of the exchange of services on behalf of the Associations of the two countries. This interchange of services shall be effected through the agency of the two Councils.

IV. *Resolved,* That the following plan shall be followed in the conduct of the common foreign work of the Associations of the two countries:

1. That there be constituted a joint Foreign Committee of the National Councils of the Young Men's Christian Associations of the United States of America and of Canada for the purpose of conducting the foreign work of the Associations of the two countries;
2. That said joint committee consist of the Foreign Division Committee appointed by the National Council of the Young Men's Christian Associations of the United States of America, and the Foreign Work Committee of the National Council of the Young Men's Christian Associations of Canada;
3. That the name of said joint committee shall be the Foreign Committee of the National Councils of the Young Men's Christian Associations of the United States and Canada;
4. That the Executive Committee of said Foreign Committee shall consist of twelve members, nine of whom shall be members of the Foreign Division Committee of the National Council of the United States of America, and three of whom shall be members of the Foreign Work Committee of the National Council of the Young Men's Christian Associations of Canada, this joint Executive Committe to act as one committee;
5. That the by-laws and the commission governing the acts and defining the responsibilities of the Foreign Division Committee of

the National Council of the Young Men's Christian Associations
of the United States of America be referred to the said Foreign
Committee and that when the said committee itself agrees upon a
revision of the by-laws of the commission, these revisions will be
submitted to the appropriate governing bodies for their consideration and action.

V. *Resolved,* That the trustees of the International Committee in distributing the income of undesignated endowment funds shall be free to
allocate funds to the joint foreign work and to the home work of the
two Councils as it may deem best. In allocating funds to the home
work of the two Councils it shall make said allocation to the two
Councils in such proportions as the actual contribution income of each
Council for its home work in the preceding fiscal year bears to the total
actual contribution income of the two Councils for their home work
in the preceding fiscal year.

VI. *Resolved,* That there shall be consultation between the representatives
of the Personnel Division of the National Council of the United
States and the corresponding committee of the National Council of
Canada with reference to determining how these two committees may
be mutually most helpful.

VII. *Resolved,* That with reference to the World's Alliance of Young Men's
Christian Associations, the present relation of the International Committee to the World's Alliance be replaced by the plan of having each
of the two National Councils become a constituent member of the
World's Alliance of Young Men's Christian Associations.

CONSTITUTION OF THE NATIONAL COUNCIL OF THE YOUNG MEN'S CHRISTIAN ASSOCIATIONS OF THE UNITED STATES OF AMERICA

(This Constitution, the work of the Constitutional Convention held in
Cleveland, Ohio, October 17-23, 1923, was adopted by referendum vote of the
Young Men's Christian Associations of North America and amended at the
Second Annual Meeting of the National Council held in Washington, D. C.,
October 27-29, 1925, and at the Fifth Annual Meeting of the National Council
held in Chicago, Illinois, October 22-25, 1928.)

PREAMBLE

We, the Young Men's Christian Associations of the United States and
Canada, through our representatives in constitutional convention assembled,
reverently and joyfully confessing our faith in Jesus Christ our Lord and only
Savior and our unswerving allegiance to His Church, recognizing humbly the

creative hand of God along the pathway of three-quarters of a century of corporate experience, and dedicating ourselves afresh to our great mission of bringing under the sway of His Kingdom the young manhood and boyhood of North America and of the other lands served by our Associations, and with the desire of conserving all the values of our past and likewise of unifying and strengthening our work so as to enable the North American Associations to meet the requirements of the modern age and of the coming day, hereby adopt the following Constitution of the National Council of the Young Men's Christian Associations of the United States of America.

ARTICLE I
MEMBER ASSOCIATIONS

SECTION 1.—Those Associations shall be entitled to representation in the National Council which signify their acceptance of this Constitution and which annually certify to the National Council that their voting membership and governing board have been elected or appointed in conformity with the basis of voting membership and control as determined by the International Conventions of the Young Men's Christian Associations of North America.

SECTION 2.—The autonomy of the Associations herein described shall be preserved. All ultimate authority concerning said Associations not delegated to any other body shall remain vested in said Associations.

SECTION 3.—The Associations shall, through their representatives, have control of their General Agencies as herein provided.

SECTION 4.—The Associations having control of the General Agencies as herein provided shall be responsible for their moral and financial support.

ARTICLE II
COMPOSITION OF THE NATIONAL COUNCIL

SECTION 1.—The member Associations of each state or interstate[2] area or group shall, in convention assembled, divide their Associations into electoral districts according to territory or types of Associations. Each electoral district shall be composed of each complete 4,000 voting members of member Associations, sixteen years of age or over, provided, however, that the Associations of any state or interstate area which, in addition to one or more units of 4,000 each, have additional voting members in excess of one-half of 4,000 shall be entitled to the formation of an additional electoral district for such major fraction, and provided that the member Associations of each state or interstate area shall have at least one electoral district.

SECTION 2.—From each electoral district there shall be elected to the National Council three council members, two of whom shall be laymen.

SECTION 3.—The National Council shall have power to change from time to time the ratio of voting members composing electoral districts provided that

---

[2] At its meeting on June 3, 1924, the Committee of Thirty-three ruled "that wherever the words 'state or interstate' appear in the Constitution they shall be understood to apply equally to a territorial organization."

the Council shall be composed of not less than 300 or more than 400 members, all of whom shall be voting members of member Associations, sixteen years of age or over.

SECTION 4.—The members of the National Council shall hold office for three years. The first Council so elected shall divide itself into three classes, one of which shall hold office for one year, one for two years, and one for three years. Thereafter, all members shall be elected for three years.

SECTION 5.—There shall be twenty-one members-at-large of the National Council additional to the members elected from the electoral districts. These shall be nominated by the Nominating Committee, in consultation with the chairmen of the divisions concerned, and elected by the National Council in a manner to meet the need of representation by the several committees.

SECTION 6.—The general secretary and not less than ten or more than thirty additional members of the staff of the National Council, including representatives of the foreign field, the senior secretary of each state and interstate organization, and the president of each Y.M.C.A. college, as selected by the National Council, shall have the right to a seat and voice in the annual meetings of the National Council but without vote. Such staff members shall be subject to interpellation in accordance with the rules of the National Council.

ARTICLE III
MEETINGS OF THE NATIONAL COUNCIL

SECTION 1.—The National Council shall meet annually at such time and place, and at such other times and places, as it may itself determine.

SECTION 2.—The officers of the National Council shall be a president, four vice-presidents, and a recording secretary, all of whom shall be elected annually.

SECTION 3.—The National Council may make provision for auxiliary assemblies of the various types of Associations to meet preferably in conjunction with or immediately prior to the meetings of the National Council. Such assemblies may formulate plans, policies, and programs for work in their respective departments. All findings shall be subject to approval by the National Council.

ARTICLE IV
POWERS AND FUNCTIONS OF THE NATIONAL COUNCIL

The National Council shall have power:

SECTION 1.—To elect its officers and such committees as may be required and to make its own by-laws and rules of procedure. All committees of the Council shall be directly responsible thereto.

SECTION 2.—To create such committees and other subdivisions as may be necessary for the execution of the policies which it may determine; to delegate to them its executive functions, and to define the distinctive field and functions of each. Membership on such committees or other subdivisions may, and as a rule shall, include not only members of the National Council, but also those who are not members. All actions of such committees or other subdivisions shall be subject to approval by the National Council.

SECTION 3.—To determine the policies to be followed by its committees and other subdivisions and to instruct them concerning the methods to be followed in executing such policies.

SECTION 4.—To devise ways and means necessary for the financial support of its various committees and other subdivisions and to approve the budgets necessary for the same.

SECTION 5.—To establish state and interstate organizations where not already established and to strengthen them in their work of extension and supervision.

SECTION 6.—To extend Association work through its own regional organization by means of personnel or by financial assistance, into fields which local, state, or interstate organizations are unable effectively to occupy, and to place such missionary activities and fields upon a self-sustaining basis at the earliest practicable moment.

SECTION 7.—To encourage, train, and strengthen state or interstate organizations so as to enable them effectively to take over the financial support and close supervision of such missionary activities and fields; provided, however, that nothing contained in this section shall prevent the National Council from exercising close supervision itself, so far as possible, in co-operation with state or interstate organizations, over such activities or fields which are clearly beyond the power of any one state or interstate organization closely to supervise effectively. The National Council shall commit to state organizations as rapidly as can be done effectively its entire supervision of local and intrastate work.

SECTION 8.—To review and report concerning the efficiency of state or interstate organizations as provided in Article VII, Section 4.

SECTION 9.—To represent the Associations, nationally and internationally, in their relations to governments, to Church bodies, to the World's Alliance of Young Men's Christian Associations, and to other national or international bodies, and also in any other spheres where national or international action of the Associations is required or desired.

SECTION 10.—To initiate work in other lands and to co-operate with national committees in such lands.

SECTION 11.—To have prepared and to review the budgets of the National Council, the state and interstate organizations, and the training agencies as provided in Article VIII.

SECTION 12.—To take and hold property and trust funds through proper committees or trustees either with or without incorporation.

SECTION 13.—To employ a general secretary and such other secretaries and other employees as may be required to enable the National Council to discharge the functions herein named.

SECTION 14.—To have general oversight of the plans of the national secretarial cabinet as herein provided.

SECTION 15.—To suggest goals and ideals of work for local Associations and state and interstate organizations.

SECTION 16.—To enact all necessary legislation to carry out the powers herein granted.

ARTICLE V
ORGANIZATION OF THE NATIONAL COUNCIL

SECTION 1.—The National Council shall establish a General Board consisting of not less than twenty-five members selected from the members of the Council, to which shall be assigned such regular and special responsibilities as the Council may deem necessary.

SECTION 2.

(1) The National Council shall establish a Home Division, a Personnel Division, a Student Division, and a Foreign Division through which its services at home and abroad shall be distributed.

(2) Each division shall be composed of twenty-seven members, to be selected by the Council from within and without its own number with due regard to equitable representation thereon of geographical areas and groups or types of Associations. The Association colleges and the Association summer schools shall have representation on the Personnel Division.

(3) Each division shall create such subdivisions and appoint such committees as may be necessary or desirable for the discharge of the responsibilities assigned to each.

SECTION 3.—There shall be a national secretarial cabinet composed of the general secretary, the chief executive secretary of each principal committee or other subdivision of the National Council, including the regional executive secretaries, the senior secretaries of the state and interstate organizations, and the presidents of the Y.M.C.A. colleges, for the purpose of insuring the unity and efficiency of the secretarial forces of these agencies. The General Board shall have general oversight of the plans of the national secretarial cabinet.

SECTION 4.—There shall be stated conferences of groups of national and state specialist secretaries for the purpose of furthering united planning and action.

ARTICLE VI
REGIONAL ORGANIZATION

SECTION 1.—In each region there shall be a regional cabinet composed of the regional executive secretary and the senior state or interstate secretaries of the region. The purpose of the regional cabinet shall be to insure the unity and efficiency of the secretarial forces of the region and to avoid duplication of effort.

ARTICLE VII
STATE AND INTERSTATE ORGANIZATIONS

SECTION 1.—In those states which do not already have state or interstate organizations elected by thoroughly democratic processes, local Associations shall effect such organization. Voting for representatives in such state or interstate organizations shall be by electoral districts or in some other democratic way.

SECTION 2.—Each state or interstate organization shall be responsible for the development of the national policies and programs within its area, in accordance with the national policies established by the local Associations in National Council assembled.

SECTION 3.—Each state or interstate organization shall elect its state or interstate secretary after approval by the National Council, which secretary shall become the executive in the area concerned of the state or interstate organization and of the National Council. He shall hold office so long as he may be acceptable to both agencies. His salary shall be paid by the state or interstate organization concerned.

SECTION 4.—Upon petition of 20 per cent of the local Associations of any state or interstate area, the National Council shall appoint a special committee to review the efficiency of the work of the state or interstate organization of the area concerned and report its findings and recommendations to the officers of the state or interstate organization, and to its regular convention, and to report the action taken thereon to the National Council.

ARTICLE VIII
ANNUAL BUDGETS

SECTION 1.—Each state or interstate organization and each training agency shall prepare its proposed budget for the ensuing fiscal year and submit the same to the General Board of the National Council at least sixty days before the opening session of the annual meeting of the National Council.

SECTION 2.—The General Board of the National Council shall cause to have prepared the total budgets of the National Council, the state and interstate organizations, and the training agencies for the ensuing fiscal year, and shall have the same distributed in analyzed form with the suggestions of the General Board to each of the state or interstate organizations, training agencies, and the member Associations at least thirty days before the opening session of the annual meeting of the National Council.

SECTION 3.—Each state or interstate organization shall review and may make to the National Council suggestions concerning the proposed national budget.

SECTION 4.—Where there is any disagreement concerning the budget of any state or interstate organization or training agency between the agency concerned and the General Board, after further review by the two agencies involved, the state or interstate organization or training agency shall have power to adopt its own budget.

SECTION 5.—The national budget shall be finally adopted and apportioned by the National Council.

ARTICLE IX
JUDICIAL BOARD

SECTION 1.—The National Council at its first meeting shall elect from members of member Associations, excluding members of the General Board of the National Council, a Judicial Board of nine members who shall serve, three for a term of one year, three for a term of two years, and three for a term of three years; thereafter one-third to be elected annually by the National Council to serve for a term of three years. Two-thirds of the members of the Judicial

Board shall be laymen and one-third employed officers. A majority of the Board shall consider all cases, except as hereinafter provided:

SECTION 2.—The functions of the Judicial Board shall be:

(1) Upon request of the National Council or of its General Board, or of any General Agency of the Associations, to interpret and construe this Constitution;

(2) Upon like request, to advise as to the interrelation and scope of the activities of any agency or agencies created, authorized, or recognized under the terms of this Constitution;

(3) Upon petition of any one or more Associations or agency or agent, to compose differences involving the construction of this Constitution or of any act or resolution of the National Council;

(4) Upon request of both parties to any controversy not necessarily involving a construction as above defined, arising from the conduct or the activities of any Association, or of any agency, or of any representative of either, to decide the same, or to bring about conciliation, so as to clear up misunderstandings, define responsibilities, and promote harmony in cooperative activities. One or more members of the Board authorized by the chairman of the Board may function under this subsection.

SECTION 3.—The findings, conclusions, decisions, and recommendations of the Board or of its members shall be final and conclusive, subject to review, upon petition of the aggrieved parties, by the National Council.

SECTION 4.—The expenses incident to the work of the Judicial Board shall be included in the budget of the National Council.

SECTION 5.—The Judicial Board shall formulate and prescribe rules to govern its organization and procedure.

ARTICLE X
RELATION TO INTERNATIONAL CONVENTION

SECTION 1.—In adopting this Constitution, the Associations of the United States desire and understand that their historic union with the Associations of the Dominion of Canada in the International Convention of the Young Men's Christian Associations of North America be and is continued, and that no provision of this Constitution shall affect such union save as such provision shall have been approved by the International Convention of the Young Men's Christian Associations of North America.

ARTICLE XI
PROVISIONS FOR INITIATIVE VOTING

SECTION 1.—The governing body of any member Young Men's Christian Association may petition the other Young Men's Christian Associations of the United States in behalf of any proposal, and when any 10 per cent of the whole number of member Associations reported in the latest Association Yearbook shall have united in an initiative measure, they shall have the right to file with the general secretary of the National Council their initiative petition proposing any act, resolution, or motion that might be legally proposed and passed by the next meeting of the National Council in open session. Every such initiative petition shall include the full text of the act, resolution, or motion demanded.

SECTION 2.—The general secretary of the National Council shall cause said initiative petition and the act, resolution, or motion demanded to be printed in *Association Men* in the next ensuing issue going to press after the filing of such petition. The petitioners and those opposing said measure shall each be entitled to not exceeding two pages of argument and explanation thereof in each of the two succeeding consecutive monthly issues of *Association Men,* after the publication of the measure and petition. In case more words shall be submitted by either those favoring or those opposing the measure than can be printed within the two pages of space so allotted, the editor shall have authority to reduce same to the limit allotted.

SECTION 3.—At the same time as the first publication in *Association Men* of any initiative petition and the act demanded, the general secretary of the National Council shall send a copy of the complete text of said initiative petition and act to the president of each member Young Men's Christian Association listed in the latest Association Yearbook. He shall also send with such petition and act full notice of the election to be held thereon and the blank ballot for the use of the local Association concerned.

SECTION 4.—In voting thereon each member Association shall be entitled to one vote for the first 200 active members or fractional part thereof, and to one additional vote for each 300 active members or major fraction thereof, additional to the first 200 active members as reported in the latest Association Yearbook.

SECTION 5.—The board of directors, committee of management, cabinet, or other governing body of each member Association shall determine the manner in which and by whom, the votes of said Association shall be determined and cast, according to its own rules, providing that the voting shall be either by ballot of its active membership, or by formal resolution of its governing body.

SECTION 6.—If a majority of the votes cast on any such initiative measure by all the Associations voting thereon shall be in favor of any initiative measure so submitted, it shall thereby become a law of the National Council the same as though passed in open session.

SECTION 7.—Any act, resolution, or motion so proposed by initiative petition and approved by a majority of the votes of the Associations voting thereon shall be subject to repeal or amendment by any succeeding meeting of the National Council in like manner as though said act, resolution, or motion had in the first instance been passed by the National Council.

SECTION 8.—Voting on any petition shall close ninety days following the date of the first issue of *Association Men* containing said petition and act. Ballots shall reach the office of the general secretary of the National Council not later than midnight of the ninetieth day following the date of said first publication. If such a day falls on a Sunday or a holiday, the next succeeding business day shall be counted as the closing day for the receipt of ballots. Ballots received thereafter shall be null and void.

SECTION 9.—The ballots shall provide for each Association to vote "yes" or "no." The number of votes of each Association shall be computed by the tellers who canvass the returns. Each ballot shall certify that it is cast by a vote of the active members or the governing board of the Association concerned, and shall be valid only when it does so certify, and is signed by the president or the duly authorized official of the governing board of the Association concerned. No vote shall be valid except when reported on a duly certified official ballot. After having filed its ballot with the general secretary of the National Council, an Association may not change its vote.

SECTION 10.—The initiative petitioners in proposing and filing their petitions shall also designate the names of two or more persons from whom the general secretary of the National Council shall elect one to act as teller and canvasser of the vote, and said general secretary shall also select and appoint two other persons to act as tellers and canvassers of the vote. Within three days following the close of said election, the general secretary of the National Council shall call together the three tellers provided for above who shall open, count, and canvass the vote on such measure and certify the same to the general secretary of the National Council. The latter shall cause the same to be published in the next succeeding issue of *Association Men* going to press, and shall also report same to the next succeeding meeting of the National Council.

ARTICLE XII
PROVISIONS FOR REFERENDUM VOTING

SECTION 1.—Any 10 per cent of the total number of member Young Men's Christian Associations reported in the latest Association Yearbook shall have the right to file their referendum petition with the general secretary of the National Council any time within ninety days after the closing session of a meeting of the National Council, demanding by such petition the submission to all the member Associations of any act, resolution, or motion approved by said Council, said submission being for approval or rejection of said act, resolution, or motion by a majority of the votes cast by the Associations for and against same.

SECTION 2.—The general secretary of the National Council shall cause said referendum petition and the act, resolution, or motion against which it is filed, to be printed in *Association Men* in the next ensuing issue going to press after the filing of such petition. The petitioners and those opposing said measure shall each be entitled to not exceeding two pages of argument and explanation thereof, in each of the two succeeding consecutive monthly issues of *Association Men* after the publication of the measure and petition. In case more words shall be submitted by either those favoring or those opposing the measure than can be printed within the two pages of space so allotted, the editor shall have authority to reduce the same to the limit allotted.

SECTION 3.—At the same time as the first publication in *Association Men* of any referendum petition and the act against which it is filed, the general secretary of the National Council shall send a copy of the complete text of said referendum petition and act to the president of each member Young Men's Christian Association listed in the latest Association Yearbook. He shall also send with such petition and act full notice of the election to be held thereon, and the blank ballot for the use of the local Association concerned.

SECTION 4.—In voting thereon, each member Association shall be entitled to one vote for the first 200 active members or fractional part thereof and to one additional vote for each 300 active members or major fraction thereof additional to the first 200 active members as reported in the latest Association Yearbook.

SECTION 5.—The board of directors, committee of management, cabinet, or other governing body of each member Association shall determine the manner in which, and by whom, the votes of said Association shall be determined and cast, according to its own rules, providing that the voting shall be either by ballot of its active membership or by formal resolution of its governing body.

SECTION 6.—If a majority of the whole number of votes cast by all the Associations voting be against any measure so submitted by referendum petition it shall thereby be repealed and in no more force or effect in like manner and in like effect, as though it had been repealed by a majority vote at a meeting of the National Council in open session, provided no referendum vote shall be effective unless the total vote cast shall at least equal the total number of voting delegates present at the last preceding meeting of the National Council as recorded in the report of said meeting.

SECTION 7.—Voting on any petition shall close ninety days following the date of the first issue of *Association Men* containing said petition and acts. Ballots shall reach the office of the general secretary of the National Council not later than midnight of the ninetieth day following the date of said first publication. If such day falls on a Sunday or a holiday, the next succeeding business day shall be counted as the closing day for the receipt of ballots. Ballots received thereafter shall be null and void.

SECTION 8.—The ballots shall provide for each Association to vote "yes" or "no." The number of votes of each Association shall be computed by the tellers who canvass the returns. Each ballot shall certify that it is cast by a vote of the active members or the governing board of the Association concerned, and shall be valid only when it does so certify and is signed by the president or duly authorized official of the governing board of the Association concerned. No vote shall be valid except when reported on a duly certified official ballot. After having filed its ballot with the general secretary of the National Council, an Association may not change its vote.

SECTION 9.—The referendum petitioners in proposing and filing their petitions shall also designate the names of two or more persons from whom the general secretary of the National Council shall elect one to act as a teller and canvasser of the vote, and said general secretary shall also select and appoint two other persons to act as tellers and canvassers of the vote. Within three days following the close of said election, the general secretary of the National Council shall call together the three tellers provided for who shall open, count, and canvass the vote on such measure and certify the same to the general secretary of the National Council. The latter shall cause same to be published in the next succeeding issue of *Association Men* going to press, and shall also report same to the next succeeding meeting of the National Council.

ARTICLE XIII

AMENDMENTS

SECTION 1.—This Constitution may be amended by vote of two-thirds of the members present at any regular meeting of the National Council, provided notice of such proposed amendment shall have been given at the next preceding regular meeting of the National Council. It may also be amended by initiative petition of 10 per cent of the member Associations of the United States by two-thirds vote of all the votes cast in such election.

THREE YEARS' PROGRAM OF THE NORTH AMERICAN ASSOCIATION MOVEMENT[3]

It is always difficult to look far ahead. If this be true in the case of an individual, much more is it in the case of an organization. Lord Ronaldsay, when asked to speak on the future of India, replied, "God forbid that I should attempt anything so rash."

We are passing through a period when it would seem to be particularly hard to forecast developments and obligations. The situation almost everywhere is still confused, more or less chaotic, yet happily plastic. Such conditions, however, accentuate the importance for a Movement, like that of our Associations, to have clearly defined goals, objectives, and policies, and not to become the creature of emergencies, changing now here, now there, as a result of conflicting voices. True, there will always be crises and unanticipated situations.

Difficult though it may be, we should seek to look further into the future than one year. This is particularly desirable in an organization world-wide in extent.

Without assuming the role of prophet, let us with such knowledge as we possess of the fields we are called upon to serve, of the conditions and trends which are apparent, and of our guiding principles, attempt to forecast the cardinal points of policy on which we as a Movement shall unite for the next three years. In the program which I now outline I will seek also to reflect the chief points of emphasis which have been brought out during the two meetings of the past few days here in Atlantic City.

1. In the very front line of our policy let us place the augmenting and strengthening of the leadership of the Movement. We should seek to realize the high hopes entertained throughout the brother-

---

[3] As outlined by John R. Mott at the annual meeting of the National Council Staff at Atlantic City in November, 1925.

hood regarding the mission and proper functioning of the Personnel Division. To achieve this we must mass the best experience, thought, and effort of the ablest and most influential men of the brotherhood, on the discovery and enlisting for the Association secretaryship of at least a few hundreds of the choicest men of the new generation. The aim should be to win these men one by one and, in placing them, to be influenced by the requirements and the possibilities of each individual case. For the purpose of equipping young men we should perfect and correlate the training processes of the Associations.

To this end, we need to enlist the best thought, not only within the Movement, but of all such men outside Association ranks as are best-qualified by experience to give counsel on the training of workers for religious leadership. It would seem wise to make effective the best features of the Certification Plan. In furtherance of this aim there should be carried forward intensive educational processes with boards of directors, and the chief executive officers of leading Associations, with reference to insuring more fully the satisfactory economic status, the stability, and the permanence of the profession. These leaders should become fully acquainted with the whole personnel program and policy in order that they may understand the great importance of the necessity for discriminating selection and proper training of employed officers. The chief executive officers of the Associations and the General Agencies should from time to time thoughtfully review the secretarial forces with reference to desirable elimination, transfer, and promotion of men.

May it not be well to consider the adoption of a plan to let the workers devote six months out of every given five years to advanced study or to some specialized work in a new field, at home or abroad?

Wisely directed, concerted plans should be put in operation to increase greatly the voluntary lay forces of the Movement. We should endeavor to enlist more mature young men of the type represented by Charles P. Taft and William Speers. At this time, may we not well revert to the proposal of Mr. John D. Rockefeller, Jr. at the Cleveland International Convention? Could we not well afford to organize a special effort to draw a large force of laymen into active service in the Association?

It is through enlistment of the right personalities that the Association will achieve the most vital success. Our main quest, therefore, should ever be that of the discovery of these right personalities. Having enlisted them we should constantly seek to further their development and largest expression.

2. During the coming years there should be a great increase in the material resources of the Movement. We should add in the

United States alone $50,000,000 to the investments in modern buildings and endowments during the next three years. In our new buildings we should enter into the heritage of the rich experience of our Association agencies, in particular our chief authorities as to building plans, programs, and management. This period should also see the successful launching of the fifth foreign Association building program to establish model buildings in another chain of important political, commercial, and educational centers throughout Latin America, Asia, and Europe.

We should also finish the series of buildings for the service of the United States Army and Navy made possible by the war fund.

The long-deferred effort should now be put forth to increase the endowment funds for the national Association work, including also the proposed fund for establishing the educational work of the Associations and some similar provision for the religious work.

In view of the unquestioned financial resources and prosperity of the United States the period right before us is one of which our Movement should take advantage.

3. The financing of the General Agencies must be placed on a more satisfactory foundation. One might almost say it is now or never. Profiting by all the favorable and unfavorable experiences of the brotherhood we should perfect a system of financing the General Agencies which will serve as a model for other religious and philanthropic organizations. We should lead the way in helping to work out a wise policy with reference to community chests and financial federations. No organization has accumulated such a wealth of successful experience in finance, or is so able to command brains, time, and influence of men of financial ability and sagacity, as is the Association Movement. Surely that which has led us in triumph in so many local financial undertakings, and in so many vast and significant national campaigns, will not fail us here. It always seems harder for God to help us this time than the last time. It is not without its advantage, however, that we are by our baffling experience placed repeatedly in positions where we are driven to discover new and better ways, where we are obliged to liberate hidden and sacrificial energies and where we come to have a realizing sense that the influence and the power are from God and not from ourselves.

4. The Association Movement must minister to vastly greater numbers of young men and boys. There is something disconcerting and solemnizing in the fact that for so many years our total membership has hovered so near the million mark instead of sweeping past it from strength to strength. The multiplication, enlargement, and strengthening of the regular Associations will help greatly to extend

our field of service. This must ever be the foundation of our most intensive and productive work, the base for the projection of the largest outreach of the Association beyond its own borders. We must break the apparent deadlock with reference to Christlike expansion, particularly in colored, railroad, industrial, and student fields as well as in totally unoccupied areas.

The Association forces must project the activities under their own direction far more widely in the communities where they are established. They must not lose their propagating power, and to this end their work must be of such high quality that it will be worthy of propagation. To this end vastly more attention must be given in the days right before us to the qualitative aspects of the membership, its distinguishing features. This problem of vitalizing membership, of putting into it a spirit of service as its essential content, is a matter of supreme concern.

Moreover, in some much more masterly and comprehensive way the Association must on its own initiative, place its experience, knowledge, organization, methods, and trained forces at the disposal of the churches and of other agencies which are in a position to influence aright the character, faith, and conduct of young men and boys. Here the highest unselfishness constitutes the highest statesmanship.

5. The Association must be brought to realize the power it possesses for helping to solve the most serious, most emergent problems of our generation. It is not difficult to suggest the serious problems of the present era. We find keen social unrest, especially in industrial areas. Racial antagonisms have become more and more acute and inflamed in recent years in every continent where the American Associations are at work—Asia, Africa, Europe, North and South America and in the island world. The growth of crime and lawlessness among our youth is a serious menace to Christian civilization. International misunderstandings, fears, ambitions, maladjustments, bitterness, and strife show no abatement. Compared with the situation just before the World War there are now more men under arms, more military dictatorships, and more actual wars in progress. Through the friction of economic competition the United States is building up a hatred on the part of other nations. The spirit of war and selfish nationalism must be exorcised.

Another group of serious problems is represented by our failure to dominate and utilize for the highest purposes the enormous material energy, the incomparable scientific enlightenment, and the penetrating philosophy of the modern day for the furtherance of the Kingdom of God in the life of men.

We cannot close our eyes to the question of the readjustment of relationships between men and women. This problem is accentuated by the new position of women and the larger understanding of morals. Increasingly it is becoming apparent that society as a whole will not stand for a double ethical standard for men and women. Will the single standard be a low or a high one? Forces tending to break down our homes are revealed in the startling increase in divorces. In getting at this issue we shall have to work hand in hand with our sister Movement, the Young Women's Christian Association.

The existence, strength, and gravity of these perils, the world over, might well cause consternation were it not for the absolute sufficiency of the Lord Jesus Christ to meet this appalling array. The Association is uniquely fitted to do more perhaps than any other agency to meet, avert, or overcome these momentous dangers. Is it not worldwide in extent? Does it not blend in its membership all nations and races? Has it not evolved a program, methods, and agencies which enable it to become literally all things to all men? The chief difficulty is that the Association leadership and membership have not begun to realize the contribution they might make toward the solution of these grave problems. Therefore they are still unaware of the magnitude of their responsibility.

6. The inquiry now being conducted under the guidance of the World's Committee, with special reference to the attitude of youth toward religion, organized Christianity, Jesus Christ, one another, and the emergent questions of the day has advanced far enough to prompt the startling query as to whether the Young Men's Christian Association in America and elsewhere may not have lost touch with reality.

This should be a period of self-examination. Do we know our facts? Do we know what youth is thinking about, what it believes? Are we aware of the tides of new thought and social passion which are surging through their minds and hearts? Have we sounded the depths of their present-day needs? Are we acutely sensitive to the springs of ideal and motive which most quickly and powerfully move them? Are our program, methods, and message calculated to arrest their attention and to call forth their heroic and sacrificial allegiance? Do we know that we have a new generation in a new environment on our hands, that "the dawn does not come twice to awaken man"? Are we really in the crosscurrents of the most vital interests of this generation? Above all, are we alert to the implications of the timeless Gospel of Jesus Christ for this day and age?

The next three years must see the frank, thoroughgoing, satisfying answers to these penetrating questions, questions which will not be downed. The discovery of these answers may mean nothing less than a reorientation, perhaps a rebirth of the Young Men's Christian Association. All this emphasizes the great importance of our plan to center attention in program and effect on young men of the ages of eighteen to twenty-four. In this connection, we are reminded that co-operation with the Young Women's Christian Association is demanded by the situation, for the destiny of young men in this age is inextricably bound up with that of young women.

7. We are summoned to improve during the next three years the one opportunity which has come, or is ever likely to come, for American Associations to place their experience in the upbuilding of young men and boys at the service of the religious forces of Europe.

This opportunity was not opened to us before the World War. It comes as the chief by-product of the work for Allied armies and prisoners of war. It is an urgent appeal for help from all the neediest nations of Western, Southern, Central, and Eastern Europe, and offers the greatest opportunity for what we believe is the true America to express herself in Europe through the Association.

8. We must help guide the foreign Association work of our Movement in different parts of Asia, Africa, and Latin America through the present most difficult, yet most hopeful stage—a period when these other Movements are passing from foreign leadership and financial backing to indigenous control and to an ever-increasing measure of self support.

This transfer of responsibility is taking place over the whole world. It is taking place at a time of economic, social, intellectual, and political confusion. For that reason every country presents an extremely delicate situation, yet it is a most hopeful sign of the times, for is it not our basic ideal to help those other Movements to a position of final independence? It is hardly necessary to emphasize the fact that only the very strongest and wisest American leadership is of any service in our foreign posts during this critical time. It is a matter for profound thoughtfulness that in these difficult times the Associations of the United States and Canada stand together in the demonstration and support of this foreign work.

9. Scientific surveys, original research, enrichment of program, and the development of the creative aspects of all our work must during the years before us bulk much more largely than hitherto in the thought and policies of the General Agencies as well as of the Associations themselves.

10. How to augment the spiritual vitality and productivity of the Associations must become the chief concern of the leadership of the Movement in all its parts.

We must not be misled by the minor conflicts of the day. The real dangers to our Christian faith lie within, and very deep within. We must face the question as to whether naturalism or supernaturalism shall conquer in our own lives. The moral forces of the world are not now being called out in any such force as will make possible the overcoming of dangers both within and without. If we permit ourselves to think or to give others the impression that our Gospel is not powerful enough to overcome all difficulties, we shall witness the complete devitalization of our Movement. Religious education must come to have its truly central place in our Movement.

We must take upon ourselves in earnest the task of maintaining an abounding spiritual life, of acquiring and preserving at all costs those attitudes, practices, and hopes on which the preservation of such a genuine spiritual experience and such overflowing triumphant spiritual vitality depends. It is not enough to repeat the phrase, "Jesus' way of Life": we must go His way. We must test ourselves. Are men being related to Jesus Christ as a reality through us? Are men being led to a deeper, more vital, more fruitful spiritual experience because of the lives we lead? Are men led to hunger and thirst after righteousness as a result of contacts with us? Are young men being moved mightily to lives of devotion and sacrificial achievement as a result of our service and leadership? Are we in reality "enlargers of the Kingdom"?

BASIC CONFIDENCE ESSENTIAL AND THE SECRET OF INSURING IT

STATEMENT AT NATIONAL COUNCIL MEETING, THURSDAY MORNING, OCTOBER 29, 1925

As I view the whole matter, there are three great elements that must enter into a triumphant united effort for 1926. In the first place, there must be what I would call basic confidence, and the unity that comes out of that. In the second place, there must be a plan that is likewise so elementally sound that it will carry at least measurable conviction on the part of the vast majority of us; and in the third place, we must have the momentum behind us as we run into 1926, of an assured victory beyond question in 1925. I think with these three elements granted, there can be no shade of doubt, long before the end of the year 1926, about where we shall land.

Now, as to this basic confidence let me share with you my own deepest feelings. I have been very much impressed by the way in which this Council has faced up to the larger and somewhat startling proposal of the budgets of 1926. I have been impressed by the thoroughness of the processes employed here in these crowded two days that lie behind us. Much more than by that degree of thoroughness, I have been impressed by the spirit that one was vividly conscious of as he passed from room to room, and as one entered into conversation with little groups of members in the halls and in the rooms. I have also found a spirit of fairness, and a spirit of conscientiousness. Thank God, I will take no memories away of men that have been lacking in candor and lacking in that fine conscientiousness on which any great work ever must rest. I am proud of the spirit of my brothers in this Council.

But there is something about you that has impressed me still more than the thoroughness and the spirit that has been vibrating in your breasts, and that is a sense that I have been conscious of here—and it has meant much to me because there come moments of loneliness with anyone who bears burdens like the burdens you have placed on me —I have been made vividly conscious of a sense of partnership and brotherhood. That word, brotherhood, has a large connotation to me. I think larger if we were to adjourn right now than any previous time in my life. I have seen men here entering into fellowship with what is admittedly a difficult situation, and I thank God for it if it brings us into this deepening fellowship. I have seen men here fulfilling the law of Christ which is clearly expressed by St. Paul when he said, "Bear ye one another's burdens," and notice the context, "and so fulfill the law of Christ." That is, so fill with vital content, with reality, that it is not a form, the law of our Lord. That is the only way it is ever done when men break out of the clutches of their own selfish opinions and considerations to seek honestly to share one another's burdens. It is reasons like these that have given me a sense of joy in the midst of a grave sense of responsibility and burden as I have faced my brothers, and as I have had contacts with them in these busy hours.

Another thing that has pleased me very much, Mr. Chairman, is the conscientious efforts to effect desirable reductions wherever possible. I have been very much gratified. That figure may not look large to some of you, that net saving, that column here in the aggregate as the result of the labors in these different rooms, but to my mind after the exhausting months spent on it, and the months that my colleagues have spent on it, and the General Board, it has meant a great deal to me that men such as we have here have been able to find ways in which we could effect savings that aggregate these few thousands of dollars.

I think something has meant more to me than that, however, and that is that you have discovered certain processes. You have indicated certain measures and asked the General Board if they will adopt them. You have a board here instantly responsive to your desires. We are not something separate from you. We are your exponents. We are on our toes to know your wishes. A number of men have made suggestions in these Council meetings as to measures and processes, concerning which I know I speak for the General Board and my executive colleagues when I say we are only too eager to follow these leads.

I heard a man make a statement that I am quite sure he did not mean in all its implications, and that is that there was an element of resistance on the part of the General Board and staff. My brothers, that is the last thing. We, who are put forward by you to be a continuation body between the meetings of this Council, who must bear the heat and burden through the year, are only too eager to have this burden lightened. My hope is that others who have not had time to speak here in these days, but in the subsequent days on further reflection, if you see here and there a place where you believe with advantage we could reduce this work, with advantage to the brotherhood, that is, to the end that we might have a better service, that we might have a larger fruitage, that by cutting out a man here, or combining two projects there, or in some way can do away with further undesirable duplications and expenses, you will find a ready response. I say that advisedly, a ready response, an eager response. The hardest thing in the world is for one to stand in the presence of uncertainty. The thing we want to do is to be sure that you have found what in your judgment is better, maybe, than ours.

What I am implying in what I am saying here from the heart is that I have long since learned that if you are to have triumphant unity, basic to it must be confidence, and confidence is not built on uncertainty, or mental reservation on the part of a man here or a group there, that the best thing is not being done. It is tantalizing for men to see a thing going forward that we believe is not in the interest of the largest efficiency and fruitage. Therefore, not with any ulterior motive save of the one that you would have dominate me—I say ulterior in the sense of a far-reaching view, that you would wish to have dominate me—I enter the plea that we continue to collaborate not only here in these crowded days, but in these coming months in the study of processes of economy and existing efficiency.

There is all the difference in the world between standing for a policy and effecting economies with resulting efficiency on the one hand, and making an equally conscious and constant endeavor on the other hand to recognize and follow the lead of God as to the larger and better meeting of the needs, and of the opportunities in our service among men. As I see it, these are not contradictory propositions. Some men at times would give you the impression that we are against each other. I do not so see it. I believe that simultaneously we can possibly economize here and there, by combinations as well as eliminations, and at the same time be keenly sensitive to the beckoning hand of Christ which I find is always leading to the constant widening of opportunity and enlargement of service. I have never known Christ to lead men to do less today than they did in the days before to meet the needs of living men. I have never heard Him say, "Call a halt on serving more men tomorrow and serving them a little better than you did today." I do not so read the parable of the talents.

Some of you were at the Cleveland Constitutional Convention and you remember I was asked to give my hopes regarding that Convention, and somewhat offhand, because I had had but a few moments to formulate. I indicated, and it is found in the little pamphlet which was issued after the Convention on the significance of that gathering in which many men shared their vision and thought, a number of the things that I said I hoped we would do before we left the Hollenden Hotel, and I will now read it. I said, "In the second place, we should not leave until something has been done that will issue in great economies. I do not mean that we shall necessarily spend less money. We shall spend vastly more than we have ever dreamed of spending if we are to do the will of God! This country and Canada are not suffering from lack of money. But it is contrary to the will of God that we should waste a dollar. It is not so much the amount of money as it is the widespread conviction that through unnecessary duplication, overlapping, friction, and misunderstanding, we are not spending the money to the very best advantage. I find that the rich men and the poor men are not resenting the spending of their money, if it is in line with the wisest economy, and if every dollar is made to count to the maximum." That expresses better than what I can say today one of my dominating convictions.

So I say the first factor in 1926 that we may well have, and I have no doubts whatever under that heading, we must have this basic confidence in turn resting upon the belief that we are all of one mind in eliminating anything that is wasteful of the talents that God has given us in time and money and plan.

Now having said that, let me come to that second factor that to my mind is essential, and that is that we must in this year 1925 so meet the situation that we shall enter upon 1926 without a handicap. There can be nothing more serious, no matter how good the plan, than for us to enter upon that new year with a deficit. I said to a group yesterday when we were talking about a deficit, This is no day to talk about a deficit, two months before the end of the year 1925. I do not propose to let that word deficit get into my vocabulary until the clock has struck twelve, the last day of December." We have not yet had a deficit. In reality, one year the Foreign Department had a deficit, which I explained yesterday to some men, by having to close the books because we could not count some subscriptions that came in after the closing of the books. We have not yet had a deficit, in over forty years. This is a matter of many, many days of reflection; this is the last year that I have known in my life when we should even contemplate a deficit, and I give you my reasons.

We are not yet at the crest, but there is a rising tide that is rapidly mounting toward a crest. A rising tide certainly of prosperity. There were issued from the Bureau of Census and also from the Department of Internal Revenue of the Treasury a few months ago, two documents that I have been studying with a great deal of care, that indicated that the latest statistics of 1922 showed that then the United States of America was worth over $320,000,000,000 in gold. The man does not live who can take in the figure. But we can grasp it quickly when that means that the wealth of the United States today is more than the combined wealth of Canada, Great Britain, Ireland, France, Germany, Norway, Sweden, Denmark, Finland, Holland, Spain, Italy, Australia, New Zealand, and South Africa. This country therefore is not starving.

Somebody may say, "You talk about 1922, but have we not begun to wane?" Well, I saw Herbert Hoover when I went down to invite him to accept the invitation to speak at the International Convention, and after we finished that business we entered into conversation and I took rapid notes. I asked him whether this country was heading toward economic difficulties and he said things like this: "At present we have very little serious unemployment. Even in the coal area it is not so serious as some people would indicate. But taking the country generally and in contrast with every nation under Heaven, there is very little unemployment." If you had been with me in England, with a million and a quarter of men still unemployed, you would see the vividness of the contrast. His next fact was, that labor was receiving the best wages in all the history of the United States. He added that there have been marvelous increases in all the principal industries and showed me a list of forty. All but three were showing increases. His next statement was that the volume of trade was the largest that it has ever been in the history of our country at this time of the year; that we are producing 30 per cent more now than we were fifteen years ago and that the payments made through the banks to conduct this business are the largest they have ever been known to be. He then stated that we have had the greatest exports thus far this year that we have had in any year save 1920, when the prices then were 30 per cent higher than now, so that in reality, from the money point of view, it has been our greatest export trade year. He insisted that the surplus of exports this year, up to this time, aggregate over $1,000,000,000, and that there has been an unprecedented absorption of new securities in the United States. His next point interested me very much; that the private investment of Americans abroad, not including moneys loaned by the government, is now over $9,500,-000,000.

Some of you heard him state that there has been a most wonderful diffusion of wealth during the last ten years. The popular impression goes that it is the richest men only who are getting it, and then he showed me the statistics of this most fascinating and encouraging general diffusion of wealth, and he summed it up with this point: The financial position of the United States is unquestionably the strongest in all of its history. And last night I read President Coolidge's Thanksgiving Address which came out yesterday morning, and right after I noticed this sentence: "God has blessed us with resources whose potentiality in wealth is almost incalculable." I think that is better than I can sum up what Mr. Hoover said in a sentence of our President, "that God has been a party to it." That ought to give us a sense of solemnity.

It is not only a time of rising tide of prosperity but a rising tide of beneficence. The Boston *Transcript,* in an issue some months ago, said that the gifts of individuals in the United States last year, apart from religion and apart from the gifts of municipal, state, and national governments, were $2,500,000,000 and my studies in other years have showed me that a vastly disproportionate share of that giving is by the Christians and the Jews. I do not suppose if you were to add religion and not speak of governments that anybody would question it. In the whole annals of time there has been nothing like this in any other country, or in our own country.

By the way, this is the better America. This is the America that is not so well understood as it should be. It is the America of unselfishness, of idealism, of imagination, that does not let its right hand know what its left doeth. At a time like this when there is this rising tide of beneficence, surely it is not a time for us to feel that we cannot close the year without a deficit.

And let me say, it is a rising tide of interest in the Young Men's Christian Association. The people have given us in this country over $170,000,000 for buildings and endowments. Besides that, more money has been given by Americans to this organization the last ten years than in the preceding sixty-five years. A man said to me in California not many months ago, "Isn't the Young Men's Christian Association losing out since the period of criticism? I reminded him that we have had more given us since the period of criticism than in any other period in our history and we have never had so much money subscribed to Young Men's Christian Associations, as we have had during the last year, not only for current expenses, but in such large bequests as in these very recent years. Along with all these vast sums given for buildings here at home, you remember in these last years we have gathered about $5,000,000 for buildings abroad. We secured over $1,000,000 for the rehabilitation fund in Japan. We have raised nearly $4,000,000 of our accrued liability in connection with the retirement fund, all in these recent years. So I say, it is a time of growing interest. I do not think I exaggerate when I say that, judged by their giving, we have ten friends now where we had one before the war.

But I would prefer to have you forget the points I have made up to now, although I think they are substantial. The point I now mention, is that it is a time of rising tide of faith. My good friend, Neville Talbot, whom I used to know at Oxford, now a Bishop in South Africa, came out with a little booklet, the title of which I love. The title is *The Returning Tide of Faith*. Most of you men have been on the seashore. I have spent a good deal of time not only on the shore but on the waves. What a different impression it is when the tide begins to come in, and when at times it overleaps the banks. Some of my friends in China have seen the great Hangchow bore where the tide rushes up with dangerous momentum. Some of you have been in St. John, New Brunswick, Canada where the tide rises seventy feet. We know what this returning tide of faith means. My contact through three world organizations shows me that there has never been a time like the present Christward movement among men. It seems as if they are losing confidence in every other source.

You ask what is the bearing of this on the budget of 1925? My brothers, Christ taught that you can do more when you have a rising tide or when you have atmosphere, than you can do in long, weary periods without this advantage. Even Christ could not do His mighty works in Nazareth because of the prevailing unbelief. I sincerely believe there is an atmosphere of belief now surging all around us— an atmosphere of divine resource. I need not say I would not stand here before my God and say what I now say unless it possessed my soul. I believe there is an atmosphere of superhuman resource; therefore, I cannot let my mind dwell on it and believe the things we are talking about are impossible for this great God. I say, forget the millions and this rising tide of prosperity, of beneficence. Let us shut ourselves in alone with Him, and let that be the principal consideration. I have seen many a difficulty melt away in His presence, whereas if we confine ourselves to our own devices some things seem impossible.

Then there is the rising tide of vitality. I may be a poor observer, but Mr. Wanamaker used to call me an expert in opportunity. I said to him, "It would be strange if after all these years of specializing on open doors I could not see them." I am reminded in these recent journeys of the time when I was sent by President Wilson as a member of Senator Root's Commission to Russia. We crossed the breadth of Russia twice at the time when the flowers were coming out. What I saw then reminds me of what I seem to see today, vitality springing from the ground.

I like to think of this organization of ours, not as an organization in the popular sense, but as an organism. Emerson said of Montaigne's words, "They are vascular, cut them and they will bleed." So I think of the Young Men's Christian Association as vascular, as an organism, not a machine. You cut it and it bleeds. I am so glad it is vital. If it ceases to be that and this organization of ours ceases to grow; if the process of atrophy begins to set in, then you and I lose our interest. I said to a man in my room yesterday, if the time ever comes when I am convinced that this time has arrived, I certainly have more important service for my Lord than in the Young Men's Christian Association. Our Lord taught that there should be pruning, and that is what I meant at the outset when I said I am glad the pruning process has been carried forward, not only here but by some of us through long and sacrificial years before this place. I have had to see this work pruned in every department and every field. It is not easy. It is sacrificial. I say it advisedly, but notice the pruning was in order "that the vine might bring forth more fruit." That is the objective, not a end in itself, but with the vision right ahead of more fruit.

There is another tide and then I must stop. That tide we want to remind ourselves here in this very solemn hour is the tide of sacrificial devotion that we are each man a part of. With some of us it is the devotion of our money. I suppose it should be with all of us whether we are rich or whether we are poor. It is hard to tell which is the most potent, the associated rivulets of poverty or wealth. I think Christ meant to put us on a level. If we can use it in that way each one will be equally fruitful. With some of us the sacrificial devotion will be our time, and some men would rather pay in any other coin than time, but I suppose there is not one of us who will escape if we are to win out in these successive enterprises of co-operation. With some of us it is going to be with our advocacy. I suppose it ought to be with all of us. It must be our influence. The man is not here that does not have a range of influence, if we can just place it all here this morning on the altar and let this tide of sacrificial devotion engulf us. Money, time, advocacy, influence—if we can associate it with these, what may not be possible?

I was called out of one meeting the day before we assembled here in this Council, the day the International Convention closed. The General Board was to come together at five-thirty and a man said, "There is a man over here in a hotel who is going to leave on a train at seven o'clock and we think you ought to lay before him our needs." "Well," I said, "can you get me back here in time for the General Board meeting?" He said, "Get in the cab and we will talk that over on the way." We got over and we found he was not in the lobby. We had to hunt up his room. When we got in there he had his coat off. He was on the bed and I said, "Now my friend we are in a very difficult position. Apparently we have got to get between five and six hundred thousand dollars, as it were, out of the blue, in new money —approximately $100,000 for the Home Division and $400,000 for the Foreign Division between now and December 31," and I said, "I have not had time to formulate any long appeal to you but I know you are a man animated by unselfishness, and I am asking you now to trust my judgment. I am making an appeal; would you, or would you not, set apart this calendar year $50,000 toward meeting this great need?" He said, "Mr. Mott, I have given all my profits." I said, "I did not come down here for profits. We are here to deal, if necessary, with principal." I said, "Do there not come moments in the business world when you have to use part of the principal?" He said, "Yes, there are times when we have to do that." I said, "Do there not come moments in your lifetime when you have to meet serious situations, the safeguarding of the interest of Christ's Kingdom, when men have had to look into their principal?" I reminded him that that morning I had a letter from a man, not of large wealth, in which he had said, "I cannot give you any from my income but I send you one hundred shares that are nearly $85 each." I reminded him of that. He said, "I had not thought of it in that light." I said, "By the way, you cannot anticipate your death, you cannot take that money out of the world with you." Then he said, "Would you let me count in what I am already giving toward this work of the National Council?" I said, "Certainly. My appeal was for $50,000 toward the work this year." He said, "Under those conditions I will do it." And I said, "Now let me make clear that we understand ourselves." I said, "I will just write it out and see if we have got it right. 'In addition to what I have already given, or have promised to give in the year 1925, to the different projects of the foreign work, conducted under the supervision of the National Council of the Young Men's Christian Associations of the United States of America, I will give an additional amount to make up with the foregoing, a total of $50,000, payable to the National Council of the Young Men's Christian Associations of the United States of America, on or before December 31, 1925.' " And then with trembling hand (he could not even use my fountain pen) he used my pencil and signed his name. I did not need a witness, but I could have had no better one than Mr. Brockman.

I got back to the General Board just a little late. We had a meeting there about which there is a sense of sacredness. You have a board not concerned simply with the mechanics and money and the popular view of money, although we look upon it in a sense of sacred trust, but you have men there who try to take God into account. It was not on the agenda, but one of our number rose and said he believed that if we were going to meet this Council and share with them our burdens we ourselves must in a very intimate way enter into the fellowship and, perchance, the sacrifice. It was admittedly a sacrifice because every man in the room had made his subscription. But one man said, "I have decided in addition to what I have pledged, I will promise some more toward this balance we must meet." I forget now who it was, but I think Mr. Taft said, "Cannot we have the paper passed that we all may share in it?" Somebody else wanted to speak and then another, and then Mr. Taft, who seems to be quite persistent, said, "I want this paper passed." It was passed back to me. I have never yet revealed those names and I am not going to, but it caused my heart to beat when I saw that twenty Council laymen had subscribed special gifts over and above what they had already given which averaged over $1,000 each, ranging to $6,000. There was also a cluster of ten secretarial members of the General Board of executive officers whose gifts averaged a little over $100 each. It was not the amount of these gifts so much as it was the evident desire to enter into the fellowship. I wish you could have heard the remarks of a colored member of this group who said, "We do not have much of this world's goods to give, but I am willing to go out and give my time, which is still more difficult to give. I am going to put myself alongside of Tobias and go with him to get $5,000 from the colored men toward this money we have still to get." Another man there, who, to my knowledge is a man of very meager income, wrote on his card, "Besides that I am going to get $10 each from the twenty members of our Board of Directors." He said, "I am going to make an earnest effort to get every active member to give something." I said, "If that spirit were to become contagious we have got enough men in this National Council without strain on anybody, except the strain we always like to put upon ourselves under the compulsion of the love of Christ that passeth knowledge. We have enough members here. If all entered in the fellowship with Christ and one another what a wave of teaching might we not sound over the whole brotherhood! What a sense of reality!

I have spoken about tides, my brothers, but I want to leave another word. There is something better than tides. They rise and fall but rivers that proceed from eternal springs do not. I sent my secretary this morning, because I did not trust my memory, to get my New Testament, and I want this message to linger with you from this man of vision. I read from the closing part of the Scriptures, "He showed me the river of the water of life clear as crystal issuing from the throne of God and from the Lamb." You remember what that made possible on the banks of that river—the tree of life, the leaves from which were for the healing of the nations, which is our great mission, to heal all the nations, our own and the others. But the secret of it was that they were on banks that proceeded from the throne of God and the Hand that gave Himself in sacrificial devotion. Let us fix our gaze on that stream, clear as crystal, nothing selfish in it, nothing worldly in it, from the throne of God and of the Lamb.

RESIGNATION OF JOHN R. MOTT FROM THE GENERAL SECRETARYSHIP OF THE NATIONAL COUNCIL OF THE YOUNG MEN'S CHRISTIAN ASSOCIATIONS OF THE UNITED STATES OF AMERICA

June 27, 1928

To the Leaders of the
Young Men's Christian Associations

DEAR FRIENDS:

Dr. John R. Mott, the general secretary of the National Council of the Young Men's Christian Associations, who has been related to this Movement for forty years, placed in the hands of the General Board at its meeting at Meridale Farms on June 22, his resignation, to take effect at the October meeting of the National Council.

The call to a higher and larger service in the presidency of the International Missionary Council which unites the missionary forces of the world, including those of the Association, made it necessary for him, he felt, to sever his official relation as secretary of the American Young Men's Christian Association.

His call to this new service together with his position as president of the World Alliance of the Young Men's Christian Associations, and his intimate relations to work for boys and young men the world around for forty years, places him in a peculiarly favorable position to continue to give counsel to the Associations of America on matters of large policy and on occasions of importance.

His resignation was received with deep regret but not without a recognition of the force of the larger call.

Since his resignation, if accepted, will not take effect until October, no action or official consideration has been given to a possible successor.

We enclose a copy of Dr. Mott's letter of resignation.

Sincerely yours,

ADRIAN LYON,
Chairman of the General Board

MONTCLAIR, NEW JERSEY, June 20, 1928

*To the Members of the General Board
of the National Council*

DEAR FRIENDS:

On my way homeward from Jerusalem I had time and detachment for prolonged and prayerful consideration of the united request of the recent enlarged Meeting of the International Missionary Council that I rearrange my plans so as to devote chief attention to furthering the advanced program adopted at that significant gathering. Subsequent reflection has served only to confirm the decision then reached. Three times before such a call has come to me, but in each case was declined in view of commitments made to the Association, and in deference to the wishes of the brotherhood. With reference to this last appeal of leaders of the missionary forces of the Churches of fifty-one countries at the close of their creative deliberations on the Mount of Olives, I came to see that the path of duty for me is to respond favorably, and, that I may do justice to the new requirements, to lay down at an early date my present responsibilities both with the National Council of the American Associations and with the World's Student Christian Federation. The considerations underlying this conviction and decision may be briefly stated.

The mandates which came to the International Missionary Council during the wonderful Passiontide on Olivet are of such momentous, exacting, and urgent character as to require from its chairman the exercise of all his powers.

In the period just before us our own National Council, in its vital and expanding work in the United States and in the thirty and more other lands which it is serving, will demand the undivided attention of its general secretary.

While I have recovered from the setback my health suffered last year, it is doubtless the course of prudence not to continue to make the demands on my vital energies which I have made for so many years.

The brotherhood well know my oft-expressed conviction that the Young Men's Christian Association, raised up to serve primarily as a youth Movement and happily in North America reverting increasingly to this type, should more and more be led by men of a younger generation than the one I represent. I cannot with a free conscience longer defer acting on this conviction.

Through all the years I have emphasized the central obligation of the Association to serve the Churches and loyally to respond to their call. It has been made unmistakably plain to me that, in addition to any services I may have been privileged to render the Church of Christ through the Association and other channels, this recent authoritative call of the leaders of the Churches has come to me under such circumstances as to constitute a clear mandate.

In view of these considerations, therefore, I place in your hands my resignation from the office of general secretary of the National Council of the Young Men's Christian Associations of the United States of America with the request that the resignation take effect at the coming October meeting of the Council.

By the early autumn I shall have devoted forty years to the service of the North American Association Movement. I cannot without profound emotion contemplate severing this official tie. I am indeed a debtor to the Young Men's Christian Association. It was through that godly Quaker, J. W. Dean, on one of his evangelistic visits to my home village in his capacity as secretary of the state committee of Iowa, that I was led to Christ. It was through the Student Association of Cornell University, as fostered by the New York state committee and the International Committee, in a period when my faith was shaken and I was bent on a selfish course in life, that I discovered Rock Foundation and later received the vision of world service which has never faded and which has dominated every subsequent decision. Again it was that Christlike secretary of the International Committee, Charles K. Ober, and that model layman, Cleveland H. Dodge, chairman of the Student Committee of the International Committee, who drew me by unselfish guile into Association work. It has been the Association which has opened to me doors of service the wide world over —opportunities the like of which have come to few men. Would that I could have improved them better! In the intimacies of the wonderful fellowship which we speak of as the brotherhood, what an unnumbered host of friendships, among secretaries and laymen scattered throughout almost every land under Heaven, have enriched my life. Such bonds cannot be severed no matter what one's official ties. For the confidence, the patience, the loyalty, the affection so unfailingly and so generously shown me during all these crowded years of glorious life I am unfeignedly thankful. In days to come I shall ever esteem it a privilege in a voluntary lay capacity, or as president of the World's Alliance of the Young Men's Christian Associations, to do anything in my power to further the Association and to strengthen the hands of its leaders and members.

To a little band of unnamed friends who for thirty-three of the forty years of my service have provided funds so that my salary and expenses and likewise those of my personal staff have not been a charge on the budget of the Association or of the other agencies to which I have been related is due a tribute of deepest gratitude. Above all would I humbly acknowledge the guiding, protecting, strengthening hand of the loving and ever-creative God vouchsafed on land and sea.

Faithfully yours,

JOHN R. MOTT

TESTIMONIAL DINNER IN HONOR OF DR. JOHN R. MOTT

IN RECOGNITION OF HIS COMPLETION OF FORTY YEARS SERVICE WITH THE INTERNATIONAL COMMITTEE AND THE NATIONAL COUNCIL OF THE YOUNG MEN'S CHRISTIAN ASSOCIATIONS, AT EDGEWATER BEACH HOTEL, OCTOBER 22, 1928

Following the dinner more than 700 associates of Dr. Mott gathered for the occasion, rose and sang "Faith of our Fathers," and "When I survey the wondrous Cross." Judge Adrian Lyon of Perth Amboy, New Jersey, presided as toastmaster.

TOASTMASTER JUDGE LYON: Dr. Mott, honored guests, ladies and gentlemen: This gathering tonight was conceived in an endeavor to do honor to our friend Dr. Mott. Of course any celebration that we might have here would be entirely inadequate to represent the love and affection we have for him, and so it was decided that we should have here tonight what might be called a family party. Now this is going to be a family party in the fullest sense of the word and there are not to be any long faces here tonight. If they are unduly long, we are going to send the men down to the beauty shop and have their faces made over. We are here tonight to have a good time of fellowship and I am glad the men have brought in the women. What would the Young Men's Christian Association be without the help of the women! We have not come in hiding behind their skirts tonight. In fact, we can't do that any more. Someone has said that it is not a coward that hides behind a woman's skirts, it is a magician.

Now I think that you are a mighty good-looking lot of people. I am glad you are, because of this circumstance: When I was coming down in the elevator, I think the first day that I came here, there being another convention in the hotel at the same time, one of the men who was undoubtedly one of our number, asked me about some meeting in connection with our conference, our National Council meeting. I did not have a button on, and as he asked the question, he said, "I assume by your face that you belong to the Young Men's Christian Association." Now just what he meant by that I don't know. It was a peculiar, happy thing to me, because of another circumstance: I was in one of the Superior Court rooms of my state some time ago, and a man came up to me and said:

"How do you do, Judge X?"

I was not the man he thought I was, and I said:

"Excuse me, sir, but I am not Judge X."

"Oh," he said, "I thought you were."

The significance of that is that a few days before that I was at a bankers' banquet and at the table sat Judge X, and a friend of mine who was sitting by me looked up at the man and said:

"That man has the face of a bank burglar, hasn't he?"

Now I am here tonight to introduce some speakers to you. I had an experience summer before last. Coming over in an Atlantic liner, I fell in with two men who were used to sailing on those boats, and they enticed me to bet on the speed of the ship. Those two men were John R. Mott and Fred W. Ramsey. The sad part of it was that I lost. But since they don't sell anything on those ships stronger than lemonade, that was all I lost. I think we are having a good time here tonight. This banquet is well set up and it is due to the man I am going to call on now to make the first speech or to bring the first greetings to Dr. Mott. If we want anything done in the National Council, and want it done properly, we ask Fred W. Ramsey to do it. Mr. Fred W. Ramsey, chairman of the dinner committee.

MR. FRED W. RAMSEY: Mr. Chairman, ladies and gentleman, Dr. Mott: We were having a good time, Judge, all of us, until you told that story. You have ruined this meeting for me. I am rising simply to disobey orders. Our secretaries have been busy these days handling mail coming from friends all over the country who would love to be with us tonight, but who could not come, expressing their profound admiration for our friend and all he has done for us and for the world. I am under strict orders not to refer to any of these communications, but inasmuch as the chief is resigning all authority over us all in the next few days, I do not hesitate to violate his orders.

We had hoped very much to have Mrs. Mott with us tonight and we hoped up to the last that she might be able to come. But as Dr. Mott and Mrs. Mott are sailing in just a few days, preparations for the long journey they are about to make made it impossible for her to come on, but she did send her greetings to us all and her appreciation for this recognition that we are giving to Dr. Mott tonight. I wish at this moment, in recognition of this lady, who through all the years has with infinite devotion supported our great friend and made possible the great services he has rendered us all in the world, that we rise in appreciation of her.

[The entire gathering rose and applauded.]

Among the letters we have had, have been letters from certain of Dr. Mott's great friends, men who themselves have been in the greatest movements of the country and the world. I just want to read a partial list of these. I wish I might read them all. We have had wonderful letters from all of the following: Bishop Charles Brent, Captain Robert Dollar, Arthur Curtis James, and a great host of others who have sent messages to us these last days with regret that they could not be here in person, wishing to express their appreciation and love for Dr. Mott. I have a telegram from R. F. McWilliams, president of our brother organization, the Canadian National Council, with which we are so closely united by historic bonds of love and mutual devotion. Also, one from Henry A. Atkinson, general secretary of the Church Peace Union, and a letter from President Faunce, President of Brown University. There is also a very precious letter, I know it will be precious to Dr. Mott, from Bishop William F. McDowell, a lifelong friend. Also letters from Major General Summerall of the War Department, Newton D. Baker, formerly Secretary of War, Dr. John H. Finley, editor of the New York *Times,* the Chief Justice of the Supreme Court of the United States, William Howard Taft, Mr. Albert Alexander Hyde of Wichita, from Alfred E. Marling and many others.

[Mr. Ramsey read parts of many letters and telegrams.]

Judge Lyon, our chairman, has asked me to share with you, before I sit down, that never-to-be-forgotten hour some of us were privileged to share, some of us who are members of this Council, when the world cause of Christian missions represented by the International Missionary Council, meeting on the Mount of Olives last Eastertide, reached out in appeal for the leadership of Dr. Mott for the great forward movement of missions to the peoples of the world still living amid the shadows. It was the greatest privilege of my life to be there—fifteen wonderful days of fellowship with the world's missionary leaders, with men and women of fifty-one different countries of the world, carrying in their hearts and upon their shoulders and in their hands, the burdens of the millions who are yet without Christ and without God. We were amid the scenes fragrant with the memory of Jesus, walking in the paths that were pressed long ago by His dear feet, and in that wonderful environment this great call came to our friend. We faced it, those of us who were of this brotherhood, with mingled feelings of dismay and gratification; with deep dismay as we contemplated carrying on without him and his wonderful place of leadership, but with great gratification and joy in our heart that this our great Movement was to have the privilege of surrendering him and yielding him up to this greater and still more important cause. We had thought he belonged to us. We had been jealous of the claims and demands that others had made upon him, his time, his strength, his mind, his heart, but as we sat there together on the Mount of Olives we came to realize, those of us who represented you there, that he did not belong to us alone, but that he belonged to the world.

I shall never forget that hour. I sat in a position in that old German hospice on the Mount of Olives where I could look into the faces of that great company of men and women from fifty-one different countries of the world, representing in their offered lives the whole spirit and genius and power and beauty of the Christian missionary cause. I sat where I could look into their faces in that hour when the call came to Dr. Mott. I have never seen men and women with so much of yearning and desire in their faces, faces so expressive of all that they were feeling and wanting and yearning for with respect to the great cause to which they had given their lives. But behind their eager faces, full of hope and expectation, as the business of the call proceeded, I thought that I could see the faces of those millions of boys and girls and men and women across the world who are still living in the shadows, waiting for the coming of the morning. I knew and we all know that Dr. Mott belongs to the nations, belongs to the world. I want to share with you a few notes that I took in that hour, of what others said, in placing Dr. Mott's name in nomination and seconding the nomination. I find in my notes these few fragments of that wonderful hour:

The Lord Bishop of Salisbury, chairman of the Missionary Council of the Church of England, himself a great world figure, and a man of infinite charm, arose to second the nomination. He represented the great British Empire and far-flung missionary enterprise of his great Church. He said quite simply:

"This has been a living conference, full of hope, and the chief and constructive figure throughout the long period of preparation and through these days of wonderful consummation, has been Dr. John R. Mott. God has raised him up in this generation to lead us."

And then our own Robert E. Speer followed him, and I have preserved these sentences from his affectionate expression: "I claim that I may support this nomination out of deeper affection and a longer and more intimate friendship than anyone else of this Convention— forty years of the truest and richest friendship and no one can support this proposal with more pride and satisfaction than I. We are doing something more vital than just asking him to continue in this service. We stand in a critical place and time. It is said that we are nearing the end of our missionary task. We are. But it is the first end; not the last. We must gird ourselves for far greater sacrifices than we have ever made. We are indulging in the hope that we may have more of Dr. Mott's time and presently all of his time given to this, the deepest and the greatest cause in all the world."

There was another word that deeply impressed me, from S. K. Datta, a native of India, the national secretary of our missionary work in India, a man possessing outstanding gifts of statesmanship, one who had suffered all things for the Gospel—we shall never forget his words as he arose to second, for India, the nomination of our friend to the leadership of world missions. He said: "I too recall most intimate and affectionate relationships running back through many years. I made my decision for Christ in one of his meetings in India nearly forty years ago. At first I refused, but was finally persuaded by the irresistible logic and reasonableness of the thing he presented. He came to us years ago as a new discoverer of the East, of its need. Yea, but more, he made the discovery that there might be those in the East who could themselves make a contribution to the cause of Christ. There were those who insisted that the East would never change, never respond to the Christian appeal. He knew better, and insisted that the opportunity must be given to the East. I am persuaded that a great day must await the Church. I am overwhelmed by the thought of what the Church might do if she were only awake to the need and opportunity. We look to Dr. Mott to lead us through."

And then, finally, came another speech that was most touching and inspiring — Professor Martin C. Schlunk representing the Churches of Central Europe, and particularly Germany, said: "I first met Dr. Mott at the Edinburgh Conference. Previously he had just been a name to me, a great name, synonymous of high achievement, but unknown to me personally. I sat at his feet at Edinburgh for many days—" And then he said with a warmth and enthusiasm that went straight to our hearts, "and now I know him, who he is. I know his deepest desires; I know the passion of his heart for the world's redemption; I know his absolute trustworthiness and high faith and am glad to represent the undivided sentiment of the Christian leaders in my country in supporting his nomination."

And so that great hour passed, as the representatives of the missionary program in the many countries of the world and of the Protestant Churches of all the world, reached out in appeal for our friend and we knew that he belonged to the nations and we were glad that he belonged to the nations. Joy was in our hearts, even we who knew how much we were giving up, that so great a claim should come on his devotion, his time, his strength—his all.

TOASTMASTER JUDGE LYON: It has been thought fitting to have tributes by the general secretaries who have labored with Dr. Mott so many years. So Mr. E. T. Colton, the executive secretary of the Foreign Division will speak on behalf of the secretaries on the foreign field. Mr. Colton.

MR. E. T. COLTON: Charged as I am tonight with the duty of being spokesman for the men and women in the foreign service and in other lands, I cannot express the craving I have to be a faithful spokesman, to voice what individually and corporately is in our hearts to say. You are aware that a few minutes cannot suffice to do more than to give only a little of the flavor of the fellowship that has stretched for a generation across the world. It is an experience that somehow defies analysis. We have been aware of a wonderful relationship with a man to whom we trusted our lives, and, what is more precious if possible, who trusted us. Some spiritual alchemy has wrought a work which leaves us wondering as to whether he has meant more to us as a father, a brother, a friend, or a chieftain.

You must realize the strong impulse there is to yield to the pain of removal, even so much as a step from this relationship, in its effective capacity. But the heritage that he has left us is not regret. Nothing could more completely belie the admonitions and example and training and trust of these privileged years than to falter for a

moment, even if the worst were true, and the worst is not true—
thank God. The Chairman of the International Missionary Council
is the chief of staff and the field marshal of the Grand Army, of
which this Movement is an organic part. The brotherhood that
we know as the Young Men's Christian Association is an official
unit and from what we have heard this afternoon and have known
for many years, is a force making for the world-wide expansion
of Christianity. The Chairman of the World's Committee is the
division general of that unit. So granted that you give us a new
brigade commander of God's own commissioning, there will and
can open out before us a total position that nobody need contemplate
meaning retreat or losses for the King, but fresh advances and more
glorious action. If there is any flagging will or drooping spirit, there
is tonic in these words with which Lord Morley finished his remi-
niscences. He said: "In common lines of thought and action as in the
elements, winds shift, tides ebb and flow, the boat sinks, only let the
anchor hold."

Only that imagery fits a skeptic more than it does a Mott, who
comes toward the end of his life as he began it, with the anchor up—
steaming seaward.

Now mankind is in search for the secret that sends a soul voyaging
further as he has done and that can account for the quality of the
seamanship and so, when the story is written and men have assembled
and interpreted, so far as men can, who have lived near, I believe
that it will be read that this man was governed by a rule that governed
another Apostle.

Miracles have followed that Apostle that the world has noted,
but those of us who have had open windows upon the near life would
bear our testimony upon the miracles of grace there. Year on year,
more prodigious labors, wider horizons, heavier tasks, under burdens,
there always glowed that wholesome humor that flashed out even
when there were great outward solemnities; patience with the mistakes of associates—I know one who has made as many as any, but
who has yet to have his first rebuke; a love for the slow of heart, for
the confused and the obstinate; a loyalty that bore the blame which
belonged to others; a vision that would comprehend the biggest project that any colleague could ever bring—and would go beyond it.
And so the list would run on into those sacred intimacies that go into
the archives only of the hearts that have the experiences, and as we
go on in the relationships that are so old and so new, whether to be
together or apart from the familiar figure of the leadership that we
have followed for a lifetime, we do not have to look wistfully on what
God has wrought in the life of another, because lesser talents truly

dedicated have in them also the supernatural powers. We know a Way.

The first inspiration that ever came from the leader, whom I did not know then, was on the front page of the *Northwestern Christian Advocate* that found its way out into the remote farm belt where I lived and these pregnant words of his were under a radiant face:

"If Mount Hermon could reveal its secrets, if the hill back of Nazareth could tell its story, if the Wilderness of Judea could disclose what it has witnessed, we should be deeply moved by the prayer life of Christ. We should be impressed by its unhurried character, by its range and depths, and above all by the Godly fear which made it so irresistible with deeper meaning. We should be constrained to come day by day to our Master with that prayer of the disciples, 'Lord, teach us to pray.'"

That was firsthand testimony and reporting over thirty years ago, and that experience has gone on, ever richer with the years, and therein lies the clue to the mystical reality of the life we are honoring tonight; that for which the world hungers, that which characterized and explained the life of every prophet and apostle and saint of the ages that have passed and of the ages that will be yet ahead. God grant us grace to follow in their train!

TOASTMASTER JUDGE LYON: I am sure there is no one who could better represent the secretaries of the United States than the one who is about to speak—Dr. A. G. Studer of Detroit.

DR. A. G. STUDER: Mr. Chairman, Dr. Mott, and friends: I would that it were possible for me to represent the brotherhood across the American continent, local, state, and national, but I feel wholly inadequate to undertake such a task at an hour like this; for no words of mine would in any wise interpret what is in the hearts of the brotherhood toward this man who has been our leader and guide during these many, many years. I would that I could somehow or other bring out of our own hearts and lives the things that are there regarding this man whom we so esteem with so much affection and love, because of what he is and has been to us in his own personal life. For he has been one to whom we could have gone time and time again in the days that have gone, as one who was (as has already been said) like a brother or a father, and never has he turned any of us away. But in that deep love that he has for all men who have been his associates in this work, he has given to us out of the richness of his life that friendship and love and that counsel and that help that has been our strength through the years. He has been our dear leader. He has been the inspirer of our lives. He is the inspirer of our lives today and we are here tonight because he has inspired us, and because that inspiration has brought us here tonight and no words of ours can in any way convey to him what we have in our hearts and lives for him. I look down through the vista of the years that have gone and I see John Mott, the student secretary, way back there, and somehow even in that early day he left his impress on my life. I see him coming down through the years, a man who knows where he is going, and as someone has said, the world stands aside for the man who knows where he is going. If any man has ever known where he was going and is going, that man is John R. Mott. The men stood aside and he went by and the world fell in behind and followed him down through the years as he came with steady stride as a student secretary, taking on increasing responsibilities until today, as has been so well said, he has become the great world figure—the great lay leader of the Church.

Probably there are two things which Dr. Mott has said that have come to me over and over again. I remember years and years ago, Dr. Mott in one of his addresses said these words and I repeat them because they have come to me in times of stress and have strengthened me. Those words were these: "Christ is Lord of all or not Lord at all." Many a time in my life and I am sure in the life of the brotherhood individually, when we have come up against some problem we have heard the words of our leader ring in our ears: "Christ is Lord of all or not Lord at all," and we have held steady to the tasks because of those ringing words that have come to us. Another expression of his is, when, with uplifted hand he says: "I see the beckoning of that Pierced Hand." Many a time have I seen that picture, where Dr. Mott lifted up his hand and talked of the pierced, beckoning hand, not of defeat, but of victory; not One that was weak but One that rose triumphantly over the power of death and now lives and because of the things that fell from the lips of this wonderful friend and leader of ours, He has been our inspiration and our strength through the years.

Dr. Mott, I just want you to know that from our hearts we love you. Oh, there have been times when there have been differences, times when the way has been made heavy for you, but we love—we love you as we love few men. We love you for what you are, and what you have been. We love you because you to us have been the one who has, might I say reverently, been the perfect example of what Jesus might be in our midst, in your loyalty, your steadfastness, your consecration, in your oneness of purpose. Nothing has swerved you from the path of duty as you saw it—and we love you for what you are. We love you and nothing can in any wise weaken that love of our hearts, and our hope is that, as you go out from us, as you go out from us into that larger field of service for the Church of Jesus Christ you may go out with the assurance in your heart that that larger field is going to make the years ahead the richest and fullest years of all that you have had. As you go out, you are carrying with you our prayers. We will remember you in our prayers as you go out carrying a part of our hearts and our lives, because in return for that which we give to you, you have given to us a memory of these years and what they meant to us, and if some of us have been able to stand the stress and strain of these years, it is only because of what you have been to us as a brother, as a leader, as a friend. May God bless you, my brother. I know I am expressing the deep heart wish of every member of the brotherhood. May God bless you, keep you in His care; may He give you the health and strength that you need and may you see the glorious realization in the years ahead of that which you have in your heart for the cause of Jesus Christ, of the extension of His Church on earth.

TOASTMASTER JUDGE LYON: There is one other man who has been closely associated with Dr. Mott in many fields of labor, especially in the International Committee, and in the National Council since it has been organized, and he is going to say a few words, bringing to us his greeting to Dr. Mott. Mr. James M. Speers of New York.

MR. JAMES M. SPEERS: Mr. Chairman, Dr. Mott, ladies and members of the National Council: I have already on another occasion, publicly and in Dr. Mott's hearing expressed my admiration and love and respect for our great leader, as well as my gratitude for the privilege of having been associated with him through a long period of years in Christian work of various kinds. Some of us are very deeply conscious of the great honor that has been ours in the Association, and, notwithstanding that I feel utterly unworthy to speak in his presence this evening, but I do want to express my love and admiration in the privilege that I have had. I have recently been reading Paul's Epistles with the purpose of discovering to how many of his fellow workers he refers in those Epistles. All the while I was doing it, I was thinking of Dr. Mott. As you will look them through, I think you will discover that he referred to something more than seventy different people with whom he has worked. In the last chapter of Romans there are twenty-eight different names of people mentioned, who have worked with Paul, and the first of those is a woman, Phoebe, he speaks of as a servant of the Church, a friend to many and to himself among the rest. He refers to Priscilla and Aquila, as those who had put their own lives in jeopardy on his account, and he expressed his gratitude to them and he says not only is he grateful, but the whole Gentile Church is grateful for that service of theirs.

Then he refers to Andronicus and Junia, as two of his fellow country-men who had shared prison with him and who were Christians of longer standing than himself. He refers very lovingly again to an-other woman, the mother of Rufus, who he said had been a mother to him also. Then I am sure you recall the very tender and affectionate way in which he refers to Timothy, as his dearly beloved son, one who had worked with him as a child along with the father, in the promo-tion of the Good News. I think that is quite significant, a very human point of view, and perhaps an expression of affection from a source where we wouldn't have looked for it. Well, friends, some of us have discovered that our apostle is a great human also in this regard. We have of course realized the sheer massiveness of his life as Dr. Stanley Jones so fittingly expressed it last night, the sheer massiveness of his life. We have realized it, but if we have not realized that this great apostle of ours is a great human, if we have not realized his great humanity and his great loving-kindness, then we do not know Dr. Mott. Turning again to those people to whom Paul refers in his letters, can you imagine what it must have meant to some of those simple people, to have the great Apostle refer to them appreciatively as he did in those letters? Can't you imagine how much of stimulus and inspiration and new courage it gave them? I imagine some of them just walked on air for days after they heard from him in that way. I want to take this opportunity of expressing my appreciation for the great thoughtfulness of our apostle John Mott in this same regard. I am expressing the feelings of a lot of you tonight when I say that I don't believe he can appreciate what it meant to a lot of us to have just a simple word of commendation or a brief note that he took the pains to write commending some piece of work that we had attempted to do. I want to take this opportunity of expressing to him our appreciation for this thoughtfulness in this particular. And men, may I not say to you that I think we have an example be-fore us here that we ought not to miss. Most of us, perhaps all of us, are in positions in life where a word of commendation or encourage-ment from us to some discouraged worker will just mean new life. Well don't let's fail to meet the opportunity, with so good an example before us as the two great apostles—Paul and John. And as Dr. Studer has already intimated, wherever Dr. Mott goes, our thought and our interest will follow him, even though we may not be in close contact with him, and we certainly shall not forget to pray for him.

TOASTMASTER JUDGE LYON: Dr. Mott has woven his heart into the hearts of men of all walks of life. We have an example in one of New York's great businessmen and eminent citizens who came to Chicago simply to do honor to Dr. Mott tonight. He did not expect to speak and was only persuaded by me a few moments ago to say a few words for his friend. I have the pleasure of introducing to this audience Mr. John D. Rockefeller, Jr.

MR. JOHN D. ROCKEFELLER, JR.: Mr. Chairman, Dr. Mott, and friends: A man walked into the sheriff's office in a western town not long since and said to the sheriff, "Sheriff, I have just shot and killed an after-dinner speaker." The sheriff replied, "Young man, you are in the wrong office. They give the bounties in the auditor's office."

I hope that no one present thinks me so ungracious as to think that I may have pointed it at those who have preceded me. I am giving it to you more that you may be hopeful with reference to my very brief address. The Chairman has said that we were to enjoy ourselves here tonight. You surely will enjoy yourselves more, now that I am on my feet, after you know that three minutes will suffice for what I am to say. I count it a very high privilege to have the opportunity to join my voice with those others that have been heard tonight, in bearing testimony to my personal admiration and esteem and affection for the man whom we are here tonight to honor. For over a quarter of a century I have been proud to call him my dear friend and I feel that Dr. Faunce has very beautifully expressed the thought that is in the minds of all in speaking of him as one of the great outstanding world's leaders.

As I was thinking last night on the train of this meeting and its purpose, I sought to analyze in my own mind the qualities which have made this man so great, and two, in addition to the many which we have all thought of, stood out in my mind. Most important, is his utter unselfishness. During the years that have passed, when he has been faced with great decisions, Dr. Mott has on occasion done me the honor to seek me out for conference and never has there been the slightest suggestion of selfishness as he faced these great decisions in regard to his own life. The only thought always has been where his duty lay, and where he could serve in the best and the highest way. The other quality is his complete devotion to the cause to which he gives himself. Nothing else enters in. Who can imagine a man giving himself more absolutely, his waking and his sleeping hours, to the task in hand, than Dr. Mott!

Of course, I realize tonight that those of you who have stood so close to him in this great work during the years are viewing with some apprehension the future without his leadership, and yet I would quickly say to you that such thoughts are unworthy of him. If he has been the leader that we know that he has been, then he has built well and this great organization must go on and will go on to do greater and finer and more far-reaching service than he, even, has been able to lead it into. And I am sure that no one more than he would urge that as this group faces the future of this great organization, it should face it not only with confidence, but realizing that with every new decade, new methods must be adopted. It is hard to get off the rails. I have five sons and I am realizing that the future is in the hands of youth, and that we older people must see the problems that they face through their eyes if we would help them to face these problems wisely. And so, instead of feeling any sense of lack of loyalty to Dr. Mott in adopting new methods, new avenues of approach, in discarding those things which have been done for years, instead of feeling any sense of disloyalty, I am sure he would be the first to say—"Forget the past, and do each day in the future the thing that is best adapted to the needs of each day."

And it seems to me fitting to say at this time that while the loss of this leader is great to this organization, nothing could be more flattering and complimentary to the Young Men's Christian Association than the fact that the man who has had his broad experience in your midst is being called now to this great world field of exceeding usefulness. So, while we mourn in our hearts the thought of his last close connection in this work we rejoice and thank God that he has been chosen as the leader of this great enterprise to which he goes.

TOASTMASTER JUDGE LYON: My friends, we are nearing the hour for which you have been waiting, and the message from the guest of the evening. When the committee was talking to me about this meeting tonight, one in charge told me that he was sure, because of the messages that would be given to Dr. Mott, that this meeting would tend to be very solemn and he said to me. "Won't you tell a funny story?" That was Knebel who asked me that. I wondered how any funny story could find a response in his heart. I told him that I didn't know any funny stories and furthermore that I never told any, also if I did, my memory system was out of order. It is a hard thing, you know, to tell a story if you have not something to connect it with. Now there is not anything before me tonight that looks very funny that I can see.. I heard Billy Sunday once preach a sermon and he said that people went through the world with a long face and he said that they ought not to do it. He said that God himself had a sense of humor and that was the reason He made donkeys and monkeys of some of you folks.

I did hear of a man once who had a memory system. He went home one night and his wife sent him to the drugstore to get something. He had been out with the boys and he went to the drugstore, leaned against the showcase and said to the clerk,

"I want something."

"Well," the clerk said, "what do you want?"

"I don't know, I have forgotten."

"Well, what can I help you with?"

And the fellow said,

"Just name everything you got in the store, will you?"

Well, for a drug clerk to do that was an impossibility, but he said,

"We have stationery."

"No, 'tain't that."

"We have a few drugs."

"No, not that. Say mister, name the Great Lakes, will you?"

The clerk answered,

"What did you say?"

"I said, name the Great Lakes."

So the clerk started in:

"Lake Michigan, Lake Superior, Lake Erie—"

"That's it. Say mister, who was the fellow who had the scrap on Lake Erie?"

"I don't know what you mean."

"Who was the sailor who had the scrap on Lake Erie, I said."

And the clerk replied,

"You don't mean Commander Perry, do you?"

"Yes, that's it. Give me ten cents worth of perry-goric."

My friends, it would be hard to estimate the place and influence of any great man in the period in which he lives. Time and the space of years must give their aid to this interpretation, but if we read history aright, we know that the influence of any great man grows with the years. We believe that the influence, for example, of Woodrow Wilson and Theodore Roosevelt is greater today than it was when they lived and will be greater ten years from now than it is today. After the rivalries and jealousies of life pass away, a man in his true worth stands out.

My friends, we have come tonight to do honor to this man who has been with us for so many years. He spoke last night in the service of the books that he was wont to read. The character of a man is known by the books he reads and also by the books he writes. I took from my shelf in my library some weeks ago, a book from which to cull thoughts for the help of young men and I wrote down some fifty or more quotations from that book. They were gems in themselves, each one. I would have given some to you tonight had the time permitted. But that book was the book written by John R. Mott, *Confronting Young Men with the Living Christ.* It is a book full of inspiration for youth and help to those who would be the leaders of youth. My friends, while this is an hour of regret, it is an hour of promise; an hour of depression, and yet an hour of inspiration; an hour of doubt and yet an hour of hope; an hour of good fellowship, and yet an hour when the heartbeats proclaim a deeper theme; an hour when we would weave the mystic words of memory into a mantle which we would throw over our guest. But we know at the same time that his mantle of a different sort must fall upon us. But as Mr. Rockefeller has suggested, there is a glory in it all. In the position to which he has been called, he raises this organization to a new plane of endeavor. The name of George Washington raised the Colonies in the respect of the world, and our European orators frequently pay their tribute to America in the terms of Abraham Lincoln. My friends, we could not wish for Dr. Mott after he goes from us, that his pathway might be strewn with roses, but that when his sun should at last set, it should set in glory in a cloudless sky.

DR. JOHN R. MOTT: As I listened to the all too generous words of appreciation of my friends they reminded me of a word of President Coolidge. In the White House one time, after I had given him a number of reasons why I thought he should be re-elected, he looked over my statement quietly, and then almost as quietly and in his characteristic laconic New England manner said, "I hope some of these things are true." To those who should share these tributes of confidence and affection I think first of my father and mother. On my father's side the lineage came down from England; on my mother's side, from Holland and likewise from England. My father, my grandfather and my great grandfather were lumbermen, cutting down the forests of hemlock and pine in Sullivan County and the neighboring part of New York State, binding the timbers into small rafts and taking them in times of freshets down the tributaries of the Delaware River and the Delaware itself, then tying these together in still larger rafts, then on down through the famous Water Gap to Philadelphia where they disposed of the logs and rough lumber. As these were not the days of many miles of railway, they returned most of the way by stagecoach. Carving out the wilderness, they were pioneers and hard workers.

On my mother's side they were woodsmen, hunters, and farmers. I was born in Sullivan County. When I was under two years of age our family pushed out into the upper Mississippi Valley, then regarded as the Great West, and settled down in the Northeastern corner of Iowa alongside the "military road" that stretched from McGregor up to Fort Snelling in Minnesota. They grappled there with the wild prairies and lived a life of struggle. Our home, all those years of my earliest recollection, was one of great simplicity and hard work. And in that atmosphere, and in the presence of the elemental forces of nature, and with primitive surroundings, there were inculcated habits of industry, order, appreciation of the value of time, and scrupulous honesty. In boyhood I was drilled in the whole range of the trade of the lumberman. My companions in childhood and young manhood were not only youth of American descent but even more of Scandinavian and German parentage—a fact that proved to have more than incidental value in later years of service in all parts of Europe. I owed much to the discipline, object lesson, and fellowship of my father, who has gone on before. When I was fourteen my father said he would give me a complete set of the Encyclopaedia Britannica on condition that I would not drink intoxicating liquor or use tobacco before the age of twenty-one. It was a memorable day when he by faith in advance presented me the twenty-one volumes of the leather-bound edition. I need not add that I kept the faith. Even more was I indebted to my mother. The list would be long and meaningful. There are two things in which you may be interested. To her I owe much of my physical vitality. My father broke down under thirty bearing the burden of a large family. His father died, drowned under a raft although a splendid swimmer, for as he came up, under the raft, he struck his head on a log and was knocked senseless. Under the strain of his impossible load my father broke and became prematurely grey, although he lived to the age of eighty-two. It was from my mother that I inherited a strong constitution. There have been only three times in forty years, and all those in recent years and beyond one's control, when I have had to miss an appointment. When I think of my mother, however, I think of something infinitely more precious. The truly Christlike life she lived created in me, even in the tender years of childhood, as I look back upon it now, the longing and inclination and purpose to go Christ's way. Her religion was not simply thought out, it was not talked out, it was lived out. In the deepest sense it was contagious. I was always impressed by her love of flowers, by her passion for reading, by her interest in all foreign countries and in great rulers and other eminent leaders in foreign lands. She inculcated also a genuine loyalty to the Church and such of its institutions and activities as the Sunday School, the midweek prayer meeting, the camp meetings in the pioneer days, and above all a reverential regard for the Christian minister. Through all the years in our home town the presiding elder, or the bishop, or other church officials were entertained in our home.

Although I had thought I would say nothing tonight about persons who are living I must say a word about my wife, especially in view of what you have so beautifully and deservedly said and which likewise touched the deepest depths. She is after all the head of the combination. I know there are great debates, in different places, about who is the head of the family, the man or the woman. I was talking with a friend of mine in Paterson, New Jersey, the other day who has become a specialist on this subject. He said to me, "There is no doubt about it, Mott, the women are going into the lead." He had a real controversy with a friend of his who took issue with him. The friend said, "I don't feel that way at all, Arnold. I am inclined to think the men are holding their own." They got into a great discussion and became bitter, and at last this man undertook to do a thing which was somewhat peculiar and costly. He said, "I will try you out." So they picked out a certain area and took a lot of chickens in crates in a wagon and also led behind the wagon two horses. They decided to go to one house after another and leave a chicken in every house where the woman was really the recognized head, and if perchance they came to a house where a man could be demonstrated as being the head, they would leave a horse. They started out and had quite a busy time in the forenoon. They cleared out four or five crates of chickens off the top of the wagon, and were working down into the second tier of crates. Then they came to a place where the head of the house, as he claimed he was, said, "There may be some doubt about some of the families where you have been, but I am the head of this place." "Very well," they said to the man, "you may have your choice of these two horses, the grey or the bay." The fellow replied, "I believe I will take the grey." But his wife broke in and said, "Now, John, you had better look into this matter. I am inclined to think that the bay is the better of the two." And she gave the points or reasons. So the so-called head of the house said, "Well, I think perhaps I did make a mistake; I will take the bay." "No," said the owner, "you will not take the bay; you will take a chicken." Undoubtedly you would have to leave a chicken at our house.

Let me say that my wife has led me, from the day I first knew her, to the higher levels, and has kept me on the uplands of God. She has been to me a living conscience and God knows how necessary this has been. I hope it could not be said of me, as I heard spoken of another man not long ago who said of himself, "I am striving to keep on the narrow path between right and wrong." I have had my soul struggles and it has been a marvelous thing to have at hand a living conscience. She has been indeed a faithful critic—a person who could and would tell the truth in love. Moreover, she has ever been responsive to the largest visions and plans. I have never known her to call a halt. Notwithstanding one's limitations, I have never known her to pass a word of discouragement or have an attitude of silence that chills one's zeal for wider visions and larger plans. She has

shared with me the vicissitudes of extensive travel in many lands, but
has also had the courage to stay behind, with entire responsibility
for home and children.

I am anxious also to pay a tribute to Iowa and the fact that in
my most impressionable years I was taken into that spacious, forward-
looking, progressive commonwealth—a land of literally large dimensions, of vast unconquered prairies. Some of you saw in the last
Sunday *Chicago Tribune* the cartoon they repeat every few years entitled "Indian Summer." It certainly makes a powerful appeal to the
imagination of all of us who recall those pioneer days. I trace to
those days in the great open spaces my later responsiveness to far
views, to retreating horizons, to regions beyond, world-wide programs. From early days to this hour the words of Robert Burns have
continued to make their powerful appeal,—"There are hills beyond
Pentlands, there are firths beyond Forth."

As I look back on my life three great phases of nature have un-
consciously, increasingly, and profoundly influenced me. One which I
have just emphasized—the wide prairies and plains. Another has
been the desert. As I told Mr. Rockefeller this evening, I have found
the deserts of Northern Africa, Western Asia, and also of our south-
western states, contrary to the popular impression, among the most
creative of all places. If God spares my life I hope to spend more
time in the deserts. It may be possible to do so for they confront me
as I think of my maps and possible unformed plans. The third of
these and greatest has been the sea. On my errands of service I have
traversed almost every sea. These many and extensive voyages, comparatively free from the turmoil, the hurry, the pressure, the conflicting
voices of the inhabited earth have afforded limitless and ideal conditions for rest, meditation, reinvigoration, and creative thinking.

Moreover, the fact that I had implanted in me somewhere, somehow, the instinct for travel, or as the Germans say the *Wanderlust,*
must be considered in analyzing my career. My mother told me one
day that when I was only a little over two years of age, I used to
plead in the only way I could, that they take me out and show me the
trains, because we were then on the farm in front of which stretched
the Chicago, Milwaukee, and St. Paul Railroad tracks paralleling
the old military road. My earliest recollection was, when only three
or four years old, of our German helper taking me out and holding
me in his arms that I might see the train sweep past. One thing
I look back on was one of my first Christmas presents (as a very
small boy) the now battered little tin train of cars that are still in
the family. As a small child I thought them quite wonderful. The
next stage in my evolution was when eight years old I laid out a rail-

way system. This was on the north side of our house where the grass would not grow and where there was plenty of stiff clay in which I cut furrows which served as the railway lines or tracks along which we ran our trains. Main line and feeders or branch lines were laid out, also sidings or switches. Stations and roundhouses were constructed. Passenger and freight trains and engines made with blocks and spools and other materials.

The next step was a dangerous one. When I was about eleven or twelve I organized the boys of our village into a railway system. The town, although still a village of only a few hundred inhabitants, was incorporated, and had put in a great many wooden sidewalks. The boys brought into action their wheelbarrows. The only bicycle in the town was also enlisted. We ran not only day but also night trains. We got on fairly well with the day trains, but when we put on night runs we had one dark night a bad wreck—that is one of our wheelbarrow fast trains ran into a leading citizen and shattered him and his basket of eggs. My father, who was the first mayor of our town, dealt with me conclusively—and shut down our whole system.

My railway interest then advanced another stage. It took the form of assembling the printed timetables and maps of all American railroads. I succeeded in winning the interest of the railway station agent and others and within two years had a very nearly complete set of all American railway timetables. My friend, General Hugh Scott, formerly head of the American army, told me once on our way to Russia as members of President Wilson's Commission, that he could find his way in the night on horseback from the Canadian border to Mexico. He had worked for years in connection with Indian warfare over that entire area. As a result of poring ceaselessly over these myriads of timetables I believe I could find my way all over this country. It became almost a second nature.

The final stage in the evolution was when the Burlington, Cedar Rapids, and Northern Railway, as it was then called, extended a branch to our town. As it was a terminus, they put up a roundhouse (although it was really square) and a turntable. Without my parents' knowledge I was able to win the consent of engineers and firemen to help wipe or clean the engine, and also to turn it.

Someone asks me now and then how far I have traveled. I have never kept track of my total mileage. Among my friends are some who, with mathematical minds and abounding in curiosity, have convinced themselves that my mileage throughout the years has averaged over 40,000 miles a year.

With reverence I would acknowledge the protecting hand of Almighty God in the midst of the countless perils of a traveling life.

There have been wrecks before me and behind me. I have been in grave peril on the seas and shielded in a way that I can only explain as God overruling. For example, for some inexplicable reason, I gave up the plan to take passage on the "Titanic" on its maiden voyage and took a parallel boat the time the "Titanic" went down.

Another source to which I would pay a sincere tribute is the state committee of the Young Men's Christian Association of Iowa. The secretary of this committee, J. W. Dean, who was also a Quaker evangelist and a remarkable Bible teacher or expositor, visited our town of 700 people and, for a period of three weeks, conducted a series of evangelistic meetings and Bible classes. During that never-to-be-forgotten series he led my father, two of my sisters, and me to Christ. What do I not owe to him for coming into my life in my early teens! Another minister of remarkable qualifications for achieving profound and abiding practical spiritual results was the Reverend Horace Warner. He was a man of the highest culture and one holding university and seminary degrees. He exemplified three vital processes. One was that of exceedingly thorough preparation of all, not some of his sermons. He would let nothing crowd him out of his study for the better part of two days and a half every week. He preached sermons of distinction in our little village. He reminds me of the contention of Bishop McDowell that the best educated men should be assigned to the most destitute fields. This rarely equipped pastor identified himself with me. Again and again he visited me while I was at my work in the lumberyard. He interested himself in my reading. He generated in me the desire and purpose to get a college education and convinced my parents so that they made this possible.

I shall never cease to be grateful that one of the smaller Christian colleges, the Upper Iowa College at Fayette, was the one to which I was sent for the early part of my course. Out of that college came David B. Henderson, for five terms Speaker of the House of Representatives, also Dr. Clough, one of the most distinguished missionaries of India and the pioneer of the great mass movement. You will recall that Lord Bryce, in his great work on the American Commonwealth, paid a high tribute to the important part our small colleges have had especially in the foundation-laying period of most of our states. Personally I can never repay my indebtedness to the one I attended before passing on to the university. At the moment I recall illustrations of the formative influence exerted upon my own life. One was what I gained through membership in the Philomathean Debating Society. Another abiding influence was a sermon by a minister whose name I do not recall on the text, "They that be wise shall shine as the brightness of the firmament, and they that turn many to righteousness as the stars forever and ever." I would also pay a tribute to my favorite professor, Chauncey P. Colegrove. He literally identified himself with me. He not only did his work in the classroom in a masterly way but he also spent long hours with me in intimate conversations helping me to make great decisions, including the passing on to Cornell University for my advanced work.

My going to Cornell came about in an interesting way. I had made up my mind that I wanted to enter the profession of law and the pronouncedly religious college in Iowa was becoming somewhat uncomfortable. That was undoubtedly a main motive. I went to Cornell because of its large toleration, because of its reputation for free thinking, as well as because of the scope of its courses of study, particularly in the faculty of history and political science. I was attracted by its president, Andrew Dickson White. He unfortunately resigned soon after I entered although not until I had the opportunity of coming under the influence of his matchless lectures on history. I owe much to Moses Coit Tyler, the greatest professor of American history in the country at that time, and likewise to Jacob Gould Schurman who soon after I entered established the famous Sage School of Philosophy.

The Student Christian Association at Cornell got hold of me through a simple but effective device. I refer to their handbook for new students, the first of its kind. It was not devoted to the plans of the Christian Association but to providing just the kind of information most helpful to men entering the university. Their work for new students was organized as in no other college in those days. They welcomed one in the most effective way, and put me at work to help others even though I myself was drifting, so far as matters pertaining to religion were concerned. Under the influence of this Association a prominent athlete of Cambridge University, England, Mr. J. E. K. Studd (later Sir Kynaston-Studd, Lord Mayor of London), was invited to visit Cornell not long after I entered the university. He was a member of the famous Cambridge Band of evangelistic and missionary fame. At Cornell he was advertised as coming with a message from the students of England to the students of America. From curiosity I went up the hill to the botanical lecture room to hear him. I reached there late and sat down at the back of the room after he had begun speaking. The first three sentences I heard marked a turning point in my life:—"Seekest thou great things for thyself; seek them not. Seek ye first the Kingdom of God." These were words which were meant for my condition. They struck deep into one's motive life. They sent me away to spend a sleepless night. On the following day I mustered up courage to call upon the speaker, who had invited students with serious unanswered questions on matters of faith or conduct to take counsel with him. That was a never-to-be-forgotten hour. With great wisdom he led me into a reasonable and vital faith; by reasonable I mean a faith for which one can give reasons which satisfy honest questioning, by vital I mean a faith which changes one's life at the center—that is one's motives and disposition. From that hour I became increasingly active in the Association and its service. Not long after I was elected to serve as one of the leading officers, and the following year as the president. In this period our Association expanded from a membership of a few score to over 300, and assumed a leading position in the entire Christian Student Movement of North America. In this administration we secured the large sum for a model Association building.

Each year for three years I attended the New York State Convention of the Y.M.C.A., at Elmira, Utica, and Harlem, which brought me into intimate relation not only with the students but also with leading laymen throughout the state. At the last-named convention William E. Dodge, President of the convention, and his son, Cleveland H. Dodge, chairman of the Committee of the North American Student Christian Movement, invited me to become a traveling secretary of the Movement. I took this under consideration but ultimately declined the call. The call was renewed twice by Charles K. Ober, the chief secretary of the Movement. On the occasion of the last call when after prayer he challenged me to try the work for a year to make sure whether or not God wanted me to devote myself to this vitally significant work, I consented to make the trial. Thus this became for many years the great work of my life because it led eventually to a world-wide ministry. From the autumn of 1888, following my graduation at Cornell, until the latter part of 1915 I served as a chief executive of the Student Department of the International Committee of the Young Men's Christian Association of North America. You can imagine the experience and training it would give any young college man to enter a work which involved visiting again and again nearly all of the universities and colleges of the United States and Canada on errands of service with the governing objective of making these centers of higher learning strongholds and propagating centers of pure and aggressive Christianity. Beginning at the same time, the autumn of 1888, and continuing to the end of the Volunteer Convention in 1920, I held the position of chairman of the Student Volunteer Movement for Foreign Missions. This was the fruitful agency of all the Protestant missionary societies of North America for enlisting and training candidates for the foreign mission field. During this period over 14,000 student volunteers recruited by this Movement finished their preparation and sailed to mission lands—the largest offering of life for the missionary career in the history of the Christian Church. In the service of these movements it was my duty and priceless privilege to visit repeatedly all parts of the United States and Canada and also the great battlefields of the Christian faith throughout the non-Christian world of Asia, Africa, Latin America, and the Pacific Island world. Parallel with most of the years of leadership in these two North American countries, namely from 1895 to 1920, and largely as a result of the experience and training essential to this leadership, I was one of six men from as many countries to lay the foundation of the World's Student Christian Federation, then its general secretary for twenty-five years, and following these years for nearly a decade served as its chairman. Along the pathway of this service a score or more of national Christian student movements were organized and bound into this world-wide fellowship. In this relationship a long series of significant international Christian student conferences were held and many national evangelistic campaigns for students conducted. Another very great responsibility rested upon me from the beginning of the present century to 1915 and that was the post of chief executive of the Foreign or World Service Department of the International Committee of the North American Y.M.C.A. In this period the Association was extended to over a score of new fields on all the non-Christian continents, and the staff of foreign secretaries increased from a small group to five score. During those years in many of the chief political, commercial, and educational capitals of the non-Christian world the Association became a most important factor. In 1915, having repeatedly declined the call, I recognized it as my duty to accept the invitation to become general secretary of the entire complex work of the International Committee. This led me to resign my executive relation to the Student and Foreign Departments and to concentrate on the problems and challenges for advance of the entire Association Movement of this continent. I continued to bear this responsibility until 1928 when, in accordance with age limits, I handed over the great trust to younger shoulders.

I was chosen to preside over the great World Missionary Conference of all Protestant missionary forces of the world at Edinburgh in 1910 and was then made chairman of its Continuation Committee. This evolved into the International Missionary Council in 1920, and I have continued to serve as its chairman. In this relationship of chairman I have had the honor of helping plant and develop over twenty National Christian Councils and I have assisted in weaving

them together for the all-important purposes of fostering on behalf
of world-wide missions united thinking, united planning, and united
action. While life lasts I shall not cease to thank God for the priceless privilege of serving all these interdenominational, international,
interracial bodies, and through them of helping prepare the way for
the developing ecumenical Movement — the world-wide Christian
fellowship.

The building and serving of these various, comprehensive, truly
world-wide bodies has involved a life of travel. Such trusts cannot
be administered from an office chair. The infinitely more sacrificial
process of traveling far and wide repeatedly, yes constantly, and
actually identifying myself with those to be served, has been absolutely necessary. It has been costly, as my wife and children know,
and as all who exercise their imagination know; but it has unmistakably been along the path of God's appointment.

Such a trust, such a life, and such a work have taken me over the
world again and again. Repeatedly I am asked how may countries
I have visited. Even now I should find it difficult to tell. One time
as a dinner guest of His Grace, the Lord Archbishop of Canterbury,
I was seated by the Dean of Westminster who, by questioning, had
discovered that I had traveled widely here and there. He took a
menu card and began to scribble on it, and then handed the card to
me and said, "Does not that represent your life?" Here's what he
wrote:

> "The wide world traveled,
> The whole world's guest,
> The end of his life,
> The beginning of his rest."

I replied that I was not dead sure about the last two lines but that
I could testify as to the truth of the first two.

From my earliest foreign journey, the first of over eighty cross-
ings of the Atlantic, I have approached nations or peoples as a learner
and have never, right up to my latest visits abroad, changed this
attitude. My archives are overflowing with notes gathered from
countless interviews and group consultations the world over. These
materials are priceless. They cannot be found in books. My list of
questions, even on the first round-the-world tour, kept growing until
by the time I reached Japan I had a list of twenty-eight questions.
They were not inquiries that could be answered by "yes" or "no."
It took from three to seven hours to answer them, that is if a man
answered them thoughtfully. I did not risk leaving the questions in
a man's hands to deal with in writing after I had gone, because I

wanted to cross-question him. I remember that my friend, Dr. De Forest of Sendai, was overheard saying to another missionary, "Have you passed Mott's examination?"

Another attitude I have tried to maintain the world over, from the beginning right down to my most recent journeys, has been the attitude of sharer. This, I trust has been increasingly fruitful. What wonderful truth I have tested and proved in the pathway of the injunction, "Cast thy bread upon the waters—for thou shalt find it after many days."

This reminds me of another profound lesson learned in the pathway of my journeys, and that is that you never understand a people until you try to move the will of that people—to win them to some point of view, or summon them to some line of action. Then you discover their background, their antecedents, their ambitions, their governing motives, their lines of least resistance. It was said of Count von Zinzendorf that he prayed that "he might be baptized into a sense of all conditions that so he might enter into fellowship with all." Would that I had prayed this prayer more faithfully. I am glad I can say that I find myself at home in all nations and among all races. I have come to recognize that each of them has a valuable contribution to make to our common humanity. I would pay my tribute also to the various Christian communions, and even to other faiths. At Cornell I was interested not only in the Christian denominational and interdenominational bodies but in another society we founded and called the Religious Union. Through this agency we drew into a common fellowship not only Christians, but also Jews, Buddhists, Moslems, and Mormons. I am grateful that in those days there fell into my hands the book on comparative religion by Principal Grant of Queen's University. Still later I attended and participated in the Parliament of Religions here in Chicago. On subsequent world journeys I entered into fellowship with many adherents, teachers, and propagators of other faiths. I trust that I let pass no such opportunity to impart as well as to receive. The keynote of the recent World Missionary Conference in Jerusalem was the word "creative." We came together not to attack other faiths but to fix attention on their valuable contributions. Our attitude was constructive, positive, sympathetic, and appreciative. Before we left the Mount of Olives Christ loomed higher in our lives than ever before. The more we could recognize the good in other faiths the more there stood out the uniqueness and supremacy of Christ.

I would acknowledge tonight my indebtedness to different personalities. The list I give cannot be complete. I think of the elder Professor Tyler of Amherst College whose book, *Prayer for Col-*

leges, brought out over a generation ago and now out of print, fell into my hands when I was at the beginning of my work for students and in doubt as to whether I should continue. It made such an impression on me that nothing in all the intervening years has been able to deflect me from this my first love and what I am constrained to believe will be my last love.

Then there was Dwight L. Moody, the world's greatest evangelist in his day. I sat at his feet at the first intercollegiate Christian Conference held at Mount Hermon in 1886, and from that time to this the evangelistic impulse he imparted has never lost its power nor have I ceased to give, as he did, right of way to evangelism.

I would at once add to these two Henry Drummond of Scotland. Much can be traced, in any service I have been permitted to render, to his books and to possibly as many as a score of unhurried periods of collaboration which we had on both sides of the Atlantic. Besides the photographs of the last two named, Moody and Drummond, you will find a third one in my study, that of Henry Clay Trumbull. To this remarkable chaplain in the American Civil War, and most fruitful Sunday-School worker and editor of recent decades, I am indebted for lifting into a place of central prominence in my advocacy and practice the most highly multiplying method of personal work.

Only twice had I the privilege of hearing Phillips Brooks preach and it left a profound and ineffaceable impression. He was indeed a great Christian—great in physical stature, and marvelous in intellectual comprehension, in religious tolerance, and in prophetic power.

Archbishop Nicolai of the Russian Orthodox Church Mission, with whom I had intimate fellowship on all my early visits to Japan, was in a class by himself in his leadership and spiritual achievements.

In the case of the eight presidents of the United States, with all but one of whom I maintained highly valued personal contacts as well as official relations in furthering the various international Christian movements I have served, I found all of them responsive to the claims of the Christian program and genuinely co-operative. Theodore Roosevelt stands out as the most versatile, most forceful, and as possibly the one with most courageous initiative. All in all Woodrow Wilson was the most internationally minded and statesmanlike. This estimate of him may be due to the fact that I knew him more intimately. First and last I had scores of consultations with him. These began with many contacts during his days as a professor at Bryn Mawr, Wesleyan, and Princeton. He gave me generously of his time and became a real formative influence in my life and plans. He was the most helpful critic of the manuscripts of two of my books. After he became President my contacts became frequent, especially through-

out the entire World War and after. I recall with emotion the last
interview near the end of his life. There he was propped up in a
chair, evidently in pain. I had just returned from an extensive journey
throughout Europe and the Near East. I was able to bring him words
of encouragement about the influence of his ideas and policies. When
I remarked that the new generation across Europe still believed in his
"fourteen points" he broke in and exclaimed: "Mott, I must get well
and help them." In a few days he passed away but the memory of
this great man will abide in power. I must desist, although I have
only started on what I might call the major list of those who have
greatly helped or influenced me. There is a minor list. I should really
not say that. It reminds me of a schoolboy in England who in an
examination paper was asked to list the minor prophets. He wrote
in reply, "God forbid that I should make any such distinction." And
the boy's answer continued, "Rather let me give in chronological
order the Kings of Israel." So I will not attempt this minor list. I
have it here and some of you may later want to see it. It included
quite a number, and in my room this afternoon I had a fight to separate the two lists. Well, as for the so-called minor list, and still
confining myself to names of persons who have died but who became
an influential factor in my life, I would mention with great gratitude:

Dr. Lyman Abbott, Editor of
   The Outlook
Bishop Baldwin of Canada
Kali Charan Banurji of India
Bishop C. H. Brent
Dr. John A. Broadus of
   Louisville
Dr. James Buckley, Editor of
   The Christian Advocate
Archbishop Davidson of England
Principal Fairbairn of Mansfield
   College, Oxford
President Charles Cuthbert Hall
Professor Harper of Australia
Bishop Honda of Japan
Dr. Kuyper of Holland
Bishop W. F. McDowell
Dr. Theodore Monod of France

Bishop Handley Moule of
   Durham
Baron Nicolai of Russia
Pundita Ramabai of India
Professor Rudin of Uppsala
Professor Sanday of Oxford
Bishop Söderblom of Sweden
Hudson Taylor of China
Bishop John H. Vincent of
   Chautauqua
Baroness Vrede of Finland
Professor Johannes Warneck of
   Halle
Booker T. Washington of the
   United States
Robert P. Wilder of India
Archdeacon Williams of New
   Zealand

As I think of my countless visits to the colleges and universities
of our land and Canada, not to mention other countries, the names of

literally hundreds of professors come surging through my memory. I venture to mention only a few chief college presidents who are typical in point of helpfulness and influence.

Sir William Dawson of McGill
Principal Forrest of Dalhousie
Principal Grant of Queens
President Sawyer of Acadia
Sir Daniel Wilson of Toronto
President Angell of the
    University of Michigan
President Bashford of Ohio
  Wesleyan
Professor Noah K. Davis of the
    University of Virginia
President Dwight of Yale
President Eliot of Harvard
President Gates of Amherst
President Gilman of Johns
    Hopkins

President Harper of Chicago
President Jordan of Stanford
President King of Oberlin
President Low of Columbia
Professor John B. Miner of the
    University of Virginia
President Northrop of the
    University of Minnesota
President Patton of Princeton
President Raymond of Wesleyan
President Scovel of Wooster
Provost Smith of Pennsylvania
President Tucker of Bowdoin
President Andrew Dickson
    White of Cornell
President Wilson of Princeton

Nor must I forget the laymen—especially the men of large affairs in the realms of industry, commerce, and finance, not to speak of the so-called secular professions. They have entrusted to me for altruistic purposes, especially for pronouncedly Christian enterprises and programs, tens of millions of dollars. In some respects they have made an even larger contribution—that of sharing with me principles, practices, experiences underlying the accumulation, the custody, and the wisest use of funds. Here again I give but a few of what, I repeat, are typical examples all of whom have gone to their reward and with all of whom I have had priceless experiences in relating the money power to plans for the widening of Christ's Kingdom.

J. B. Atherton
F. W. Ayer
Henry Birks
Andrew Carnegie
William E. Dodge
D. Stuart Dodge
John J. Eagan
John V. Farwell
D. B. Gamble
Philip Grey
J. L. Houghteling

D. Willis James
Joshua Levering
Chester Massey
Samuel Mather
Cyrus H. McCormick
Mrs. C. H. McCormick
D. W. McWilliams
Thomas J. McPheeters
George W. Perkins
H. K. Porter
Henry Proctor

John D. Rockefeller, Sr.	Benjamin Thaw
L. H. Severance	Cornelius Vanderbilt
Hiram Sibley	Henry Wallace
James Stokes	John Wanamaker
J. Livingston Taylor	Lucien T. Warner
Mrs. J. L. Taylor	David Yuile

Almost as remarkable a list, of laymen still living, and of women as wise and unselfish givers might be given.

It would be difficult to overstate my indebtedness to my secretarial colleagues or associates. I find it impossible to particularize among this goodly fellowship. I recall none quite like it in wide-ranging vision, in bold initiative, in creative ability, and, above all, in loyalty and unselfish devotion. And whenever my mind turns to my intimate personal or private secretaries I do not trust myself to voice my sense of obligation and undying appreciation. All who are in the know are aware of the truth of my contention that I am indebted to them for much of the spacing out of my life span and likewise for much of its fruitage.

Before these hours of intimate fellowship and sharing draw to a close I would venture to answer briefly an important question as to what have been the governing ideas and objectives of my life and work. This is important for such factors have been quite as vital and formative as other grounds of my indebtedness or obligation which have been shared with you. First and foremost, I would mention the supremacy and sufficiency of Jesus Christ to meet the deepest longings and the highest aspirations of the human heart and of the human race. At His name ultimately every knee shall bow and every tongue confess that He is Lord of all. He not only was but is the Living Christ. My lifework has not been built around a dead Christ but One alive for evermore. He communicates Himself to us as truly, as manifestly as any other fact of human experience. Our great work, as I have been trying to emphasize in my addresses, papers, and public conferences, as well as in personal conversations, is to make Jesus Christ known, trusted, loved, and obeyed, in the whole range of one's individual life and in all relationships.

The sense of the immediacy of Christ and His work has been and is central with me. He is not static, but the fountainhead of spiritual vitality and the generating source of all of the profound spiritual changes which have taken place and of the great creative work yet to be.

Another dominating fact with me, from the day I began a life of service, has been the recognition of the supreme importance of taking advantage of the age of adolescence. As I look back over the years of planning and of action the one great change I would make, if I had these years to live over again, would be to give far more right of way to the claims and possibilities of these wonderful years of youth.

To use by design a phrase which I esteem it an honor to have had associated with my name and practice, I mention that of the strategic importance of the students of the nations. It will be recalled that the title of my first book was *Strategic Points in the World's Conquest*. I could not do better were I to write a book today dealing with the present world upheaval and outlook. What larger or more pivotal task have we than to make the universities, colleges, and higher schools, more than ever before, strongholds and propagating centers for the leadership of the forces of righteousness and unselfishness.

All this involves not only augmenting the number and quality of the Christian ministry of the nations, near and far, but also the liberating in the years right before us of the all-too-latent lay forces of the Churches. Valuable as have been the contributions to this end of the Movements I have served, the time has come for them to revise, enlarge, and in many cases revolutionize their programs and plans. Pre-eminently is this necessary if we are actually to Christianize the impact of our so-called Western civilization upon the non-Christian world.

Possibly the most highly multiplying method, in point of influence, employed through all the years, has been that of multiplying the number of intercessors. Christ was familiar with the problem of the paucity in the number of workers. His solution of the problem was absolutely unique. Note His unmistakable direction and emphasis: "The harvest truly is great, the laborers are few; pray ye, therefore, the Lord of the harvest that He thrust forth laborers into His harvest." This is the most truly Christlike action for "He ever liveth to make intercession."

Another means I have sought to emphasize, from my first round-the-world tour, is set forth in three addresses given by me in the conferences of workers in all the lands then visited, namely, *Bible Study for Spiritual Growth, Secret Prayer,* and *The Morning Watch.* The central thought in all, which should be kept central with us all, is that of the deepening of acquaintance with God and the releasing of His superhuman guidance and power through right habits of isolation, meditation, communion, and appropriation. On my last visit to the Holy Land I went out alone to revisit the Mount of Olives. I was prompted to make this pilgrimage as in my morning meditation there broke upon me more powerfully than ever these words about our Lord Jesus Christ: "He went, as His custom was, to the Mount of Olives." Take note—out of the busy city, out of the noisy city, out of the crowded city, out of the sin-bound city—out to the zone of silence under the peaceful olive trees—there to meditate, to be attentive unto God, to hold unhurried communion with His Heavenly Father. My dear friends of the many and fateful years, if our blessed Lord Who is our perfect example in everything else found it necessary, or desirable, thus to hold unhurried and responsive fellowship with the Heavenly Father, what presumptuous and alarming folly for us to assume that in these busy, noisy lives of ours, and in the midst of the dangerous crosscurrents of the modern world, we can do without this truly Christlike practice.

ADDRESS AT THE SATURDAY MORNING SESSION OF THE SIXTEENTH MEETING OF THE NATIONAL COUNCIL OF THE Y.M.C.A., DESHLER-WALLICK HOTEL, COLUMBUS, OHIO, OCTOBER 25, 1941

As we draw near the close of our first century, it certainly is fitting that we should, if I may use the language of the Psalmist, "abundantly utter the memory of God's great goodness." I remind you that it has been a century of adventure, of pioneering, and of pathfinding —pathfinding across almost every part of this wide world. I have had the honor and rare privilege of visiting now over eighty countries, on all of the continents, and our brotherhood has extended its ministry to over sixty of them.

It has been a century, likewise, of foundation laying. You know, there is only one foundation-laying period in the life of a man or of a movement, and that is all-important. My lifelong and world-wide studies have shown me that these foundations are broad, deep, and solid. Having Christ as the cornerstone, they are capable of sustaining a colossal superstructure which we are now rearing. There is only one foundation-laying period, and we must be true to that.

It is not strange that our predecessors across the years have found the doors, and entered so many of them. As a result, we are here today.

Then it has been a century of the unwearying proclamation of the eternal evangel, that is, the fronting of successive generations of youth with the central figure of the ages and of the eternities, the

Lord Jesus Christ. They have been bowing down before Him all through these many years. Herein we find the hiding, as well as the releasing, of the power of this organization.

It has been a century, likewise, of character building. Symmetrical personalities have been built the world over. They have personalities characterized by manliness, by open-mindedness, by sympathy with overburdened men, and by loyalty to Jesus Christ the Lord. It is not surprising that in my world-wide journeys, I find this type of character highly contagious.

Furthermore, it has been a century of ceaseless conflict with the ageless enemies of mankind — ignorance, poverty, disease, strife, superstition, aggression, intolerance, and sin. I say these have been the agelong enemies. We have come to close grapple with them in every area of the Young Men's Christian Association, and we have come to successful grapple with them.

It has been a century, also, of strategy and statesmanship applied to the use of the highest talents and the greatest powers, and relating those energies to the world-wide spread of the reign of Christ.

Thus it has been a century of developing the highest order of citizenship in land after land, across the breadth of the world. The pillars of strength in these nations are those that have been fashioned by these processes to which I have referred.

These have been marvelous years. The century draws to a close. As you and I stand before it, it is fitting that in a spirit of reverence we should this morning acknowledge these foundations, these architects, these contributors of life and substance, these believers through thick and thin, and these valiant warriors. Well might we repeat again the words of the Psalmist, that we "abundantly utter the memory of God's great goodness."

But I am reminded that the century is not quite over and we find ourselves in the midst of one of the most tragic, most alarming, and most fateful moments of all the centuries. It is a time, literally, of wars and rumors of wars. It is a time of something quite new in wars, suggested by words like this: "White wars," "nerve wars," "undeclared wars," "lightning wars," "total wars," "all-out wars," yes, and "all-in wars"—wars employing such instruments and powers of cruelty and destruction as this world has never before known. This is a war in which not only men under arms but also millions of women and innocent little children and the aged and the unprotected, are slain or called upon to suffer.

This tragic moment is witnessing tens of millions of people torn out of their homes, cast adrift, homes broken and destroyed; and the aspect of this presented by the little children lays such hold of me that it haunts me in the watches of the night.

Think of the unnamable cruelties due to the Gestapo, the Comintern, and the other nefarious organizations, the like of which this world has never before known.

But God be thanked, it is also a time of creation and of recreation. I agree with Helen Keller when she says that the world is filled with troubles, but she continues that it is also filled with the overcoming of troubles. There has been nothing like it in the annals of mankind, when there was such a black background, which every traveler here will say I have not made too black. But against this indescribably awful background you and I may see this morning the beauty that is in the world. That leads me to say that by far the best days of the Young Men's Christian Association lie in the future and not in this last century, marvelous as that may have seemed to be as we let it unfold before us in memory. Yes, our best days are in the future.

You ask why? Because of our numbers. I think of that little band—unacknowledged and almost despised, who met there in the building in London that has been destroyed by the bombs, and where I met our founder again and again in prayer, Sir George Williams. The beginnings of that little band—I say unacknowledged—were in the beginnings of this past century. And here we are about to start a new century with not only millions of members but uncounted numbers of interested people who have been members and who have not lost the vision and the outlook, the purposes and the habits, that came to them in their young boyhood and young manhood. What have we not a right to expect, as we launch a new century, with this marvelous fellowship cast across the breadth of the world!

Think not only of the numbers, but also of the knowledge and experience, much of it acquired at infinite cost and much of it most bitter. What prices have not had to be paid! We have had our martyrs across the world, integrated with all the churches to which we belong.

We remind ourselves, as we start a new century, not only of our numbers and our far greater knowledge and experience, but of the fact that we have evolved certain unerring guiding principles that are as unerring as the North Star. What a price we paid for them! Where may they not lead us!

Think, likewise, of the momentum we have acquired. Momentum is the most costly thing in the world. What can you not do when you have it!

Moreover, we have evolved a trustworthy leadership. My heart has been fully responsive to what we have been saying these busy days here about our leadership—professional, clerical, and lay. That is most strategic, in the sense that granted this, all else may follow.

Why do our best days lie in front of us? Because of the challenges sounding in our ears. When has a generation of the Young Men's Christian Association had such stern challenges? When have we had so many major unsolved front-line problems? When have we had such a plastic world, such an upheaved world, where anything is possible?

The ground of my quiet and unshakable confidence this morning in a far brighter, more significant, and more eventful future than the past, lies in the fact that we are now passing through unexampled sufferings and unexampled trials or testings. And I, with you, in the language of St. Peter, would say, "My brethren, rejoice greatly, though now for a while if need be you find yourselves hard-pressed by manifold trials." Not one trial, but a veritable network of trials. We should, as Peter said, thank God under these circumstances, not because of the evil, but because of the inevitable triumph of the good.

Of course our hearts leap high when I say our best days lie in front of us, because we have a larger Christ. Notice I do not say a new Christ. He is the same—yesterday, today, and forever. But I maintain He is larger, in this sense: that there are so many more millions of interpreters of Him; there is so much more authentic knowledge now of His mighty works than ever before.

Then, there are so many communities where this has been tried out on a community basis—of what Christ's principles and superhuman power might do in contrast with any time in the past.

Above all, Christ is proving again that the things that are impossible with men are the very things that are possible with Him. In other words, in Christ and in Christ only, we have the key to all the problems that vex us—personally, socially, and across the world.

Therefore, with you I maintain this morning that wonderful though the achievements of the century that is to close in three years have been, there is something far more meaningful and possible in the one that lies before us. I find everywhere expectations that cheer me. I could not be a pessimist if I tried to be. You say, expectations of what? Of whom? Well, expectations of discerning men of large affairs. I say "discerning men," on watchtowers, on mounts of vision, are revealing an expectation from us which is most humiliating, as we consider our lack of ability right at this moment to cope with their expectations.

Then there are expectations also of noble rulers. Those men who are bearing impossible burdens are looking to us. They have had an opportunity to see us more particularly these last three decades, beginning with the last World War. They got acquainted with us, and they have expectations in this war that have been so moving to some of us that we find it difficult to bear the burden they put upon us.

If that is true of the leaders of the nations and of these men of large affairs—in industry, commerce, finance, the various professions, and all walks of life, what shall I not say about the leaders of the Church? Some of you know I am in several official relations there. I am chairman of the International Missionary Council, that weaves together all the foreign missionary societies. I am also the American vice-president of the committee that is working to bring into being a World Council of Churches, and in not a few other relations that have thrown me with what I would call the outstanding leaders of Christendom—Protestant, Greek Orthodox, and, to some extent, Roman Catholic. I say they have expectations concerning us that we might easily forfeit if we fail to put ourselves more intimately in touch with them and sit more at their feet and help weave together our and their plans more effectively.

Above all the expectations that move me are those of the youth —and I suppose these help to keep me alive.

Somebody asked me what is the secret of my longevity. I told a few of you the other day about Bishop Denny of the Southern Methodist Church. I went to see him the last time I was in Richmond. I found, by telephoning, that he was at home, and he said, "Come right out, Mott, and see me." I went out to see him—retired, over seventy, but with hair as black as jet. I said, "Bishop, what is the secret of your longevity?" And he said, "Mott, I drink all the black coffee I can get hold of; I smoke steadily; I sleep very little; and I take no exercise." When I mentioned that to my friend and your friend, Fletcher Brockman (God bless him!), he said in reply, "Why, Mott, if he would only gamble and drink whisky, he would live forever!" I do not need to tell you that those are not my remedies. I have been true to Richard Morse. I do not let a morning go by without my setting-up exercises, although he did me one better—he could do them in a sleeper, and I have not been able to do that.

But I was going to say that I suppose I owe my life to the Canadian wilderness, where I had a chance to become acquainted with my children, and now with my grandchildren. I owe my life, in the second place, to the fact that I have spent on an average thirty-four days a year on the high seas. I owe my life, in the third place, to the tides of youth that surge around me. I owe to these three things, I suppose, the fact that I am here and alive.

Now, I was going to say, therefore, that we have these expectations of the youth. What a tragedy it would be if we, of an older generation on the home stretch of this century and at the all-important beginning of the next century, were to disappoint their expectations!

My mind continues to travel over the past. I remember that word in Hebrews which to me is the source of remarkable inspiration where it says, after that wonderful galaxy of the heroes of the faith, "That apart from us they shall not be made perfect." Remembering these ninety-seven years of our first century, I say that apart from us in this room and those whom we shall inspire and guide and inform in the first decade of the new century—not to mention our world-wide brotherhood—apart from us they cannot be made perfect.

But, higher than all, my friends, I remind myself of the unsearchable riches of Christ—unsearchable. I felt very much at home this morning when we got into discussion on what amounted to the basis of our organization. I began such discussions fifty-three years ago. I have had a battle under that heading in almost every college over the round world, until at last I got to the point of summing it all up in the language of St. Paul. St. Paul, you know, with all of his mental acumen and vision and profundity, finally gave it up and threw up his hands and said, "Thanks be unto God for His unspeakable gift." It is not possible in the language of men to define adequately this marvelous Central Figure of the Ages, and of the eternities. What an inspiring task it is to make Him known, trusted, obeyed, loved, and exemplified in the whole range of individual life and in all possible human relations! We should reverently fall at His feet this morning and thank Him that He permits us to share with Him in His sacrifice.

In view of all that is behind us in our significant and never-to-be-forgotten history, and still more, in view of the vista of the coming days that breaks upon us, what shall we say and do? In the first place, let us put our house in order. We must put our house in order economically. There is an economic base to every enterprise that amounts to anything in this world, even the most spiritual. Some people are very superficial in assuming that we are drifting out of the zone of spirituality when we deal with economics. Not so. Our conscience here as a brotherhood should not allow us to rest in a time like this. We must devise ways and means of wiping out our crippling debt. I have seen much bigger things done in my lifetime by our brotherhood. How many times have we come together in a zone of doubt, and taken counsel first with our fears, and then finally, after that, with our hopes and our prayers. I remember the time when we hesitated up in Lake Geneva about whether we should go out for the Retirement Fund. After over half a day of taking counsel with our fears, some of us then suggested swinging over and prayerfully taking account of our faith. This we did and what seemed impossible at the beginning of the discussion of our gathering, the raising of $4,000,000 in a few months for that beneficent object, was achieved.

I had the honor of participating in five successive foreign building programs, two of them in times of great financial stringency, greater, by the way, than now. One was a campaign to get $100,000. In that day of beginnings this looked hard but we got $200,000. Another was to get $400,000, but in a few days we secured this amount from four or five persons and before we were through secured over $800,000. The next was to get $1,080,000 and we swept past this goal to a total of $2,000,000. The next was to obtain, if possible, $4,000,000, and ultimately we secured $5,000,000. The last of these campaigns was launched before America entered the last war. After the United States entered the war, some of the donors wanted to take back their pledges, in order to give more to the war projects. This course was followed and some time after the war the campaign was renewed in the teeth of new difficulties, but with the almost unbelievable triumph I have indicated. Our series of three great war work campaigns literally abounded in signal triumphs over what at first seemed the impossible. I know you could also call a long list of victories in securing great buildings and in wiping out serious debts in the case of local Associations.

I have never known the Young Men's Christian Association of this country to fail to achieve a thing which we unitedly set out to achieve, and the number of triumphs over the impossible has been legion. The least of my fears is your inability to do this thing of which I am speaking this morning. I endorse heartily all that Mr. Harbison and Mr. Barnett have so well said. To my mind, their statements are absolutely convincing, and show rare realism and appreciation of the gravity of the difficulties that confront us. Let me reiterate what I have so often said, that our difficulties are our salvation. It seems to require the impossible to call our faith into full action. I mean we are apt to lean back on our own resources, our own wisdom, and our own devices. It is not until we take God into account that impossibilities turn from stumbling blocks to stepping-stones.

Is it not a tragic thing that we seem to have to have times of suffering like the present to call out the best that is latent within us?

Must the present war extend to this continent before we shall be moved to do our part? Is it going to be necessary for us to go much further and literally by way of the Cross before we discover the releasing, as well as the hiding, of our power?

But I am persuaded that this will not be done if there are divisions among us. I have faith that we shall blend our divisions, and discover a larger synthesis than we have yet found, and thus be swept into a greater triumph than ever.

My next word is that, as we face the last years of this century, and the first ones of the next, we must concern ourselves primarily with the qualitative. I do not worry about the quantitative in the Young Men's Christian Association, providing we have the qualitative. But we will do well to heed this startling thought that if we stop becoming better in this organization, we shall inevitably cease to be good. There is something alarmingly incongruous in an organization becoming static which is built around the Living Christ, or counting itself as having attained. Nothing should so drive us to our knees as such a menace.

Our whole program, therefore, should be essentially qualitative. Therefore, I have endorsed everything that has been said here about special commissions and worth-while and scientifically thorough research projects. How grateful we are that we have had such a pastor of this conference as the one who has led us into the deeper things of God.

Let us, therefore, in this organization, in the language of St. Peter, gird up the loins of our minds. Let us get the reputation of being concerned far more with the quality of our work, the motives that lie behind it, and our hidden superhuman resources, than with externals. The things which then take place will transcend our fondest dreams.

Notwithstanding what I have said about the qualitative, let me say that we simply must augment greatly the number of active and effective laymen. Today the lay forces in all our churches are all too latent. Think of the total membership of the Protestant churches alone on this continent, and then see the relatively small number we have in our organization; or forget this organization, and go into individual denominations and see the relatively small number of men whose names are on church books and who are inactive but who might constitute an apologetic of what the Living Christ does when He actually breaks out through men. When I see all that, I would not be content this morning to have you go away and say that Mott in defining his conception of the challenges is contented with things as they are, with reference to the number of men we have lined up with us who are ready to take on great burdens.

Therefore, I have listened with great attention and joy to the report of the Commission on the Student Work and everything that has been said concerning other groups here who should be called far more largely into action. I am hoping also that in a like way we shall attack the rural problem afresh under modern conditions, and by all means also the industrial. That, of course, is to be the battle-ground of the next half generation, and therefore our programs need to be rethought, restated, revised, and, in my judgment, largely revolutionized.

The next challenge is that we must concern ourselves even more largely (I say it advisedly, because in not a few areas we are doing splendidly) with reaching the boys in the plastic years of adolescence, the years of forming life attitudes and tendencies, the years of surprise, of discovery, of invention, and of the morning. Oh, what may they not mean! The danger is that in this time of war we are going to be so occupied—and properly occupied—with the older age brackets, that we may overlook the boys. There could be no greater mistake or calamity as we take the long view. All of the other things ought to be done, but this must not be left undone. I should not be true to my best intuition and my great burden if I did not say what I have just said.

The next thing we are called upon to do is to enter upon what I call the larger evangelism. The verse in the Bible that has buoyed my wife and myself in these recent momentous years more than any other is this word from Isaiah: "When thy judgments are abroad in the earth, the inhabitants of the world learn righteousness." Notice, it does not say they *should* learn righteousness. It states the fact that under these conditions they learn righteousness. The judgments of God in a double sense. In the first place in the sense that there are being visited upon us the results of the sins of omission, as well as commission, of ourselves and of our ancestors; also in the sense that in these days of tension and suffering the loving Heavenly Father is drawing near His children, revealing to them His sympathizing, and guiding hand. His almighty hand also is being manifested. How true that is now all over the world—"When thy judgments are abroad in the earth, the inhabitants of the world learn righteousness." That is, they are humbled, they are chastened, they are eager for light, they are seeking light, they are ready to be guided. What a tragic thing it would be for an organization like ours, that was called into being in the midst of evangelistic action not to be in the front line of evangelism in days like these!

Mark my word—and I have had wide observation and experience—I do not know of any part of the wide world where what I am now saying is not true: that men are ready to learn righteousness.

"Blessed are the pure in heart, for they shall see God." What a calamity that we do not furnish a sufficient number of wise guides and true interpreters who will give themselves with the passion that made this organization what it was in order to enable it to reach you and me in our day!

I remember how I was first led to Christ by the state secretary of Iowa, J. W. Dean, who came to our little village in Iowa. He led my father, as well as one of my sisters, and myself, to go Christ's way. He gave us the true sense of direction. Then I was left for a period to drift without guidance. It was not until I got into the university when an athlete from Cambridge University visited our institution and conducted evangelistic meetings that I was brought into a vital relation to Christ. Thus I owe both of these creative initiatives to the Young Men's Christian Association.

Let me summarize the aspects of what I call the larger evangelism. It must be evangelism characterized by larger desires, by larger understanding of the changed psychology all over the world now and of the antecedents of these people for whom we want to work, also by larger plans. How pitiably small our plans are in contrast with the designs of our Savior, with His illimitable spiritual resources, and with the indescribable depths of human need. It must be larger evangelism in the sense of larger adaption of our ways and means to these infinitely high ends. And, of course, it must be larger in the sense of larger unity. Listen to Christ as He prays that we all may be one, that the world may believe. That is indeed the triumphant apologetic which an apologetic world has never been able to resist— the weaving together in a solid front of those who bow down before the Deity of our Lord.

The larger evangelism calls also for a larger message. At the Jerusalem Conference over which I presided in 1928, we had a commission that brought in a report of thirty pages on our message. Robert Speer and the Archbishop of York were cochairmen of the commission and with their colleagues accomplished a wonderful work. It will reward our best study. In this notable document there is one short sentence reading: "Our message is Christ." It is all there.

There we are called upon to buttress our nation. Here, again, this USO work has made a strong appeal to my imagination and memory. It took me back to my experiences in the other war, when I was director of the National War Work Council, and its great campaigns.

As I see it, friends, we have the opportunity of the ages now to serve our nation, not only by working among these initial hundreds of thousands, soon to be literally millions, in the training camps, but we have also the most difficult task, in some ways, of getting ourselves oriented in time to serve the many millions of those in industry who are going to call for a like special ministry. And in the midst of this, do not forget the boys. They are watching their fathers and their older brothers. They are in an attitude that will not last forever.

That leads me to another thing we are called upon to do, and that is to be Good Samaritans. I am inclined to agree with what Herbert Hoover recently said to me, that nine-tenths of the Christian Gospel is found in the parable of the Good Samaritan. That is Christianity in action. That does not stop with conventions and resolutions. That goes out to illustrate Christ and becomes lost in unselfish causes. What a chance we have right now! I ask you when has the area of human need been so wide as it is now? When has the depth of human need been so tragic, so profound? We can hardly believe what we are hearing. I say that surely, at a time like this, there would be something alarming in our position if the United States of America, most favored in its location and in its resources, were not to place itself at the service of suffering millions. As some of you know, I am a cochairman of a joint committee of our Churches on the matter of relief. We are responsible for validating projects we can conscientiously recommend to the Churches in this time when relief is needed. It is a very responsible task we have. Many a project passes before us. I know of no single project right now in the vast realm of human need that I would bracket with that presented by the prisoners of war. Would you believe it that we already have behind the barbed wire over 4,000,000 of them? We are not taking the statistics of Russia from either the Russians or the Germans, as yet. In my judgment, within a few weeks we shall be talking of over 5,000,000, and more likely 6,000,000. We had only 6,000,000 prisoners at the end of the last war who were behind the barbed wire. These men are largely about twenty-three years of age. Here we have behind the barbed wire, with time on their hands, men chosen by rigid processes of selection, with their lives largely in front of them. We have to answer this question: Shall this period of enforced confinement be one of physical deterioration, mental stagnation, and moral collapse? Or, as a result of our initiative and action, shall it be made a period of physical invigoration, of mental enrichment and strengthening, and of spiritual and moral growth? That is the question. What a limitless opportunity! Remember, those men are not criminals. They are soldiers out of luck. But they are brothers and sons and husbands and fathers. May the human touch just grip each man here, no matter what he has thought of this work in the past, and put a key in his hand. Let us all go back using our efforts to share with the people at home the knowledge of this tragic need.

I have been so pleased that some of you spent a full day here before we began our official sessions, discussing what a Young Men's Christian Association can do to help in this process of bringing in a just, righteous, and enduring peace. I belong to several committees which are working on this problem. I would go so far as to say this: I fancy that there are today at least twenty committees, or groups, or whole organizations dealing with this problem, where we had one at the middle of the last war. This is very reassuring. There is a purpose now seizing men, with the idea that we are not going to miss the switch at the end of this war, as we did before. We are going through the painful process of having to retrace our steps, but we are going back there where we lost our way, and from there we shall proceed where we should have proceeded together at the end of the first World War. I am glad our organization is in the heart of this vital process.

Let me now emphasize one of my deepest convictions and that is that if our World Service was ever needed, it is needed now. I go further and say it is far more needed now than ever. Why? Because so many nations are orphaned. They are nations that want to help, but they cannot get their money and their workers out. This indispensable help has to come from us. Secondly, there are so many other nations that are shattered in this war. When you think of some of these countries by name, you quickly say that anything God will permit us to do for those shattered countries, we will do now. Then there are countries that are war-opened countries, which would not have been opened except for this struggle. If, for example, we all do our duty, as Good Samaritans and in other ways, for the great Russian peoples who are now being tumbled into ditches, we may again have our opportunity. Some of you know my deep attachment to Russia, from my many tours there. The most discerning remark with regard to Russia came to me from a Russian who said, "You may not understand Russia, but you must believe in Russia." I do not understand Russia, but I am free to say that I believe profoundly in the limitless resources and possibilities of the Russian people. When I think of the most strategic part of this world, the Near East—not only Russia, but Turkey and Iran, and all the fringing lands—and think of how relatively little we are doing for this part; when I think of my journeys in Africa, and realize that, with the exception of that marvelous work in the Nile Valley we are practically not touching that continent; and when I think of my five tours in the last two or three years in Latin America, in which I was able to cover virtually all the twenty Latin-American republics—I realize keenly how little we are doing compared with what we might do. And that is not to mention what is to be the reconstructed Europe. I say that if we ever are to expand the work of the World Service, it must be now, and in the time just before us. May God help us to see the day of our visitation, and to seize it. A lot of men see opportunity but they do not seize it. Let not that be said of our brotherhood.

In view of all I have said, we should get behind the commission you have authorized today, the one to foster preparation for the centennial of the Young Men's Christian Association.

Secondly, we should back the Mother Country, which will have the heavy burden of the World Conference in 1944. We should support her to the limit.

Thirdly, we must strengthen the hands of the World's Committee. It is our committee. It is in reality ourselves working in unity with all the national Young Men's Christian Association Movements of the world. It is the only body right now that is working on both sides of all these tensions—for example, Japan and China, Germany and England, Finland and Russia. I say we shall be serving men on both sides of all these tensions. Let us back this World's Committee, that it may be true to its great trust.

May God help us to select the men who will best represent us in this solemn hour! May God help us to raise a fund which will enable us in this tragic hour to afford a leadership the like of which the world has never known. Above all, let us lay a mine of prayer which will upheave any obstacle which may confront us.

Christ, and Christ only, can make this world a safe place, and flood it with good will. He made the most stupendous claim that has ever been made on this earth when He said, "I am the Way, the Truth, and the Life." Think also of His other equally stupendous claim: "I, if I be lifted up, will draw all men unto Me." How does He do it? By His unerring, guiding principles which have never led a country or an organization into a blind alley. He does it by His revolutionary commands, which have never been repealed. He does it by His irrevocable word of authority. He does it by His sure word of prophecy. He does it by His agony on that Cross.

"He still remembers in the skies,
His tears, His agonies, and cries."

He does it by breaking the bonds of the tomb—life evermore. He does it by the power of the Holy Ghost. And, wonder of wonders, He does it by His Body, which is the Church of which He is the head, and *of which all of us in this room are members.*

THE PRICE THAT MUST BE PAID

ADDRESS AT THE MEETING OF THE NATIONAL COUNCIL OF THE YOUNG
MEN'S CHRISTIAN ASSOCIATION, HOTEL STATLER, BUFFALO,
NEW YORK, OCTOBER 22, 1944

I do not trust myself this afternoon to voice emotions that surge
through one with overpowering force. My life, I sometimes think,
has been spent in conventions. My wife says I could preside over one
in my sleep—and she knows. I have been in literally hundreds of
gatherings—national, international, interracial, denominational, interdenominational. I mean all that I say when I say that this one has
moved me as profoundly as any other in what it illustrates, what it
exhibits in its deeper aspect, and, by the law of association, in what
it represents. I want to commend the texture of the personnel of this
assembly. I have received the distinct impression that we as a Council
have found ourselves. I was present at the origin of the National
Council here in this hall some twenty years ago. I believe now I can
say that in the intervening years we have found ourselves in what we
then had as vision. This has impressed me greatly as I have studied
the personnel and the volume and the quality of experience and insight
manifested here these creative days.

One has been impressed with the management of the Council
meeting. I refer not only to my good friend, the presiding officer, who
has brought his heart as well as his head and his fine business sense
to his task. He has been splendidly supported by his colleagues and
the wonderful organization, supplied with such fine insight by my dear
friend, Barnett, and his colleagues—an organization that has been
invisible, but that has been so highly efficient that we have probably
accomplished more here in three days than many bodies accomplish in
ten days or longer periods.

Again I think of what has been achieved here. I do not know of
a finer piece of diagnosis than we have had in terms of our time, our
world, and our destiny. That is saying a great deal. I also think of
the constructive, forward-looking and courageous decisions at which
we have arrived. I use every one of those words advisedly. We have
not been concerned with the past so much, except to conserve it and
go from strength to strength, as with the realistic forward view.

And, I repeat, we have been constructive. I would use a stronger
word, perchance—creative. There have been quite new things accomplished here, some that have vitality and germinating power and that
should be widely transplanted.

I reiterate, we have been courageous, and we have been counting the cost. We have just been reminded in moving terms by our chairman of the price that must be paid as we face a new generation, the like of which this world has never known, and with a situation the like of which the world has never seen.

More important than what lies behind us in the way of preparation for this wonderful gathering, and in the way of immediate achievement, is what I want to characterize as the sense of solidarity, of brotherhood, of fellowship which we have experienced here. When I can say that of a gathering, I need not have any question as to what will come out of it. If I can be sure there has been solidarity, a sinking of minor differences, a blending of great contradictory convictions in sincerity, so that we have a spirit of brotherhood and even of affection, I have long since learned (as you have) that that constitutes a truly creative atmosphere. There Christ finds His opportunity and always improves it. So, with a sense of gratitude and yet with trembling, you and I pause in this closing hour to remind ourselves of the significance of it all.

And here I am not going to yield to pressures and to dwell upon our past. I have been doing that so much in the last few months, in connection with our centennial observance, that it has got on my nerves. I am glad I don't have to say what two women were overheard saying the other day. One said, "My, how you have aged since last I saw you!" That was not calculated to call out the finer sensibilities. But the other got even. She said, "I would not have recognized you if it were not for that dress you have on."

By the way, speaking of our past reminds me of a conversation I had with my dear friend, Rufus Jones of Haverford College, over at Lake Mohonk. He had been back at his summer home on the Maine coast, and said that he had been there three days without the gardener, from whom they got their vegetables, turning up. His wife said, "Rufus, you'd better go down to the cottage and find out what is the matter." So he went down and found the gardener in a rocking chair on the porch looking out over the ocean. He said to him, "How are you getting along?" To which he replied, "I am in the right place, right here in this chair. I like looking out here at the sea. I enjoy my vittles. They say I have lost my mind, but I don't miss it." I hope you men who have been congratulating me on having rounded out so many years are not thinking of me in these terms. I want to get that past behind me and get my mind fixed on the coming day.

I am surely familiar with that past, let me pause to say. It began with me when I was a boy of twelve out in Iowa. I was born in Sullivan County, New York State, but my father was a lumberman, as had been his father before him. He went out into the Mississippi

Valley and took me as a child to Iowa. There, when I was twelve years of age, the state secretary of the Young Men's Christian Association in Iowa, a Quaker by the name of J. W. Dean, visited our little village, to give Bible readings and evangelistic addresses. (People say we ought to overlook the villages.) He led my father, myself, and an older sister to Christ. That was my first contact with the Association. That was afforded by a state secretary of the Young Men's Christian Association visiting a village and expounding the Bible. And then I got my first training in Iowa in what you would call the beginning of county work. Would to God we had it in all of our 3,000 counties now! Then I came East to Cornell University. There the Association got hold of me by guile. I was trying to dodge religious impressions. They led me along tactfully into the Association there. A year later they elected me to the presidency of the organization. Then Charles Ober of the International Committee got his eye on me and extended a call to me to become one of the two student secretaries of the Committee. I turned it down. He extended it a second time and I again turned it down. He came a third time and when we knelt in prayer up in the coal shed near the station where I was seeing him off, I had in mind to say to him, "It can't be." He said, "Now, Mott, won't you be willing to try this one year to see whether or not this is the will of God for you?" That struck me as a fair deal—that I might possibly invest a year to be sure whether or not God wanted me in this work. So began one year. It has widened out into fifty-six years. But I have been related to the Young Men's Christian Association for sixty-seven dating from that visit of the state secretary of Iowa. That is two-thirds of the first century of our brotherhood.

With that as background, having visited some eighty-three countries, and most of them again and again, and having sat at the feet of the many nations, races, and communions, and being under lasting obligation to all of them—I say, with that as background, I want to be remembered as having said this afternoon that in my judgment the century that now opens up before us is going to transcend by far the one that lies behind. This I earnestly believe; and, friends, it must be so. I say this without argument. What could be so dishonoring to our past, to those foundation layers, to those pathfinders, to those leaders in adventure—what could be so dishonoring as to say they had not prepared the way—by their sacrifices, their self-denial, their seed-sowing, their watering with tears and at times with blood—for something far better? So I say it must be so. But that may not satisfy the more penetrating minds here this afternoon. Therefore, I will give you quite concisely my reason why I am not doubtful and why I honestly

believe our best days are out there in front of us. I say it because of
our vastly larger knowledge and experience. Those have ever through
the centuries been the wisest teachers—knowledge and experience.
And how these riches have been accumulated; and at what a price
throughout a wide world, under all conditions, year in and year out!
Now it stands to reason and common sense, that this knowledge, this
insight, this marvelous elaboration of the scientific spirit that takes
account of all facts—not simply in one area of the world, but across
the world and across the years—spells something greater. It stands
to reason that this penetrating discernment and costly experience
(especially, my friends, the experience of failure, of shortcomings, of
sins of omission and sins of commission), are absolutely invaluable.
I am humbled but free to say that I have learned more by way of my
mistakes, my stumblings, and my fractional views, than I have learned
by the opposite. Our wider knowledge and our larger, richer, and
more tragic experience, surely spell something greater.

Then again, there is our organization. What is organization?
It is the means of distributing force most advantageously. What is
wrong about that? The more you dwell on that definition, the more
you see the significance of the word "organization." We have built
an organization, not simply a letterhead. There are so many so-called
organizations which in reality are merely letterheads.

Neither is our society simply a chain of conventions, although I
am proud of them. I have been at every international convention
since the one in Philadelphia in 1889. I have attended all the World
Conferences, beginning with 1891 at Amsterdam, save one, when I
had to be on the other side of the world. I have been at countless
state conventions, provincial conventions, district conferences, and
many others, not to speak of various denominational assemblies. So,
having them all in mind, I would say that we are more than a chain
of conventions.

We are also more than a series of findings. I have accumulated
already 130 sets of findings or resolutions adopted largely in the last
two or three years and bearing on the world order which should follow the present World War. Many of them were adopted in the
British Isles. Far more of them in this country. A few of them in
Canada. A still smaller number in other parts of the world. I have
130 sets, I say, not counting some that I have put in the wastebasket
as not worthy of consideration. Thank God, we in this meeting are
something more than our own work book, although it is the best of its
kind I have seen. How it has saved time for us and made possible
doing here in three days what might otherwise have taken weeks and
then left us in a jumble. Don't misunderstand me. I have probably

stood for as many findings as anybody in this room. But our organization is something besides a letterhead, something besides endless chains of meetings and endless talk, and something besides resolutions.

I repeat we are an organization prepared, as none other of which I can think, to cope with the present great world situation. We are an organization with a membership of not less than 2,100,000 men and boys, not counting, I estimate, nearly 3,000,000 older men who caught the vision in their youth and have not lost it, have not lost the habits then fastened on them, and have not abandoned their great unselfish purposes. They constitute largely to this day the backbone in our great supporting enterprises.

Here we are, with this vast living membership. Our organization is now established in all the great political capitals of the world, in all the great financial and commercial capitals of the world, in all of the greatest industrial capitals of the world, and in many of the greatest educational capitals of the world—here we are, at the strategic positions from which we can best dominate the outlying areas and regions beyond.

Contrast our large cosmopolitan membership with that little band of a dozen people around George Williams and with other little bands I am familiar with—God bless them—as I've gone on in my efforts as a pioneer trying to plant this work in country after country. I say, in contrast with those little unacknowledged and at times unpopular and poorly equipped bands, here I point to 2,000,000 to 5,000,000 bound together in a triumphant solidarity. Truly this means something far greater in the future.

Then, with you, I think of our money power. That is not to be despised. What is money? Money is so much stored-up personality. It is the equivalent of so many days of labor and sacrifice. It is a sacred possession. I have come to regard it so, increasingly. I suppose that is the reason God permitted me to liberate more of it than otherwise would have been the case. I have regarded its use as a sacred matter. My money raising has been primarily a matter of prayer. We have had money co-operation. The money tide of the rich and the poor has flowed out. I want to pause here to commend my good friend, Pence, and those who have supported him, in having brought out a book that is historic. That is an easy word to say, but it is a word that will take on larger meanings. It will be a book that we cannot do without, right on down through every one of the hundred years of the next century. I have spent a good many hours over it. I mean to make wider use of it in introducing it among other organizations. I suggest that you get a copy of it. I refer, of course, to *The Hundred-Year Book*.

In the first year I began my traveling life, the property of the Young Men's Christian Association at home and abroad, including buildings and endowment, was estimated at $14,000,000. Last year it was estimated at $271,000,000. And we are just gathering momentum. As you study that development in stages of ten years each, you will see what I mean by the word "momentum." That brings me to another reason why the greatest is in front of us—it is because of our momentum. What can you not do in an organization—as with an individual—when you have momentum, as contrasted with when you don't have it! Every automobile driver here knows what I mean. And if I might change the figure, the contrast is something like this: the contrast of a great ongoing, rushing tide. I have spent on the average of thirty-four days a year on the ocean since I began my traveling life. That has made me fairly acquainted with the tides as well as the waves. There is a great contrast made on your mind when you see a great tide rushing in, sweeping up the inlets and carrying everything before it, compared with the impression made when it is lazily, slowly ebbing away at your feet. I think of the Young Men's Christian Association as a rising tide. It has risen against the most obstinate cliffs, stretching up into the interiors and reaching out wherever it is given an opportunity. Surely, the added momentum means something ahead in contrast with all that has taken place. It is a solemn reflection that the opposite will take place if we don't press our present unprecedented advantage.

That brings me to another ground of my confidence, that our future is going to be something that will so far surpass in outlook and achievement and impression anything that lies behind us that it will be almost unbelievable, and that is because of the atmosphere that has been generated. The older I become, the more widely I travel, and the more deeply I ponder and read, the more importance I attach to atmosphere. You know there is such a thing in an organization as an atmosphere in which men come to loathe to differ and to determine to understand. It is a great thing in an organization for leaders and members to loathe to differ; but is it not far more significant for them to determine to understand one another?

Jesus Christ placed the greatest strain on the imagination that has ever been placed by a teacher, when He taught the golden rule, that is, that we are to do unto others as we would be done by. This right atmosphere that leads me to want to understand my brother, and therefore to put myself at his point of view, how greatly this expands the creative possibilities of an organization! Our President has reminded us in most penetrating illustration how calamitous it would be for us to assume that something mighty had not taken place here in Buffalo—that the power of the Living God has not broken out here summoning us to do something in addition to anything we've done in the past.

Another reason why the best is out there in front, my friends, is the open doors. John Wanamaker, the great storekeeper, one day said to me, "Mott, I look on you as an expert in opportunity." I said, "Mr. Wanamaker, it would be a very strange thing if after these years of ceaseless travel I had not learned how to discover whether a door was open." And, by the way, I helped him to open some.

I remember, as though it were yesterday, a time when I was speaking in Calcutta at an evangelistic meeting and we had got down to the after meeting with about 200 inquirers, and I was giving instructions. It was a most critical moment—the last time a man wants to be interrupted. Just at that moment who should walk up the central aisle but John Wanamaker. He came up to me before all those waiting inquirers, when I was at this very delicate point in my meeting, and said, "Mott, what can I do for India?"

Well, God gave me an answer, and I said without time for reflection, "Mr. Wanamaker, if you will give money for a boys' building for the Young Men's Christian Association to serve the 30,000 schoolboys, you will never regret it," and I went on with my evangelistic meeting. When he got to Bombay, ready to sail a few days later, his conscience evidently had done its work. He telegraphed back, "I will give the building."

That reminds me that later I met him—it must have been three or four years after that—in Paris. We were having a meeting of the World's Committee and Mr. Wanamaker turned up. We invited him to the meeting. After the meeting—he had his chaise there—(it was before the day of many automobiles) he said to me, "Get in and ride with me, Mott." I got in. He said, "That man of yours, Fisher of Japan, wants me to give a building for the Young Men's Christian Association at Kyoto, the ancient capital of the country. Now Mott, is that the best thing I can do?" And I said, "Mr. Wanamaker, no, it is not the *best* thing you can do. Far better would it be for you to give not only a building for the old capital of Japan but also simultaneously for Seoul the capital of Korea, and one for Peking the capital of China. That would be much better." He said, "Well, I didn't get you in this carriage for that reason." We talked a little more, and then he said, before we got down into the city, "Come back this afternoon and we will talk it over." I went back. We got up into his little purchasing office which he had in one of the large buildings in Paris. He locked the door and sat down. I can still see that old roll-top desk. He took one of his large cards—he had a very large one—

and began to write in his bold hand that he would give so much money for these three buildings. And he lived long enough for us to bring the plans to him and to see them carried out. We showed him a plan for the building in Korea. He said it would not do. It was too narrow at the front. He said, "You have to square that out or else we can't put money in it." We said, "But it will cost more money," and he merely replied, "But you'll have to square it out." It did cost him more. I am glad to add that this generous donor and friend of the Association lived to see these three buildings completed and paid for.

But let me amplify my point by saying that I will accept Mr. Wanamaker's statement that I ought to be an expert on opportunity. I, therefore, would be glad to be remembered by every man here this afternoon as having said that I do not know of one door on this earth which is today closed to the friendly and constructive ministry of Jesus Christ and His Church, and the auxiliary agency of the Church, the Young Men's Christian Association. Should someone think of a door which he believes to be closed, let him recall the promise of Jesus Christ, "Knock and it shall be opened unto you."

With that in mind, what content we should all read into what I am now saying! How much we should take at their word every member of the World Service Department of our National Council and our International Committee, about the open doors across the world!

I have had the honor of opening the doors in thirty-nine countries of the fifty-five where we have national organizations. There is Persia. I have been invited there five times across the years and have said each time that I hope I am going to get there. There are other areas of this world where I wish, before I die, I could witness for you. How many doors have been apparently sealed that we have talked about in these days—by which I mean very difficult situations—for meeting which we may think we have no precedent? But man's extremity, I have long since learned, is God's opportunity. That is the primary reason, then, that we should go. We should not say that it is too difficult or that the time is not ripe. No, let us hold the unshakable conviction that something greater will characterize our future than our past because there are so many more unentered open doors and also doors that Christ wants to open in answer to prayer. There are no two interpretations to that language, "Knock and it shall be opened unto you." Opened unto you, for what? Opened unto you to let Him through. Now, He might have had a different plan. I have sometimes wondered why He did not have the plan of direct action—of leaping right down out of the heavens and not working through human instrumentalities. But have we discovered that He has another plan? Has it not been through the prayers of others, and at times through their sacrificial devotion even unto death, that He has liberated His power?

Therefore, I rejoice. I cannot be pessimistic knowing what I do about difficulties. In the last two days, as I have listened and noted the difficulties—and you did not, in my judgment, exaggerate their gravity—I said to myself that there is all the greater chance for Christ. That is the reason why the Young Men's Christian Association on this next stretch, may have unexampled triumphs. Here is something that people honestly think is going to baffle us—that we cannot do it. That is not so. My dear friend, Barnett, we are going to be with you to a triumphant end on that debt business. That ought not to take us long. There are enough of us here this afternoon, if we all take seriously what has been said in our meetings, to open up the doors of privilege and sacrifice and achieve our goal before what you have so well called our centennial year is over. We will go Mr. Rockefeller one better, when he gives us until the fifteenth of October next year. I do not know of a thing, incidentally, that will please him more than for us to come in on the homestretch saying, "You put the lever in our hands and we have not used it in vain; we have lifted here and there, among the rich and the poor, and victory has been achieved."

Now I come to another ground of my hope. Besides the momentum, the atmosphere, and the open doors, I would remind us that we are now facing the greatest concentration of major unsolved problems that the Young Men's Christian Association and the Christian Church have ever faced. To me that is an added attraction. It necessitates our having superhuman wisdom, superhuman love, and superhuman power, as well as superhuman unity. That is all to the good.

The best days are out there in front because of the magnitude of the issues. There is the tragedy of the present world situation with its ever-widening area of neglect and its ever-deepening depth of human need, that haunts me in the watches of the night. Believe me, there are opportunities on every hand that are not simply as great as last year, but that transcend that which was crowded into last year.

That leads me to remind us of another reason why the best is in front of us. It is because of this global war and what it makes possible. Martin Luther said one day that before every great opportunity God sent to him some special trial. Let me repeat: before every great opportunity—not every little opportunity. I have had some opportunities that people did not call great, but which turned out to be among the greatest. And before every really great opportunity

I have had, God has sent some special trial or at times more than one severe testing. Surely this global war has been a special trial.

Our President's penetrating words about the boys "got me" because I have had the same response. When I think of what this war is costing in terms of these unending hospitals! One of my sons is in the medical service. All of my four children are related in one way or another—two sons and two daughters—to this world struggle. When I think of these unending hospitals, these lonely prisoner-of-war camps, these tens of millions on trek without home, with all of the loneliness, suffering, sorrow, and insanity, I say that God has some great design that will transcend any of the plans that men have projected up to this time. It is going to call for the exercise of the super-human and likewise, on a vastly larger scale, of the human. Of this there is no question. Surely it is going to be a better future than a past!

And I give as a climax reason the one that my good friend, Tracy Strong, quoted me as having said last night. I would like to repeat it right now. The great reason, the incomparably great reason why our best is in front of us is that we have a larger Christ. I did not say a new Christ, for He is the same, yesterday, today, yea, and forever—but larger. You ask, larger in what sense? Larger in the sense that there are so many more millions of men and women and children now than a few decades ago who did not previously know Him, who have become acquainted with Him, and who have had authentic, indubitable, convincing evidence of who He is, where He is, what He does. I say so many millions. Let me repeat again what I said about direct action. He might have worked directly, without human intermediaries, but, I repeat, it has always been His method to work through human instrumentalities. Therefore, we have a larger Christ, because we have so many more millions of men and women who know Him, and through whom He can communicate Himself than when I began my traveling life. We have a larger Christ, because He has shown His ability to transform whole communities as well as individuals. If anybody doubts this, I wish you would go out where I have a dear daughter in India. Part of her work is in the villages. I would like to take you to some of those villages and other so-called mass movement villages, where there were to be found the very dregs of human society, and where there were to be found the most obstinate and difficult situations I have ever known in my world travels. Whole communities of those outcastes have been transformed and from among them have been raised up men and women of saintliness and might. I have found that some of the leading clergymen were converts from those outcastes—the shadow of whom cast upon a person would spell defilement.

The fact is we have a larger Christ because there are so many more present-day evidences of what Christ can do collectively as well as individually.

Then, of course, there is the climax reason that has been evidenced in your findings in this Conference, and that is, Christ's ability to break the strangle hold of the greatest evils that bind us—like race prejudice, economic injustice, international bitterness, and hatred. Christ has shown His ability to make men strongest where once they were weakest; and where sin did abound grace does much more abound. Surely, the best is out there in front.

Now, while what I have said is all true, it must not stop there. It all hinges on what our attitude is going to be as we go from this place—we who are gathered here in this conference assembly. I am going to indicate some things we must do in order to fill with living content all that I have said.

In the first place, we must give and hold for Christ the central position. He is either the Lord of All or He is not Lord at all. He is the cornerstone of the structure we are striving to build. There is no other name under Heaven given among men whereby we must be saved. This Christ is able to do everything we are talking about, and therefore we regard Him as our cornerstone—our great basis that binds us—the Paris Basis. Thus, regarding Jesus Christ as our Lord and Savior, according to the Scriptures, we desire to be His disciples in our doctrine and in our lives and to associate our efforts for the extension of His Kingdom among men. In this respect let there never be uncertainty in our findings, in our plan of studies and lectures, or in our personal dealings. Let there be no ambiguity about our relation to Christ and our giving Him the supremacy and following His lead and proclaiming Him as actual Lord.

We must give the front-line place to the vital processes in our work. And what are these? First and foremost, exposing men to the Living Christ—not to the dead Christ, but to Him Who is alive forevermore. "But we all, with unveiled face beholding as in a mirror the glory of the Lord, are transformed into the same image from glory to glory, even as from the Lord the Spirit." Thus the most vital process we have in the Young Men's Christian Association is that of unveiling the face of Christ. He then does His work. He makes His own impression. If He makes it, it is profound. If He makes it, it is revolutionary. If He makes it, it is enduring. That is the superhuman aspect of our faith. But do not forget that He requires us to insure the unveiling of His face.

That leads me to the second vital process and that is the promotion of the intensive and assimilative study of the original writings of our faith—the Old and New Testament Scriptures. I am somewhat pained—I hope it can be shown to me that I am wrong—when I discover we have not had over 20,000 of our members in Bible classes last year. I remember a year when we had over 80,000, most of those in the student Associations, with the most marvelous Bible teachers this country and Canada could produce, training hundreds of other Bible teachers.

When I remember that Christ requires these writings through which to break out in contagious, superhuman, highly multiplying power, then I say, one of our most productive processes is going to be that of promoting what I call the intensive and assimilative, to make it a part of ourselves—this original study of the writings of our faith, without which we should not have our faith.

The third one of these highly multiplying processes is that of prayer. There were times when I did not believe in prayer, or was sorely perplexed. It was not a reality to me. Two things led me out into a profound belief in prayer and into an authentic experience of its power. One was the simple fact that prayer is something that can be verified only by praying, not simply by reading about prayer. I have nearly 300 books and pamphlets on the subject. It is not listening to others talk about prayer, and not listening to other people pray. Prayer, I say, is something that can be verified only by shutting the door, in secret seeking His face, where there is no possibility of hypocrisy.

A second thing that led me to prayer was the simple reflection that Jesus Christ prayed. Yes, He taught prayer. He taught us not one Lord's Prayer. There are thirteen of them. He taught us many things about how to pray. The results of my Bible study of an hour a day for two months I could put on two large pages. This included His prayers, also His teachings on prayer. The greatest thing, however, was not so much that He commanded prayer, taught prayer, and gave us models of prayer, but that He, Himself, prayed.

When I was in Jerusalem next to the last time, this passage stared me in the face: "He went, as His custom was, unto the mount of Olives." Think of it, the perfect example, the perfect teacher, the one who never led any man into error! Out He came from the crowded city, out of the noisy city, out of the busy city, out of the sin-bound city—out under those peaceful olive trees, where some of us have gathered for prayer—to hold unhurried communion with the Heavenly Father. My fellow members of the Young Men's Christian Association, what presumption and worse than folly, if Christ found this a desirable or necessary practice, to assume that we can do without it. So I say, a third one of these vital processes that we must promote among our members, no matter what things we leave unpromoted, is prayer.

And then there is a fourth process, and that is to become ourselves recruiting officers. If I had my life to live over again, how much more attention I would give to that. As the great British statesman, Morley, put it, "He who does the work is not so profitably employed as he who multiplies the doers." That should become true of every Young Men's Christian Association secretary here and, likewise, of every layman. We who are doing the work are not so profitably employed as we would be if we were multiplying the numbers of those who will go and do likewise.

This brings me to another thing we must bear in mind, and that is what Herbert Hoover said to me the other day at the Waldorf-Astoria Hotel. I met him first as a student in Stanford University the year it was opened, and when I planted a Young Men's Christian Association there. In this interview to which I refer he said, "Mott, I have come to the conclusion that nine-tenths of the Christian religion is set forth in the parable of the Good Samaritan." I could not take it all in at that time. I went away to reflect, and when I went to see him shortly after the death of his dear wife, I said, "Mr. President," (as I continue to call him) "I have come to believe what you have said, and that is, that nine-tenths of the Christian religion is gathered up in the parable of the Good Samaritan." What led me to this conviction was the word of Christ: "Why call ye me 'Lord, Lord,' and do not the things that I say?" Christ went about, as He said, doing good, illustrating good, making good contagious. And so I say, let us all go and do likewise. And what an opportunity there is, in view of what Tracy Strong has taught us, and others here, about the tragedies that are all about us today. I could have enlarged upon it to include the 50,000,000 in China who are refugees, and some tens of millions in France still, and on the whole Russian front that are refugees—without homes; or I would remind us again of those wounded. I saw the printed list in the papers yesterday of our numbers of wounded. It is enough to solemnize us all right here as we think of those, as well as the number who have been killed and the number who are missing. And we must not and cannot forget the millions of lonely men in the many prisoner-of-war camps.

Then I think of the little children. I cannot get away from thinking of them. A letter from Greece not long since—before the Allies pushed in there—said that nineteen out of every twenty babies born in Greece die from malnutrition. It reminds me of a Quakeress who came into a meeting in New York, where I was presiding, of representatives of the different Protestant denominations, on our relief problems. A note came up to me saying, "A young woman has just landed from France, one of the Quaker workers. I suggest you call her out." I did. She rose up and spoke. She had her notes on library index cards. She said, referring to her notes, that we must send a worker to this place, and two, or better three, to that place; that we must send so many jars of a certain medical ointment to another place, and so on. Once she stopped reading and said, "I must stop and tell you a story about a person I met the last time I was here in America before I went back to France. He told me that he would like to give a generous meal to 150 little children in France who were not being sufficiently fed. He emphasized that they should be little children." She described what she had done. She had gathered 150 small children, nine years or under, as I recall; she had put together the 150 meals in little paper boxes and placed them in the front of a schoolroom. She described their countenances as they looked at those boxes before them before they were given out. Here were 150 little children with spindle legs, all of them with little wasted bodies. She said that some of their faces were wrinkled like old women's faces. Then she described their faces when she had given the boxes out. She described their tearing them apart and the great avidity with which they ate up every morsel. But the thing that got me was the last part of the story—how they looked after they had eaten up all the morsels and there were no more. As much as to say, "No more! no more!" I went out and resolved that if God would spare my life I would do vastly more before the end of the year to help the innocent little ones. My daughter in India, in a famine region, has, I think, nine kitchens with forty-five in each, and she does not invite anyone to come to those kitchens who gets more than one-half of one meal a day. The places are always crowded, day after day. So I say, I cannot get out of my mind what my friend Hoover said. He is right. "Why call ye me 'Lord, Lord,' and do not the things that I say?" He who went about doing good and not simply talking good; He who went about working miracles, helping the hungry and the starving, the emaciated, the deaf and the dumb and the insane!

Another reason we must occupy ourselves diligently is that of the difficult jobs there are to be tackled. I hope there is not a delegate here of whom it can be said after a few months that he has gone back to do less than when he came here; but rather, that it can be said of everyone of us, in one way or another, that we have got hold of something down here at Buffalo which has called out our all-too-latent powers. The Master summoned us here to an almost impossible task, and we counted the cost and went out to do it. Why not let this example of life, of the larger Christ, become contagious? Why not let us be able to say after this conference that we have caught the spark, not only in these findings which we have adopted (and which, by the way, we should never have adopted unanimously unless there had been good thinking back of them), but in what may grow out of them? Let us give effect to those. But let us permeate the whole thing with the spirit of unselfishness.

Another thing we must do. Let us have more retreats. The Roman Catholics last year in thirty-six states, had from one to thirty retreats of laymen. I have been familiar with the retreats of the priests in my reading and in my travels, but had not known of their use of this method among the laymen. We may well pay heed to their experience. By the way, the Detroit Association has had a plan of retreats that for years has been very helpful. Twice a year a goodly company of their laymen spend a day in a wonderful chapel in one of the country places. They find it facilitates holding communion with God. There they spend the time unhurriedly, recollectedly in God's presence and under the penetrating blaze of the Scriptures. This practice enables one to understand the deeper notes faithfully struck by the Detroit Association. One longs to have this practice—each one of us in our own way—multiplied. I recall also the practice of the Kansas City Association. I remember I attended one of their retreats held on Sunday in town. It has proved to be a veritable powerhouse. But especially in this busy time, in this most demanding of all times, let us do things that we are not now doing which will help get men right with God, and provide an open and unhindered channel through which He can break out with irresistible power.

That leads me to the next thing. Let us multiply the number of small groups or so-called cells. I have always belonged to at least one group. There are only three of us yet living out of that group which we started forty years ago—Robert Speer, Del Pierson and I are the only ones still living. We did have twelve. Some have gone into the land of larger dimensions and others have taken their places. What do we not owe to those quiet days together—one day each year! I don't tell you what we talk about. But we share with the greatest intimacy and helpfulness our unsatisfactory as well as our most rewarding spiritual experiences, our burdens, and the vistas ahead; also the secrets of largest spiritual discovery and fruitage. Month by month we share with one another objects of intercession and answers to prayer. What do we not all owe to this fellowship!

Someone asked me the other day, "Dr. Mott, if you had your life to live over again, would you make a change in it?" And I said, at once, "Yes, one change at least. I would spend vastly more time on the age of adolescence than where I did spend it." Most of you know I spent it on the student age from about eighteen up to twenty-five and beyond. If I had it over, my life would be spent working primarily with young people between the ages of eleven and twelve, and sixteen or seventeen. With you, this afternoon, I see these boys in the vision-forming years. Do not old men have visions? Yes. But when did they get them? When they were young. I see them in the vision-forming years, in the habit-forming years, the years of determining life attitudes and tendencies; in the years of surprise, in the years of awakening, in the years of dedication, in the years of adventure. Yes, I would win and serve them in those incomparable years which never come back. It is the time of times. It is indeed the creative time.

I will sum up now in two things all that I have said. If every man here would give heed to these two things I should not be concerned about the others. One of them is that we cultivate attentiveness unto God. I have been more helped by the Russian Orthodox Church and by the Society of Friends—the Quakers—than by any two denominations, not excepting my own, and that is saying a great deal. You ask what is there about the Russians which has helped me? Well, it is the attention they pay to the doctrine of the Resurrection. The Church of Rome, you know, rivets it on the Crucifixion. The Russian Orthodox Church is centered on the Resurrection. Their watchword is "He is Risen!" Not only that, but they lay great stress on this article of the Creed—the Communion of Saints. You and I are in the habit of rising almost every Sunday and among various articles we say that we believe in the Communion of Saints. What meaning does that have to us? It has infinite meaning to the Russians. It means not only the fellowship of those gathered around them as they stand or kneel in prayer; not only the fellowship of their relatives and friends who are living, but far more, they have in mind those who have gone before into the land of large dimensions, where they see the King in His beauty and where the heavenly host are occupied with the high offices of praise and worship. Are they not likewise ministering spirits, as we are told in the Scriptures? And so, how much these Russians are enriched! We sometimes think of them as poverty-stricken. But I say to you that we are living relatively poverty-stricken in contrast with what we might do if we had gathered around us not only loved ones from over in that other Land with whom we should still have the center of communion, but the ever-enlarging host of the Church of Christ purchased by Him—alive forevermore.

The second thing is like unto this, and that is, that we try to live under the constant sense of immediacy. Some people say, "Mott, that is your hobby." And I think they have in mind when they say that, that I, in my early days of travel, wrote my second book on the evangelization of the world in this generation. (Think of the presumption!) The other day a Bishop of the Church of England wrote me and said, "Mott, if you were to rewrite that book would you change it today?"

I went back to the book. It was written over forty years ago. I went through it critically. I could not change it in any detail except, as I wrote him, that I would have to add more illustrations, especially of recent years. But the argument would stand.

In some lectures that I gave at one of the universities in Georgia, my last lecture was on this subject: "Is the Watchword of the Student Volunteer Movement, the Evangelization of the World in this Generation, Still Valid? If Not, Why Not?" To the best of my ability I still adhere to this great conviction. Therefore, I am urging with this larger context in mind that we all cultivate a sense of immediacy. But I have a smaller context. I have in mind what Christ had in mind when He said, "Say not ye there are yet four months and then cometh the harvest"—four months after Buffalo. "Lift up your eyes and behold the fields that are already ripe unto harvest"—for the sickle. Say ye not yet that there are four months to put into effect that which has been borne in upon us these days by the power of the Spirit of God.

WORLD'S ALLIANCE OF THE YOUNG MEN'S CHRISTIAN ASSOCIATIONS

THE OFFICER'S COUNCIL OF THE WORLD'S ALLIANCE OF YOUNG MEN'S CHRISTIAN ASSOCIATIONS, AUGUST, 1929.

WORLD'S ALLIANCE OF THE YOUNG MEN'S CHRISTIAN ASSOCIATIONS

✦✦✦

REPORTS OF THE COMMITTEE OF DELEGATES, AND REPORTS OF JOHN R. MOTT AT SERIES OF WORLD CONFERENCES PRIOR TO THE HELSINGFORS CONFERENCE

REPORT OF THE COMMITTEE OF DELEGATES OF THE FOURTEENTH INTERNATIONAL CONFERENCE OF THE YOUNG MEN'S CHRISTIAN ASSOCIATIONS AT BASEL, JULY, 1898

YOUR COMMITTEE RECOMMENDS to the Conference the adoption of the following resolutions:

1. The Conference expresses its profound gratitude to Almighty God for the marked blessing bestowed upon the work of the Central International Committee during the last four years, which have been characterized by greater evidence of growth than any similar period in the history of the Association Alliance.

2. We note with satisfaction that helpful visits have been made among the Associations in many lands, that in various countries national alliances have been formed, that national conferences have been held for the first time in different countries, that promising Associations have been established in several leading cities, that the work of correspondence has been carried on in eight different languages, that the usual publications have been issued, and that the other work of the Committee centering at the headquarters has been successfully prosecuted.

3. We recommend that the Committee continue the work on the following lines approved by experience:

a. The formation and development of national alliances, and of strong Associations in great cities.

b. Co-operation in the organization of continental conferences of secretaries.

c. The holding of training courses for secretaries at places where the local Associations offer a good object lesson of the principles and methods of Association work. The greatest care should of course be exercised not only in the arrangement of such courses, but also in admitting only such men as are strongly approved by their local and national committees.

d. The conducting of Bible courses and courses of Young Men's Christian Association instruction, to be carried on as far as possible in quiet places.

e. The promotion of the observance of the Universal Week of Prayer in November. We suggest that Associations invite pastors to preach sermons bearing on work among young men the Sunday preceding this week.

f. The issuing of the *Messenger* as a valuable means of information and communication among the Associations, and such other publications as have been found useful to the Associations.

g. The making of journeys with the objects as here indicated in view:

In France, general development;
in Belgium, general development;
in Spain, raising up of the work, if possible, and formation of a national alliance;
in Portugal, to give greater support and form a national alliance;
in Italy, general development;
in Hungary, to give greater support and form a national alliance, as well as to start a central Association in Budapest;
in Austria, general support and formation of a national alliance;
in Russia, general support and formation of a national alliance;
in Denmark, general support and making known the principles of the Paris Basis;
in Germany, Holland, Scandinavia, Great Britain, America, and Switzerland, tours in order to make the International work known and to gain interest in it;
in the Oriental countries, especially China, Japan, and India, missionary journeys if possible;
in other countries, journeys in order to create interest and to promote closer international relations between us.

These journeys will only be undertaken after the national or local committees have been communicated with, and as far as they are in harmony with them.

4. We suggest that the Committee continue the negotiations now

in progress with the Danish National Committee with reference to joining the International Alliance on the Paris Basis.

5. Recognizing the great importance of the Christian Movement among the students of the world which has been organized since the last conference, we wish to express our special thankfulness to God, to convey our brotherly greetings to the coming conference of the World's Student Christian Federation at Eisenach, and to express our hope that the friendly and intimate relationship which now exists between the International Alliance of Young Men's Christian Associations and this Federation may continue to their mutual benefit.

6. We urge that the attention of the Associations be called to the necessity of special efforts on behalf of railway men, seamen, commercial travelers, miners, waiters, and such other classes of young men as are in need of such help as the Associations can give.

7. We advise the development of junior branches in the Associations—a work to which we attach great importance. We express our conviction that this work should always be carried on as a department of the Associations.

8. We gratefully accept the cordial invitation of the National Committee of Norway to hold the Fifteenth International Conference in Christiania.

9. We authorize the International Committee to hold plenary meetings in addition to the one in 1900, the exact time and place to be determined by the Committee, provided this does not involve extra expense on the part of the Committee. While it is most important that the members of the Committee should all be present at such meetings, if this should be found impossible, it is understood that they can delegate their powers to men approved by their respective national committees.

10. We desire to express our warm and affectionate sympathy with our brother Mr. Robert R. McBurney in his illness, and our earnest hope and prayer that through God's blessing he may be speedily restored to health and to his wonted activity among young men.

11. Feeling very grateful to the senior secretary of the International Committee for his devotion, and for the manner in which he has performed his duties during the twenty years of his general secretaryship, we place on record our conviction that Mr. Charles Fermaud has merited well of the Associations. In consequence of this we again assure him of our confidence and faithful affection, hoping that the Lord will renew his youth like the eagle, and uphold him in the post of honor to which he has called him.

12. We highly appreciate the action of the Committee in calling to their service Mr. Christian Phildius. We recognize the very valu-

able work which he has accomplished, and trust that this marks but the beginning of a long period of usefulness on behalf of the young men of the world.

13. We express our sincere gratitude to those members of the Central International Committee who have so generously given their time, strength, and money to the work of visitation in different countries, thereby setting such a worthy example to the whole Association brotherhood of the principle and spirit of voluntary service, conspicuously to that member who has recently made a tour around the world in the interest of the Associations.

14. We are glad to learn that the deficit of over 10,000 francs, mentioned in the report of the Committee, has been entirely removed; and we most heartily thank the friends in different countries whose gifts have led to this result, and thus enabled the Committee to continue their work without embarrassment.

15. We authorize the Committee to adopt a budget of 34,000 francs, per annum, until the next conference; and we request the delegates of this Conference to enlist the co-operation of the members of their Associations in obtaining the entire amount, and as much more as possible, in view of the enlarging work and opportunities of the Committee. We would advise that an opportunity be given to the members during the Week of Prayer to make a thank offering for this great work.

16. We hereby elect the following as members of the Central International Committee to serve until the next conference:

Executive: Professor Edouard Barde, Henry Fatio, Ernest Favre, Charles Fermaud, Adolphe Hoffmann, Louis Perrot, Max Perrot, Christian Phildius, J. A. Porret, Gustave Tophel.
South Africa: J. D. Cartwright, Cape Town
Germany: Pastor A. Klug, Barmen; Superintendent K. Krummacher, Elberfeld; Count A. Bernstorff, Berlin
America: James Stokes, New York; Cephas Brainerd, Indiana; H. B. Ames, Montreal, Canada; Honorary Secretary R. C. Morse. New York
Austria: H. von Tardy, Vienna
Belgium: Jean de Looper, Jumet
Denmark: V. Schousboe, Aalborg (corresponding member)
France: Professor Raoul Allier, Paris
Great Britain: Sir G. Williams, London; Honorary Secretary W. H. Mills, London; D. Dreghorn, Glasgow, Scotland
Holland: E. Sillem, Amsterdam
Hungary: A. de Szilassy, Budapest

India: W. R. Arbuthnot, Madras
Italy: Comm. E. Piovanelli, Rome
Japan: Taizo Miyoshi, Tokyo
Norway: Professor P. Waage, Christiania
Oceania: D. Walker, Sydney
Portugal: A. H. da Silva, Porto
Russia: A. Findeisen, St. Petersburg
Spain: Luis de Vargas, Barcelona
Sweden: Prince O. Bernadotte, Stockholm
Switzerland: R. Sarasin-Warnery, Basel

17.   Finally, we would abundantly utter our gratitude for the most
hearty welcome which we have received in Basel; for the admirable
local organization of this Conference which may well serve as a model
for coming conferences; for the cordial hospitality extended to us by
our hosts and hostesses; for the self-sacrificing work of the ladies' committee and those who have assisted them; for the influential recognition
of the Conference by the government of Basel, for the valued co-operation of the pastors of the city; for the assistance rendered by service,
gift, and prayer on the part of the members of the Young Men's Christian Associations of Switzerland; for the help given by various societies
of Basel, especially by the musical organizations; for the enjoyable
reception given by the St. Chrischona Mission; for the able leadership
of the Conference by Mr. Reinhold Sarasin-Warnery; and for the
appreciated co-operation of the many friends who have not only in
public but also in quiet ways contributed to make the Fourteenth
International Conference such a conspicuous success and, with the
continued favor of God, a steppingstone to larger achievements in
the world-wide Association brotherhood.

On Behalf of the Committee of Delegates:

JOHN R. MOTT, *Chairman*

REPORT OF THE COMMITTEE OF DELEGATES OF THE FIFTEENTH
INTERNATIONAL CONFERENCE OF THE YOUNG MEN'S CHRISTIAN
ASSOCIATIONS AT CHRISTIANIA, AUGUST, 1902

Your Committee recommends to the Conference the adoption of
the following resolutions:

1.   We would recognize with sincere and profound gratitude the
hand of God in the continued development of the united work of the
Young Men's Christian Associations, as expressed in the varied
activities of the World's Committee. The progress of the four years

which have elapsed since the memorable conference at Basel is inexplicable apart from the direct working of the Holy Spirit.

2. We note with satisfaction that effect has been given to the general policy recommended by the conference at Basel, and would call attention to the progress achieved on the following lines:

    a. The organization of over eighty new local Associations, and of three or four national unions;

    b. The visitation and encouragement of hundreds of existing Associations, scattered throughout many lands;

    c. Helpful co-operation rendered at numerous conventions and conferences;

    d. The organization and direction of secretarial conferences and of special training courses, as well as the selection and locating of secretaries at a number of centers.

    e. The continued publication of the *Messenger,* and the conduct of the varied and extensive work of the central office.

The fact that all this work has been accomplished without incurring a financial deficit gives cause for special thankfulness.

3. The Committee records its deep sense of appreciation of the arduous and devoted labors of the two general secretaries, Messrs. Fermaud and Phildius, and of the loyal and conscientious co-operation rendered by their assistants, Messrs. Schlaeppi, von Starck, and others. The invaluable voluntary service rendered by the chairman, Professor Barde, and other members of the World's Committee, not only in committee work, but likewise in special visitation, also calls for grateful recognition, as a helpful example to the whole Association brotherhood of self-sacrificing effort in the interests of young men.

In the death of M. Max Perrot of Switzerland, Superintendent Karl Krummacher of Germany, Mr. Robert McBurney, and Mr. Dwight L. Moody of North America, Professor Peter Waage of Norway, and Pastor Wilhelm Beck of Denmark, the world-wide work of the Associations has sustained a loss the extent and significance of which we are destined increasingly to realize. Let us unite our prayers that God may raise up more men of like consecration and ability to guide our counsels and lead our forces in the coming years.

4. We would recommend as general lines of policy to be pursued during the coming three years:

    a. The work of visitation should include not only the strengthening of Associations already established, but also the creation of new organizations, both local and national. In carrying on this work in fields already possessing a national organization, continued care should be taken to act in harmony with the national committees, and to lead them to assume as large a burden of responsibility as possible. Moreover, as in the past, effort should be concentrated on building up model Associations at strategic points.

b. In view of the benefit attending the conferences for secretaries, the Committee should continue this feature of their work, at the same time encouraging the holding of similar gatherings, under the auspices of national committees, as well as training courses for Association workers generally at suitable centers.

c. The Correspondence Department of the administrative work should be still further developed, to the end that the central office may become of additional value as a bureau of information and advice, particularly with reference to the more isolated Associations and workers.

d. In regard to the Publications Department, we endorse the suggestion of the Committee that in addition to the improving of the *Messenger,* a fortnightly duplicated news circular for distribution to the Association press and among leaders of the work, be inaugurated. The pamphlet literature of the Committee should also be enriched.

e. Effort should be made to secure a wider and more thorough observance of the Week of Prayer for young men. Too much care cannot be expended upon the preparation of the program, with a view to insuring the best spiritual results! National committees should co-operate in this matter in ways to be suggested by the central office, as well as in encouraging every Association to take a collection during the week in aid of the work of the World's Committee.

f. The policy should be continued of encouraging the national organizations to work for special classes, such as railway men, soldiers, sailors, waiters, and such other classes as from the nature of their calling require specialized effort. Particular stress is to be laid upon work for boys, making sure that all such effort is organically related to the local Associations. In so far as the work undertaken by the Central Commission of the French-speaking Junior Branches will help to develop activity along these lines, we approve of the action taken by the World's Committee in affiliating this organization.

In employing the various methods and means which have been mentioned, the Committee should lead the Associations to keep in the forefront the chief objects of the Movement; namely to lead young men to become disciples of Jesus Christ as their only Savior and Lord, to help them in the battle with temptation and forces of evil, to build up strong faith and Christian character, to form right habits of devotional Bible study and prayer, to develop among them the true missionary spirit on behalf of the young men of the world, and to accentuate their oneness in Jesus Christ—all of which is implied in the fundamental declaration of the World's Alliance, the Paris Basis.

5. In view of the fact that 1905 will be the jubilee year of the world's conference which adopted the Paris Basis—the first world's conference ever held—we advise the World's Committee to hold the next conference in Paris that year, provided that satisfactory arrangements can be made. Realizing the advantages of having a registration fee, we authorize a fee of 25 francs for each regular delegate. Approval is given to the plan introduced at this Conference of presenting a general topic at a plenary session and discussing it subsequently by sectional meetings according to language—excepting such matters as affect the policy of the World's Committee.

6. Recognizing the close relation which already exists in many countries between the national branches of the World's Student Christian Federation and the general Association Movement, we express the hope that such relations may be further strengthened and established wherever possible and that all overlapping be carefully avoided in the cultivation of the student field.

7. The spiritual need of the young men in non-Christian lands is so great that the national committees of Christian countries should be led to feel their responsibility to help them. Why should not each national union undertake work on behalf of some part of this great field? A national committee in undertaking such work in a given field should do so in perfect accord not only with the national committee of Young Men's Christian Associations in that field, but also with the Association committee of any Christian country already at work there.

A national committee should not begin work in a colony of a country which has a national committee without previous consultation with that committee.

The World's Committee should co-operate in promoting the most harmonious and effective effort on the part of the different national committees engaged in such service. In all this foreign work a special burden of responsibility should naturally be laid on the national committees of the non-Christian countries.

8. While recognizing the tasks awaiting us in non-Christian countries, let us not forget the pressing claims of different parts of Europe in which the work is not yet fully established. A number of these fields, so far as experienced Association leaders are concerned, are even more destitute than some of the fields of Asia. Every effort should be put forth to meet the crisis confronting our work in several of these countries.

9. In view of the enlarged opportunity and responsibility of the Committee arising out of the last-named and the various other matters dealt with in this report we authorize the appointment of a third general secretary to rank with the two already at work.

10. We authorize the Committee to adopt a budget of 45,000 francs per annum until the next conference. This is understood to include provision for but one additional secretary, with the necessary traveling and general office expenses involved in such enlargement. We urge the national committees proportionately to increase their contributions.

11. We recommend that the World's Committee make a careful study of the best plan for improving the world's conferences, and for arranging such other international meetings as may be found essential to the best development of the work; reporting their recommendations to the next convention.

12. We hereby elect the following as members of the World's Committee, to serve until the next conference:

Executive: Professor Edouard Barde, Pastor A. Hoffmann, Professor E. Martin, Henry Fatio, Louis Perrot, Charles Fermaud, Christian Phildius, J. Johannot, R. Sarasin-Warnery, Pastor J. A. Porret
America: James Stokes, New York; Cephas Brainerd, New York; H. B. Ames, Montreal, Canada; Honorary Secretary R. C. Morse, New York.
Austria: Dr. C. A. Witz-Oberlin, Vienna
Belgium: Jean de Looper, Jumet
Denmark: Count J. Moltke, Copenhagen
France: Professor Raoul Allier, Paris
Germany: Count A. Bernstorff, Berlin; Pastor A. Klug, Barmen; Pastor F. Berlin, Berlin

Great Britain: Sir G. Williams, London; Honorary Secretary W. H.
  Mills, London; D. Dreghorn, Glasgow, Scotland
Holland: E. Sillem, Amsterdam
Hungary: A. de Szilassy, Budapest
India: Professor S. Satthianadhan, Calcutta
Italy: Dr. R. Prochet, Rome
Japan: Dr. Ibuka, Tokyo
Norway: Stiftsprobst C. Hall, Christiania
Oceania: David Walker, Sydney
Portugal: Pastor Alfredo da Silva, Porto
Russia: Pastor A. Findeisen, St. Petersburg
South Africa: J. D. Cartwright, Cape Town
Spain: Pastor G. Fliedner, Madrid
Sweden: Prince O. Bernadotte, Stockholm
Switzerland: G. Wagner, Basel

13. This Conference, consisting of 2,100 delegates, representing
Young Men's Christian Associations in thirty-one countries and being
thus the largest conference ever held on the continent of Europe,
desires to express its hearty acknowledgment of the gracious kindness
accorded to it, alike by His Majesty the King of Norway and Sweden,
the Storthing of Norway and the City Council of Christiania; by the
heads of the Church and War Offices, the Commandant of the
Fortress, and others in granting the use of buildings for the various
sessions and services; and by the many families which have so hospi-
tably opened their homes to receive the delegates. Special thanks are
tendered to the Kristiania Elektriske Sporvei and the Kristiania
Sporveisselskab, for the generous offer of the free use of their trams
to all foreign delegates; also to the editors of the Norwegian press
for the sympathetic attention they have given to the Conference.
    Finally, we would congratulate the local organizing committee
and the many young men who have supported them upon the most
successful and efficient way in which they have fulfilled their onerous
duties, and convey to them the warm gratitude of the whole body of
delegates for their self-denying and devoted labors in the interests of
the Conference. It it our united hope and prayer that as the result of
the work of the Spirit of God, in and through this assembly, the Kingdom of Christ may be widely extended among the young men of
Norway and throughout the world.

On behalf of the Committee of Delegates:

JOHN R. MOTT, *Chairman*

THE WORK OF THE WORLD'S COMMITTEE OF YOUNG MEN'S CHRISTIAN ASSOCIATIONS

REMARKS AT THE MEETING OF THE WORLD'S COMMITTEE, GENEVA, SWITZERLAND, 1903

On this the twenty-fifth anniversary of the World's Committee, it is fitting not only that we recount the achievements of this central agency of supervision during the first quarter-century of its history, and abundantly utter the memory of God's great goodness to us as an organization, but also that we set before us the main purposes for which this Committee exists, and which we should continue to emphasize in our policy. It may be well at this time to call attention to the main lines of work which should occupy us in the new epoch on which we have entered.

Manifestly it is our duty to carry on a thorough study of the young men of the world. We should become increasingly familiar with their physical, intellectual, social, moral, and religious conditions; with the forces of evil which tend to undermine them; with the agencies and influences which shield them and build them up; with their dominating ideals and ambitions; with their attitude toward Jesus Christ and His Church; with the problems involved in reaching them for Christ, developing them in faith and character; and enlisting them in Christian service; with the opportunities of extending among them the Kingdom of Christ; and with the most approved means and methods of work on their behalf. Such studies are being carried on in a more or less fragmentary way by individuals and by societies in different parts of the word. But there is need of a group of men, such as our own Committee, standing on a high watchtower, looking out over all lands and races, making a comprehensive study of the young men of the world, and then placing their knowledge at the disposal of the leaders in work among young men in the different nations.

It is one of our most important functions to establish and to help develop efficient national Young Men's Christian Association organizations. These should be adapted to the conditions which exist in the various countries. As quickly as possible, they should be made independent or self-directing and self-supporting. With reference to the cultivation of the fields which they occupy, our policy should be to decrease and to lead them to increase.

We should aim to build up, or to have built up, at principal centers, Associations of such strength and vitality that they will determine the character of the Association work throughout the region or land in which they are located. Such has been, and is, the influence of Associations like those in Stockholm, Paris, New York, and Tokyo. Who can measure the far-reaching influence our Committee may exert on whole nations and peoples, by building up during the next ten years model Associations at Madrid, Lisbon, Athens, Budapest, Sofia, Belgrade, and Bucharest? In each land we should promote the type of work which is best-adapted in that particular land to realize the spiritual purposes of the Association. As a Committee we should discover and propagate the best ideas of all nations as to how best to carry on Association work. God has not revealed all of His mind regarding the Young Men's Christian Association to any one nation. His Spirit works in divers places as well as in divers manners. A world's committee should reflect faithfully and impartially this wonderfully varied and rich manifestation of the mind of God as seen throughout the world field.

The World's Committee should unify or bind together in aim, in effort, and in spirit, the various national Association Movements. This should be done, in the first place, in order that these Movements may be most helpful to one another. It would be difficult to overstate the great good which the Committee has already accomplished in introducing the national Movements to one another, and in setting them to acting and reacting on one another. It has enabled the strong to help the weak, and, alike important and in accord wth God's manner of working, has enabled the weak at times to help the strong. This most desirable process is going on constantly as a result of our conferences, the visits of our secretaries, the dissemination of our literature, the promotion of intervisitation, and the direct work and influence of the members of the Committee itself. And the good which is being accomplished is worth many, many times more than all that the work costs. Another reason why this unifying work of the Committee is so important, is that it enables the Young Mens Christian Associations, scattered throughout the world, to present a united front to the world. Let us not forget that there is a united worldliness, a united sinfulness, a united unbelief, a united indifference. If we are to overcome such an opposition and make a real impression on an unbelieving world, we must realize the answer to our Lord's prayer, and be one indeed. To accomplish this larger and stronger unity, let us as a committee in all our activities and plans emphasize the things on which good Christians of all lands are agreed, and not the things on which they differ.

Have not the different nations a right to expect that the World's Committee will lead in forward movements? There are regions beyond, in every direction, in this wonderful work for young men. There should be enlargement or expansion in every nation and in every department of the work. The unorganized fields should be occupied. Efforts should be put forth on behalf of classes of young men now untouched. New phases or features of the work should be undertaken. In season and out of season the Association should be summoned to stand for work of higher quality. In the last analysis the measure of our permanent influence will be not the extent of our work, but its genuineness and thoroughness.

Possibly the greatest service rendered by this Committee has been its constant insistence on the supremacy of the spiritual work. Through all the years, it has been unswervingly loyal to this vital principle. So let it ever be. May it continue to exalt Jesus Christ as Lord, to magnify the Word of God in the hearts of young men, to advocate and to exemplify the efficacy and reality of prayer, to stimulate the Associations everywhere to more aggressive evangelism, to hold forth as the inspiring objective the reaching of the young men of the whole world, to hasten the answer to the prayer of our Lord "that the all may be one."

THE ACHIEVEMENT OF HALF A CENTURY OF THE WORLD'S ALLIANCE OF YOUNG MEN'S CHRISTIAN ASSOCIATIONS

ABSTRACT OF AN ADDRESS AT THE WORLD'S CONFERENCE JUBILEE AT PARIS, MAY, 1905

The Young Men's Christian Association has constituted the first great and comprehensive lay Movement in the Christian Church. It was organized by laymen. It has been developed chiefly by laymen. Its leaders are laymen. It has powerfully stimulated lay effort among all branches of the Church.

The Association has emphasized before the world and done much to realize the ideal of true Christian manhood. It has recognized its mission to the whole man—body, mind, and spirit. Both psychologically and sociologically this has been a contribution of incalculable importance in the direction of developing symmetrical young manhood. It has helped to develop the most attractive type of Christian manhood—a type characterized by manliness, reality, open-mindedness, sympathy for men, and loyalty to Christ.

The Association Movement has consolidated the forces of Christian young men of all the churches and has enabled them thus to present a united front to the influences which tend to destroy faith and character. Under its leadership, and as a result of its methods, a far more scientific and effective warfare has been waged against the great evils which assail young men than in any previous period in the history of Christianity.

The Young Men's Christian Association has developed an organization and varied agencies which have enabled it to a remarkable degree to lay hold of and deeply impress young men of all types— social, intellectual, and racial. In organizing one class of men to reach other men of that class—for example, students to reach students, railway men to reach railway men, soldiers to reach soldiers —it has recognized a principle and employed a method which have achieved the largest results. One of the best definitions of organization was that given by a missionary in China. "Organization," said he, "is the means of distributing force most advantageously." Judged by this standard, the Association may well rank as one of the most effective, if not the most effective, religious organization of modern times.

The Association Movement has done much to break down barriers between man and man and to fuse together all classes of men of right impulses. Who can measure what it has accomplished in drawing together the rich and the poor, the brainworker and the artisan? Think also what wonders the Association has accomplished in drawing together men of all religions and of no religion! In the Madras Association, for example, with its 600 members and more, you will find men of probably twenty different religions.

The Associations have carried forward on behalf of young men an evangelistic campaign of mighty sweep and power and of ever increasing results. The evangelistic note has ever sounded out clear and true from this Movement. It is not strange, therefore, that under its influence not only the number, but also the proportion of young men led into a vital faith in Christ, has increased from decade to decade. This is true, not only among the masses of young men, but also among the educated classes, as is strikingly seen in the Association work in the colleges and universities. These growing evangelistic triumphs have been witnessed in the pathway of the activity of the Associations, not only in Christian lands, but also in the more difficult fields of the non-Christian world—Japan, China, and India.

The Young Men's Christian Association has afforded a fresh demonstration to the world in a materialistic age of the reality of the great spiritual facts and forces. What organization has more faithfully and effectively emphasized the dynamic power of the Word of God, the mountain-moving energy of prayer, the sufficiency of the work of Jesus Christ and of the Holy Spirit? This Movement has for half a century been unswervingly loyal to the cardinal points of the Christian faith. It has stood as immovable as the eternal hills for the inspired Paris Basis, which we have so solemnly reaffirmed during these days.

While working out its own specific mission the Young Men's

Christian Association has either directly or by example and suggestion led to the organization of other great spiritual Movements. The Evangelical Alliance is a significant example. The Young Women's Christian Association, which in some respects has already surpassed the men's Movement, is traceable to the Young Men's Christian Association. The founder of the Young People's Society of Christian Endeavor, which in turn has led to other extensive movements among the young people of the churches, has repeatedly borne testimony to the influence which the Associations have had upon that Movement. The founder of the Brotherhood of St. Andrew, which is the most efficient young men's society to be found in any one body of Christians, has said that he derived the idea of establishing such a society from his connection with the Association. The Student Volunteer Movement for Foreign Missions, which is without question the largest and most fruitful enterprise in behalf of the world's evangelization ever organized in the Church, is a direct outgrowth of the Associations. The World's Student Christian Federation, which embraces a membership of over 100,000 students and professors in nearly 2,000 universities and colleges, was organized and developed under Association leadership.

In some ways the greatest result of this Movement within the fifty years has been its extension to the young men of the non-Christian nations of the world. In building up at the great strategic centers of Asia, Africa, and South America model Associations which are reaching for Christ the most aggressive and progressive class of society —the young men—this Movement is meeting the greatest need of these vast continents. In seeking to make the universities and colleges of the non-Christian nations strongholds and propagating centers of Christianity, the Associations are influencing the very leadership of over two-thirds of the population of the world. In laying on its members in all these countries a burden of responsibility for the evangelization of their own people the Association is helping to solve in the most effective way what many deem to be the greatest problem of foreign missions.

The Young Men's Christian Association has done more to promote and to realize true Christian unity than any other agency. By accentuating the points on which true Christians are agreed, by actually drawing Christians together in a common work, and by fusing together in its student Associations the future leaders of all denominations, this Movement has accomplished wonders in the direction of uniting the disciples of Jesus Christ. It is a striking demonstration of the fact that "there is one body, and one spirit, even as ye are also called in one hope of your calling; one Lord, one faith, one baptism, one God and Father of all, who is above all, and through all, and in you all." Without doubt it has accomplished more than any other influence in hastening the answer of the prayer of our Lord, "that they all may be one." This, the motto of our World's Alliance, fittingly epitomizes the distinguishing spirit and crowning achievement of our whole Movement. Who can measure its power as an apologetic to the unbelieving world? Well did Ambassador Porter point out the other evening that the Associations are doing more than treaties and diplomacy to unite the peoples and nations.

Great as has been the achievement of our first half-century, is there any reason why the next fifty years should not far surpass it in advancing and establishing the reign of Jesus Christ in the world? On the contrary, is there not every reason to expect a tremendous advance in the years right before us? We know our field as the founders of this Movement never knew it. We have access to the young men of the whole world, which could not have been said even a few years ago. We have at our disposal fifty years of rich experience. We have the priceless heritage of the example of the heroic spirits who have gone before us. We have an army of well-nigh a million members to be molded and wielded. We have financial resources which are simply inexhaustible. We have developed the type of work to be propagated, and have perfected the supervisory organizations which made possible the wide and rapid extension of this type. More important still, God has been pleased to give us the vision of the young men of the world to be evangelized. Along with the vision He has given us the courage and the determination, with the help of the triumphant God, to realize this vision. Above all, we have the immeasurable divine resources— the unsearchable riches of Jesus Christ.

THE JUBILEE DECLARATION

Prince Bernadotte, of Sweden, presented the jubilee declaration in the three languages of the Conference, French, German, and English:

"At this time, when the Alliance of the Young Men's Christian Association is commemorating in Paris, the place of its origin, the fifty years of its foundation:

"We, the authorized representatives of all Young Men's Christian Associations of the world, wish first to express our gratitude to Almighty God, who, during these fifty years, has granted so much blessing on the work He has entrusted to us.

"We further wish to witness our deep thankfulness to the men who founded the Alliance, and gratefully recall the noble examples of faith and life which they have given us.

"We desire formally to declare the supreme importance of the fundamental principles which have formed a bond of union between the Associations from the beginning."

Consequently the conference solemnly reaffirms the Basis adopted in Paris
in 1855, as follows:

ALLIANCE OF YOUNG MEN'S CHRISTIAN ASSOCIATIONS

THE DELEGATES OF VARIOUS YOUNG MEN'S CHRISTIAN ASSOCIA-
TIONS OF EUROPE AND AMERICA, ASSEMBLED IN CONFERENCE AT
PARIS THE 22D OF AUGUST, 1855, FEELING THAT THEY ARE ONE IN
PRINCIPLE AND IN OPERATION, RECOMMEND TO THEIR RESPECTIVE
SOCIETIES TO RECOGNIZE WITH THEM THE UNITY EXISTING AMONG
THEIR ASSOCIATIONS, AND WHILE PRESERVING A COMPLETE INDE-
PENDENCE AS TO THEIR PARTICULAR ORGANIZATION AND MODES
OF ACTION, TO FORM A CONFEDERATION ON THE FOLLOWING FUNDA-
MENTAL PRINCIPLE, SUCH PRINCIPLE TO BE REGARDED AS THE BASIS
OF ADMISSION OF OTHER SOCIETIES IN FUTURE:

*"The Young Men's Christian Associations seek to unite those young men
who, regarding Jesus Christ as their God and Savior according to the Holy
Scriptures, desire to be His disciples in their doctrine and in their life and
to associate their efforts for the extension of His Kingdom among young men."*

REPORT OF THE BUSINESS COMMITTEE AT THE PLENARY MEETING OF THE WORLD'S COMMITTEE, UTRECHT, JUNE 13, 1921

PREAMBLE

The World's Committee, coming together this year in a period
still characterized by great social and industrial unrest and by grave
international misunderstandings, irritation, and want of unity, would
record its sense of profound gratitude to God for the fact that it is
possible for leaders of the Association Movements of so many lands
to meet for purposes of promoting international thinking, international planning, and international action. Notwithstanding the
continued reaction and economic hardship experienced in virtually all
parts of the world, it is highly reassuring that the Associations have
been able to such an extent to maintain ground and, in not a few
countries, to expand their program on behalf of young men. The
past year in the Associations throughout the world has been one characterized by readjustment to greatly changed conditions, redefinition
of relationships, re-emphasis of vital principles and ideals, and revival of spirit exhausted by years of impossible strain. The work of
the World's Committee has necessarily been affected by the general
world conditions and trends. It has been a year of reorganization
and preparation for a larger leadership inspired by the Spirit of
Christ in helping to usher in what may be and should be a new era in
the life of the Association Movement.

I.

We would express deep appreciation of the faithful and close attention which Dr. Des Gouttes has bestowed upon the work of the World's Committee, and heartily unite in calling upon him to continue to serve as president of the World's Committee. We would also propose that Mr. Louis Perrot and Pastor Frank Thomas serve as vice-presidents.

II.

We desire to place on record our indebtedness to the National Council of Sweden for its self-sacrificial action in releasing Dr. Karl Fries, thus enabling him to accept the call given him a year ago to become general secretary, and our satisfaction that the Association Movements in North America and Great Britain have fulfilled the request made to them among others by the appointment of Messrs. D. A. Davis and Oliver H. McCowen respectively to be associate general secretaries of the Committee. These appointments have been made possible by the generous co-operation of Denmark, Finland, Norway, and Sweden, North America, and Great Britain. It is our conviction that by this combination the foundation has been laid for the building up of an international executive staff adequate to the growing demands made upon the World's Committee. It is hoped that in accordance with the action of the last Plenary Meeting the next associate general secretary may be chosen from a Latin country. It is a pleasure to record that a cordial welcome has been extended to these new officers by Mr. Christian Phildius and the staff at headquarters and that they have begun their work under the happiest auspices. We would express our belief that the secretaries should devote longer continuous periods in the field in helping to develop indigenous national Movements in countries where the work is still relatively undeveloped and weak.

III.

In response to the request of officers of the Executive Committee that the present Plenary Meeting place on record its conception of the distinctive responsibilities and powers of the World's Committee we would indicate them in the following outline:

1. To prepare and adopt the budget within the general instructions of World's Conferences.
2. To authorize the enlargement or reduction of the staff of secretaries of the World's Committee and to designate their fields and duties.

3. To define the terms of any agreements entered into by the World's Committee with other organizations.

4. To consider and pass upon applications of national groups of Associations for affiliation with the World's Alliance.

5. To see that the general lines of policy authorized by World's Conferences are carried out, and likewise, to authorize any modification in policy demanded by changed conditions.

The chief function of the Executive Committee is to carry out the general policy and instructions of the World's Committee, as expressed in its Plenary Meeting and at World's Conferences.

Nothing in this resolution shall be interpreted as changing the resolutions dealing with the same subject at the last Plenary Meeting.

IV.

Having in view the World's Committee's responsibility for coordinating the international service of the Associations and for developing and deepening world fellowship, we are more than ever convinced that this work calls for the active participation and leadership of Christian laymen and we urge that every member of the Alliance should leave no stone unturned in persuading gifted leaders in national life to give time and strength to the fulfillment of the tasks confronting the whole Movement.

It is particularly desirable that the lay representatives on the World's Committee should be regular in their attendance upon Plenary Meetings.

V.

We recommend that members of the World's Committee in the different countries be authorized to bring with them to the Plenary Meetings of the Committee their national general secretaries, who will be present for purposes of counsel.

VI.

1. We endorse the action of the Executive in receiving into the World's Alliance as a national group or union, the Associations of New Zealand, in view of the status of the Movement in that country and of the extent and quality of the work which it has accomplished.

2. We have learned with great pleasure of the marked progress in recent years of the Associations in Czechoslovakia and the Kingdom of the Serbs, Croats, and Slovenes. With reference to the applications of the Associations of these two countries for affiliation with the World's Alliance, we would propose that final action be deferred for at least another year, thus affording time for representa-

tives of the World's Committee to visit these countries, and to help extend and consolidate the work. It is recommended that in the meantime these Movements be invited to send representatives to the Plenary Metings of the World's Committee.

3. We instruct the Executive Committee in consultation with the national Movements and preferably through an international commission to make a special study of the principles and considerations which should govern the reception of new national groups into the World's Alliance.

VII.

We draw attention to the valuable historical library, now housed at Geneva, which is available for the use of the Associations throughout the world, and urge that visitors from countries represented in the Alliance be encouraged to inspect and use the library, and that Association workers and other students of Association problems who are unable to come to Geneva, secure by correspondence, so far as practicable, the assistance of the librarian in their investigations; and that copies of all Association documents, pictures, etc., be sent in duplicate on publication to be filed, and that lantern slides, films, etc., be forwarded to complete the collection now being made at headquarters.

VIII.

We welcome the concern manifested by the Executive regarding the urgent need for Christian literature of a high standard, specially prepared to meet the need of the youth of the nations, but are not satisfied that we have adequate proposals to accomplish the ends in view. We therefore refer the matter back for further consideration with the expression of the conviction that nothing short of the full-time service of a man highly qualified by scholarship and organizing ability and who can command the co-operation of a circle of competent and forcible writers can secure the results desired. Pending the time that the Committee may be able to employ the services of such a full-time worker, we recommend that the present arrangement be continued and that the department should concentrate primarily on carrying out plans for the benefit of countries that, for one reason or another, are not able themselves to make adequate provision for the literature they need.

IX.

In regard to the training of secretaries, we desire to reiterate the principle laid down at the last Plenary Meeting as follows: That "Mr. Siordet's attention should be given to establishing and strengthening self-supporting training agencies in the affiliated Movements and in, or on behalf of, countries as yet without national organizations."

We are of opinion that the conducting of an international training school is a very complex and difficult matter, and, while sanctioning the fulfillment of the obligations already entered into towards enrolled students, instruct the Executive Committee to make a full inquiry into the best means of helping the most needy countries in the enlistment and training of suitable men for the secretariat. The steps already taken are to be regarded as only experimental and no commitments are to be made beyond the next Plenary Meeting.

X.

We recommend that the international importance of the Week of Prayer be emphasized by making the observance a truly "international week." During the seven days the fullest thought and deepest prayer should be devoted:

1. To the development of the foreign or extension work of the national Movements.

2. To the removal of interracial and international friction and misunderstanding.

3. To the Christianizing of international politics and commercial and industrial relations.

4. To the creation of that moral and spiritual atmosphere and that knowledge of the fundamental problems of foreign affairs which are essential to the life and development of a truly Christian fellowship of nations.

During this week special effort should be made to call forth sacrificial giving from young men toward the world-wide program of the Young Men's Christian Association.

XI.

We recommend that the Executive Committee obtain the views of the various national Movements in the Alliance and make a full investigation regarding the extent and method of the use of the authorized badge and of the Red Triangle and other modifications of the badge which have been adopted by various countries, and report with recommendations to the next Plenary Meeting of the Committee. It is understood that pending the report of the Executive Committee on this special study no change is made in the matter of the official badge.

XII.

We confirm the action of the Executive in consenting to preliminary arrangements being made for a World Conference of Workers Among Boys to be held in the neighborhood of Geneva, in May, 1923. In view of the unparalleled opportunity for work among boys, we trust that all members of the Alliance will co-operate in the preparation of the program, in securing full and competent delegations, and in making this conference the beginning of a forward movement on behalf of the boys of the world. It is proposed that a preliminary report be prepared for the next Plenary Meeting on the conditions of boy life, especially in Europe.

XIII.

We recommend that the next Plenary Meeting of the World's Committee be held in the year 1922, preferably in one of the Scandinavian countries; that during the same year 1922, there be held one or more Leaders' Conferences, each confined to the leaders in Association work in a particular group of countries, e.g., Latin countries; that in 1923 the Plenary Meeting of the World's Committee be held in Geneva in association with the proposed World's Conference on Boys' Work. It is suggested that the Executive Committee begin to give thought to the possibility of holding a World's Conference some time within the next three or four years.

XIV.

We have received the comprehensive and timely report of the Executive on emigration prepared at its request by Mr. Fred. H. Rindge, of the International Committee, and would recommend:

1. That the emigration work now being conducted by national or International Committees be continued and increased in efficiency and volume.

2. That national committees which have not yet undertaken work for emigrants be influenced by the Executive Committee to do so.

3. That the World's Committee be held responsible for coordinating, unifying, and, in countries where there is no national committee, initiating and promoting the entire emigration program, and to this end, that a secretary be added to the staff of the World's Committee to devote his full time to directing this work.

4. That the work should be planted as seems best in countries from which men are coming, at border towns, ports of embarkation,

on ship board, at ports of entry, on railroad trains and at stations, and at the final destinations throughout the world.

5. That attention should be given by all engaged in this special branch of service to the matter of doing what is possible to counteract the exploitation of the emigrant classes by selfish interests which have no concern for their welfare.

XV.

We resolve that an international commission be appointed by the Executive Committee to make a full report at the next World's Conference on "The Young Men's Christian Association and the Application of the Principles and Spirit of Jesus Christ to the Social and Industrial Order and to International and Interracial Relations." The report should include, first, a full survey of the extent to which each national Movement is a vital factor in the national life in seeking a Christian solution of the pressing social problems of the day; and second, a statement of the principles and programs which would enable national Movements to take their place in giving leadership to public thought in the establishing of a truly Christian order in commerce and industry and in all the intricate, social relationships of modern life.

XVI.

We confirm the general understanding entered into at the Plenary Meeting last year by representatives of national committees which were before or are definitely planning to send and support workers in other lands. We are gratified to observe the signs of growing interest and participation in this extension work. We would urge that the various national committees continue to regulate their extension work in accordance with the principles laid down at the conference in connection with the Plenary Meeting last year and that they seek to co-operate to the extent of their ability in such work.

XVII.

The supreme responsibility of the World's Committee, as of all the national Movements, is to hold in true prominence the spiritual objective. The events of the recent tragic years have served as by a vast process of exclusion to create distrust in other supports and to fix the gaze of confidence upon the Lord Jesus Christ. He was never more unique, never more necessary, never more sufficient.

In every land under heaven the young manhood and boyhood are open, accessible, and responsive to the Christian message of reality and to the messenger of vital experience. The moment has come for large, wise, unselfish action. "The dawn does not come twice to awaken man." The demand for the world-wide expansion of the Association is irresistible.

With the boundless opportunity have come many and grave dangers. To the Christian those constitute an added attraction. But we must reassert with all power the truly religious, pronouncedly Christian, and aggressively missionary character of the Association Movement.

The World's Committee would sound out the call through all the national Movements to every Association and group of Christian men to confront the present generation with the Living Christ. This is incomparably our most highly multiplying and enduring work. We stand on the threshold of remarkable spiritual developments. Years of suffering, sacrifice, and humbling have ever been a precursor for something truly great. Therefore, we must avail ourselves far more largely of the limitless resources of God. The wider our outreach, the more important that we, through Bible study, through prayer, through Christian fellowship, and through serving men in need, deepen our experience of Christ.

On behalf of the Business Committee:

(Signed) JOHN R. MOTT, *Chairman*

(Signed) T. Z. KOO, *Secretary*

THE WORLD'S CONFERENCE, HELSINGFORS, FINLAND, 1926

IN QUEST OF NEW VALUES

ARTICLE IN *Association Men,* JULY, 1925

The first World's Conference of the Young Men's Christian Association since 1913 is to be held at Helsingfors, Finland, August 1-6, 1926. The conference is to be one event in a search which has already commenced and which will continue through the conference into the following years. This search has been defined as "an inquiry as to the Christian way of life in personal, social, and international affairs." The main process will not take place at the conference but in discussion groups of boys and young men in every quarter of the globe. The United States will be entitled to send more than 200 delegates. Because these 200 delegates are to be largely representative

DELEGATES IN ATTENDANCE AT THE WORLD'S CONFERENCE, HELSINGFORS, FINLAND, 1926.

of hundreds of groups throughout the country who have been meeting to discuss the Helsingfors topics, it is desirable that we take this opportunity, a full year in advance of the conference, to get a picture of some of the difficulties which are inherent in the holding of a great world conference. It will be a truly great religious gathering. The process of preparation which has already begun and which will develop through the conference and continue to unfold thereafter, is equally a great educational venture.

The educational process will begin from the very day when we and our friends take down the atlas before the trip: some to study the best route; others (from distant lands) to find out just where Helsingfors really is. As our fingers trace on the map the course our steamer will take, our eyes will catch the names of some of the Baltic cities: Riga, Reval, Helsingfors—just to the left of Leningrad. Many of us will thrill to think that in July, 1926, we shall be steaming along where 500 years ago sailed the ships of the Hanseatic League, laden with cloth and cutlery, to be exchanged for furs, honey, and flax in the markets of Russia. Those were courageous spirits who made their way year after year by this northern route into "Muscovy." Something of the romantic flavor of their day has come down to us through their title—merchant adventurers.

In those days a trip to Finland even from Germany was an event preceded by the writing of a will; nowadays it is a mere trifle of thirty-six hours on a comfortable steamer before one is put ashore on the edge of the picturesque little market place in Helsingfors.

But our band of 1,500 men from all parts of the world who will arrive there in August, 1926, will be adventurers, too. Ours will be a quest, not for trade, but for new spiritual values. We shall return, not with merchandise, but with new ideas to enrich our own lives and that of our Associations and communities.

It will take but a short flight of the imagination to find a special meaning in the selection of Helsingfors as a meeting place. Only a few hours away are Leningrad and Moscow, where other groups of men have set themselves the same problem as that of our commission —to find a better way for men to live together. That group believe that they have no need of Christianity or religion in any form. They have pointed out our many failures in a society which professes to be Christian to provide justice for our fellows. We shall need no further reminder that at Helsingfors must be no evasion of issues: ours must be a quest for realities.

If we look forward to the conference in that spirit, we shall be able to learn much from the very difficulties inherent in holding an international Christian gathering. The first obstacle will be that of language. One recalls that those merchants who sailed up the Baltic long ago earned in Russia the title of "The men who are dumb" because of their difficulties with a new tongue. As some of us in the first hours of the conference try to make ourselves understood, we shall probably have occasion to recall that old phrase, and to reflect that our predicament gives us one more bond of sympathy with the past. At least three languages will be necessary when the entire assembly meets. Men who speak two languages will be urged to join groups in which there are few of their own countrymen, in order that we may have the greatest possible sharing of ideas.

A second obstacle will be the variety of our interests, experience, and responsibilities. Each national group and even each individual will bring these in a fresh combination. Discussion in the conference will take on meaning, and plans for united action will get men's strength behind them in proportion as we recognize that we do not break into two or three or four groups; but that we have beneath many superficial differences one great common interest—to find out what is preventing our boys and young men from living the best possible lives, and of searching out new ways to help them.

A third obstacle will come from the fact that, this being the first world conference since the war, for the most part it will be made up of boys and men who are attending a world conference for the first time. We shall have no memories of previous common experiences on which to build acquaintance and fellowship during the seven days in Finland.

A fourth obstacle will come from the differing war experience of the delegates. About two-thirds, or 1,000 boys and young men, will have come from nations which took part in the war. Mingled with them will be four or five hundred delegates from countries which were neutral but near enough to feel the shock and horror of those years. One of our great spiritual assets will be the common impulse of those who are setting out afresh to discover what contribution a more Christian way of life may make to world brotherhood.

A fifth obstacle will come from the divergence in form of government in the different countries. The political system in which we have lived, will, of course, shade our language in ways that men of other countries cannot fully understand. If we are alert, however, in interpretation, there will be in our discussions of international relations a richness and variety of experience which should be of infinite value to us as we seek, after Helsingfors, to interpret the meaning of men and movements in other lands.

A sixth obstacle will be our varying interpretations of Christianity, due perhaps to the accident of our being born in one country rather than another, or on one side of a city instead of the opposite. But each of us recalls the impression made when, through a friend's mind he first caught a glimpse of the riches of some mode of Christian belief other than his own. Our week at Helsingfors will be filled with these occasions. There will be among us Lutherans, Calvinists, Anglicans, Wesleyans, Baptists, Orthodox Catholics, Roman Catholics, and men of a dozen other communions. The world "Church" will call up in our minds mental pictures of almost infinite variety. Some of these associations will be so highly personal that the inner meaning of many of our remarks in discussion will be unintelligible to other Christians equally sincere and earnest. Our mutual faith in Christ and our common concern for the welfare of youth must teach us a new international language—a kind of Esperanto of Christian experience the textbook for which is the life of the boys and young men with whom we live.

A seventh obstacle will be the widely differing conceptions of the central function and work of the Y.M.C.A. itself. What indeed will the words Young Men's Christian Association mean to us? To A it may bring to mind the picture of ten or twenty friends in a little rented room seeking through the study of the Bible and through Christian fellowship a better way of life; to B it may suggest crowds of people in a huge building, dormitories, gymnasiums, swimming pools—a vast and complicated organization, the meaning of which is difficult to find until one catches a glimpse into the minds and hearts of a little nucleus of men. To C it stands for no material equipment at all but rather as a spiritual youth Movement losing its own organizational identity in impregnating civic, recreative, educational, and political institutions with Christian ideals. How can A understand what B and C are talking about? If B spends much time talking about buildings and budgets, A and C may be impressed but may be wondering just what these have to do with the Christian way of life. How can each appreciate the work of the others?

Differences we shall have in plenty but just as the "impassable barrier" of the oceans a few centuries ago has been changed into a great highway linking the continents, we believe that all the vitality in our varying traditions and beliefs may become a bond drawing us together.

The Helsingfors Conference Committee is asking all the National Councils to choose the delegates with unusual care, and as far as possible, sufficiently far in advance so that it may prepare for conferences by actually leading discussion groups of boys and young men. Delegates who have not had this preliminary preparation will be at such a disadvantage that it has been recommended that all

National Councils give preference to those who have participated actively in discussions and studies for which the program calls. Happily, a large number of Associations throughout the United States have already begun or are about to organize discussion groups to prepare for Helsingfors so there should be no difficulty in securing an adequate number of thoroughly qualified delegates to represent at Helsingfors the boys and young men of this country. The General Board at its meeting in Detroit on April 16, authorized the appointment of a committee to have entire charge of working up the representation of the American Associations and of other preparations for the coming historic event.

DR. MOTT ACCEPTS THE PRESIDENCY OF THE WORLD'S COMMITTEE OF YOUNG MEN'S CHRISTIAN ASSOCIATIONS

At the meeting of the World's Committee on Saturday, July 31, 1926, at Helsingfors, Finland, Dr. Mott made the following statement, in response to the call to him to become its president.

"After prolonged and prayerful consideration, in face of the highly complex character of my existing responsibilities and relationships, I am ready to accept your call with the following understanding:

"1. That you do not call upon me to serve in this capacity for an extended period. It is my understanding that you want me to help in an important transitional period. It is my conviction and desire that, because of the character of our world-wide brotherhood as essentially a youth Movement, this responsibility should as soon as practicable be transferred to one belonging to the younger generation, and it will be a special satisfaction to help realize this objective.

"2. That my responsibilities and functions as president are to be those of a chairman and not of a general secretary, that my relationship like that of other members of the World's Committee will be concerned primarily with the determination of policies rather than with their execution. To this end, I understand that we are agreed on the building up of a symmetrical and thoroughly qualified staff, and that the president will naturally collaborate in the choice of those who are to fill major positions.

"3. That I continue to sustain a vital official relationship to the other interdenominational and international movements which I am now serving.

"4. That the other members of the newly reconstituted World's Committee and of its enlarged Executive Committee will join me in assuming and discharging the heavy responsibilities which come upon us as an international group of laymen responsible for uniting the

Association forces of all nations and races in fellowship, plan, and action for great world tasks. The least that this means is that in filling the membership of the Committee men will be chosen: (1) who are qualified to think internationally, and who command the confidence and following of the Association leaders of their respective countries; (2) who will attend the relatively infrequent meetings of the Committee; and (3) who on their return from the meetings will see that effect is given to the plans adopted.

"5. That the Committee is to be developed as truly a World's Committee and that we are to stand for a policy of real world co-operation in which each national body, whether large or small, will be afforded opportunity to make its contribution.

"6. That we continue to rest our World's Alliance on the Paris Basis with its enduring cornerstone principle, Jesus Christ, the Divine Lord and only sufficient Savior—the same yesterday, today, and forever, and to regulate our lives, our plans, and our activities by its ecumenical, prophetic, and heroic implications.

"7. That we stand for a forward-looking, true progressive, and pronouncedly Christian evangelistic and missionary policy, with special reference to commanding the confidence, the loyalty, and the sacrificial devotion of the new or oncoming generation.

"8. That the call which comes to me is a unanimous call and that I shall have behind me the united human support and intercession of all the national groups in our world-embracing fellowship. This is a superhuman enterprise and to carry it forward you and I will be in constant need of superhuman discernment, superhuman sympathy, and superhuman power. To this end let our prayers for each other be not a form but a great reality."

The World's Committee by a rising vote, unanimously and with great enthusiasm expressed their full acceptance of these conditions and their gratification at Dr. Mott's acceptance of their invitation.

OPENED DOORS IN FRONT OF THE YOUNG MEN'S CHRISTIAN ASSOCIATION

ADDRESS AT THE WORLD'S CONFERENCE OF YOUNG MEN'S CHRISTIAN ASSOCIATIONS AT HELSINGFORS, FINLAND, AUGUST 1-6, 1926

The Young Men's Christian Association confronts today the greatest opportunities of all its history. To it may we not apply the language of Revelation which represents Christ as saying to the Church at Philadelphia, "This is what the Holy One and the True says, He that openeth and none shall shut, and that shutteth and none open. . . . Behold I have set before thee a door open which none can shut." As we, the representatives of the world-wide Association brotherhood, during these coming days of fellowship and common counsel, share with one another our experiences, our problems, and our visions, may we have a realizing sense of the tremendous challenge Christ thus presents to the youth of this generation. What are some of the opened doors which He has set before us?

I. OPENED DOORS BEFORE THE ASSOCIATIONS

1. Without doubt Christ has set before the Young Men's Christian Association an opened door to the nations. This impression has been borne in upon me with overwhelming force in the pathway of my recent journeys which have taken me to nearly all of the continents of the world. There may have been times, as a matter of fact there have been times, when in certain parts of the world the doors to the friendly and constructive ministry of the Association were as wide open as they are today; but we make bold to assert that never in the annals of the Movement have doors of opportunity throughout Europe, North America, Australasia, Asia, Africa, and Latin America stood simultaneously so wide ajar as they do today. The unselfish service of the Associations during the war to tens of millions of men under arms and in prisoner-of-war camps has served to widen enormously the opportunity of the Association across the breadth of the world. It would be difficult to mention a country of which we could say with certainty that it is absolutely closed to all Association influence.

While our organization is securely established in over forty nations the challenge comes to us today, as we look into this opened door, to enter and place at the disposal of the youth of many another country the inestimable blessings which the Association has already brought to us. Think of the totally unoccupied fields of Asia, such as Indo-China, Siam, Persia, Syria; of those in nearly every part of the African continent, North, South, East, West, and Central; of the ten or more unentered Latin-American republics of North and South America and the West Indies. At the same time do not overlook the vast relatively unoccupied fields in countries in which the Association has already been introduced, for example, China, Japan, India, the Philippines, the Nile Valley, Brazil, Argentina, and some of the important parts of Europe and North America. In virtually every land our brotherhood is well able to minister to vastly greater numbers of young men and boys than we are now serving. A door, an open door, a door opened by Christ Himself, and an ability to enter the door brings with it inescapable obligation.

2. The Young Men's Christian Association has had set before it an opened door to some of the most important and baffling problems of the world. Not only do we have access to the nations, but we also have an organization, an experience, methods, a program, and a Gospel which within these nations enable us to make helpful contributions toward meeting their serious and emergent situations. All over the world we find keen social unrest, especially in industrial areas. Through the friction of economic competition human relationships are being greatly inflamed. Racial antagonisms have become more and more acute and aggravated in recent years on almost every continent and in the island world. The growth of crime and lawlessness among our youth is a serious menace. International misunderstandings, fears, ambitions, maladjustments, bitterness, and strife show little abatement. Much of the spirit which leads to wars remains still to be exorcized.

Another group of serious problems is represented by our failure to dominate and utilize for the highest purposes the enormous material energy, the incomparable scientific enlightenment, and the penetrating philosophy of the modern day for the furtherance of the Kingdom of God in the life of men. Moreover, we cannot close our eyes to the question of the readjustment of relationships between men and women. This problem is accentuated by the new position of women and the larger understanding of morals. Increasingly it is becoming apparent that society as a whole will not stand for a double ethical standard for men and women. Will the single standard be a low or high one? Influences tending to break down our homes seem to be gathering strength. In a word, we are summoned to more aggressive warfare against the agelong enemies of mankind—ignorance, poverty, disease, strife, and sin.

The existence, strength, and gravity of these and other perils, the world over, might well cause consternation were it not for the absolute sufficiency of the Lord Jesus Christ to meet this appalling array. The Association is uniquely fitted to meet, avert, and overcome such momentous dangers. Is it not world-wide in extent? Is it not located at nearly all the principal friction points between peoples? Does it not blend all races of mankind? Does it not include in its membership all classes and all social groups? Has it not evolved a program and agencies which enable it to become literally all things to all men? Above all, has it not in the Biblical Gospel Christ's own adequate answer and, therefore, that which covers and meets the whole bleak field of human need?

3. Before the Young Men's Christian Association stands the opened door of the minds and hearts of the youth. Never has there

been such a generation as the one now oncoming. It is the most alert intellectually. Surging in the minds and hearts of its members are tides of fresh thought and social passion. In their company in every land one is vividly conscious of the ferment of new ideas. They are dissatisfied with the past, and still more with much that obtains in the present, but surely they have a right to be. They are an inquiring generation, calling into question long-established traditions, standards of authority, and social sanctions. They are extremely critical. What do they not criticize? This is not without its advantage; it certainly is better than the old mental inertia and indifference. Everywhere we find them in revolt against dominating and unreasoning authority, but without this spirit of revolt there would be little hope of progress. They hate cant and hypocrisy, and are responsive to the note of reality wherever they find it. This passionate quest for truth is most hopeful. At times the new generation may tend to go to extremes, but has not the time come when we should welcome the spirit and the courage which make possible the discovery and charting of new courses for mankind?

We cannot but be responsive to the real passion animating the youth to build a better world. In many lands both in the Occident and in the Orient they feel that they have entered into the heritage of suffering and sacrifice and they are vividly conscious of the fact that a great responsibility rests upon them as nation builders. Their hopefulness, idealism, vision, spirit of adventure, and readiness to lose themselves in great unselfish causes afford ground for great encouragement for the coming day. All over the world this new spirit is manifesting itself in all sorts of youth movements. Some of them are highly organized; some are not. Some are national; others are international. They vary in their notes of emphasis—social, political, racial, ethical, religious. They differ as to origin, aims, goals, and methods. However, with certain exceptions which give ground for solicitude, they give evidence of being movements of the human spirit reaching out for something freer, fairer, nobler, and more unselfish.

These movements, and more especially the present-day attitude and trends in the life of the youth, present a wonderful opened door. They afford the cause of Christ, and in particular the Association Movement as the most comprehensive society in contact with youth throughout the world, marked advantages. What an opportunity for providing a satisfying apologetic to this most inquiring of all generations! This will encourage the study of the teaching and program of Christ. This in turn and inevitably will serve to prepare the way for Christ by leading to a larger understanding of Him and of His marvelous Gospel. Again, the social interest and concern which so largely animate the more serious-minded among the youth of today afford to a Christian Movement like ours a great advantage, because the religion of Jesus Christ holds a unique position with its ideal and method of social conduct and amelioration. Such an opportunity should stimulate us to pray and to search for teachers, writers, and speakers who will serve as wise spiritual guides. Association leaders should not stand, as it were, as spectators on the bank of these great tides of interest and action among the youth, but should rather plunge into the middle of the stream and identify themselves with their struggles, aspirations, and purposes, and thus help relate the new generation to the Association program with all that this will make possible in the way of realizing our highest hopes. This door to the youth, to the new generation, simply must be entered by the Association. What is more important than to reach them for Christ, for His Church, for His program, and for His warfare? If we fail in this, what hope is there of fulfilling the great unselfish purposes of the Kingdom of God on earth?

4. One of the most impressive facts about the Young Men's Christian Association in modern times is the fact that there has been set before it the opened door to the confidence of other constructive forces. In this connection we think at once of the intelligent, sympathetic, and influential co-operation of forward-looking rulers and enlightened governments. On my recent journeys to the countries around the Pacific Basin, and before that to those along the shores of Northern Africa, Western Asia, Southeastern and Eastern Europe, I was profoundly impressed by the large place which the Association has won for itself in the confidence of the most unselfish and able leaders of nearly all these countries. Such friendly attitude and keen appreciation have greatly widened the Association's opportunity to serve young manhood and boyhood. What has been said of these parts of the world is but typical of the general attitude and feeling manifested by men of character and of unselfish concern among those in authority in other lands. We think also of the centers of learning and of leaders in the realm of thought in general. The large attention which Association leaders have paid to the student field in so many countries, including the enlistment of the collaboration of professors who are sympathetic with the Christian position and the Association program, is now beginning to show its large results. The Association has not begun, however, to utilize the great talent thus placed at its disposal. The thought content and basis of every aspect of its program may be greatly enriched and strengthened by enlisting much more largely the contribution of thinkers and scholars.

Among religious and social betterment agencies the Association is almost in a class by itself in respect to the degree to which it has won the confidence and called forth the co-operation of men and women of consecrated means. The great and increasing outpouring of gifts of the wealthy, as well as of associated poverty, notably during the last half generation, has been most impressive. Nevertheless, the Association is virtually only at the blueprint stage in its utilization of financial energy. The money power should be much more largely related to the expanding plans of the Association brotherhood, but in this it is supremely important that giving should be prompted by unselfish motives, and the use of material resources should be dominated by the spirit and passion of Christ. Otherwise this power will be a stumbling block rather than what Christ evidently designed it to be, a steppingstone into the heights of unselfish achievement and attainment. Another constructive force whose confidence in the Association has been so markedly enlarged in recent years is the Christian Church. Of this there have been many encouraging evidences both during the war and during the period which has since elapsed. Here we have in mind not only the traditional and vital relationship sustained to the many branches of the Protestant Communion, but also the new doors of access and confidence with reference to the other great Christian Communions such as the Russian, the Greek, the Bulgarian, the Rumanian, the Gregorian, the Syrian, and among so many of the lay forces of the Roman Catholic Church. Thus the Association Movement has assumed a much more widely ecumenical aspect. What great accessions of spiritual life and power and what widening of opportunity to serve await the Association in almost every land as it faces this wide opened door of confidence!

Apart from such forces and factors as have been mentioned in this connection, attention should be called to the almost unbelievable opportunity which has come to the Association in recent years in multiplied contacts with members of non-Christian religions and cults. It has been deeply moving to observe how in large and ever increasing numbers the followers of these religions have availed themselves of the privileges of the Association and have come under the influence of its vital, dynamic, and transforming message and spirit. This great door, the vast significance of which we are only beginning to realize, has been opened and placed in front of us in such a way as to be inexplicable apart from the belief that Christ Himself accomplished this wonderwork. We have mentioned only a few of the great constructive forces and influences the powers of which should be increasingly related to the enlarging plans of the Association, and which in turn should be served in increasing volume and helpfulness by the Association. A ruler of one of our great nations remarked not many years ago that the thing about the Young Men's Christian Association which caused him most surprise was the fact of how little the Association leaders themselves seem to realize the opportunity and influence which their Movement possessed.

5. Another opened door which Christ today summons the Young Men's Christian Association to enter is that of enlarged co-operation between the nations and the races. He it was Who first imparted the vision to bands of earnest Christian youth well-nigh three-quarters of a century ago, the beginning of the realization of which was the formation in Paris in 1855 of the World's Alliance of Young Men's Christian Associations. Through the intervening years this Alliance has been the means of weaving together into closer intimacy, through strands of understanding, fellowship, and brotherhood, as well as of faith, the Christian Association Movements of various nations. More recently our Divine Lord has been reuniting bonds which had been strained or broken, and restoring our world-wide fellowship. He confronts us in this Conference with a great and effectual door of possibilities to be realized in the realm of much closer collaboration, co-operation, and unity. The world has yet to see the marvels which will be wrought by the Associations of all lands and races when actually united in common quest for truth, in corporate thought for constructive program-building, in warfare against all enemies and influences which are seeking or tending to disintegrate faith and blast character, in international action to extirpate the causes of war and to insure right racial relationships, and in determined effort to Christianize the impact of our so-called Christian civilization upon the non-Christian world. By His Incarnation, by the inclusiveness and comprehension of His wondrous Gospel and Kingdom, by His breaking down the middle wall of partition on the Cross, by the world-wide sweep of the program committed by Him to His followers, and by His high-priestly prayer that we all might be one and His ever-living intercession, He has indeed opened the door to the realization of this high hope—a door which none can shut.

6. Above all, Christ has put in front of the Young Men's Christian Association an open door to superhuman resources. Ours is not simply a human or an humanitarian, but essentially a superhuman enterprise. Its origin is traceable to the Living Christ and His Church. Its name and basis, its governing purpose and guiding principles, its message and program, its spirit and genius, its spiritual anchorage and resources are Christian. Were it not for the Lord Jesus Christ there would be no Young Men's Christian Association. He is the Fountainhead of all there is in the Association which is most distinctive, vital, and enduring. As the leader of the German

Movement has said, "Our message is the Biblical Gospel in the center of which stand the Cross and the Resurrection of Jesus Christ. . . . It is valid for all times." In reality He it is Who has opened the door of hope to the young manhood and boyhood of every land, race, and condition.

Through a life of ceaseless travel my intimate contacts with the youth of other faiths and cults have convinced me that, not as a matter of dogmatism but of scientific generalization in the sense that science takes account of all the facts, "there is none other name under Heaven given among men whereby we must be saved." In the light of human experience, who besides Christ has opened up a fountain for the washing away of all uncleanness? Who besides Christ has manifested power to redeem men absolutely unto God? He is the only Being in all history who has shown the ability to call out absolute trust. He came not alone to proclaim a gospel, but more especially that there might be a gospel to proclaim. He Who died, lives, loves, forgives, serves, is longed for, satisfies, is not the dead Christ of formal Christianity, but Christ, the Savior, the Redeemer, Christ of the Cross and the Atonement, Christ, the Victor over sin and death, Christ alive forevermore. He is the Fountainhead of spiritual vitality, and has, therefore, opened up the realms of eternal life. He liberates in and through the lives of men energies infinitely greater than their own. His supreme quest is to communicate Himself inwardly to men—to clothe Himself with men. Let us, wherever necessary, seek to recover the fullness of our wondrous Gospel. Let us range over the amazing vastness of our inheritance, Let us recognize that Jesus Christ, the Living Christ, Christ the Leader and the Conqueror, is the One Who can arouse the enthusiasm, command the loyalty, and call forth the undying devotion of the youth of all lands.

II. WHAT WOULD HINDER ENTERING THE OPENED DOORS

1. Although the Young Men's Christian Association in its world mission is today confronted with more opportunities and with greater opportunities than at any time in its history, we must not hide from ourselves the fact that there are serious obstacles and opposing forces which would hinder our entering them. Notwithstanding what has been said with reference to the favorable attitude of many and increasing numbers of adherents of the non-Christian religions toward the Associations, the fact remains that in certain instances their revival and their inauguration of new enterprises and activities have created attitudes and aroused opposition which constitute a distinct hindrance. Even more, the anti-religious movements such as the one raised up in China during the past four or five years, and the one

associated with the present anti-religious government of Russia, are a menace to the ideals and objectives of the Association Movement and the Christian Church. The marked development of the forces of materialism and the spirit of secularism throughout Christian as well as non-Christian lands, the influence of which is apparent within the Churches themselves, must be regarded by us as an enemy to spiritual progress. Naturalism in its many manifestations is a most insidious danger exerting a devitalizing and paralyzing influence. Add to these perils the aggressive forces of organized evil such as the liquor traffic, the opium curse, licensed vice, gambling and all else that tends to deteriorate character, disintegrate faith, and undermine family life, together with the spiritual hosts of wickedness arrayed against us in the Heavenly warfare, and we recognize the stern challenge which comes to the Association Movement in times like these.

All these opposing forces, however, to those of us who are bound together around the Person of our Divine Lord with His illimitable resources, constitute not so much an obstacle as an added opportunity. Should we not view them and face them in the spirit of St. Paul who was able to say, "A wide door stands open before me which demands great efforts, and we have many opponents." Notice he did not say, "A wide door stands open before me which demands great efforts, *but* we have many opponents; that is, I have a great opportunity but there are so many enemies and hindrances that it is hopeless to think of improving the opportunity or entering the open door." Oh no, the great Apostle, who should be our pattern in times like this, said in substance, "I not only have a wonderful opportunity, but along with it the additional attraction of adversaries who would keep me from improving the opportunity or entering the open door. Let me at them." Let us, therefore, as leaders and members of a great world-wide brotherhood under the banner of Christ, as we front far greater and more wondrous vistas of opened doors, not only thank God for them, but likewise that we have the additional incentive and attraction of waging a determined and successful warfare against all influences and powers which would stand against Christ and His unselfish and sublime program. In reality such an array of seemingly impossible difficulties constitutes God's greatest opportunity. Is it not true that He concerns Himself not so much with things which we can do in our own wisdom and strength, but especially with those which are impossible for us? Thus that which we might superficially have thought threatened or narrowed our opportunity has but widened the door. "Greater is He that is in us than he that is in the world." Or, to reiterate the word of Christ as given by St. John, "He that openeth and none shall shut."

2. This brings us to the serious reflection that while no other can shut the door, Christ can, for the full expression is, "He that openeth and none shall shut, and that shutteth and none open." Recently when I was in the lands of Northern Africa I was reminded that at one time there were over 10,000 active Christian churches across the northern end of that great continent, churches planted by the early missionaries of the Christian faith and possessing massive and true creeds. These churches had ceased to exist and even their ruins were literally covered with the sands. On that journey I visited in other parts of the Levant certain Christian churches still existing in name, still possessing sound creeds, but churches without vitality and conquering power. These experiences occasioned solemn reflection. One came to realize vividly that if a Christian community has placed before it an opened door and long neglects to recognize and enter the door, the One Who places the opened door in front of them in His own time likewise shuts it. We do well, therefore, at the threshold of our Conference and during these coming days, to examine ourselves as to our attitude and purpose with reference to the wide open doors which unmistakably confront the Association Movement, and which alike unmistakably Christ Himself has set before us.

What is there within us which would prevent our recognizing the opened door and following His hand which beckons us to enter? At times without doubt our neglect is due to want of spiritual vision. We allow ourselves to become so preoccupied and absorbed with what is immediately before our eyes that we fail to see what lies just beyond as well as far away, or we fail to dwell with Christ sufficiently in the Mount of Vision from which height only can men see with clearness the kingdoms of this world becoming the Kingdoms of our Lord. Moreover, at times as we stand in front of an opened door we are kept from entering it by unbelief that the Lord Himself has opened it, and, therefore, that He may be depended upon to give us the courage, the wisdom, and the power to enter it. Again, it may be, we falter, procrastinate, and fail to enter an opened door because of lack of spiritual energy. A most serious reflection comes to me again and again, and that is whether the discipline of our lives, the culture of our souls, the thoroughness of our processes and, above all, our habits of appropriating fresh accessions of spiritual power are such as will enable us to meet our ever-widening opportunities and ever-growing responsibilities. God grant that through no such neglect on our part we fail to recognize and enter opened doors which He has placed in front of us, He may shut them, possibly never to be opened; or, if ever again opened, opened to those of some future day who will be found more sensitive to the Divine leading and to the day of God's own visitation.

III. THE CHALLENGE OF CHRIST TO THE HELSINGFORS CONFERENCE

What then is the central challenge of Christ which comes to us here at Helsingfors? Is it not that we who, in His Providence have been brought to this place, may recognize the opened doors which He has placed in front of us and prepare ourselves in these days that we may return to the lands from which we have come to guide our world-wide brotherhood to enter them? What is an opened door for? Is it not for the sole purpose of being entered? We have assembled at a moment when if ever, these words quoted by St. John apply, "I have put an open door in front of you which no one can shut." We have come together from over forty nations, representing all the principal races of mankind. To what land represented here do not these words apply, "I have put an open door in front of you which no one can shut." For long months before coming here we have in our different countries been inquiring, searching, and collaborating, under the guidance of the World's Committee, as to the attitude of youth as it faces the world, especially with reference to ascertaining the Christian way of life and of life's relationships. It is the first time in the history of the world when the youth of all lands have been united in such a vital quest.

Notwithstanding the limitations and shortcomings of this first stage of our united study, who can measure the results flowing from such fellowship in research, discussion, and interpretation on the part of many hundreds of groups of earnest Christian youth the world over with reference to their most vital problems. This beginning should lead into a continuing and more adequate study of the mind and heart of modern youth in every country and of every race, and in increasingly effective service based upon the fuller and more exact knowledge of their real conditions, problems, and aspirations. If the Young Men's Christian Association is to continue to exist as a vital, active power in the field of youth, it must command their confidence and pay the price of fulfilling its part in realizing God's plan for the youth of today. There is danger in some quarters lest our Movement lose its consciousness of its distinctive mission, that is, a mission primarily to the youth of the world. Herein we begin to see the significance of Helsingfors. It is not an end in itself. It is but a stage in the journey we began before we came to this place and on which we are to continue as we go hence. Helsingfors should generate new and expanded thoughts of our great mission, and should mark the beginning of a new epoch, and, so far as the youth are concerned, the setting of the world on new courses.

We, and many whom we represent, have been praying that the Living God might begin here to accomplish in and through us a new, a creative, a truly wonderwork, and that this gathering might furnish a real lead for many years to come to the 10,000 Young Men's Christian Associations planted throughout the world. We should be solemnized with the thought that the answer to this prayer depends in large measure upon the personal attitude and spirit of each individual delegate of the Conference. On the human side, what are the conditions on compliance with which depends the desired fresh manifestation of Christ's presence and creative working in our midst during these momentous days and during the great days which are to follow as we seek to enter the opened doors set before us so unmistakably by our Living Lord?

1. The life of each one of us should be characterized by a spirit of certainty. Real leaders must know the way. The men who have led in every forward movement have been men of clear and strong conviction. Men of divided, or uncertain, or vacillating mind do not have a great following. We are living in a time of much uncertainty and unrest. There is added need in such days of leaders who can with conscientiousness and conviction make a stand for some great affirmations. We have not come together as atheists, but as believers. We have not assembled to debate or discuss who is our Lord. We believe with unshakable conviction in God Almighty and in Jesus Christ, His only Son, our Lord. We believe that every man stands in need of a power infinitely greater than his own. We believe that God has manifested Himself in Christ to meet the deepest longings and the highest aspirations of the human heart and of the human race. We believe in "the Biblical Gospel, in the center of which stand the Cross and the Resurrection of Jesus Christ." We believe that in Christ and in Him only will be found satisfying answers and solutions for the personal, social, international, and interracial problems that press upon us. We believe that the processes of inquiry, corporate thinking, and honest application already instituted and which are to be advanced another stage during these days in Helsingfors, will, if continued with open mind, scientific method, and moral passion, lead to further clarification and strengthening of conviction as to the scope and content of our program, the enrichment of our message, and the opening up of new realms of united unselfish endeavor.

2. Each one should be filled with a spirit of loyalty to our Divine Lord. You will recall that the reason given why Christ confronted the Church at Philadelphia with an opened door and kept it open was that they had honored His word and had not denied His name. We must be of like mind as we stand in front of the opportunities which He has placed before us. Therefore, in the midst of this great as-

sembly we bow down and acknowledge Him as Lord and reverently lend ourselves to His creative processes. We recognize His rightful place as the Master, the Owner, the Director, the Lord indeed of our lives. We acknowledge His rightful claim upon all our powers whether little or great. We here rededicate ourselves to Him because of Who He is; because of what He has done on the Cross; because of what His dominance over us makes possible in us and through us; and because of the requirements and implications of His Gospel and world-wide program. As we are silent unto Him during the coming days in our united meetings of worship and of vision-forming, or in the intimacies of our fellowship in the open forum groups, or alone in hours of meditation and prayer and appropriation, we will hear His voice and will heed His call and will resolve to follow Him whithersoever He leadeth, cost what it may.

3. We should enter upon these days in the spirit of expectancy, and go forth in the spirit of triumphant faith. Christ is here. It was said of Him at the time of one of His visits to His home town, where of all places He undoubtedly most intensely longed to accomplish a wonderwork, that "He could do no mighty work there because of their unbelief." One of the greatest functions for us, one and all, to perform is that of generating in this Conference an atmosphere of belief; that is, the supplying of this condition on which the great creative works of the Living God have ever depended. Without shadow of doubt Christ is in our midst, and will remain in our midst and will increasingly manifest Himself as here to forgive, to cleanse, to enlighten, to enrich, to create or vitalize, to commission, to embolden, to energize, and to unite. We are too prone to relegate His wonderworks to the foundation days of the Christian faith in a faraway past or to an ever-retreating horizon, or period in the future. We do well to remind ourselves that it is characteristic of the Living Christ to work here and now. May it not be said of any one of us that through lack of yielding to the spirit of expectancy and of true faith, as was said of another group in an ancient time, "They hindered the Holy One of Israel." Let the Young Men's Christian Association become known increasingly in all lands as specializing on the impossible, thus making possible present-day evidences of the reality and conquering power of our faith.

4. If the opened doors set in front of us are to be entered, we ourselves must receive a fresh baptism of the spirit of adventure and of abandon to our great unselfish cause. He that saveth his life shall lose it; he that loseth his life in the service of his generation shall find it in ever-deepening, ever-widening, ever-multiplying influence for

good. It is through such men that Christ has ever effected the great, beneficent, permanent changes in the life of the world. Is this not the secret of the undying influence of St. Francis of Assisi, and of the spiritual conquests of St. Methodius, St. Cyril, and St. Ansgar? Does it not take us to the heart of the triumphs of Christianity in all these lands of Northern and Central Europe in the periods of most significant advance? Does this not explain the rise of the world missionary movement on the continent of Europe, in the British Isles, and in North America over a century ago? Does it not let us into the secret of the recent marvelous triumphs of the Cross of Christ on the continents of Asia and Africa and throughout the Pacific island world? This also explains the rise, progress, and contagious power of the Student Volunteer Movement, which, in the face of impossible difficulties, has been the instrument in the hands of God of projecting within our lifetime over 12,000 student volunteers throughout the world-wide field of Protestant missions. God is not through working in this way. It is our belief that we are on the threshold of something new and more wonderful. These are great days in which to live and to have a life to place at the disposal of the Lord of Life. There will never come a time when it will not be necessary for Christan youth to take up unpopular causes and to stand by them until these causes win out and become popular as did Wilberforce in England and Lloyd Garrison in America in the last generation, and as we recognize in the case of Kagawa of Japan in our own day. Herein lies the glory of our spiritual warfare. Christ in these days at Helsingfors is summoning young men to great renunciations, to fearless breaks with precedent, to daring and lonely adventures— in a word, to wholehearted commitment to His way and to His sway.

5. The demand comes that those of an older generation, who still so largely direct the organization and plans of the Association Movement in all lands, shall give free course to the spirit of trust in youth. While we shall always need older men for counsel and to bring to bear the lessons learned only in the pathway of experience, we must look to young men for action; and if ever in the annals of the Christian faith there was a time demanding intense and persevering action, that time is during the next half generation. In recent addresses in the East and in the West I have expressed the conviction that the next fifteen years bid fair to be the most difficult in the life of the Christian religion. I have pointed out that the reason is not so much the forces which oppose the religion of Christ, although these are by no means negligible, but that there are so many more Christians now than ever who have waked up to the serious implica-

tions of the Christian Gospel and who believe with soul-gripping conviction that Christ in proclaiming His program meant what He said. This, therefore, inevitably means bold initiative, sustained action, the prodigal expenditure of vitality.

Moreover, we do well to remind ourselves at this time that most of the delegates of the first World's Conference of the Young Men's Christian Association held in Paris in 1855 were young men under twenty-five years of age, and that the man who framed the Paris Basis, which has proved to be such a prophetic and adequate unifying bond for the complex world-wide Association Movement, was but twenty-one years of age when he drafted this remarkable affirmation. The youth have likewise furnished the pioneers who have spread the Association over the continents of the world. To the youth primarily have come the visions to which we trace many of the most beneficent and fruitful forward Movements in the life of the Association brotherhood. Youth must be given the credit for some of the most germinating or creative ideas and plans. It will be recalled that one of the principal opened doors set before us is that to the hearts and minds of the youth. All experience shows that it is an idle dream to think of entering adequately that door save under the initiative and largely under the leadership of the youth themselves. No law has been tested and proved more completely by the Association than the law that it takes like to reach like. The challenge that comes to us, therefore, is that we should seek during the period right before us to weave into the responsible leadership of the Movement—local, national, and international—the new generation to a far greater extent than has hitherto been deemed practicable. Only in this way shall we insure the freest expression of the ideals and convictions of youth, and only in this way shall we arrest the attention and command the confidence and following of the new generation. Without doubt this will involve risks, mistakes, and some apparent losses, but such have ever been prices which have had to be paid to provide an adequate training school for true leadership. Christ, Who constituted the Apostolic band so largely of young men, and Who committed to them and to other youth the launching of His world-wide Movement, still abides as a living, guiding presence in His Church, and in the Association, the child of the Churches, and we make no mistake in following in His train. If He trusted the new generation then, we may be sure that He does so now.

6. A precursor to many of the great wonderworks of Christ through all the centuries has been the spirit of triumphant unity among His followers. From the night when in an upper room He

taught them His deepest lessons underlying triumphant unity, and from the time when He sent them again to the upper room to tarry until they had complied with the conditions on which depended the coming upon them of the Holy Ghost in power, in the heart of which conditions unquestionably was the achieving of unity, down to this very day, this has been one of the secrets of the largest manifestation of His presence and creative power. Helsingfors will be no exception. We come together from almost every nation under Heaven. Among our number are men of many races. Here are members of countless Christian communions. Wide cleavages and chasms have existed between various groupings of our number. A great many of us are ignorant of the languages of our brothers here assembled. What a vast and complex variety of antecedents, backgrounds, mentalities, outlooks, prejudices, and convictions are to be found in our midst! On the human side it is almost unthinkable and unbelievable that such complexity, such variety, such diversity, such divisions, should be blended or transcended into a genuine, recognized, wondrous unity. But it is precisely such an extremity on the part of man which furnishes Christ, Who is in our midst, His opportunity. In terms that we cannot mistake, and to the end that His heart's desire and prayer that we may be one may be realized, He summmons us to join Him in the mountains. He calls us to abide with Him these days on the Mount of Vision. From that inspiring height, where we shall see the lands of large dimensions to be occupied and the unending vistas of opportunity through which we must pass, we shall come into a realizing sense of our need of one another and of our indispensability to one another, and shall be drawn together irresistibly like comrades in common warfare. He summons us to join Him on the Mount of Transfiguration. There, where we come to see no man save Jesus only, we shall be drawn into such a wondrous fellowship that we shall shrink from going down from this place on the seventh day of August, but when we do go, we shall go forth, not with a sense of loneliness, but of a new and inspiring comradeship and of an unbreakable spiritual solidarity. He summons us to join Him on the lonely Mount of Sacrifice, reminding us in His most penetrating teaching that except a grain of wheat fall into the ground and die, it abideth by itself alone, but if it die it bringeth forth much fruit. There with Him, in the observance of the Holy Communion, reminding ourselves afresh of the price that He paid and its far-reaching significance, we shall be ushered into the heart of the secret of transforming, truly creative unity, and of lives and works the influence of which can never die.

AT THE CROSS ROADS

ADDRESS AT THE WORLD'S CONFERENCE OF YOUNG MEN'S CHRISTIAN
ASSOCIATIONS, HELSINGFORS, FINLAND, AUGUST 1-6, 1926

The leaders and members of the World's Alliance of the Young Men's Christian Associations stand today at a fork in the road. This is pre-eminently true of the delegates who have had the unique privilege of attending the present World's Conference. What we have heard and experienced during these never-to-be-forgotten days constitutes a tremendous challenge. As a result of what has come before us in the intimate discussion groups and in our large plenary sessions, we are all called upon to make some momentous decisions. What are some of these decisions which should not be evaded or deferred?

We are summoned, in connection with our future planning and action, to make the choice between guiding on the future and guiding on the past. Surely none of us will be contented with harking back to the prewar past. Still less can we look to the years of confusion in the war and postwar periods for our guidance. Certainly we shall not fail to use our memories and to draw from the experiences of other days, both favorable and unfavorable, the lessons they have to teach us. Moreover, we should never cease to utter abundantly the memory of God's great goodness. Above all shall we continue to go back to Christ to learn ever deeper lessons and to enter into ever deeper experiences as a result of what He has taught and what He has wrought. At the same time, we shall not fail to let the unmet needs, the unentered open doors, and the unappropriated spiritual resources profoundly affect the making of our program and the calling forth of our sacrificial devotion. In another sense this Conference has taught us to be influenced by the future. I refer to that which has been the central organizing idea of the Helsingfors Inquiry and discussions, namely, the effort to find out the conditions surrounding the new generation and to ascertain their opinions, desires, and needs, and then to have the Young Men's Christian Association govern its action by the result. In other words, the unspent years, the unexhausted energies, and the limitless creative possibilities of the youth should dominate us in our thought and purpose even more than the attitudes and trends of the older generation which, from the nature of the case, will not live long enough to bring about the extensive and profound changes called for by the program of Christ. To this end we need to rethink, revise, and restate our strategy. We need to reorient the Young Men's Christian Association.

We who are responsibly related to the Associations are called upon to choose between a policy of expansion and a policy of contraction. Our Movement, which is and should continue to be a youth movement and which is emphatically a Christian movement, was never intended to be static. The very word "movement," which we are in the habit of using to characterize the Association, at once suggests the incongruity of marking time. We have had brought before us in this place vast areas of the world where the Young Men's Christian Association has not yet been planted. The penetrating question which we simply must answer is: Shall the young men and boys of entire nations on nearly all the continents of the world continue for another period without having the inestimable benefits and privileges which have come to the youth of our own lands through the Association agency? Can we rest contented to come back to another World's Conference four years hence and be obliged to report that we have done nothing to influence our National Alliances to assume larger missionary responsibility. I cannot but believe that the Living Christ Himself is tonight appealing to some in this great company to take sacrificial initiative in the matter. Let us follow the beckoning hand of Christ which, let it be reiterated, invariably points to ranges of boundless opportunity and depths of indescribable need.

Are not many of us impelled, as a result of our reflection upon the requirements of our great task, a task which surely never seemed so difficult and exacting as it does today, to choose between living deeper lives and continuing to live lives which have been all too shallaw or superficial? In speaking to an audience of workers in a distant land not long since I remarked that one of my most serious misgivings is lest we as Christian workers may be producing Christian activity and Christian organization more rapidly than we are developing Christian experience and Christian faith. If we wish to see great and enduring results flow forth from our labors, there must be at work within our lives greater causes.

Our wills must be called into action in choosing before we go hence whether or not we will live in the mountains of spiritual attainment and achievement, or permit ourselves to be drawn down into the mists of the valley or live on the dead level of mediocrity. Surely the appeals of the prophetic voices which have sounded in our ears in this place, and the quickening work of the Holy Spirit in our periods of united worship and intercession, and the notes of reality which we have heard in the discussion groups, have created in us a holy discontent with much of our Christian experience and accomplishment, and have awakened in us desires and purposes to live on the higher levels and to abide with Christ in the Mount.

We are summoned unmistakably, every man of us and every boy, to wage uncompromising and heroic warfare against the enemies of Christ, and, therefore, of the young manhood and boyhood of the nations, as contrasted with affording any occasion for the charge that the Association lends itself to weak acquiescence and compromise with the evils of our time. The splendid manner in which leaders of the Association in China have come to close grapple with the opium curse should put many of us to shame as we think of how weak and futile our own resistance is in front of other dangers which beset the youth. Without a shadow of doubt the Son of God calls us to go forth with Him to war in every land represented here against the agelong, unconquered enemies arrayed against Him.

I come now to the most momentous of all the decisions Helsing-fors demands of each one of us, and that is the decision whether we will govern our plans by our visible, human resources or by our invisible, superhuman resources. Are we not deeply moved as we remind ourselves that surging all around us in Johannes Church tonight is an atmosphere of divine resource, and that we may continue to live in that atmosphere whithersoever we go. It is not the desire of an all-powerful God that any of us should live lives of weakness or that any Young Men's Christian Association in any land represented here should work solely with human energy and wisdom. The Lord hath commanded our strength. From His point of view it is not optional, but obligatory, that we be men of power and that our Associations vibrate with power more than human. This Conference has been built around the Living Christ. I would solemnly remind you that it is characteristic of the Living Christ to work here and now. He is here to make you strongest where, when you came here, you were weakest. He is eager each day and hour to work in us and through us that which is truly creative and undying. Let us so order our own lives and so direct the plans and activities of our Associations, therefore, that even the keenest critic as he observes the outreach of influence and the extent and character of the fruitage will be obliged in honesty in his endeavor to account for it all to admit that a power infinitely greater than human is the only adequate explanation or cause.

In a word, we might sum up all of these decisions and others which God has been calling upon us to make and then to put into full effect as we go back to our respective countries, by saying that it is a choice with all of us between vitality and atrophy — a choice between drinking at gushing, living fountains or dwelling on the scorching hot desert sands. Therefore, let the closing reminder in the last quiet moments of our World's Conference be that Christ Himself is in our midst. "He showed me the river of the Waters of Life, bright as crystal, issuing out of the throne of God and of the Lamb. On either side of the river was the Tree of Life . . . the leaves whereof were for the healing of the nations." "Healing of the nations!" What nations? Your nation, and my nation, and every nation. "The river of the Water of Life"—the Living Christ. At all costs may we until we meet again preserve unbroken union with Him, our Fountainhead.

RESOLUTIONS OF THE NINETEENTH WORLD'S CONFERENCE OF YOUNG MEN'S CHRISTIAN ASSOCIATIONS, HELSINGFORS, FINLAND, AUGUST 1-6, 1926

I. THE PRESENTATION OF JESUS CHRIST

We recognize that the supreme task of the Young Men's Christian Association is that of fixing the attention of young men and boys, both within and outside the Movement, on the Lord Jesus Christ, and that at the present time as revealed by the Helsingfors Inquiry, there is urgent need in all lands of such a presentation of Christ and His message as will arrest the attention of the youth of our day and afford satisfying answers to their questions relating to life and relationships, and develop a firmly founded and vital faith. We believe there would be marked advantages in uniting the intensive thought and action of the Associations throughout the world on the realization of this central objective. To this end we instruct the World's Committee to appoint a commission which, in collaboration with the Executive Committee, will undertake the following:

1. To work out a comprehensive plan of enlisting the co-operation of the various National Councils in fresh, intensive study of Christ and His message: a study in which youth in every land would be confronted with the fulness of the personality of Jesus Christ and would be given opportunity to express in its own way its experience of Him, with a view to bringing together from all peoples one living impression of our Master; and of devising and putting into effect new and more fruitful methods of insuring the presentation of His message to and by the youth of our time.

In carrying out this plan each national Movement is called to take advantage of such conditions, events, and circumstances as will insure the largest results in its own field, and at the same time make its most suggestive and enriching contribution to the world-wide Association brotherhood. Among these constructive measures to be emphasized is the furtherance of the plan of Bible study centering on the personality and work of Jesus Christ adopted at the recent annual meeting of the World's Committee.

2. To assemble, and through the Geneva headquarters make available throughout the World's Alliance, information regarding the most rewarding studies and experiences which have been taking place in the various countries.

The World's Conference expects that the World's Committee will bear witness in all its activity in a clear and penetrating way, especially through the yearly Week of Prayer, to the liberating grace of God in Jesus Christ.

II. EXTENSION OF THE ASSOCIATION TO UNOCCUPIED FIELDS

That in view of the many extensive areas such as in Asia—Siam, Indo-China, Persia, Iraq; in Africa—East, West, Central, North-western and much of the South; at least ten Latin-American republics, and the Netherlands Indies, to all of which fields our attention has been directed in this Conference as fields where the Young Men's Christian Association has not yet been established, and in view of the requests for larger co-operation which have come from certain countries where the Association has already been introduced, the World's Committee give special attention to enlisting more of the national alliances in sacrificial effort to enter as many as possible of these lands before the next World's Conference.

III. THE ASSOCIATION AND THE CHURCHES

Having heard with emotion the appeal that the Churches united in their recent Ecumenical Congress in Stockholm have addressed to the Christian youth of the world, the Conference desires to affirm its profound and respectful gratitude to the Churches, to which the Young Men's Christian Association is indebted for vital inspiration.

The Conference observes with deepest satisfaction the many signs of sympathetic appreciation and confidence in the Association manifested by the Churches and of multiplying opportunities on every hand for the Association to render larger and more efficient service to the Churches in their efforts for the upbuilding and training of the young manhood and boyhood of the nations. While the Association in no sense is or can be a substitute for the Church or can perform any of the distinctive functions of the Church, it is recognized that the call comes to the Association today as never before to place at the disposal of the Church its experience, its specialized knowledge, and its ever growing secretarial and lay forces in the critically important work of reaching and holding for Christ, His Church, and His Mission young men and the boys of the world.

IV. BOYS' WORK

The Conference records its gratification that the official delegation includes 240 boy members of the Associations, and thus gives recognition to the important place taken by the boys in the work of the Movement. It rejoices in the success which has attended the World Conferences of Boys' Workers held at Oxford and Pörtschach and the resources in personnel and money which have been made available to the World's Committee for the prosecution of this branch of service. It is gratified at the progress achieved in many countries during recent years and that the needs of boys are claiming a large share of the thought and effort of Association leaders. It desires that the World's Committee maintain and develop as an integral part of its whole service the leadership and assistance to national alliances successfully inaugurated by the Pörtschach Conference, emphasizing always the need for continuous research of boyhood and of the methods by which the Association can render its best service in this field. The Conference further urges upon the Associations everywhere the recognition of the principle that the Association's ministry is both to boys and young men and to make adequate provision for the application of this principle in their policy and program.

V. LITERATURE

The conflicting tides of thought that are challenging the moral and spiritual standards of boyhood and young manhood in every continent, the incessant flow of literature that disintegrates and degrades, the almost entire lack in many countries, and the defective nature in all countries, of the existing Christian literature for youth, together with the highly multiplying power of literature to spread its influence in all lands, are factors that lead to the conviction that this instrument is capable of untold development in Christ's service throughout the entire Association brotherhood. The experiments and inquiries carried through recently from Geneva in numerous countries in the development of the literature policy at the World's Committee headquarters in the service of national alliances, make it certain that the Committee and its staff can perform a service of high value and worldwide range to youth and the leaders of youth. Those experiments and inquiries do not point to a setting up of an extensive publication work in Geneva. They do, however, demonstrate convincingly the necessity for expanding work in at least the following directions:

1. The preparation of basic manuscripts to meet specific needs that are, by inquiry through national alliances, clearly seen to be wide in range, pressing in their nature, and not easily met by the separate national alliances.

2. The securing of the right to make the copyright of valuable books for youth and its leaders that are already available in some countries, available for translation and such adaptation as may be necessary in other lands.

3. The service to the world brotherhood of the Young Men's Christian Association through periodicals either produced in Geneva (*e.g., The Sphere* and the English edition of *World's Youth*) or editorially produced in manuscript in Geneva and published in other lands like *Jugend in aller Welt* and the Czechoslovak edition of *World's Youth*.

4. A service of the press through the national alliances in all the countries where our Association is at work with a view both to disseminating news of its work in each country throughout the other countries and to educating our public in the larger principles and policies, the ideals and trends of thought and faith that are at once the foundation of our work and its aim. We would also emphasize the importance of giving attention to the development of international radio and film services.

5. The work already in process, the demands made from other countries, and the program of pamphlets and books already agreed upon for production, indicate work at least adequate to absorbing the whole time of the existing staff at Geneva for literature for boys and for their leaders alone. The demands that it seems certain the Helsingfors Conference will make not only for carrying farther the processes initiated in the Inquiry, but for an intensive Bible study in all grades of our work in relation to the person of Jesus Christ, will inevitably greatly expand the existing program.

6. These demands call for a staff with at least two ranges of qualification: (1) editorial, that is the securing of authors, the defining of content, and having manuscripts written on the lines outlined above; (2) managerial, that is, the arrangement for the interchange of copyrights, the passing of the manuscripts through the appropriate channels to the publishing organizations, of contacts with the men responsible in those countries, and the handling of all the business related to these processes. It has already been proved that in this connection a source of income to the World's Committee can be developed.

7. While specialization of capacity is needed with a view to securing or to writing the best material on the one side for boys and their leaders and on the other side for adult manhood, the whole production of literature should be looked on

as a unity. Not only so, it should be intimately integrated to the processes of research with a view to enriching the contacts, and to all the travel and field work with a view to securing that the material produced is fully known throughout the nations of the World's Alliance.

8. In view of the need, the possibilities, and the existing developments already outlined we commend to the favorable notice of the World's Committee in building up its staff the importance of making provision for a highly qualified secretarial officer to direct and administer the policy outlined above, as the World's Committee shall direct, as it watches the expanding demands of the Association throughout the world.

VI. RESEARCH WORK

Strong, able, progressive leadership of boys and young men by the Association is everywhere hampered by lack of knowledge. The World's Committee can do work of inestimable value to the national alliances by a service of information of a kind that may help in the framing of policy and practice, in the presentation of our message to youth, and in making known our work to the supporters of the Association.

The information needed for such a service would include knowledge of existing movements among youth all over the world (outside as well as inside the Association Movement); developments in educational theory and practice, in physical culture and psychology, in the main currents of religious, philosophical, and ethical thought that impinge upon our work; the state of national feeling in different parts of the world in so far as it affects our development or can be affected by it; movements and organizations parallel to or opposed to our own; the whole current life of the Association throughout the world; and the actual facts of the race problem, its causes, and the best lines of thought and action for its solution. This conception of an information service to the national alliances clearly involves a highly skilled work of research. We desire the World's Committee to take such steps in framing its policy as shall develop a department which, though directed by one secretary, would mobilize the research activities of the staff as a whole and all available voluntary service, working in contact with existing research work carried out by bodies specializing in this kind of service.

The carrying into effect of such a research policy would involve: (1) an expansion of the library, which so far has concentrated largely upon creating highly valuable archives of Young Men's Christian Association history; (2) an increase in the incoming periodical and book literature; (3) the correlation of the inquiries undertaken during travel by the secretaries and others; and (4) equipment for a careful scientific analysis of the material secured in these separate ways.

Other elements entering into the efficient use of such research, when made, would include: the development of definite provision for skilled translation work in a way that will not place impossible burdens on the shoulders of men responsible for other work, and that will be more nearly adequate to the highly sensitive and varied demands of our work of interpreting the knowledge required by the different nations within our Alliance. It would also be related to the channels through which the information can be passed on for the benefit of the Association brotherhood throughout the world, including periodicals produced in Geneva, correspondence and occasional bulletins, special articles, speeches of secretaries when traveling, the knowledge provided through conferences, and in other ways. We are convinced that such a policy and practice of research and study would lead the World's Alliance increasingly to turn to the Geneva office with demands for fresh light and guidance in making the Association a more and more powerful Christian force in the world.

VII. THE SEX QUESTION

The Conference has ample evidence that members of the Association as well as boys and young men in general are influenced by the intensified interest in, and wide publicity given to what is called the sex question. It behooves the Association to press upon parents the obvious duty of including accurate knowledge of sex life as one of the vital elements in the education of young people and to unite with Christian doctors and teachers in finding the best methods of imparting scientific truth in a Christian setting and in making available suitable literature whenever needed on this subject, affording help on the one hand to parents, teachers, and Association secretaries, and on the other hand presenting facts to boys and young men for their guidance. It requests the World's Committee to collect, study, and disseminate the best available experience of other Christian bodies. The Conference declares that the solution of our problems in personal life cannot be found in knowledge alone, but requires along with it the effort of will surrendered to God in Jesus Christ and controlled by Him.

VIII. RACE RELATIONS

In view of the fact that the Association is at work among men of all the great races of the world, most of whom we rejoice to see represented in the fellowship of this Conference, and in particular that the

Young Men's Christian Association is located in the principal areas of racial friction throughout the world, we cannot in fidelity to Christ, in whom there is no racial division, rest without pressing further our efforts towards the practical solution of this problem. We recommend, then, the adoption and practice of a definite program with a view to grappling with the situation. That program would include the following processes:

1. To accumulate and co-ordinate existing knowledge upon the situation throughout the world, making special use of the facilities afforded at Geneva in the library and files of the League of Nations and of the International Labor Office and elsewhere through the Institute of Social and Religious Research, the Commission of Interracial Co-operation, the Institute of Pacific Relations, the Phelps Stokes Fund, etc.

2. To devote, whenever possible, special man power for carrying forward this accumulation of scientific knowledge with a view to making it available for the information and use of all the alliances.

3. In co-operation with the individual National Councils to encourage research into the actual concrete facts of racial friction in the areas of those Councils. The range of this research, both centrally and locally, would include not only a scientific analysis of the situation but inquiry into the basic causes of the problem, an indication of the promising elements, a record of what is being done to mobilize helpful influences as well as of the actual results accomplished.

4. Special work should be done in analyzing the New Testament foundation of our faith and in particular in discovering the mind of Christ with reference to the application of His principles to the race problem, and making that thought available throughout the Association brotherhood.

5. Every use should be made of existing literature for individual and group discussion. New literature especially suited to Association purposes should be provided through the operations of the World's Committee as well as the national alliances. The example of the Commission on Interracial Co-operation in the southern states of the United States of America, and similar experiments in gathering together, e.g. in South Africa, local influential interracial groups for handling and diagnosing local cases of friction and applying principles to their solution, should be widely extended. The special facilities and experience of the Association in promoting personal friendships should be mobilized for interracial comradeship through discussion groups, social gatherings, sports, camps, and in other ways.

6. We recognize with humiliation that the Associations are not

able at this stage to achieve interracial unity within their own borders. At the same time we note with satisfaction and high hope that in some of the most difficult areas the Association is pioneering in the practice of interracial fellowship. We would, therefore, press on the Association the obligation to promote such sentiment and practice as will lead to closer co-operation and interrelationship and a more deep-seated mutual understanding. The World's Committee is urged to press upon national alliances the carrying out in local Young Men's Christian Associations of the views here expressed without entering into political entanglements.

7. Every opportunity open to the Association, whether separately or in alliance with other organizations, for the formation of right public opinion, and the removal of misunderstandings and suspicions should be utilized. In particular, effort should be concentrated in relation to agencies such as the cinema, the public press, the theater, and schools (in particular, textbooks).

8. In addition to the above-mentioned areas of co-operation with other organizations, common action should be taken with agencies that are interested in the welfare and mutual understanding of the races such as the Federal Council of Churches, the missionary bodies, national and international, governments in their educational and other aspects, etc.

9. Every opening should be utilized for unselfish service on a large scale between the races, both for its own sake and as a means of developing interracial good will.

10. The continued intercession of the Associations should be stimulated in relation to this pressing problem that is so central to the work of the world-wide brotherhood, and in particular, a central place should be found for it in the program of the Week of Prayer shared in by the national and local Young Men's Christian Associations in all lands.

IX. INTERNATIONAL QUESTIONS

In view of the international character of our Association and our allegiance to Christ as the Prince of Peace, special and continuous thought should be given throughout our Movement to the problem of developing international understanding and furthering world peace.

To this end first of all we must work for that fellowship which can only be most intimately achieved in Jesus Christ.

1. Study should be made of international subjects in an atmosphere of Christian fellowship with a view to deeper understanding of the life and teaching of Jesus Christ.

2. An international program should be pursued in each national

Movement to stimulate the thought and action of the members. The World's Committee should explore the possibilities of correlating these studies in the various countries for the benefit of the Movement as a whole.

3. International camps and area conferences (such as were held for instance at Vaumarcus and at Mölle) should be held with this element in their program. National conferences should be enriched by inviting foreign delegates on a still larger scale and giving time to these problems.

4. For these purposes and the help of discussion groups, literature should be provided on: (1) Questions of international relationships; and (2) Christian thought and practice in different lands so that the national Movements may have fuller understanding of each other.

Co-operation should be given in work for the production of textbooks of history from an international point of view.

5. The national Movements should examine how they could give greater help to students and others from foreign countries within their own borders.

6. The World's Committee and the national alliances should promote and develop co-operation in relationships with the international organizations on the lines recommended in Resolution VIII on race relations.

X. WORLD'S COMMITTEE REPORT

The Conference accepts the report of the World's Committee on the work during the years 1913-1926 and commends this interesting and suggestive survey of the Association service and development throughout this period to the attention of the members of the Associations everywhere.

XI. REVISION OF THE CONSTITUTION

That the revision of the constitution of the World's Alliance approved by the national alliances and submitted to this Conference be approved, it being understood that the officers of the World's Committee mentioned in the first paragraph of Article XI are ex officio members of the World's Committee and of its Executive Committee.

XII. THE LAY LEADERSHIP OF THE ASSOCIATION

Recognizing that the Association Movement from its earliest years has been maintained through voluntary leadership, and that the importance and necessity of a trained and consecrated secretariat to meet ever-expanding needs does not in any sense decrease the necessity of the leadership of laymen but rather increases it:

The Conference would reiterate its abiding conviction that sacrificial voluntary leadership in all departments, branches, and activities is essential to the fulfillment of the Association's great responsibility with the boys and young men of the world.

The Conference recommends that in the composition and leadership of committees and in the attendance at and participation in conferences, both national and international, there should always be a much larger proportion of laymen than of secretaries.

XIII. WORK AND STAFFING OF THE WORLD'S COMMITTEE

The Conference notes with satisfaction the careful study which the World's Committee, through a special commission, has made of the work and staffing of the Committee. It endorses the definition given of the various kinds of service which the national alliances should expect from the World's Committee, welcomes the emphasis laid on the importance of the service of information, research, and literature, and approves generally of the scheme of organization suggested, in particular of the provisions for insuring that the staff, so far as is consistent with the highest efficiency of the service, be representative of the different cultures in the Movement. It urges the World's Committee to give special attention to the necessity of assuring that the work shall be prosecuted as a unified and symmetrical service both to boys and young men.

XIV. YOUNG MEN'S CHRISTIAN ASSOCIATION INTERNATIONAL ATHLETIC CONTEST

The Conference is gratified at the development of educative activities in the Association physical program and reaffirms its conviction as to their great importance in contributing to the building up of strong harmonious Christian character. It cordially commends the First Young Men's Christian Association International Athletic Contest to be held at Copenhagen in 1927 and trusts that many national alliances will participate therein.

XV. NEW ALLIANCES

The Conference has with gratitude to God noted the fact mentioned in the report of the World's Committee that the number of members, secretaries, and buildings has greatly increased during the years that have passed since the last World's Conference, and that progress has been made in the strengthening of their organization and in the widening of their service.

The Conference welcomes the alliances which have been affiliated since the last World's Conference, viz., those of South America and Czechoslovakia.

XVI. FAR EASTERN CONFERENCE

In line with the general policy of the World's Committee of holding area conferences for workers with boys in order to unify, strengthen, and develop the work by helping leaders to face their problems in the light of the world situation and in face of the present position in the Orient in regard to religious education, the Conference recommends that the World's Committee, after further consultation with the committees concerned with the organization of a Far Eastern Area Conference, proceed with the organization of a conference in the Far East at the earliest date possible (the summer of 1928 having already been suggested) the conference to be in association if practicable with such organizations as the Young Women's Christian Association, the World's Student Christian Federation, and the International Missionary Council with its constituent National Christian Councils.

XVII. MEMBERS OF THE NEW WORLD'S COMMITTEE

That the following be elected members of the World's Committee:

Europe

Austria: Mr. Rudolf Stroh

Belgium: Mr. Henri Sauveur

Bulgaria: Mr. S. Botcheff

Czechoslovakia: Mr. B. Jerie, Professor E. Radl, Dr. A. Sum

Denmark: Mr. K. Hee Andersen, Mr. S. Bögh, Mr. E. Frederiksen, Mr. H. Jessen, Mr. S. Rehling

England: Mr. F. J. Chamberlain, Mr. R. M. Gray, Mr. C. R. Hemingway, Mr. Frank Pratt, Sir Arthur Yapp, Major F. H. Young, and one other to be designated

France: Mr. Jean Laroche, Mr. E. Meyer, Comte P. de Pourtalès

Finland: Professor A. Hjelt, Dr. P. Virkkunen, Mr. Axel von Weissenberg

Germany: Mr. C. Engel, Mr. A. Friedrich, Mr. P. Herzog, Mr. P. Humburg, Mr. F. Humburg, Mr. H. Lüst, Mr. Meissner

Holland: Dr. Liebrandt, Mr. C. D. van Noppen, Mr. Quarles van Ufford, Mr. A. Sillem, Mr. P. Veen

Hungary: Professor A. Karacsony

Italy: Mr. Mario Falchi

Norway: Mr. O. Grasmo, Mr. L. Koren, Mr. K. Stub, Mr. Fr. Wislöff

Portugal: Mr. R. Moreton

Scotland: Dr. G. F. Barbour, Mr. John Craig, Mr. John Forrester Paton, Mr. H. Lightbody

Spain: Mr. Julian Saco

Switzerland: Mr. P. Bots, Mr. Karl Egli, Mr. P. Juillard

Sweden: Prince O. Bernadotte, Mr. Hugo Cedergren, Mr. J. Noren

Asia

China: Dr. Fong F. Sec, Dr. Poling Chang, Dr. Y. T. Tsun, Dr. David Z. T. Yui, Dr. G. C. Yen, Mr. T. T. Pun

India: Dr. S. K. Datta, Dr. John Mathai, Mr. K. T. Paul

Japan: Dr. K. Ibuka, Mr. R. Ishikawa, Mr. S. Kimura, Mr. K. Mizusaki

Korea: H. Cynn, and two others to be designated

Africa

South Africa: Mr. W. McEwan

Australasia

Australia: Mr. James Allen, Mr. T. Thomas, Mr. A. T. Wreford

New Zealand: Mr. H. W. Kersley, and two others to be designated

North America

Canada: Mr. E. G. Baker, Mr. H. Ballantyne, Mr. G. E. Barbour, Colonel G. E. Birks, Mr. R. F. McWilliams

United States: Mr. W. W. Fry, Mr. John Hope, Mr. W. F. Hypes, Mr. Adrian Lyon, Mr. Alfred E. Marling, Mr. F. W. Ramsey, Mr. J. E. Smitherman, Mr. William Speers

South America

Brazil: Dr. Erasmo Braga, Mr. Fernandez Braga, Professor Henrique Lindenberg, D.D.

Continental Committee: Dr. A. Abeledo, Professor E. Monteverde, Mr. W. E. Wotherspoon

XVIII. PROPOSALS FOR APPOINTMENTS ON THE EXECUTIVE COMMITTEE OF THE WORLD'S ALLIANCE

1. That the following be elected as the seven members residing in or near Switzerland: Mr. Ayusawa, Dr. J. van Walré de Bordes,

Dr. P. Des Gouttes, Mr. C. R. Hemingway, Mr. A. Koechlin, Dr. A. Riddell, Reverend J. E. Siordet.

2. That the following National Councils be represented permanently on the Executive until the next World's Conference: China, Denmark, England, France, Germany, Czechoslovakia, and the United States.

XIX. RECOMMENDATIONS OF THE DISCUSSION GROUPS

Recognizing the rich value of the recommendations and suggestions of the fifty discussion groups which have come out of the deep spiritual experiences and intimate fellowship of these days, and the significance of the process they represent for the development of personal conviction and united policy, we recommend that the report of these recommendations and suggestions now in preparation and to appear as a part of the official report of the Helsingfors Conference, and which has been presented on the first draft of the Conference, be taken into consideration by the World's Committee in shaping its policy and in giving effect to the foregoing resolutions; and that, so far as they concern the National Councils and the local Associations, they be referred by the World's Committee to the national alliances for their favorable consideration.

XX. THE NEXT WORLD CONFERENCE

The Conference hopes that the next World Conference be held in the year 1930, and that the exact date and place be determined by the World's Committee and announced, if practicable, two years in advance.

XXI. FINANCES

It is recommended that the budget of Swiss francs 478.645,— as examined in detail by the finance committee—be adopted, that the World's Committee be instructed to proceed on the lines indicated in the report of the finance committee, and that all alliances be urged to increase their contributions so that necessary funds may be forthcoming.

XXII. EXPRESSION OF GRATITUDE

This Conference desires to record its gratitude to all those who, since the last meeting at Edinburgh in 1913, have served the World's Alliance, during years in which all human institutions have been tested as never before. We owe it to them that we are able to meet in Helsingfors as a united world Movement.

Specially do we mention:

1. Our retiring president, Dr. Paul Des Gouttes, who has held office for thirteen years, whose name will be permanently associated with this difficult period and whose leadership will be gratefully remembered.

2. Our retiring honorary treasurer, Mr. Henry Fatio, who, in that capacity, has shared the responsibilities. Dr. H. Audeoud, Dr. F. L. Perrot, Professor E. Choisy, Professor P. Bovet, Professor F. Thomas, and the other retiring members of the Executive who have had for years such a valuable part on the councils of the Committee; Pastor Kœchlin, who has done such valuable work as an interpreter.

3. Messieurs E. Sautter and Christian Phildius who have successively served in and retired from the general secretaryship.

Dr. Karl Fries has served the Alliance during the past five years as its general secretary. By his Christian character and consecration and his unselfish devotion he has won the love of the brotherhood. His long experience of international work has given him peculiar fitness to guide our affairs during years when reconciling forces needed to be released throughout the world.

We are grateful to the Associations in the northern countries, especially to the National Council of Sweden, who made it possible for Dr. Fries to accept the call and who have supported his appointment by their generous gifts and prayers. He will carry with him on his retirement the affectionate good will of every national alliance and our prayers that he may long be spared to share in the Association's problems and triumphs.

These officers have been supported by a secretarial and clerical staff without whose unstinted service the work could not have been efficiently maintained.

A special expression of gratitude is due to the members of the staff and some occasional workers who have given unstinted help in preparing the organization of the Helsingfors Conference and in conducting the inquiry which has preceded it.

This Conference desires to express its sincere and heartfelt gratitude to the President and government and parliament of Finland for their gracious welcome and warm hospitality in their beautiful country.

To the city of Helsingfors for warm and hearty co-operation.

To the bishops and clergy and church council of Helsingfors for the use of the Johannes Church, and to the Church throughout Finland, whose generous assistance has so helped in the preparations for the Conference.

To the Minister for Education and school authorities of Helsingfors whose action in placing several spacious and well-equipped school buildings at our disposal made possible the extensive grouping arrangements as well as the housing of the delegates.

To the president, Professor Hjelt, committee, and members of the Helsingfors Young Men's Christian Association who with the local conference secretary, Mr. Louhivuori, and many young helpers have placed themselves unreservedly at the service of the whole delegation.

To the press for their understanding reports and sympathetic interpretation of our aims.

To the warmhearted people of Helsingfors who opened their homes and so kindly entertained delegates from all parts of the world.

And finally, to the president of the Conference, Dr. John R. Mott, who has, by his chairmanship, added to the ever increasing debt that this Movement owes him.

RECOGNIZING THE CENTRALITY OF JESUS CHRIST

LETTER FROM THE PRESIDENT OF THE WORLD'S COMMITTEE

S. Wirt Wiley, Esq.   January 19, 1927
Associate General Secretary, Home Division
The National Council of the Young Men's
Christian Associations of the United States

DEAR WILEY:

I write you today in my capacity as chairman of the World's Committee of the Young Men's Christian Associations. I am glad indeed that my first official communication through you to the American Association brotherhood is upon a subject of transcendent importance—a subject which, I trust, will ever hold the central and supreme place in the thinking, planning, and action of Association leaders, both lay and secretarial, the world over. Largely due to the conception and urgent emphasis of Mr. R. F. McWilliams, chairman of the Canadian National Council, the World's Committee, at their meeting held in Helsingfors, decided to call upon all of the National Councils or alliances to commemorate the nineteen hundredth anniversary of the three years' public ministry of our Lord Jesus Christ by furthering an intensive study of His personality, His work, and His message concerning the whole range of the life and relationships of men. According to the general consensus of Christian chronologists, the nineteen hundredth anniversary falls within the years 1927, 1928, and 1929. In line with this action, the following resolution was subsequently introduced and unanimously adopted by the delegates of the

Associations present from forty-six nations at the World's Conference held in Helsingfors last August:

We recognize that the supreme task of the Young Men's Christian Association is that of fixing the attention of young men and boys, both within and outside the Movement, on the Lord Jesus Christ, and that at the present time as revealed by the Helsingfors Inquiry there is urgent need in all lands of such a presentation of Christ and His message as will arrest the attention of the youth of our day and afford satisfying answers to their questions relating to life and relationships, and develop a firmly founded and vital faith. We believe there would be marked advantages of uniting the intensive thought and action of the Associations throughout the world on the realization of this central objective. To this end we instruct the World's Committee to appoint a commission which, in collaboration with the Executive Committee, will undertake the following:

1. To work out a comprehensive plan of enlisting the co-operation of the various National Councils in fresh, intensive study of Christ and His message—a study in which youth in every land would be confronted with the fulness of the personality of Jesus Christ and would be given opportunity to express in its own way its experience of Him, with a view to bringing together from all peoples one living impression of our Master; and of devising and putting into effect new and more fruitful methods of insuring the presentation of His message to and by the youth of our time.

In carrying out this plan each national Movement is called to take advantage of such conditions, events, and circumstances as will insure the largest results in its own field, and at the same time make its most suggestive and enriching contribution to the world-wide Association brotherhood. Among these constructive measures to be emphasized is the furtherance of the plan of Bible study centering on the personality and work of Jesus Christ adopted at the recent annual meeting of the World's Committee.

2. To assemble and through the Geneva headquarters make available throughout the World's Alliance information regarding the most rewarding studies and experiences which have been taking place in the various countries.

The World's Conference expects that the World's Committee will bear witness in all its activity in a clear and penetrating way, especially through the yearly Week of Prayer, to the liberating grace of God in Jesus Christ.

May I request you kindly to bring this significant action of the World's Committee and of the World's Conference to the attention of the leaders and members of the American Associations and to enlist as soon as practicable their constructive suggestions and initiative as to how the American Association brotherhood can give the largest and most fruitful effect to the plan and at the same time make the richest contribution to this world-wide observance of the Ministry of our Lord.

Very sincerely yours,

JOHN R. MOTT

REPORT OF THE PLENARY MEETING OF THE WORLD'S
COMMITTEE OF YOUNG MEN'S CHRISTIAN ASSOCIATIONS,
GENEVA, SWITZERLAND, AUGUST, 1929

STATEMENT AT THE OPENING SESSION

The August, 1929, session of the Plenary Meeting was opened
on Saturday evening, August 3, by Dr. Mott who gave a report of
his recent world tour. An outline of his address follows:

I. Dr. Mott first characterized the situation throughout Asia,
developing the following points:

1. The economic situation is most serious, particularly in India,
    and large parts of China, Japan, and Korea.
2. The spirit of nationalism is more pronounced and aggressive
    and is revealing more sense of direction than at any time, both
    within and outside the Christian community.
3. Although there are still many unfavorable aspects in the
    sphere of international and interracial relations, the outlook
    on the whole is more favorable than it has been for years.
4. Organized Christianity is working under very heavy handi-
    caps due primarily to the divisions, especially among Prot-
    estant bodies, due also to the associations of the Christian
    agencies of the West with so-called Christian powers, and
    moreover due to inadequate leadership of the Christian forces.
5. Notwithstanding this, the influence of Christ is becoming
    markedly more widespread, penetrating, and transforming.
6. There are signs on every hand of a marked quickening of the
    social conscience and of more manifold and serious applica-
    tions of the teachings of Christ.
7. A larger synthesis is being developed on the part of the varied
    altruistic and constructive forces at work in Asia.
8. The anti-religious movement, especially in the form of com-
    munistic propaganda from the Russian base, has by no means
    spent its force.
9. There are most encouraging evidences of a greatly improved
    psychology among the Christian leaders and workers in the
    various parts of Asia.
10. Jerusalem is markedly in evidence from one end of Asia to
    the other. It has evidently exerted more extensive and pro-
    found influence on Christian leaders and even on many edu-
    cated non-Christians than any previous world religious gath-
    ering.

II. Dr. Mott next presented a number of concrete proposals of special interest and concern to the World's Committee of the Young Men's Christian Association. Among these he indicated his convictions on the following points:

1. The Young Men's Christian Association throughout Asia is dangerously undermanned, both with reference to the number of foreign secretaries and also with reference to the nationals; for example, whereas ten years ago there were in India over forty foreign secretaries, there are at present in that field not more than twenty-five. Moreover in China ten years ago the staff of foreign secretaries numbered 100; now less than fifty.

2. We cannot much longer defer facing the claims upon us for launching and carrying to a successful issue another building program.

3. We must put forth efforts to strengthen the hands of the national committees of Asia as well as of other parts of the non-Christian world.

4. The policy of visitation of secretaries of the World's Committee should be worked out in such a way that, if possible, each year there might be one member of the staff on each principal continent for at least part of the time.

5. We must help to usher in the period of higher specialization in virtually all the fields of Asia.

6. The Christian character of the Association Movement across Asia is imperiled. On every hand one is made vividly conscious of the subtle and dangerous influence of secularism, naturalism, humanism, and in some cases of a dangerous syncretism.

7. The Association throughout Asia is summoned to a larger evangelism, not alone in a quantitative or numerical, but also in a qualitative sense.

8. The Association is called upon to perform far more effectively its distinctive mission, that of liberating a vastly greater lay force.

9. We must seek to foster and make more truly operative the conception of our world work as a sharing enterprise.

10. The Young Men's Christian Association, together with the Young Women's Christian Association and the world-wide Student Movement, have at present in Asia the greatest opportunity in all their history.

11. An aggressive, expanding program is absolutely essential to the vitality of the Young Men's Christian Association.

THE OCCUPATION OF THE FIELD

SUMMARY OF AN ADDRESS DELIVERED AT THE MEETING OF
THE PLENARY COMMITTEE, AUGUST 6, 1929

I. OUTLINE OF FIELDS VIRTUALLY COMPLETELY UNOCCUPIED BY THE YOUNG MEN'S CHRISTIAN ASSOCIATION

1. *Europe:* Russia, Lithuania, Albania.
2. *Latin America:* Guatemala, Costa Rica, Nicaragua, Honduras, San Salvador, Panama, and several groups of the West Indies, in North and Central America; also Paraguay, Colombia, Bolivia, Ecuador, Venezuela, and parts of Guiana, in South America.
3. *The Near East:* Persia, Iraq, Syria, Arabia, Transjordania.
4. *The Far East:* Siam, Indo-China, and the larger part of the Federated Malay States.
5. *The Island World:* The Netherlands Indies, and several groups of islands of the Pacific.
6. *Africa:* With the exception of the lower Nile Valley, Madagascar, and portions of South Africa, this vast continent is unoccupied.

The foregoing outline presents, apart from Africa, not less than ten major, and not less than twenty-four minor fields, or a total of thirty-one countries without the Young Men's Christian Association, or approximately the same number which have been entered in different parts of the non-Christian world. If we add Africa, the unentered fields embrace a population of fully 400,000,000, or one-quarter of the human race.

II.

What is the reason why the Association has not during the past ten years extended its service to the unoccupied fields? It has not been due to there being no need for the ministry of the Association, nor has it been due to the fact that the Association is not wanted in these fields, because we have on file calls from the large majority of them. It has not been due to these lands being closed, because the past decade has been a period of unexampled openness of doors. The failure to occupy cannot be traced primarily to lack of financial resources, nor is it due to the want of men who possess the spirit of adventure and sacrifice. We cannot explain the matter by the lack of success in Association work throughout the non-Christian world, because the good results in this period have been truly notable. It cannot be said that our failure is traceable to there being no element of urgency in the situation, for the opposite has been and is true. It has not been due to the discovery of some new power or agency which could more adequately meet the deepest needs of youth.

We may trace the neglect to preoccupation primarily on the part of the leaders of our organization. As a result, there has been lack of perspective or sense of true proportion in their planning and action. In too many cases our gaze has been in the wrong direction, for as truly as in ancient times, Christ has been saying, "Lift up your eyes, and behold the fields, that they are white already unto harvest." We must admit also that there have been evidences of want of world-conquering faith. Thus our leadership has been inadequate. Again we must admit that our gaze has been in the wrong direction—that is, it has not been fixed upon our Prince Leader, the Lord Jesus Christ.

Be the causes of our neglect what they may, the results have been indescribably momentous and serious. This has been true as we think of the results visible in the Association Movement itself. It has been even more serious as we think of the effects upon the young men and boys in the nations thus neglected.

The Movement drifts into the position of a selfish club, and suffers atrophy because of failure to use its will for service. It loses its greatest appeal to the men of largest caliber.

III. A CONSTRUCTIVE PROGRAM

1. Every National Council in the World's Alliance should have some definite and enlarging part in the extension program.

2. If a National Council cannot yet send and support a secretary, let it undertake some other project within the compass of its ability.

3. Don't rob Peter to pay Paul; that is, don't cut off what is now being given to some other part of the Association work, such as the support of the World's Committee, in order to perform one's duty to the extension program.

4. Let none of us who are here at Geneva delay initiative or sacrificial action.

5. The plan in each country should involve the enlisting of the interest and co-operation of the rank and file of our membership.

6. We should seek to find and enlist individuals, families, companies or firms, and Churches, to assume the support of a representative in the foreign field.

7. The time has come to set up a small but strong committee of the World's Committee to initiate efforts on behalf of the unoccupied fields, and likewise to facilitate the proper co-ordination of the extension work of the various National Councils.

8. In planning the tours of our staff, the gradual reaching of unoccupied areas should be kept in view. At the same time, the possibility of securing the collaboration of well-qualified lay members of the World's Committee and of the National Councils in the extension program should be kept in view.

9. We should keep in mind and seek to realize the advantages of giving ourselves to far larger plans and undertakings.

IV. GUIDING PRINCIPLES IN RELATIONSHIPS IN THE EXTENSION WORK OF THE YOUNG MEN'S CHRISTIAN ASSOCIATION

Principles generally accepted and to be followed by national sending committees (that is, committees which send secretaries to work in other countries and support them in such work) in their extension work:

1. The objective of all extension work should be to develop indigenous national and local committees which will as soon as possible become truly autonomous and self-supporting.

2. The indigenous national committee of a country, wherever such committee exists, is the body responsible for co-ordinating the work of any two or three foreign Association bodies (or national sending committees) sending workers to that field.

3. If there is an effective national committee already in the field to which secretaries are to be sent, it is understood that secretaries will not be sent to that field without consultation with and approval of such national committee.

4. If there is no national committee in a given field, any national sending committee is free to send secretaries to this field. If the field is a colony of a country having a national committee, this national committee should be consulted and its approval secured before sending secretaries to the colony. If there are missionaries in the field they also should be consulted in advance.

5. In case of a field without a national committee in which field secretaries are already being supported by one or more national sending committees, these committees should first be consulted by any other national sending committee which may wish to send workers to that field.

6. In a field to which one or more national sending committees have sent workers, and where no indigenous national committee has yet been established, the two or more committees concerned shall agree as to which of them shall furnish the senior secretary, and as to which of them shall be otherwise primarily responsible for co-ordinating and leading the work. Unless there be some understanding to the

contrary, this relation of leadership shall be sustained by the committee which first established work with resident secretaries giving their whole time to the serviec, or which, because of the volume and strength of its work, has the acknowledged leadership.

7. The function of the World's Committee with reference to the extension work is to influence wherever possible national sending committees (or local Associations in lands without national committees) to assume responsibility for extending the Association Movement to countries needing their help through the sending or support (in full or part) of secretaries, and also to co-ordinate and further such work of national sending committees and to facilitate the development of indigenous national committees.

It is expected that the various national sending committees will keep the World's Committee informed of their activities and plans in extension work.

A national committee which may wish to send workers to a foreign field should first consult the World's Committee.

RESOLUTIONS OF THE TWENTIETH WORLD'S CONFERENCE OF YOUNG MEN'S CHRISTIAN ASSOCIATIONS, CLEVELAND, OHIO, U.S.A., AUGUST 8, 1931

RESOLUTIONS

The Resolutions set out below were adopted in three plenary sessions held during the course of Saturday, August 8. They fall into two main categories. In the first place, the Conference gave a series of mandates to the World's Committee which will determine the general lines of its policy during the ensuing five years. In the second place, the Conference sought to express in Resolutions the mind and purpose of the World's Alliance. In view, however, of the nature of the Alliance, it is evident that the latter are not binding upon the constituent national Movements.

I. The claims of youth.

The year 1930 constituted the seventy-fifth anniversary of the World's Alliance, and it was fitting, therefore, that the Conference should preface its decisions by a Resolution of thanksgiving and dedication:

The Twentieth World's Conference of the Young Men's Christian Association assembled at Cleveland returns thanks to Almighty God for the record of seventy-five years showing the progress and development of a World Movement, especially for extension in recent years within the areas of some of the younger national alliances, and for new work established in Siam and in the Dutch East Indies.

The main concern of the Conference, however, lies in its recognition that the needs of youth amid present world conditions are more intense and urgent than ever before and that there are great groups of boys and young men still unreached by the Association or by any similar Christian movement. Too many calls for service remain unanswered.

The Conference receives encouragement from the increasing values constantly coming out of the service of the World's Alliance and its staff and organization in practical co-operation in many areas of the world, and in the growing help given in service by national alliances. It calls upon the whole membership to strive in deeper unity to share in understanding, meeting, and fulfilling the great responsibilities for youth which rest with our World's Alliance.

II. Call to youth

We, the youth and youth leaders of the Young Men's Christian Association of more than forty nations assembled in Cleveland, met together under the watchword of "Youth's Adventure with God," desire to express our gratitude for the practical experience of the reality of God in Jesus Christ which has come to us in our profound sense of fellowship, in spite of all the political, economic, racial, and national differences, and we would therefore unite in making the following appeal to the youth, not only of our own Movement but of the whole world.

While gladly recognizing the presence of many constructive forces in our time, we have been deeply impressed by the fact that we live at a moment in the history of the world when relations between individuals, nations, classes, and races are rapidly reaching a point of unendurable tension, a moment also in which great confusion and uncertainty exist with regard to the truths by which man must live.

In such a situation, we who believe in God through Jesus Christ realize with pain that because of our want of courage in applying the teachings of our Master, we have lacked the power to redeem human relationships. Furthermore, we have given no such clear and dynamic witness to the reality of God as will satisfy youth in its search for the meaning of life.

We affirm, nevertheless, in spite of our failure, our strong conviction that Christ can give us the vision and power to transform human society. In Him alone, as Lord of life and Savior of men, we also discover the true vocation, purpose, and fulfillment of our own lives.

We, therefore, call upon the youth of the world, and in the first instance upon ourselves, to pledge obedience to God's will in Christ and to the courageous and practical application of Christ's law of love to all human relationships. We would at the same time challenge youth to consider Christ's claim to reveal God and the true meaning of life.

In order to give effect to these resolutions and make good our consecration to them, we call upon the World's Committee and the national alliances to stimulate the working out of these convictions in the message and program of the Young Men's Christian Associations throughout the world.

For the same reasons, we call upon the World's Committee and the national alliances to safeguard and preserve the character of the Young Men's Christian Association as a movement rather than an institution, to make it increasingly a spiritual movement of youth itself in which the directing influence shall be predominantly youthful, a pioneer movement which ventures fearlessly in carrying the spirit and teaching of our Lord and Master into all the complicated relationships of modern life, whatever the cost to ourselves or our Association.

III. Membership

1. The Conference reaffirms the Paris Basis of 1855 as the Basis of affiliation of national alliances with the World's Alliance.

2. The Conference is of the opinion that liberty should continue to be allowed to national alliances to make their own conditions of affiliation for local Associations, including the rule of membership, so long as these conditions are consistent with the Paris Basis.

3. The Conference holds that in order to preserve and promote the Christian and missionary character of the Associations the following should be regarded as minimum requirements for those admitted to the governing or active membership:

(1) A personal commitment to the purpose of the Association.

(2) A personal commitment to the Christian fellowship of the Association and its obligations.

(3) Active participation in the work of the Association.

(4) Admission to the membership by a worthy initiation service, a public declaration of allegiance to Jesus Christ, or by an adequate ceremony, and not by the mere payment of a fee.

4. The Conference urges national alliances to re-examine the rules of membership which obtain throughout their areas and to take steps to insure that these are consistent with the Paris Basis. It is suggested that every national alliance should institute a study of the aims and objectives for which the Association exists and formulate these in a statement which will set forth clearly the meaning and obligations of membership.

5. The Conference requests the World's Committee to continue the study of the meaning of membership in co-operation with the national alliances.

IV. Leadership

1. In view of (a) the demand of the Young Men's Christian Associations for spiritual leadership by men with strong Christian conviction and clear message who recognize the personal leadership of Jesus Christ, and the regenerating power of the love of God in every area of life; (b) the response to the interests of youth made by other agencies and associations of a non-Christian emphasis under highly trained and specialized leadership, and the consequent urgent need for both lay and secretarial leaders who are equipped with specialized

skill and technique in the field of activity undertaken by the Association; (c) the too largely professional and adult leadership of the Movement as it exists at present, the Conference registers the paramount necessity for:

(1) The leadership of the Association being drawn from among men of strong Christian conviction and discipleship.

(2) Emphasizing that voluntary leadership constitutes the very heart of the Movement, and for the development of better methods for the training of lay leadership in all Association activities.

(3) Older boys and young men being given a more important place in the processes of legislation and control within the Association in local Associations as well as in the deliberative and legislative committees of national alliances and the World's Committee, and in the planning committees for future conferences.

2. The Conference further suggests that the World's Committee should:

(1) Continue to develop the International Training School at Geneva, Switzerland, and create within the national alliances in all parts of the world a greater interest and co-operation in this enterprise of far-reaching importance.

(2) Give increased attention to training processes in use among national alliances.

(3) Establish a world center of postgraduate training and research and a study exchange for experienced workers who desire to carry further their study of Y.M.C.A. work in its world setting.

(4) Devise plans for, and give aid to, a wider interchange of leadership across national borders.

(5) Conduct training schools and assemblies for voluntary leaders within national, as well as international, boundaries.

(6) Make available material on leadership to the national alliances and aid them in setting up suitable processes in lay training.

(7) Encourage the development of curricula in the training processes which consider all possible problems in their world setting, lifting them out of their limited national considerations to international and world significance.

(8) Inaugurate a study of the definition of leadership and the problems of leadership training.

V. *International relations*

1. The Conference affirms the following as the fundamental principles of the Christian attitude to international relations:

(1) Faith in God, the Creator and Ruler of the earth, is recognized as the basis of all Christian thought and action in the realm of international relations; faith in a God, moreover, Who manifests His will and establishes His Kingdom not only in the hearts of individuals but also

in the lives of nations; Who through Christ the Elder Brother calls all mankind to be His children.

(2) The Christian community must also serve not only individuals but nations; and by obedience to the Master rather than to man it will inevitably contribute to understanding and peace among the nations more effectively than through loyalty to any mere human institution.

(3) Peace and justice are in harmony with God's purposes for man; only through the attainment of justice as well as peace can God's love as Father be made manifest in the life of nations today so distraught by hatred and fear. Peace and justice being themselves the fruit of love, it thus follows that the Christian community, knit together in the life of the Holy Spirit, must ever strive to express this love-relationship within itself, in order that its unique mission as reconciler and upholder of justice may be fulfilled in the world of men and of nations.

(4) Despite the inherent difficulties and complexities of the international questions which confront the world today, God nevertheless calls Christian youth to understand and then to testify, in the spirit of bold adventure, to the saving power of His laws in this domain. Indeed, such a corporate effort on the part of professing Christians is long overdue, and conscience has been slow to respond in this domain to the constraining love of Christ.

2. Conscious of its deep responsibility in regard to the present campaign for effective disarmament, the Conference calls upon the national alliances to bring the full weight of their influence to bear upon their respective peoples and governments with a view to securing that the forthcoming Disarmament Conference shall result in an actual and considerable reduction and limitation of armaments in accordance with Article VIII of the Covenant of the League of Nations, the Preamble to Part V of the Treaty of Versailles and the official correspondence relating thereto, and the terms of the Kellogg Pact.

At the same time the Conference is deeply concerned about the causes of fear and friction in the international situation of the present day, and as armaments necessarily imply a state of fear and disharmony between peoples, affirms that it is a Christian duty to strive with hope towards the goal of total disarmament and the elimination of the causes of fear and friction.

3. The delegates from thirty-two nations present at a plenary session of the Conference of the Young Men's Christian Associations, having during four days of fellowship together become acutely aware of the spiirtual sufferings of their German brethren, while conscious of their incompetency to deal with any of the political implications of the question which they approach only by reason of their common spiritual concerns, desire, in the spirit of that international brotherhood which the Association seeks to promote throughout the world, to dissociate themselves from the injustice of attributing to one nation or group of nations alone sole responsibility for the war.

They affirm their conviction that war is an expression of the sin of men and that all international conflicts should be settled by pacific means. They solemnly pledge themselves to work devotedly for the removal of all causes of hatred and antagonism between nations, and to create amongst the youth of the world a spirit of justice, peace, and love. (Adopted in plenary session, August 8, 1931, by 203 votes to two, the German delegation and four other delegates abstaining.)

4. Without wishing to minimize the positive value which arises from devotion to a cause greater than the individual, the Conference is conscious of the very grave danger which results from that ultranationalism which challenges the supremacy of all other allegiances. There is also a manifest tendency to translate faith in internationalism into a veritable "gospel" or "religion" with the result that human brotherhood is emphasized to the virtual exclusion of God.

The Conference calls upon the national alliances and the local Associations to be on their guard against these dangers.

VI. Interracial and intercultural relations

1. The Conference endorses the following statement of basic principles which should guide the Association's policy in regard to race relations:

(1) We would set forth our conviction that racial and cultural variations offer an opportunity for enrichment of culture through fellowship across racial and cultural lines. This variation in no sense justifies a sense of inferiority or superiority on the part of any group.

(2) We further affirm our conviction that all races have a real contribution to make to the enrichment of the life of humanity. The Y.M.C.A. should, therefore, facilitate in every way possible the making of such a contribution by every group in the community.

(3) The supreme value of the personality of every man is clearly set forth in the teaching of Jesus, and is one of the unique contributions of Christianity to human relationships, therefore, it is not Christian for any institution to be indifferent to situations in which human beings are scorned or treated with disrespect.

(4) Since all people are children of a common father, we deny that stage of cultural achievement has any real bearing on inferiority or superiority of race. We believe that all races are capable of full cultural, mental, and spiritual development, and we call on Associations everywhere to facilitate this development for all men and boys in every land.

(5) The Y.M.C.A. has a common obligation to all the young men and boys of any community in which it exists. We express our conviction that in conformity with the principles of Christ, Associations should not forget or neglect any group of young men or boys living in their communities, nor exclude them from membership merely on the basis of race.

2. The Conference, while recognizing that society may not be changed in a day, and that the Y.M.C.A. must exist in the midst of society, nevertheless

declares its conviction that patience without effort towards improvement is un-christian. It, therefore, calls upon every Association to take such immediate next steps as the following:

(1) The carrying forward of an educational program of racial understand-ing. There are few subjects on which there is less accurate informa-tion and more deep-seated prejudice. It is our bounden duty to help to remove such ignorance and prejudice through all educational processes which we may be able to command.

(2) As a part of such an educational process local Associations are urged to provide frequently a platform on which different races may speak through their respective leaders, and in the various communities throughout the world to bring together from time to time the choicest spirits of differing racial groups for conference acquaintance, in order that each group may come to know the other at its best.

(3) In the organization of national gatherings of the Y.M.C.A. in any country, care should be taken to see that all delegates may be received without discrimination as to accommodation and privileges.

3. The Conference adopts the following statement as to the Association's ideal goal in relation to the above next steps:

It recognizes that there may be difficulties at present as to the distance any local Association may go in serving various racial groups together, but urges upon every Association the obligation to take the above next steps, in order that the Movement may the sooner come to what the Conference believes is the ideal, namely, the making possible of the enlistment and full participation in the Association enterprise of all classes of young men and boys in the community without distinction of race, culture, or nationality.

4. The Conference authorizes the reappointment of the Commission on Intercultural and Interracial Relations as a permanent commission, with corre-sponding members in the various nations, and recommends that it should be charged, in co-operation with national alliances, with the following tasks. To achieve these objects adequate financial and staff provision should be made:

(1) Further experimentation in interracial fellowship and co-operations already begun.

(2) The facilitation of exchange of experience within the entire Association Movement.

(3) The promotion of new experiments wherever possible.

(4) The presentation of reports at each World Conference regarding prog-ress made and suggested plans for the future.

5. The Conference supports the recommendation made in 1928 by Dr. Datta calling for the study of colonial and imperial phenomena, and recommends that the Commission on Intercultural and Interracial Relations should provide the ways and means for making such a study.

VII. Industrial relations

1. The Conference affirms the following statement of principles which should guide the Association's policy in regard to industrial questions:

(1) Work for individuals is an essential Christian duty; to unite Christian young men is, undoubtedly, one of the Association's purposes. Whatever external conditions may be in which boys and young men live, one of their outstanding needs is a Christian fellowship. The Association is primarily concerned with the development of individual Christian character and faith.

(2) Society will be transformed by individuals living a Christian life; in "associating their efforts for the extension of His Kingdom among young men" members will surely show a quality of life which will act as a leaven to transform the surroundings in which they live and work. Through individual Christians the light will be carried into the darkness of the world.

(3) Christian social education of the individual is a way of improving the social order: "The extension of the Kingdom" among all men and all nations calls for an interpretation of the will of God for the various circumstances in which there is a contradiction between the ideal and perfect life, as revealed by Jesus Christ, and the existing conditions of the world. The Association should have a part in the solution of social problems, and it is incumbent upon it to contribute to the social Christian education of its membership and of the various social groups of the community at large.

(4) Christianity has a direct and collective responsibility towards the solution of social problems: scores of theories are being proposed for the solution of the present social disorder. Many of these are built on principles entirely opposed to the conception of life and humanity revealed by Jesus Christ. Without neglecting its duties towards individuals, in order to extend the Kingdom of its Master the Association has an obligation to take a large share in making Christian principles increasingly operative in social life with a view to the achievement of a Christian social order.

(5) Under all circumstances and at all costs the Association should discharge its duties towards its members and towards society in general in an unbiased and Christian manner.

2. The Conference believes that there is necessity for nothing less than a fundamental change in the spirit of our economic life, and that this change can only be effected by accepting as the basis of industrial relations the principle of co-operation in service for the common good in place of unrestricted competition for private advantage.

3. The Conference recognizes with satisfaction the increasing tendency in many areas of the world on the part of industrial leaders to regard service rather than profit as the governing motive for the guidance and control of industry.

4. The Conference desires to emphasize the responsibility of industry for the general welfare of the worker and his family outside his wages; for his opportunity for continuous employment; and particularly for his contentment and his widened outlook upon life through some just and equitable personal participation, beyond his wages, in the fruits of his work.

5. The Conference views with the gravest concern the present world-wide economic crisis with its tragic and demoralizing effects upon our common life. Such a situation constitutes a challenge to our Christian ideals which the Association and the Church of Christ can neither ignore nor evade. The Conference regards with appreciation the efforts already made, but feels bound to urge governments and industrial leaders and trade unions and other organizations of employees throughout the world to take such further steps as may be necessary to insure the means of livelihood to the millions immediately affected by the present unemployment and also to modify the structure of the existing industrial order in such a way as to prevent in the future the recurrence of such a condition. In particular, the Conference believes that the World's Committee, through the various National Councils and other appropriate channels, should call attention to the devastating effects which the industrial situation is having on the mind, body, and spirit of youth, and should urge that immediate further steps be taken by governments and leaders of commerce and industry to give youth opportunity to gain a livelihood until economic stability is restored, and, further, should call upon the local boards of directors the world over to take immediate action in making a careful study of the economic situation as it affects youth in their various countries with a view to instituting such ways and means as may quickly alleviate the present economic distress of the young men concerned and prevent, as far as possible, the demoralization which such a condition inevitably entails.

6. The Conference recommends that the Commission on Labor Problems should be reappointed and endorses the statement of policy set out on page 211 of the World's Committee Report as a minimum of what should be undertaken by the Commission, with the suggestion that in clause (*d*) the words "and interracial" should be inserted after the word "international."

7. The Conference requests the World's Committee to make available to national alliances through their various publications reliable data regarding current industrial problems, particularly in their international aspects, and also descriptions or significant program experiments in this area being carried on by Associations in various parts of the world.

8. The Conference further desires that the following recommendations should be sent to national alliances, and through them to local Associations:

(1) That Associations everywhere should regard it as a privilege and responsibility to maintain an open platform for the public discussion of social and economic questions.

(2) That through forums, study groups, etc., a vigorous program of popular education on industrial questions should be conducted for Association members.

(3) That having regard to the historic genius of the Association in bringing together different races in a common program, the Associations should extend this ministry to the various groups in industry with a view to promoting such a frank interchange of views as may promote mutual understanding and facilitate the solution of industrial conflicts.

(4) That local Associations throughout the world should be urged to examine thoughtfully their own practices as employers, not only in relation to their secretarial, but also to their clerical and house staffs, with a view to insuring that in such matters as a living wage, conditions of labor, and adequate social protection, a practical demonstration be given in their various communities.

9. The Conference requests the World's Committee to recommend to the national alliances and, through them or through other appropriate channels, to the local Associations, that wherever practicable:

(1) The good offices of the Association should be extended towards a settlement of any dispute in the local community between employer and employee, including the promotion of friendly meetings for the mutual discussion of disputed issues.

(2) The boards of directors or other governing bodies in the local Associations should bring together the heads of the various business concerns within their communities with a view to discussing ways and means of relieving the distress and unemployment amongst the membership of their Associations.

(3) The Associations should impress upon the Churches the necessity for collaboration with them in a campaign for educating youth to understand and appreciate the fundamentals and difficulties of the present social crisis.

VIII. Bible study

1. The Conference places on record its great appreciation of the World Study of Jesus Christ so successfully inaugurated by the World's Committee and its staff in accordance with the decision taken at the Helsingfors Conference. This enterprise has stimulated the study of the Bible in many new fields. It has given a fresh impetus to Bible study in those countries where it was already strong, has also proved helpful to many individuals, and has created a new sense of unity in our world-wide Christian fellowship.

The Conference suggests to the World's Committee that it should continue its promotion of this study in such alliances which, as yet, have not used it, and urges all other national alliances to maintain this most fruitful undertaking.

2. The Conference calls the attention of the World's Committee and its staff to the desirability of furnishing a new series dealing with the message of the Association Movement. It is suggested that, in order to be of largest use, these outlines should relate the Bible studies closely to the problems faced by the Associations and their members.

3. The Conference requests the World's Committee to furnish to the various national bodies a selected list of books and courses dealing with the Bible and study of it, to the end that the best available literature may be generally shared.

4. The Conference requests the World's Committee to assemble and make generally available information regarding the most rewarding methods of promoting Bible study and training leaders of groups.

IX. *Week of Prayer*

The Conference requests the World's Committee to give consideration to methods which will cause the Week of Prayer to be viewed as a natural climax to a year of prayer, and to this end makes the following suggestions:

1. That the call for the Week of Prayer should contain:

   (1) A short key thought for each day.
   (2) A liturgical form of service giving place for silence and meditation, and subjects for intercessory prayer.
   (3) A form of service containing Scripture selections, subjects for an address, and periods for spontaneous or silent prayer.

2. That service designed for boys similar to that contained within the call for prayer of 1928 be repeated.

3. That a manual of prayer be considered as essential to the promotion of prayer life within Associations and that such a manual should include a foreword giving an exposition on prayer and suggestions as to how to pray.

4. That the World's Committee should give further consideration to the date of the Week of Prayer, in consultation with the national alliances, and in co-operation with the World's Young Women's Christian Association and the World's Student Christian Federation.

5. That every endeavor should be made to secure the co-operation of the Churches in prayers for the youth of the world during the period of the Week of Prayer.

X. *Ecumenical questions*

In view of the fact that since its beginning it has worked towards the unity of the Christian Churches and all their individual members, the World's Alliance of Y.M.C.A.'s rejoices in the progress of the ecumenical movement in the Churches. As an organization which for many years has pioneered in the realm of closer relationship between Christians of different denominations and confessions, it is willing to co-operate with all movements which work towards the goal of greater unity of the Church of Christ.

In view of the essential importance of the Church in Christian life and of the individual loyalty of its members towards their own Churches, the World's Alliance welcomes opportunities for co-operation with all Churches which are willing to accept its services. It would reiterate, moreover, its basic principle that every individual whose faith is in Jesus Christ be accepted in its membership.

The World's Alliance endorses with special satisfaction the work done in Eastern Orthodox lands and authorizes the World's Committee to continue to work along the lines laid down in the resolutions of the meetings at Sophia and Kephissia, Athens, between Y.M.C.A. leaders and leaders of the Eastern Orthodox Churches, in order that the World's Alliance may be of still greater usefulness to the youth and the Churches of these countries and in order that the spiritual treasure of Eastern Orthodoxy may be made known and available to the Alliance as a whole.

XI. The printed page, the radio, and the film

1. The Conference recommends that the literature policy of the World's Alliance should include the following:

(1) In regard to non-periodical literature:

 a. The publication of reports and documents growing out of International and World Conferences.

 b. The publication of World's Committee research findings, Bible study material, and study outlines on major questions of significance to youth, as demanded by national alliances, such as:

> "Our Christian Message in the Light of Modern Thought."
> "Capitalism, Socialism, and Christianity."
> "The Meaning, Value, and Practice of Prayer."
> "The Effect of the Use of Alcohol and Drugs on Boy Life."

 c. The stimulation of authors to write articles and books in keeping with the objectives of the Young Men's Christian Association, and the placing of such articles and manuscripts with publishers in different countries, either Y.M.C.A. publication departments, Church publishing houses, or secular publishers.

 d. The promotion of collaboration between national Movements by facilitating the exchange of manuscripts, copyrights, articles, and translations where necessary, paying special attention to countries where there is little literature of the type needed by the Association. Especially is it urged upon the national Movements to furnish materials and suggestions to the World's Committee.

(2) In regard to periodical literature:

 a. The continued publication of a periodical organ monthly, bi-monthly, or quarterly, of a more or less popular type, seeking to reach and serve leaders in the Movement, particularly members of boards of directors and committees of management, secretaries, and others responsible for Association policy and work in local and national fields, with editorial emphasis on the following:

> Fundamental problems facing international Christian leadership of youth.

The contribution to be made by the Association to international, interracial, and interconfessional movements.

The work of other national and international movements of youth.

Description of Association activities in different countries and of the work of the World's Committee.

The interpretation of contemporary currents of Christian thought, philosophy, science, and education.

Articles for the inspiration of the Christian life.

b. The continued production of *Information Service* in mimeographed form, giving news items, description of events, and other facts regarding the Association in different countries, as well as similar items regarding other youth movements; of the Article Service, which aims at furnishing editors of secular and Association papers with material for publication; and the achievement of due co-ordination between the periodical organ, *Information Service,* and the Article Service.

2. The Conference further recommends that, in pursuing the above policy, the World's Committee should:

(1) Endeavor to increase its income for publications by securing paid advertisements of suitable character for its periodicals and by adequate promotion of paid circulation through the collaboration of national Movements.

(2) Establish co-ordination and collaboration with the World's Student Christian Federation and the World's Committee of Young Women's Christian Associations.

(3) Examine the extent to which an international language such as Esperanto could be used in its publications, especially for the use of those Alliances which are unable to secure such publications in their own language.

3. The Conference is of opinion that the report of the Toronto Assemblies to be included in the World's Conference Report should be supplemented by the publication of separate accounts of both gatherings.

4. While recognizing that the cinema is an educational agency of great potentiality for the development of moral character and for the promotion of international and interracial goodwill, the Conference regrets that these possibilities are so little realized in many current productions and in particular protests against those films which portray the perversion of the decencies of family and social life and caricature the characteristics of nationalities. It suggests the immediate study by the World's Committee of the Association's position and possibilities in this field, and recommends that definite action be taken both internationally and nationally.

(1) Through direct negotiation with producers to insure positive moral value in films produced.

    (2) By collaboration with other institutions and agencies having aims similar to those of the Association in this field.

    (3) By releasing more generally and more fully through the national Movements information regarding films of positive value for the moral life of youth as is already being done in the American Y.M.C.A. magazine *Young Men*.

    5. The Conference requests the World's Committee to undertake a study of the possibilities of broadcasting for Association purposes, on the basis of the experience and of the developing plans of various national Movements, and to aid in the exchange of such experience and in collaboration between alliances by international and world relays of programs useful to the Association.

    6. The Conference recommends the World's Committee to establish a group of consultants, consisting of both men and older boys in different countries, to serve as both advisers and active agents in developing and promoting the plans outlined above.

    7. The Conference requests the World's Committee to do everything within its power to provide a member of staff who will devote his entire attention to directing its literature work and to make staff provision for carrying out the above recommendations in regard to the cinema and the radio.

XII. *The service of rural youth*

    1. Fully recognizing the importance of the present economic and spiritual needs of the rural people of the world, the Conference requests the World's Committee to assign one of its secretaries to work on their behalf. Because of its importance such work requires the whole time of a specially qualified secretary, but for the time being it could be carried on in co-operation with the Research and Information Division. The duties of such a secretary should include:

    (1) The centralization of all information, plans, and programs in regard to rural work in different countries, the study and formulation of methods of organizing and maintaining such work, and the communication of these to national alliances.

    (2) The publication of a quarterly bulletin for the use of Association leaders in rural areas dealing with questions relating to rural youth.

    (3) The preparation of special training courses for rural secretaries.

    (4) The consideration of the desirabiilty of organizing international camps for rural youth.

    (5) The publication of special types of programs at present employed in work for rural boys and rural young men.

    (6) The assistance of national alliances in furthering and extending the Association's work among rural youth.

    2. The Conference recommends the World's Committee to consider the practicability of appointing a permanent Rural Commission for the study of important problems and practical questions. Such a Commission would assign special fields of inquiry to its most competent members, would be consulted by

correspondence, and organized by a specially assigned secretary of the Committee. In particular, it would:

(1) Be responsible for all inquiries regarding rural questions and secure the collaboration of specialists, both members of the Association and others.

(2) Endeavor to secure the co-operation of the World's Young Women's Christian Association, the International Missionary Council, the Universal Christian Council on Life and Work, and other international organizations working in this field.

(3) Promote studies on sex problems, alcoholic problems, family problems, the influence of industrialism, and urban migration and influence, in relation to rural life.

3. The Conference suggests that a World Conference of Rural Leaders be held every five years and that area conferences of the same kind be held from time to time, and in particular that:

(1) These Conferences be held successively in different countries, preferably during the winter, and that the delegates attending them be chosen from amongst both secretaries and laymen who specialize in rural questions and who are active members of the Association.

(2) These Conferences comprise both meetings for study and journeys of inquiry.

4. In view of the magnitude of the rural work and the importance of the rural field as a world problem, the Conference requests that some place be given to this subject in the program of the next World's Conference.

XIII. Work for migrants, travelers, and students from abroad

1. The Conference unanimously places on record its deep appreciation of the valuable service rendered to migrants by the Migration Department of the World's Committee during the past five years, and desires to emphasize the increasing importance of this Christian service which should ever remain an integral part of the Association's activities.

2. The Conference recommends that an increased allocation be made to migration work in the World's Committee budget for 1932 in order to provide for an extension of activity in connection with

(1) the work of caring for the increased number of repatriated migrants and returnees now arriving in Europe from overseas countries,

(2) the establishment of a World Migration News Bulletin and Information Service among all national alliances associated with the World's Committee.

3. The Conference endorses the statement regarding the function of the World's Committee and desires that immediate effect may be given to it; it submits the following recommendations to the World's Committee, and asks that

such of them as receive its endorsement may be officially communicated to the national alliances with an urgent request that wherever possible the necessary action should be taken to put them into operation.

(1) *Co-operation between national alliances*

In view of the fact that discussions during the Conference revealed a grave lack of co-operation between national alliances and local Associations in respect to the service being rendered to migrants, it is strongly recommended that all possible efforts be made by the World's Committee to draw all national alliances dealing with migrants into closer association with each other so that the work of each may be in a greater degree complementary to that of the others.

(2) *Responsibility of local Associations*

Having heard with dismay the reports from delegates representing Europe, U.S.A., China, and Japan concerning large bodies of seasonal workers who migrate to other areas where no provision is made for their physical, moral, or spiritual welfare, the Conference desires to place on record its unanimous opinion that it is the duty of the local Y.M.C.A. of the country in which these people settle to care for them; and recommends that the World's Committee make a survey of the countries where such conditions exist with a view to bringing the matter to the attention of the national alliance concerned.

(3) *Free membership for newcomers*

The Conference requests the World's Committee to recommend to all national alliances that the system adopted by some Associations under which newcomers are given free membership for the first three or six months after settling in a new country be adopted as far as possible by all Associations in their respective areas.

(4) *Chinese National Alliance*

At the unanimous request of the delegates representing China, the Conference recommends the World's Committee to address a special communication to the national alliance of China, drawing attention to the great importance of the service which the Y.M.C.A. is rendering to migrants, and suggesting that special consideration be given by its National Committee to the possibility and expediency of organizing a Migration Department under its auspices as one of its activities.

(5) *Severity of immigration tests*

In view of the statements of several delegates regarding the severity of physical and intellectual tests applied by Immigration Authorities to migrants seeking entrance into their respective countries, the Conference is of opinion that such tests are resulting in the rejection of many suitable settlers, and therefore recommends that the World's Committee bring this matter to the attention of the International Labor Office of the League of Nations with a view to representations being made to the governments of the countries concerned asking that this complaint should receive their sympathetic consideration.

(6) *The conflict between emigration and immigration countries*

The Conference recommends that the attitude of the Young Men's Christian Associations in regard to this question should be that while encouraging migrants to maintain all that is best of their own national characteristics, every help should be given them to assimilate the ideals and culture of the land of their adoption, and to make their best contribution to the national life of their new home.

(7) *Co-operation with the Y.W.C.A. and other organizations*

The Conference desires to place on record its appreciation of the valuable help given by the Y.W.C.A. and the World's Student Christian Federation in certain spheres of migration activity, and recommends the World's Committee to call the special attention of the National Councils of all alliances to the desirability of entering into closer and more sympathetic co-operation with these organizations and with other Christian agencies.

(8) *Careers for boys*

In the light of a statement by the General Secretary of the Migration Department of the British Isles regarding its system of finding careers overseas for young men and boys under what is called "The Church Nomination Scheme," the Conference heartily recommends the World's Committee to bring this scheme to the notice of all other national alliances with a view to consideration being given to the possibility of an extension of such work among other nationalities.

(9) *Service to students and visitors from other lands*

Throughout the world the life of nations is interpenetrated by the presence of young men of other nations, temporarily resident for purposes of study and research, or trade and industry, or as observers of the actual life of other peoples. The Conference affirms that a grave responsibility rests on our Movement to offer hospitality and friendship to these, and to secure the co-operation of friends in order that such visitors may find our ideals of fellowship adequately expressed; and to this end recommends that the World's Committee should make a survey of the work being done in this connection by each national alliance on behalf of Association men and boys with a view to co-ordinating the service of all alliances and to making more effective use of port secretaries.

(10) *Conference of migration secretaries*

The Conference is of opinion that if practicable a Conference in 1933-34 of all migration secretaries and representatives of national alliances interested in migration would be of immense value, and recommends the World's Committee to give sympathetic consideration to such a proposal.

XIV. Physical Education

1. The Conference notes with satisfaction the statement of the First European Y.M.C.A. Physical Education Congress held in Berlin, Germany, August,

1930, relative to the place of Physical Education in the Y.M.C.A. contained in the World's Committee Report and commends it to the special attention of the World's Committee and the national alliances.

2. The Conference further desires to call special attention to the report of its subcommittee on physical education, emphasizing particularly the sections on leadership and competition.

3. The Conference requests the World's Committee to institute a study of the character-building values of physical education and the technique of integrating these with the ideals and objectives of the Association.

4. The Conference also requests the World's Committee to assume greater guidance in this field, and suggests the necessity of steps being taken to provide expert leadership on its staff at the earliest possible opportunity.

5. The Conference recommends that the subject of physical education be placed on the agenda of the next World's Conference as a topic of major importance, and that arrangements should be made for its discussion at that time by a group of delegates adequately representative of all the alliances and every aspect of Association work.

XV. Family and Sex Relations

1. The Conference recommends the reappointment of the Commission on Family and Sex Relations with enlargement, if practicable, especially on its consultative side, to include other cultural groups not now represented, and that the lines of investigation now being pursued by the Commission should be continued. Special attention should be directed to the problems of older boys and young men in view of the changing conditions in the relations of the sexes, both before and after marriage.

2. The Conference is of the opinion that while, ideally, sex instruction should be given to the parent and should start in the earliest years, satisfying the child's curiosity, it should be realized that many parents feel incapable of giving such guidance and that consequently the Y.M.C.A. has the dual responsibility of educating, first, the present generation of boys, and second, parents, to equip them for the right training of their children.

3. The Conference recommends that the subject of sex should be treated not as an isolated fact but as a vital part of the normal life experience; that, therefore, each Association secretary and lay leader, whatever his function, should be conversant with the approved methods of sex education, and that this should be considered an essential part of his training.

4. The Conference urges that in the production of literature for the education of leaders, the subject should not be approached exclusively from the point of view of religion, psychology, biology, or sociology, but from the standpoint of all four.

XVI. The policy of the Association in lands where non-Christian religions predominate

1. The Conference is fully conscious that in several national alliances a considerable proportion of the members of the Association do not profess the Chris-

tian faith and do not owe their allegiance to Jesus Christ as their Lord and Savior. Some of them are in sympathy with the Association and its ideals and are actively engaged in its program. The Conference welcomes this membership into its world-wide fellowship and requests the World's Committee to make a special study during the next few years of the message, the program, and leadership of the Association in such lands with special reference to these members.

2. The Conference understands that the ultimate control of the Association in all these countries is in the hands of those who are members of the Christian Church or who subscribe to the Paris Basis or some other basis accepting the sovereignty of Jesus Christ.

3. The Conference is anxious that the national alliances in these countries should take a full share in the work and program of the World's Committee, and it requests the World's Committee to consider ways and means to insure:

(1) The continued inclusion of at least one national of an Eastern country in its staff. As soon as possible there should be representatives from two such countries.

(2) The adequate representation of these national alliances in all plenary sessions of the World's Committee and its other important gatherings.

4. The Conference also requests the World's Committee to consider the desirability of bringing together the representatives of these countries for sharing experiences and for the consideration of common problems.

XVII. The extension of the Association in the world field

The Conference is acutely conscious of the fact that while substantial progress is being made in many aspects of the Association's work, there are still large areas of the world where it does not exist and some where its work is very meager and slow of development. It welcomes the appointment by the World's Committee of an Extension Committee "to further the planting of the Young Men's Christian Association in unoccupied fields and to help to co-ordinate the foreign work of the various national alliances," and feels that the situation with regard to youth in the areas referred to urgently demands the courageous and enterprising missionary effort of the whole Movement to extend its work to such areas, giving prior attention to those parts of the field which have made repeated appeals for help. It recognizes that no adequate plan or program of extension can be entered upon without the active and enthusiastic co-operation of the various national alliances, and urges that every alliance should accept responsibility for sharing in such a missionary program, and should strengthen its present co-operation by enlisting the interest and support of the whole membership and by lending for stated periods the services of experienced workers to participate in pioneering and development projects within plans prepared by the World's Alliance.

XVIII. Changes in the Constitution (none)

XIX. Co-operation with other national and World Movements

The Conference receives with gratification the report of the increased practical co-operation which has been established with other international youth movements, and urges its extension wherever possible with these and other organizations working in the same field. It commends the value of such co-operation with other organizations to national alliances, and would also draw their special attention to the opportunity which now offers through co-operation with educational institutions and authorities for the Association to take an influential part in the growing movement for the provision of educational facilities for adolescents and adults, inasmuch as the Association is able to stimulate and supply a considerable demand for such service in education, and to make more widely available to large numbers the resources and facilities provided by educational institutions and authorities.

XX. Expression of thanks

The delegates of the Twentieth World's Conference of the Young Men's Christian Association desire to express their deep gratitude to the many friends in Canada and the United States of America who have received them with open-hearted generosity and given themselves with unstinted devotion to the service of their guests and of the Conference, and in particular:

To the presidents, officers, and members of the National Council of United States and Canada;

To the presidents and officers of the Associations in Toronto and Cleveland, and elsewhere in centers where delightful visits have been made;

To the hosts and hostesses who have entertained them in their homes;

To the speakers who have specially participated in the Conference, including President Hoover of the United States and the Premier of the Dominion of Canada;

To the Churches for active co-operation;

To the members of the Fisk Jubilee Singers of the Fisk University, to the various choirs, and to the organist, pianist, and conductor, all of whom have made such a notable contribution through the musical program to the spiritual experience of the Conference;

To the members of the press and of the broadcasting services; and

To the President and staff of the World's Committee, as well as to all who have in any way helped the organizers of the Young Men's and Boys' Workers' Assemblies at Toronto and the Twentieth World's Conference at Cleveland.

XXI. Work with boys

1. The Conference rejoices in the indisputable evidence furnished by the World's Committee Report and the Toronto Boys' Workers' Assembly that Association work with boys throughout the world has both deepened its significance and broadened its outreach. The strategic importance of work with boys is again clearly revealed. The Conference calls upon the World's Committee and the national alliances to support with all possible resources and personnel further extension and intensification of work with boys.

2. The Conference generally approves the report of the Toronto Boys' Workers' Assembly together with the adaptations and additional suggestions embodied in its own resolutions. It urges all national alliances to use these pronouncements from both the Boys' Workers' Assembly and the World's Conference as guides in the development of work with boys in the period just ahead. It calls upon the Boys' Work forces of all national alliances and local Associations to take full advantage of the opportunity provided by these recommendations to share creatively in an aggressive effort to extend to its utmost the Association's work with boys.

3. The Conference commends the World's Committee for calling the nations together to share their beliefs and practices in Association work with boys. Its satisfaction with the recent Assembly demands that other similar opportunities shall be provided.

4. The appropriateness and usefulness of the presence of older boys in world gatherings has been demonstrated and should be further studied, improved, and made a regular part of all World Conferences.

5. The World's Committee is urged to take steps to bring together in a fellowship of consultation the secretaries assigned by National Councils to work with boys, to the end that the particular problems of national boys' work secretaries may be the more speedily solved.

6. The Conference approves, and calls special attention to, the following recommendations contained and implicit in the Report of the Assembly.

(1) That the national alliances should study carefully the implications of the Report in relation to their boys' work, and in particular of those sections of it dealing with "The World of Boyhood"; "Wherein We have Failed"; and "Our Common Task."

(2) That the World's Committee should give special consideration to the content of the Association's message to various ages and types of boys, and especially seek ways to make it more meaningful in everyday experience, and to encourage boys themselves to express their spiritual needs in their own terms within the Association.

(3) That the World's Committee should promote the preparation of study outlines dealing with some of the major questions of significance to youth which may be of use to national and local leaders; it should also keep clearly in mind the possibility of their adaptation for use with boys.

(4) That in order to fulfill more adequately its mission to boyhood the World's Committee should urge national alliances in their work with boys:

a. To serve the individual boy more effectively in all phases of life.

b. To carry the message and work of the Association to a larger number of boys of all ages, and especially to those between ten and eighteen years of age, and to all social groupings such as rural boys, high school boys, industrial boys, and underprivileged boys.

    c. To extend their work to the untouched areas of boyhood of both their own and other nations with a renewed missionary zeal and consecration.

(5) That as a special part of its mission to boyhood the World's Committee should continue to emphasize the international character of the Association, and to extend its plans for international camps in strategic centers throughout the world and for the interchange of boys through visitation.

(6) That the World's Committee, in order to emphasize the character of the Association as a Movement, should encourage new manifestations of it in small groupings of boys in business organizations, places of employment, schools, communities, etc., banded together to make certain that decisions are only taken after Christian values have been clearly seen; and that national alliances should study how such groupings may be brought into full affiliation as members.

(7) That the World's Committee and the national alliances should continue to extend the emphasis on the place of the older boy in the Association through such means as:

    a. Provision for their attendance at, and participation in, National and World Conferences.

    b. Establishment of methods of organization which will give them opportunities to express themselves locally, regionally, nationally, and internationally as members of official Y.M.C.A. groups.

(8) That the World's Committee should make a special study of the conditions under which the participation of non-Christian boys and workers may be secured without endangering the essentially Christian character of the Movement.

(9) That recognizing the importance of rightly conceived methods in work with boys and the increasing interest in the interchange of experience between national bodies, the World's Committee should prepare thorough descriptions of types of Y.M.C.A. boys' work, and of experiments and demonstrations which have developed in various countries, together with the objectives, philosophy, principles, and methods involved and results obtained. These descriptions should be made available to the Movement throughout the world for the purpose of enabling such work to be thoroughly understood and more generally shared and among them should be accounts of the use of Scouting by the Association in certain European countries, of the B. K. Movement in Germany, of the Hi-Y Movement in North America, of the Tokyo experiment in democratic control, and of the Service Club features of the Chinese Associations.

    That in this connection the World's Committee should take advantage of the work done at Toronto in the Demonstration-Exhibit and issue a booklet describing what it comprised, together with a statement regarding the place of arts and crafts in Association boys' work, with special attention to the relation of such activities to the central aim of the Movement.

(10) That the World's Committee should stress the importance of securing locally, nationally, and internationally more highly qualified leaders both as laymen and salaried officers, and should give special emphasis to the deep Christian purpose of such leadership and the growing necessity that through it the boyhood of the nations shall come to know and understand each other better.

(11) That the World's Committee should arrange area boys' work conferences which may be attended by representatives of a number of national alliances for the purpose of studying the needs of the areas occupied by them, interchanging ideas and experiences regarding their work, and securing that the whole experience of the Toronto Assembly is shared as widely as possible throughout the Movement.

XXII. Work with young men

1. The Conference views with greatest satisfaction the re-emphasis which is taking place in all parts of our Movement on the important principle that young men shall occupy a large place in the leadership of the Associations and in determining and directing their policies and programs.

2. The Conference commends the World's Committee for calling a Young Men's Assembly and authorizes it to lay plans for similar world gatherings at suitable times and places in the future.

3. The Conference regards as most hopeful and encouraging the disposition of an increasing number of younger men to assume vigorous leadership in their own Association enterprises, and urges the World's Committee and its staff to make ever larger place for such leadership in subsequent meetings and conferences.

4. The Conference urges national alliances to make the widest possible use of Sections I and II of "The Challenge of the Association's Work with Young Men" as a call and guide to more effective local and national effort.

5. The Conference urges the World's Committee to give full weight to the subject matter of Sections I and II of this Challenge as indicative of the scope of program and work which should be its concern.

6. The Conference approves the following recommendations of the First World Assembly with regard to the immediate objectives of the Young Men's Division:

(1) That the Committee of the Young Men's Division of the World's Alliance should be made as representative as possible of the various parts of the field, and that it should be composed largely of lay members, particularly of young men engaged in the active work of the Movement; that wherever practicable national alliances and local Associations should appoint committees of the same representative character to supervise and direct their work with young men.

(2) That the World's Committee should prepare full accounts of the proceedings and findings of the Assembly and make them available

throughout the field, accompanied by a considered request to national alliances to decide what steps they will take to participate in the whole project set out in the official report, and submit suggestions as to the co-operation which they will be willing to give in this urgent world service.

(3) That adequate arrangements should be made in co-operation with national alliances to secure from the various parts of the field the fullest information regarding work done with young men, the methods employed, and the results obtained, and for the study and collation of these with a view to making whatever will be useful to workers available to them.

(4) That the World's Committee should arrange to hold area conferences on work with young men which could be attended by representatives of a number of national alliances to study the needs of the areas occupied by such alliances, to interchange ideas and experiences regarding their work, and to insure that the whole experience of the Toronto Assembly is shared as widely as possible throughout the Movement.

(5) That the Young Men's Division should participate to the utmost extent in such further study of the message of the Association which may be undertaken after the Cleveland Conference, and should stimulate this study throughout the national alliances among the leaders and groups of young men in the membership.

(6) That immediate attention should be given to securing throughout the field the intensive study of the many important questions bearing upon work with young men arising out of the discussions which have taken place in groups at the Assembly, giving a leading place to that regarding the meaning and obligations of membership which is held to be of paramount and central importance to the life of the Movement and to its qualification for the accomplishment of the task which now opens before it.

XXIII. Essential financial resources

1. The Conference authorizes the proposed budget for 1932 as presented, calling for a total expenditure of Swiss francs 285,000 and refers it to the treasurer's committee for further action as the financial situation may present itself at the end of 1931. The Conference would urge that all national alliances should increase their contributions to the work of the World's Committee and should adopt the practice of making monthly or quarterly remittances.

2. In view of the needs of the World's Committee to carry on its present program and to meet only a few of the many demands made upon it; and in order to secure funds to cover the present deficit, to increase, or at least to maintain, the staff and work without crippling reductions, to provide for working capital, and to take advantage of the great opportunity in the years following this World's Conference, and further to enlarge the circle of friends of the World's Alliance, it authorizes the President of the Conference to make a financial appeal to this gathering.

RESOLUTIONS ADOPTED UNANIMOUSLY AT THE TWENTY-FIRST WORLD'S CONFERENCE OF YOUNG MEN'S CHRISTIAN ASSOCIATIONS, MYSORE, SOUTH INDIA, JANUARY, 1937

RESOLUTIONS

1. Feeling that by youth receiving a greater share in the responsible work of the Associations there would be secured the advantages of the combination of youthful idealism, initiative, and the will to serve, with the experience of age; we recommend that on the boards of directors, other councils and staffs of the Y.M.C.A., there shall be an increased representation of men under thirty years of age.

2. In order to promote appreciation of the extent and problems, as well as the essential unity of our World Movement, we urge that the World's Committee make possible the training of men in Associations of other nations, by providing for temporary exchanges of young members and secretaries.

3. We recommend that at all Y.M.C.A. conferences, the devotional period each day should include a study of the application of the teachings of the Bible to the questions under discussion during the day.

4. We, the younger delegates of the conference, affirm our conviction that in Jesus Christ, God has shown the solution to the problems arising from human relationships, but only in so far as men accept and follow Him does the will of God become operative in human lives.

   We pledge ourselves to accept the above as the dominating principle in our own daily lives and we promise personally to endeavor to assist the realization of the purpose of the Conference in our own Y.M.C.A.'s and to insure that the relevant findings are given conscientious consideration as part of the Y.M.C.A. program.

   We desire that a copy of this statement be given to every delegate under thirty attending the conference.

5. The present international tension is so poignant that it needs the maximum possible attention of all religious bodies. We say this because of the deep conviction that the final solution of the problem of peace and war is a rebirth of mankind through the Word and Spirit of Jesus Christ. Therefore it is the duty of the Y.M.C.A. as an international Christian Movement to give a Christian lead to the organizations working for peace.

   We present the following suggestions for a program of work in this direction:

   (1) The World's Alliance of the Y.M.C.A. should have a department to attend to international problems with the special objective of the promotion of world peace. Similarly, every local branch of the Y.M.C.A. should have a special department to prepare youth for a forward movement in the program of peace.

(2) In preparing for this work it is necessary that a selected number of young men belonging to different nations should be given training so as to enable them, after a certain period, to lead the movement for peace in various countries.

(3) It would be of great value in this connection to organize an international team of young men to travel in many countries of the world, propagating the Christian principles underlying peace, helping in the organization of peace departments in local Associations, co-ordinating local peace groups, both nationally and internationally, exploring possibilities of relating political groups with groups that work for peace, and canvassing public opinion by means of the press and platform.

More than all these, this international group would be helping to prepare the Y.M.C.A. groups for effective contribution to the World Conference of Christian Youth to be held in 1939.

Such teams would probably work under the auspices of the World's Committee. The initial expenses with regard to arrangements, publicity, might be met by the World's Committee. The national organizations may cover the expenses incurred by the team in each country.

(4) In order that the World Conference for Christian Youth may have the best possible influence in promoting the cause of peace, it is highly necessary that an intensive peace campaign should be conducted in each national Y.M.C.A. unit to lead to a national Y.M.C.A. Youth Congress (these national congresses might be held simultaneously in all nations where it will be possible to hold them) where the whole problem may be dealt with thoroughly, and plans of action suggested, so that the findings may be placed at the disposal of the World Conference for Christian Youth in 1939.

LIBERATING LARGER LAY FORCES

There is imperative need in virtually all our countries for calling out a vastly greater force of laymen and for relating them to the program of the Churches and of the Associations. This is due to the fact that society is more complex and more highly organized than ever, and that only as laymen bring to bear within the sphere of their daily calling the principles and spirit of Christ, can the life of the world be permeated with spiritual purpose and passion. Moreover, lay initiative, lay sense of responsibility, and full-hearted lay participation are essential to insure the proper development of the laymen themselves. More active laymen are needed on every hand to develop and maintain an adequate financial or economic base for the widening operations of the Christian movement if present-day needs and opportunities are to be met.

Again, to insure the best leadership and administration of the work of the Churches and Associations in their local, national, and international programs there must be integrated with the boards of management many more well-qualified men. Because of the insufficient number who are now assuming and discharging responsibility much needed causes and projects are languishing. To arrest the attention and enlist the co-operation of working men as well as of men of large affairs, and also to win the active allegiance of the new generation, the contagious object lesson of many more men now largely latent or inactive is indispensable. To come to more successful grapple with great national and international evils, such as the traffic in opium and narcotic drugs, the sinister aspects of the liquor power, the white slave trade, forced labor, and anti-Christian challenges to the allegiance of youth, calls for a marked increase in the lay forces across the world. It is an idle dream to think of Christianizing the impact of so-called Christian civilization upon the admittedly non-Christian aspects of the life of the world, without augmenting greatly the number of laymen, not only whose names are on the rolls of our Church and Association membership, but who also accept the implications of membership in the Christian community and devote themselves to the Christian task with sacrificial devotion.

It was precisely to meet such needs that the Young Men's Christian Association was called into being and then established in one after another of the countries in our World's Alliance. The Conference recognizes the need of calling upon our brotherhood in all its parts to consider seriously how to reassert, as possibly never before, this our most distinctive function.

In the light of rewarding experiences, where the Associations are proving to be most successful in meeting this admittedly great and alarming need, the Conference recommends the following, among other ways and means:

1. That the World's Committee consider how it can be most helpful, both directly and through the various national alliances, in utilizing laymen to win laymen, and in bringing to bear the influence of active laymen of standing and capacity for this specific end.

2. That the Associations expose them to dynamic personalities, dynamic literature, and dynamic gatherings; and to this end hold week-end laymen's retreats, summer camps, institutes on issues which are relevant to the needs and interests of men, making sure that these gatherings are under able leadership.

3. That specific undertakings be listed with thoroughness, whether in World's Committee work, National Committee work, or local work, in which volunteer lay workers of varied abilities and experience are required, in order that definite opportunities and projects may be presented to individual men.

4. That a study be made as to how to make clear to laymen that there are evils to be fought, reforms to be made, large constructive services to be rendered in Christ's name in the community, the Church, the nation, and the Association, demanding their co-operation and best efforts; in a word, showing them convincingly that they are absolutely needed.

5. In conclusion, recognizing that, as a rule, younger men and older boys can be won and trained for lives of service, by a small fraction of the effort required to enlist the active service of latent or inactive laymen of middle age, the Conference urges that well-considered and more

purposeful efforts should be employed to interest and recruit youth for the service program of the Churches and the Association Movement.

LEADERSHIP

The all-important need of leadership has been brought to the attention of this Conference again and again; first in the chapter written by Dr. John R. Mott, in the book *East and West;* second in the excellent résumé contained in the Report of the World's Committee under the title, "Enlisting and Training a Leadership for These Times"; then from time to time in the various commissions and platform presentations. Referring to the findings of the Cleveland Conference we are reminded of the several proposals there adopted, some of which have been put into effect with gratifying success, others of which have perforce been neglected. Recognizing the fundamental nature of this need, and fully aware that many of the other resolutions and conclusions of this Conference will hinge for their realization upon the adequacy with which it is met, we urge the World's Committee to give the most earnest consideration to the problem of leadership in all its major aspects, and to hasten as rapidly as possible to institute effective measures to cope therewith.

EXTENSION WORK

The Conference notes with satisfaction that the Extension Committee, authorized at the World's Conference at Cleveland, has been constituted and has held two important meetings, at which the policies were laid down, to be later confirmed by the World's Committee. Definite projects have been suggested and regular contacts with National Alliances have been established in the realm of extension work, resulting in the realization of a number of these projects.

Much still remains to be done, and the conference calls the special attention of the national alliances to their responsibility for the further development of this important phase of our world-wide work. No alliance is too young or small to take its share, to its own benefit, in the extending of the services of our Movement to still larger fields of young men and boys in new areas.

The Conference further calls the attention of the World's Committee to the pressing necessity of taking immediate steps to strengthen, or re-establish the Association work in those countries where the work has been disastrously depleted by events of recent years.

The Conference urges the Extension Committee to find the means of entering new fields, where the services of the Young Men's Christian Associations are needed, and from several of which requests have come for help since the last World's Conference, such as Gold Coast, Congo, Iran, Bolivia, Venezuela, Colombia, and New Caledonia; it further urges the Committee to be alert to the opportunities that may arise for service to young men and boys in countries at present closed to the Y.M.C.A.

The Conference authorizes the World's Committee or its Executive to take action on the findings of the enlarged meeting of the Extension Committee, immediately following this Conference.

THE PHYSICAL WORK OF THE Y.M.C.A.

This Conference notes with regret the curtailment of work and the losses in personnel reported by the World's Committee in its physical work program and views with approval the efforts and results recorded at the International Olympic Games held in Berlin in 1936.

Believing fully in the ideal of Christian manhood, adopted by former conferences and conventions, namely, the unity of life in body, mind, and spirit; appreciating that this ideal has been one of the reasons for the successful spread of Association work around the world; and realizing that it has particular significance, at present and in the immediate future, for the development of youth into Christian manhood and for society generally with the increase in leisure; not only re-affirms its belief in this ideal but places on record its whole-hearted support of the following convictions:

1. That the Young Men's Christian Associations throughout the world should take adequate steps to revise, strengthen, and in some parts enlarge their objectives and activities in the fields of health, education, sport, and physical training in the light of developments like:

   The changing ideas about the place of recreation in life;
   The increasing awareness of the importance of physical and mental health;
   The expansion of service by schools, colleges, the communities, and governmental organizations in this field;
   The larger amount of free time;
   The greater facilities for hiking, camping, and other out-of-door forms of recreation;
   The growth of activities enlisting the interest of both young men and young women.
   This Conference expresses its conviction that the Young Men's Christian Associations will need to give very earnest attention in the period just ahead to strengthening their service in this field if it is to be adequate to present-day needs, possibilities, and demands.

2. That the World's Committee be urged to regain as rapidly as possible the ground lost in personnel and program, as mentioned in its report to this Conference.

3. That the World's Committee and national alliances co-operate wherever possible with governments and other organizations interested in the physical welfare of youth.

4. That national alliances be urged to re-establish or take up sections for such work under specialized leaders in which not only the co-operation referred to above may be maintained but also the local Associations may be helped by supervision and support.

5. That particular attention be given to strengthening and supporting the existing training agencies and, when required, to providing additional training facilities, in order that leadership for this work may be adequately and readily available.

INCREASING THE STAFF OF THE WORLD'S COMMITTEE

The Conference is of the clear opinion that there is urgent need of enlarging the staff of the World's Committee. The fact that so many of the national alliances have been obliged to reduce their forces so largely owing to economic causes has greatly increased the demands upon the World's Committee to help those bodies to meet critical situations. Moreover, the disastrous cuts on the part of the overseas departments of those alliances which have hitherto furnished so many expert secretaries to other countries has placed added burdens upon the Extension Committee of the World's Alliance. The greater perils of youth in recent years and which still obtain owing to unemployment, uncertainty, prevailing pessimism, the breakdown of character of so many youth, and the claims of sinister rival claims upon the allegiance of youth makes more necessary than ever the ministry of such a unifying, stabilizing, and guiding agency as the World's Committee. Add to all this the unexampled opportunities on every hand not only for conservation and extension but also for improving programs, policies, and strategy, and it becomes evident that an early and carefully planned enlargement of the staff is absolutely essential.

It is recommended to the World's Committee that, if it be found possible, not less than four men be added to its staff within the next twelve months.

In building up of the staff the following considerations should be kept in view:

1. The desirability of having on the staff, which must serve the entire world field, a group of men who represent as fully as practicable the various cultural, national, racial, and religious aspects of our World's Alliance.
2. The members of the staff should be men of great ethical, social, and religious passion and concern.
3. They should be men of creative ability and of such intellectual background and equipment as will enable them to appreciate and to deal constructively with the problem involving the thought-bases of the Christian faith.
4. They should possess a truly ecumenical and missionary outlook and spirit.
5. Other things being equal they should be men under thirty-five years of age.

MEMBERSHIP

A study of the statistics appearing in the World's Committee report reveals the fact that the membership of the Y.M.C.A. throughout the world has remained static over a period of two decades.

The Conference viewed this situation with some concern and resolved that in view of the coming centenary in 1944 national alliances be invited to undertake a campaign for a substantial increase of membership, aiming at 1,000,000 new members, the majority of whom should be boys and young men below the age of twenty-five years.

The Conference further recommends in order that the control and management of the Association should be vested in younger hands, that national alliances consider the advisability of limiting voting membership to those not above the age of forty.

AREA CONFERENCES

Because of the significant success of the Area Conference plan as adopted at Cleveland enabling the World's Committee to keep in closer touch with national Movements, the Conference requests the World's Committee to extend this plan into the period following this conference, having in mind the usefulness of such a method in spreading more widely the benefits of this Conference and securing more effective consideration throughout the world of the subjects here discussed, the findings and recommendations adopted, and the lines of further inquiry instituted.

THE REPORT OF THE WORLD'S COMMITTEE

The Conference receives the report of the World's Committee with appreciation of the comprehensive record of the work accomplished by the Committee during the period since the last conference, together with the challenging survey of the situation now confronting the Movement, and commends the forward-looking conception which it gives of the task of the Association as it enters upon a new period. It urges national alliances to circulate it widely among Association leaders in their areas in order that the work and responsibilities of the World's Committee may become better known throughout the membership, and the sense of fellowship in a great and compelling missionary enterprise be thereby increased.

CONSTITUTIONAL CHANGES

Alterations approved

1. That Article II in Section B of the Constitution of the World's Alliance, be amended by substituting in line 3 the word, "more," for the word, "two," making the sentence to read "The officers of the World's Committee and of its Executive shall consist of a President, one or more, not to exceed five, Vice-Presidents and a Treasurer."
2. That in Article II, line 4, for the word, "Divisional," be substituted the word, "Standing," making the sentence to read "These officers and the Chairman of the Standing Committees shall be elected. . . ."
3. That Article 8, paragraph 3, be altered to read "honorary life members, such as appointed by the World's Committee."

Resolutions referred by the World's Conference, because of the lateness of the hour, to the World's Committee with power to act:

RESOLUTION
on an addition to the report of the commission on
THE WILL OF GOD AND OUR RELATIONS WITH THOSE OF OTHER FAITHS

The World's Committee, by a small majority vote, suggests to national alliances, especially those in Asia, to explore the following lines of service, which are based on the experience—with varying success—of a number of Associations.

1. A room set apart, for use by individual members and by groups, for prayer, meditation, and spiritual fellowship.

2. A carefully selected collection of books representative of other religions, for study, and for devotional use.
3. The preparation of scholarly books on the indigenous faiths of each country, such as the Religious Life of India Series, the Religious Quest of India Series, and the Heritage of India Series, which have been produced through the Literature Department of the Indian Y.M.C.A. National Council.
4. Co-operating with those of other faiths in common efforts (*a*) for constructive social service, and (*b*) for deepening spiritual life.
5. Responding to the requests of those of other faiths for spiritual service and help from Christian members of our Association.

BADGE OF THE WORLD'S ALLIANCE

The Conference, having received the request of the National Committee of Australia that a new badge be adopted and having reviewed the section in the World's Committee report dealing with this subject refers the matter to the World's Committee, with power to act, if necessary, before the next world's conference.[1]

World's Youth

This Conference requests that immediate steps should be taken to insure that the organ of the alliance, *World's Youth,* should be much more widely circulated than at present. Leaders and workers ought not to be without the benefit of its valuable presentation of the philosophy, policy, and practice of Association work. Problems of language and cost should not be allowed to hinder its adequate use. With this in view it suggests that:

1. The staff prepare a new costing scheme based on a much increased circulation.
2. National alliances give pledges of support on a two years' basis at a rate of half the present subscription for parcels exceeding twenty-five copies per issue.

The conference places on record its appreciation of the great services rendered our Movement by the National Council of Great Britain through making it possible to edit the *World's Youth* by releasing for the editorial work, Mr. Z. F. Willis and Miss Walding.

ISOLATED AND UNAFFILIATED ASSOCIATIONS

With reference to the question of how to bring into the fellowship of the World's Alliance certain isolated and unaffiliated Associations of European-American young men located in areas where there are in some cases national alliances devoted to work for the nationals, the Conference recommends that wherever practicable, these Associations should be brought into affiliation with such national

---

[1] The World's Committee authorized the staff to prepare a memorandum together with a number of samples of badges, and circulate them to all National Committees in order to determine what action should be taken regarding the badge.

alliances, but pending this they be brought into closer and mutually more helpful affiliation with the alliances of Europe and North America to which they sustain national or other ties.

THE CENTENARY CELEBRATION AND THE NEXT WORLD'S CONFERENCE

The Conference accepts with sincere gratitude the invitation of the English National Council, supported by the Scottish National Council, to the World's Committee to hold a Centenary Celebration in London in 1944.

The conference authorizes the World's Committee to determine the time and place for the next World's Conference.

VOTE OF THANKS AND GRATEFUL APPRECIATION TO HIS HIGHNESS THE MAHARAJAH OF MYSORE

Be it Resolved:

That this Twenty-first World's Conference of Young Men's Christian Associations, the first held in Asia, desires to place on record the deep gratitude of all officers and delegates to His Highness the Maharajah of Mysore.

Every possible facility has been provided for the comfort and happiness of the 250 delegates who have attended from thirty-three countries.

Unforgettable memories will be carried away of the deep interest of the Maharajah in youth and the problems before the Conference; of the generous hospitality enjoyed in many directions; as well as of the beauty of the surroundings in which the Conference was set.

His fine address at the opening of the Conference showed that His Highness was closely aware of our constituency, purpose, aim, and of our problems, whilst his understanding friendship has made the delegates feel completely at home.

We ask the President of the Conference to convey our appreciation and gratitude to His Highness.

VOTE OF THANKS AND APPRECIATION TO SIR MIRZA M. ISMAIL, DEWAN OF MYSORE

Be it resolved:

That this Twenty-first Conference of the World's Alliance desires to express to the Dewan of Mysore, Sir Mirza M. Ismail, its deep appreciation of his participation in the work of the Conference. By his sympathetic and thoughtful address, by his constant concern for the well-being of the visitors, by his generous hospitality and by his frequent presence he has given the greatest encouragement to the workers.

That this Twenty-first Conference of the World's Alliance requests the Dewan to convey the gratitude of the delegates to all those members of the Maharajah's staff and his own staff, who have served, in whatever capacity, the needs of the delegates.

VOTE OF THANKS TO DR. JOHN R. MOTT

The World's Conference wishes to acknowledge with a very special gratitude the eminent services rendered by its President, Dr. John R. Mott, in preparing and presiding over the Conference. His ever-working energy, his inspiring vision of the possibilities involved in the planning and holding of the Conference, the devoted attention he has given to all main problems as well as to the smallest questions, has rendered possible our coming together here in Mysore. His leadership during these unforgettable days of common worship, sharing, deliberating, and framing new policies will remain one of the great services he has rendered to the World Brotherhood.

VOTE OF THANKS TO THE NATIONAL COUNCIL OF THE YOUNG MEN'S CHRISTIAN ASSOCIATIONS OF INDIA, BURMA, AND CEYLON

The Twenty-first Conference of Young Men's Christian Associations meeting for the first time in India, and indeed in Asia, records its deep gratitude to the National Council of Young Men's Christian Associations of India, Burma, and Ceylon and especially to its President, Dr. S. K. Datta, and its Secretary, Mr. J. S. Aiman, on whom the major burden of the work has fallen. From the early days of preparation until the end the delegates have received kindnesses that have fulfilled the best traditions of our Movement. The Officers of the Council are asked to bring to their friends and fellow workers in India the assurance of the deepened interest of the delegates in all that pertains to the well-being of the Indian people and the progress of the Association in their land. It is hoped that the conference may lead to much more real co-operation between East and West in the service of the youth of the world through the Y.M.C.A.

SPEECH DELIVERED BY HIS HIGHNESS THE MAHARAJAH OF MYSORE

Dr. Mott, Ladies and Gentlemen:

It gives me very great pleasure to welcome this world pilgrimage of youth, which has come together at Mysore for the purpose of promoting an enduring fellowship among the leaders of the youth of the nations, and of trying to find a way to meet the fear, the despair, and the disillusionment that are dominating the thoughts of so many of us, and even our actions. I am very delighted to welcome you, Dr. Mott, and others of the delegates who visited Mysore just eight years ago, and did much to stimulate the spiritual life of our people here. I am equally glad to welcome many new delegates, and especially the youngest among you. For it is to youth, the age of idealism, that we must look for new ideals of life, of religion, and of dedication of self to the good of others.

You are met to discuss a large program, of which I will take a single item—to give a lead to youth as it faces the baffling confusions of our time and seeks a way of life in which it finds both authority and freedom. A great scientist has defined the disease from which the world is suffering as the absence of an ethical ideal. And an Indian philosopher has answered the diagnosis with a prescription. "Religious idealism," he says, "seems to be the most hopeful political instrument for peace which the world has seen. . . . Treaties and diplomatic understandings may restrain passions, but they do not remove fear. The world must be imbued with a love of humanity. We want religious heroes who will not wait for the transformation of the whole world, but will assert, with their lives if necessary, the truth of the conviction 'on earth one family.' "

A great English physician recently startled the world by proposing to substitute for the Ministry of Health a Ministry of Happiness. The fact that the world was startled is a significant exposure of the fact that its current idea of pleasure is so largely synonymous with the gratification of the appetites, the satisfaction of which brings the pleasure to a close. What I take it that Lord Horder meant was the same thing as Bentham meant when he described, as the object of good government, "the greatest happiness of the greatest number." If we regard happiness in that sense, however, not a single minister, but the whole government, ought to be ministers of happiness, or of pleasure.

The Young Men's Christian Associations over the world at large have, if I may say so, set themselves to be ministers of happiness to the youth of the world. They have among their principal objects the creation of new opportunities for what Plato called the purer pleasures, which are the only ones that endure. Such is the pleasure derived from the exercise of our bodies or of our faculties, the enjoyment of the gifts of God in birds and animals, trees and flowers, and all the wonders of the countryside, the acquirement of knowledge, the pleasure arising from music or from art, and above all the pleasure that comes from living for others. There never was a time when the youth of the world more sadly needed to have more happiness in their lives, and there never was a country in which they needed it so much as India.

For your own sake, for the sake of the world in general, and for the sake of the youth of Mysore in particular, I wish you all possible success in your endeavors to give direction to a civilization which has lost its way. And as I suggested to some of you eight years ago, so I suggest to you now again, the signposts are to be found, when you have cleared out of the way the jungle of listlessness, disillusionment, and false philosophy that hides them, in the simple truths that lie at the base of all religions, and in their application, by the aid of the great discoveries of science, to the needs and conditions of the present day.

RESPONSE OF DR. JOHN R. MOTT TO THE ADDRESS OF WELCOME
BY HIS HIGHNESS THE MAHARAJAH OF MYSORE

Your Highness:

Your most gracious welcome has gone straight to our hearts, and
has stirred the deeper depths. It has accomplished the highest office
of any welcome in that you have made us, away from our homes—
most of us far away—feel at home. By your comprehending thoughtfulness and abounding generosity you have provided us with such
pleasant surroundings and splendid facilities that we find the conditions most favorable for the important creative work which has
brought us here from the ends of the earth. We are fully responsive
to the noble sentiments you have so well expressed.

We are deeply touched that Your Highness has come to meet us
in this intimate way. We esteem it a great honor, for we have high
regard for yourself and that for which you stand. We recognize in
you one with a rare balance of qualities: one with intense patriotic
devotion and just pride in your wonderful state, and at the same time
with discerning appreciation of and fellowship with other states and
nations near and far; one with reverential regard for the great traditions of ancient India, and yet with up-to-date contacts with modern
progress the world over, and responsiveness to new visions and
plans; one, therefore, who has successfully blended the priceless heritage of the East with much that is best in the Western world. Under
your fostering care we find an impressive development of material
resources and all that we associate with the machine age, along with a
most evident love of beauty in nature, art, and architecture, and the
manifestations of the finer charms and graces. Together with devout
belief in your own faith, Your Highness has exhibited a wonderful
tolerance, amity, and appreciation of other faiths.

And so, while it is a joy to come to a land where there is so much
to appeal to the eye and the ear, it is a source of deeper satisfaction
to find ourselves guests in a country and under a noble rule where no
apology is made for religion, but rather where it is held in a place of
central prominence.

We come, Your Highness, from many lands and climes, for the
Young Men's Christian Association is a world-wide organization. We
have delegations present from over thirty countries. All of the continents of the world are ably represented—Asia, Europe, North
America, South America, and that land, a neighbor of India, which I
think of as a continent—Australia. Ours is a great brotherhood of
over 1,500,000 young men and boys. This does not take account of
other millions of men still living who in their youth were members,

and who have not lost the faith, the traits of character, and the spirit of unselfish service imparted to them by their participation in the fellowship, the studies, and the unselfish action of these Associations. There are nearly 10,000 of these societies. They are planted at all of the principal commercial, industrial, educational, and political centers of the world, not to mention the multitude of smaller cities and towns and even village communities. They blend the strongest races of mankind. They constitute the largest, the most vigorous, the most unfettered, and one of the most beneficent of all movements of young men and boys.

It will interest Your Highness to know that this Conference, which you have so kindly welcomed to Mysore, although the Twenty-first World's Conference of our organization, is the first one ever held in Asia. This is highly significant, and is a reminder of the shifting of the center of gravity in the world interest and concern.

More significant is the fact that it is the first of all our world gatherings in which the Orient and the Occident stand on a parity—not only in the matter of numbers, but also of initiative, responsibility, leadership, and participation. What may it not mean for the troubled world in the drawing together the future leaders of the nations in fellowship, in deeper understanding, in good will and co-operation!

We enter into the larger meaning of our World's Conference when we remind ourselves that we have come together to face the major problems and issues of the world at this present fateful hour. This we are to do from the point of view of youth. It is our purpose and our belief that this Conference will afford what is now so greatly needed, namely, an authentic lead to youth and the leaders of youth throughout the world for the all-important period that lies ahead.

Our central theme is The Challenging Will of God for Youth. The other day, in one of the lands of the West, I was asked for my opinion as to the world outlook. I replied that when I let my mind rest on the older generation now in power, I had sinking of heart; but I added that when I let my gaze rest upon youth, then my heart leaped high with hope. I have large confidence in the new generation —granted there be multiplied the number of wise counselors, interpreters, and friends of youth; and, above all, granted that we here at Mysore enter into a more profound understanding of the Will of God. For we come together, not as atheists, but as believers in the Living God, and that Central Figure of the Ages and the Eternities through Whom He has so wondrously revealed Himself and His mind. Ours is a Living God, and therefore alive for evermore, and therefore eager to break out in us and through us to do new things, to set fresh precedents, to chart new courses for mankind.

REMARKS BY DR. JOHN R. MOTT, INTRODUCING
SIR MIRZA M. ISMAIL, DEWAN OF MYSORE

Ladies and Gentlemen:

I esteem it a rare honor to be permitted to present to you Sir Mirza M. Ismail, the distinguished Dewan of Mysore. What do we not owe to his initiative and collaboration in making possible our Conference here at Mysore! It has been my lot, in a traveling life, to visit some sixty-eight different nations, most of them again and again, and to have opportunity to study the problems, methods, and results of administration. With this in mind, let me say that I regard Sir Mirza as one of the very small group of really front-line administrators, from the point of view of achieving ability. If I may use a word which is much overused, but I trust I may give it fresh content, I would characterize him as a great modern statesman. He most certainly possesses the traits of a true statesman. He has to a marked degree the power of vision—the ability to see what the crowd does not see, and to see it before others see. It is evident from a study of his career that he has some governing, guiding principles, and that he trusts these and follows them, no matter how many may oppose him, or how few go with him. Moreover, he has the special gift of recognizing, and then of observing, relationships, a trait that makes all the difference in the world in the quality and extent of one's leadership. He is a man of foresight. President Theodore Roosevelt used to maintain that nine-tenths of wisdom is being wise in time. How aptly this applies to our friend! Then there is another trait of the great statesman, which is often overlooked, that of sympathy, or heart-power. One of the most eminent administrators of India has maintained that "We rule by the heart." This, I think, goes far to explain the wonderful hold which Sir Mirza has had over all classes and conditions of people. He has shown genuine sympathy with both the rich and the poor. I emphasize both advisedly, because the rich, I sometimes think, quite as much as the poor, call for sympathy. Crowning all of his traits as a statesman is the spirit of service. Again and again he has made the impression of one lost in an unselfish cause.

If one were to ask what have been the achievements of Sir Mirza, one might well answer: open your eyes and look around you. This exceedingly beautiful city of Mysore abounds in marks of his genius. The same could be said of that other attractive city, the neighboring city of Bangalore. You could travel all over this great and progressive State of Mysore, and even in its most out-of-the-way corners, and find the results of his wise and beneficent action. On all sides one must be impressed by the varied and symmetrical developments in the industrial life, in financial affairs, in commercial relations, in social uplift, in educational progress, in cultural and artistic developments, in humanitarian and philanthropic achievement, and in the religious welfare of the people. All this shows what can be done under enlightened leadership to build up what has again and again been aptly called a model state.

There are two traits of the character and influence of our friend which commend him in a very special way to a world gathering such as is here assembled. One is that he is a man of wonderful versatility. Some years ago there fell into my hands a volume of his speeches. It was designated "Volume One." I became so interested in it that I did what I seldom do, ran through all of the literally scores of speeches—speeches given under a great array of quite different circumstances, and in connection with a wide range of organizations and interests. Imagine my pleasant surprise this morning upon receiving from Sir Mirza a copy of "Volume Two" of his speeches, recently issued! Busy though I have been in this absorbing day, I took time to scan this collection, which is, if possible, more remarkable in its sweep and in its fascinating variety. A marked virtue of the speeches in both these volumes is their brevity. Seldom have I read speeches into which more that was truly relevant to the themes discussed, and happy in illustration, and effective in appeal, was packed. Not a few of these deliverances revealed rare insight and flashes of genius.

Another trait of his character, which all of us in our world-wide organization appreciate, is that of his universality or catholicity. Race, color, and creed have never formed a barrier to him, nor do they today. Of this we have had abounding proofs. The night before I left England on my way to India, I was the guest of His Grace the Archbishop of Canterbury, at Lambeth Palace. When he learned that I was coming out to India, he remarked to me, "I have a new friend out there, one I hope you may see, Sir Mirza Ismail." This leads me to say that when a man of such spacious mind and such penetrating recognition of the qualities of men as characterize this great religious leader embraces such a personality within the circle of his friends, it bears impressive witness that he has found a really kindred spirit.

Be that as it may, I am sure I speak for our whole company from all parts of the world when I say that we find so many points of sympathetic contact with Sir Mirza, that we one and all claim him as our friend: and on your behalf I invite him to regard himself as one of our fellowship. I now call upon Sir Mirza to address us.

ADDRESS OF SIR MIRZA M. ISMAIL, DEWAN OF MYSORE,
IN WELCOMING THE DELEGATES

Dr. Mott, Delegates, Ladies and Gentlemen:

I am sure that all the leaders and delegates assembled here realize how warmly they are welcomed by His Highness the Maharajah and his people, and with what interest we shall follow their deliberations.

This is, indeed, a unique gathering. All honor to the great organization that has brought together so many representatives from so many parts of the world. Europe has sent representatives of eighteen nations, Asia of nine, America of four, Africa of two, and Australia of one.

In this pleasant and peaceful place, you are deliberately planning an offensive against the warring powers of evil, whose threat also is now more deliberate and more concerted and more dangerous than ever before. You stand for ideals that inspire us also—the freedom of the spirit, and unity, and peace; and we are not merely your hosts, we are with you in this fight.

This, I believe, is the kind of conference that does not fail. Of fruitless conferences the world is weary. Year after year men meet together, with honest purpose, with more and more desperate desire to seek peace and unity amidst the conflicting needs and ambitions of mankind in every sphere. But in the end the narrower interest overrides good will, and fear, more powerful even than ambition, rearms us against each other. Thus the kind of conference which is essentially a discussion of conflicting interests has so far suggested little hope of success. Unfortunately the greatest conference of all, the League of Nations, is so firmly established in that class that any faint attempt at a nobler policy is either suspected as cunningly veiled self-interest, or despised as a sign of weakness.

This Conference is of another mood, and a far more hopeful one. Here are all nations met together yet without one thought of conflicting interests. All are united in a single transcendent purpose.

I observe that in your admirable report upon interracial difficulties in Y.M.C.A. administration, the conclusion which seems to be pointed to is that an overt and systematic dealing with this difficult problem would result merely in confirmed hostility. One American Association writes thus:

> "Many local groups have organized for the avowed purpose of promoting interracial understanding and good will. Invariably they become propagandistic and fail."

It adds that good results are achieved when Negroes and whites manage to unite in *working* together. It was a wise pen that wrote this.

Differences are reconciled by turning away from them and laboring together. And if this is true in the case of any particular Y.M.C.A. branch, it is no less profoundly true as regards world relationships; and this doctrine you are practicing now. Active co-operation means understanding, respect, liking, and a new disposition to give as well as take; and in that change of attitude lies the only hope of the world.

Yet this process is so long, so toilsome, so incessantly disappointing that one may well believe success impossible without a faith so strong as actually to be invincible—a faith in man's goodness and in his destiny. And this implies that faith in God which is your impulse, and your security.

In the problems to be discussed in this Conference there is plenty to tax that faith to the uttermost. It is with the greatest admiration that one observes the thoroughness and ability with which the documentary preparation has been made. I have referred to one example. Another is found in the little masterpiece prepared by the Chinese Associations' commission, on that very comprehensive subject, the building of a new social order. Such clear dispassionate thinking is of course a large part of the battle: and evidently the Y.M.C.A. has at its disposal some of the best brains of many countries.

I suppose that the most urgent practical problem for the Y.M.C.A. organization is that which is indicated at the close of the Chinese Memorandum—whether the Y.M.C.A.

(1) should remain apart from every political and social issue; or

(2) should throw much of its energy into social reconstruction, with the inevitable political implications, and with the quite possible result of definite expulsion from certain countries, and thus lose, in those countries, its opportunities for other sorts of service; or

(3) should adopt the middle course affording only opportunity for theoretical discussion, keeping in the background the social convictions of Christianity.

It seems to me, as an outsider, that the third course, while less candid than the second, is almost as dangerous, since there are lands where even discussion, even thought, is now a crime against the state.

In this difficult decision, and in all that you have to consider regarding the continuance of your great services to humanity, may God be with you, to give both wisdom and courage. This must be the prayer of all the many thousands that in the past you have cheered and helped, and of all those who care for the increasing worth and welfare of mankind.

REPORT OF THE PLENARY MEETING OF THE WORLD'S
COMMITTEE OF YOUNG MEN'S CHRISTIAN ASSOCIATIONS,
STOCKHOLM, SWEDEN, MAY 24-28, 1938

PROLOGUE

From Mysore to Stockholm—could any contrast be greater? Yet this very contrast is an apt symbol of the variety of situations, needs, and problems with which we as a World Movement are confronted. In Mysore, we were brought face to face with the burning question of our relations with those of other faiths, and saw our Movement through Asiatic eyes. In Stockholm, we were brought face to face with the question of our relations with the Churches, and saw the tense situations in many countries through the eyes of a united people whose culture is deeply rooted in the Christian tradition. In each case, the setting of our discussions has influenced the emphases and trends of thought which find expression in our Resolutions.

Sweden is a beautiful, happy, and prosperous country. It is a land of ancient and strong traditions, as the prestige of its monarchy and its aristocracy, and no less the form of its Church life, sufficiently show. It is also a land with a progressive and courageous social outlook, as the favorable situation of its workers and the impressive achievements of its co-operative movement indicate.

Stockholm itself is a worthy capital of so great a nation. It has traditions reaching far back into the past; and these, together with the customs of the whole country, find expression in the wonderful open-air museum of Skansen, where buildings from all parts of Sweden and all periods in its history and all classes in its social life have been brought together and placed in natural surroundings, as a constant reminder of the roots of the nation's greatness. It has fine buildings out of the classical period, such as the Royal Palace and the House of the Nobility. And it also possesses two of the most notable examples to be found anywhere of the finest spirit of modern architecture — in church architecture, the Engelbrektskyrka — a daring combination of ancient Nordic conceptions with the very newest methods and ideas—and in secular architecture, the Stadshus or City Hall, which is firmly built upon an agelong tradition and yet is an essentially new contribution to the development of the city's life. All these buildings are embedded in one of the most perfect natural settings in the whole world. The waterways and lakes and many bridges, the wonderful parks with their ancient trees, and the invigorating freshness of the air combine to leave a unique impression in the visitor's mind. If ever a city had a special personality of its own, Stockholm possesses one.

Country and city have both played a great part in the development of modern Christianity. It was at Stockholm that the epoch-making World's Conference of Y.M.C.A.'s was held in 1888, from which Luther D. Wishard went out to Asia to begin the foreign work which has transformed the life of the World's Alliance. It was at the Castle of Vadstena that the World's Student Christian Federation was founded in 1895. It was at Stockholm that the World Conference of the Churches on Life and Work was held in 1925, under the creative leadership of the great Archbishop Söderblom of Uppsala —a conference which is one of the chief landmarks in the way towards the World Council of Churches now taking shape.

Sweden's welcome to the World's Committee was a royal one in every sense of the word. King Gustav V—whose eightieth birthday on June 16 was the occasion for remarkable demonstrations of loyalty and affection—gave the Committee a most gracious reception in the Royal Palace. Prince Oscar Bernadotte not only opened the proceedings of the Committee with an address of welcome and good wishes, but also, together with Princess Bernadotte, followed its deliberations throughout with the kindest sympathy and closest attention.

The city of Stockholm received the Committee in the City Hall, and expressed through the President of the City Council its appreciation of the aims for which our Movement stands. Many private citizens also showed most hospitable interest in the members of the Committee.

The Swedish National Council, and the Y.M.C.A. of Stockholm, also played a great part in making the Committee welcome. The dinner in the Great Hall at Skansen, under the presidency of Prince Oscar Bernadotte, offered in honor of Dr. Mott and Dr. Fries, on the occasion of the fiftieth anniversary of their entry (both on the same day, September 1, 1888!) into the work of the Y.M.C.A., is one of the unforgettable events in these wonderful days. And the Stockholm Central Y.M.C.A. placed its beautiful building at the Committee's disposal, offered many kinds of hospitality, and assisted the Committee's work in ways too numerous to mention.

The whole atmosphere of Stockholm helped the Committee in its work. Not only was the physical atmosphere so invigorating that even long and arduous discussions did not fatigue the members unduly, but also the psychological atmosphere calmed the hearts of those who were disquieted by events in the world outside—even when their own countries were concerned. This was no small contribution to the success of the meeting.

The World's Committee meeting was indeed successful. There reigned through all its deliberations a wonderful spirit of good will and understanding, and decisions were taken which, if carefully followed out, will exercise a great influence for good upon every aspect of the Movement's life. The members went home feeling that it had been good for them to be there; they had received a new sense of the solidarity of our World's Alliance and new heart for their often lonely and difficult work.

Twenty-eight nations were represented: twenty-four duly affiliated Movements; three (Latvia, Poland, and the Russians in Emigration) non-affiliated; and a visitor from Lithuania. Fraternal delegates were present and brought greetings to the Committee: Mrs. Hugo Cedergren on behalf of the World's Y.W.C.A.; Mr. R. H. Edwin Espy on behalf of the World Alliance for International Friendship through the Churches and the Universal Christian Council for Life and Work; and Mr. H. Johansson on behalf of the World's Student Christian Federation.

The chairmanship of Dr. John R. Mott, President of the World's Alliance, was as vigorous and constructive as always; and it was with acclamation that the Committee received at the end his decision to continue for some time longer to give it his inspiring leadership.

I. EVANGELISM

PROPOSALS AND RECOMMENDATIONS

In the light of its survey, the Committee decided:

To adopt this report unanimously, and to commend its contents to all national alliances, with a view to reaching the entire membership.

To send out a special general call to all national alliances to engage in a new program of evangelism.

It made the following recommendations for the effective carrying out of this new program:

(1) That a long-term program of study and propaganda be instituted in the field of Christian education and evangelism; and that authorization be given to make adequate provision in the staff of the World's Committee so that some member of it may accept leadership in this field as a major responsibility.

(2) That there be set up within national alliances much more adequate processes of training for Christian workers with a view to clearer and more convincing exposition of the Christian faith.

(3) That a Standing Committee on Christian Education and Evangelism be instituted in every national alliance.

(4) That the staff of the World's Committee draw up a list of speakers who may be used in the international field, and that every

national alliance be urged, not only to prepare similar lists of professional workers in the religious field, but also to search in the membership for young men with a vocation to this work.

(5) That the potential value of every Association as a training
ground in the theory and practice of Christian living be more fully
realized.

(6) That the Week of Prayer be used throughout the Alliance
for evangelistic purposes, and that the great importance of Bible
study as a means to evangelism be recognized.

(7) That the programs of the Area Conferences of the World's
Alliance be framed with these recommendations in view.

(8) That an international bibliography be prepared for the use
of workers in this field.

(9) That the study of the evangelistic responsibility of the Alliance be correlated with the study of the question of its relations with
the Churches.

II. The Young Men's Christian Association and the Church

The World's Committee has noted the increasing interest of the
Churches in youth and the tendency toward building up confessional
youth groups, some of which become united in national federations.
There are at the same time many evidences that the Churches themselves are drawing closer together, not only in local and national
federations but also in the formation of organic unions. Of special
significance are the processes leading toward the formation of a World
Council of Churches.

The World's Committee has followed these developments with
the deepest sympathy and interest. Since its inception, its purpose has
been to serve the youth of the Churches and thereby to serve the
Churches themselves. The Association has furthermore welcomed
the ecumenical vision of the Church and has eagerly sought to implant
it in the youth which constitutes its membership.

In examining the situation in the various countries, however, the
Committee has come to realize that the relations between the
Y.M.C.A. and the confessional youth movements of the Churches
require careful study, in order to insure to the Y.M.C.A. under present changing conditions the possibility of adhering to its traditional
policy of working with boys and young men whether within the Church
or not reached by the Churches.

The Committee has felt that the Y.M.C.A. can render its best
service to the Churches in the future, as in the past, by maintaining
those principles which it has considered basic and fundamental. It is a

youth movement, serving youth through youth. It is a missionary movement, whether at home or in distant countries. It calls lay forces not only for the direction and control of the Movement itself, but for service in the thinking and work of the Church. Being essentially an ecumenical movement, it draws young men from all Churches together in their efforts on behalf of the unity of the One Church of Christ. As an organization it is independent, while seeking always to be in vital relationship with the Christian Churches, especially with their evangelistic and missionary efforts, with their educational work, and with their endeavors towards a more just social order.

Considering these principles as a trust to be preserved, the Y.M.C.A. has followed a policy enabling it, through adaptation to particular needs and situations, to serve confessional youth groups within the Churches, drawing them into our world-wide fellowship through their affiliation with the respective national Y.M.C.A. Movements. These have enriched our Movement by bringing into it the more clearly revealed spiritual heritage of their confessions; and the Association has rendered especial service to those who would otherwise be isolated, in denominational or confessional groupings, by opening up to them the path to world-wide ecumenical fellowship.

The Committee would advise local Associations and national committees, in the light of these suggestions, to study the situation in their respective areas, in order that problems may be solved or averted, enabling the Association to render its full service to the Churches.

In cities, the Y.M.C.A.'s ought clearly to maintain the interdenominational and whenever possible the interconfessional principle, and these Associations should take their full part in the life of the national alliance of the country. One of their main tasks is to win for Christ the large number of young men outside any Church, and to bring them into faithful allegiance to the Churches of their choice. However, by reason of the predominantly confessional character of the populations in some cities, the Associations there face peculiar problems and difficulties in trying to fulfill this task. This is a situation which requires the special attention of the Committee on Ecumenism in collaboration with the national alliances concerned.

The Committee has noted that the Constitution of the World's Alliance and the autonomous character of national Movements imply that certain Resolutions passed by the World's Committee and accepted as the general policy of the World's Alliances are not necessarily binding upon national alliances where such Resolutions would not be in harmony with the predominantly homogeneous confessional character of their membership.

III. EMERGENCY APPEAL FROM THE FAR EAST

The World's Committee has remembered with deepest sympathy those of its members who are living in the midst of tragic conditions and suffering, especially in the Far East. It has learned with intense interest of the heroic and statesmanlike efforts on the part of the national Movements in Japan and China to meet the needs of thousands of young men and those who have been driven from their homes during the present crisis. The Committee has been stirred by the letter from the general secretary of the National Committee of China in which both the emergency needs calling for an expenditure of Ch. $120,000 (approximately Swiss francs 120,000) during the next twelve months are clearly presented, as well as the problems of rehabilitation which will confront the Movement at the close of hostilities. It has noted that the Chinese Associations are planning to secure half of the needed amount themselves. This has called forth its admiration for their courage, and at the same time a sense of humiliation that the results of our efforts, despite our vastly greater resources, have been so meager.

The Committee trusts, therefore, that the amounts now requested from the World's Alliance will be provided. It invites the National Committee of China to send Mr. Daniel C. Fu, one of its senior secretaries, to visit Europe and America to assist in interpreting this great need. It strongly urges the national Movements to continue to support this emergency work and any other like clamant need which may present itself as the result of this great struggle.

IV. EXTENSION WORK

GENERAL STATEMENT ON EXTENSION WORK[2]

Aim and purpose

The aim of Sending Movements is to establish truly autonomous, self-supporting, self-propagating, and self-directing Movements which are prepared to promote the ideals and further the purpose of the World's Alliance in agreement with the Articles of the Confederation adopted in Paris in 1855 and amplified in subsequent declarations, and which, whenever possible, will become constituent members of the World's Alliance.

---

[2] The following four sections co-ordinate decisions which have been taken at previous meetings of the Extension Committee and of the World's Committee, concerning those phases of extension work indicated; they also formulate those accepted practices which have not previously been caught up in the form of recorded decisions.

Procedure for the entering of new fields

The planning for all forms of extension work should be done more and more in the kind of setting which will insure that the purpose, emphases, philosophies, and methods which are to underlie the work and give direction to those who are to be intrusted with the implanting of the Association in a new area, may be formulated in the light of the varied viewpoints and experiences existing within our Movement. The Extension Committee, composed of recognized leaders of Sending and Receiving Movements and of designated officers and secretaries of the World's Committee, is designed through its regular meetings to be the instrument for the realization of this end.

Any national committee is free to send secretaries to any field in which there is no national committee or recognized Association, but the sending of secretaries should be preceded by consultations with the World's Committee for the purpose indicated in the preceding paragraph and to insure the co-ordination of similar efforts. If the field is a colony or under the mandate of a country having a national committee, this national committee should be consulted before secretaries are sent. If there are missionaries in the field, they and the missionary societies to which they are related should also be consulted in advance.

If a national committee already exists in a given field, it is understood that secretaries will not be sent to that field without consultation with and the approval of that national committee.

In cases where one or more national committees are at work in a field in which a national committee does not yet exist, these Sending Movements should be consulted by any other national committee which may wish to send workers to that field.

Relationships

During the period in which a Sending Movement carries responsibility for assisting in organizing or developing Association work in a given country, efforts should be made to insure the continuance of the established "direct contact" relationship, in order to keep vivid the sense of responsibility of the Sending Movements for continued support of and relationship with national Movements with which they have entered into co-operation.

The national committee of a receiving country, wherever such a committee exists, is the body responsible for co-ordinating the work of any two or more Sending Movements or Associations collaborating in the development of Association work in that field.

In fields to which more than one national committee has sent workers, and in which no indigenous national committee has yet been established, the two or more Sending committees concerned shall agree as to who shall be primarily responsible for co-ordinating and leading the work. Unless some agreement to the contrary is made, the responsibility for co-ordination shall rest with the committee which first established work with a resident secretary giving his whole time to the service, or which, because of the volume and strength of its work, has the acknowledged leadership.

Steps should be taken to insure that both Sending and Receiving Movements carry their full responsibility as constituent members of the World's Alliance. This would mean that in addition to their extension work, Sending Movements should retain such a continuity of relationship with the World's Committee and its various standing and special subcommittees as will insure constant and intimate fellowship with those Movements to which they are not bound through direct collaborating relationships. In the case of Receiving Movements, this would mean that as early as possible relationships should be established between them and the World's Committee in preparation for affiliation with the World's Alliance.

"The Past is Prologue"

Since such large areas remain unoccupied, the foreign work should be considered as being only in its beginning, and the function of Sending Movements must be an increasing and a developing one. This fact should inspire Sending Movements with long experience to transfer available resources to new fields as rapidly as possible, but it should also inspire other Movements to undertake this type of service which experience has shown to be one of the most spiritualizing forms of expression, for Sending Movements as well as for Receiving Movements, which our Associations have discovered in their years of work with boys and young men.

Experience has shown that during the period of establishment of such Movements, there has been created a sense of fellowship between the collaborating Movements which it is most important to continue indefinitely, even though active financial support may cease. Such continuing relationship is a highly valuable exemplification of international Christian brotherhood in its best sense, and should by all means be encouraged to continue to the mutual enrichment of the Movements concerned.

Every Association Movement, within its means and according to its needs, should be both a Sending and a Receiving Movement. One of the greatest needs which confront the World's Alliance is the multiplication of avenues of active collaboration between Movements and Associations new and old. It should be one of the main functions of the Extension Committee in the immediate future to help those Movements to which it is related to find ways for attaining this goal.

EDUCATION OF MEMBERSHIP IN EXTENSION WORK

Reports received from the various national Movements during the present meeting of the Committee make quite clear that the problem of enlarging this aspect of work is very intimately related to the spreading among the rank and file of the membership of intelligent comprehension of the extension work now being done and its present and future needs. This can be accomplished only by careful attention to a well-laid plan of cultivation, involving the spread of information about the work through addresses, the visits of representatives from other countries, and a variety of printed material, emphasized by specific appeals for the support of definite pieces of work.

V. BOYS' WORK

STRENGTHENING LAY LEADERSHIP IN BOYS' WORK

The World's Committee decided: (1) that there be formed, in the various nations, lay committees whose particular business shall be the recruiting, development, and care of lay leaders; (2) that the importance of using the young lay leader in the activities of the boys' work national committees be kept steadily in view; (3) that the staff of the World's Committee establish and maintain close relations with the various national boys' work committees, or, where these do not yet exist, with the national committees, in order to exchange with them information concerning the recruiting, development, and care of lay leaders; (4) that the staff of the World's Committee organize international camps or conferences for boys' work leaders in neighboring countries, with a view to the fuller sharing of experience; (5) that *World's Youth*, while maintaining its present intellectual standard, should also include simple descriptions of boys' work which may be readily understood and used by all leaders; and that in view of the language difficulties, the material it provides should be made available on request in any of the three official languages.

BOYS' MEMBERSHIP IN THE Y.M.C.A.

The Committee decided: (1) that in working towards the desired increase in membership, every boy shall be given a chance to become a member but the importance of a high quality of membership shall be steadily borne in mind; (2) that a suitable initiation ceremony be introduced in Boys' Departments, whereby new boys may be given a clear understanding of the meaning of membership in the Y.M.C.A., especially its fundamentally Christian character and evangelistic objective; and that this beginning be carefully and consistently followed up, since "the Y.M.C.A. is a Movement with a missionary objective"; (3) that a careful study of membership in the Y.M.C.A., on the basis of the material supplied in the Spring, 1938, number of *World's Youth* and reprinted in a special pamphlet, be made, and its results be applied in practice as far as possible.

EVANGELISM FOR THE BOYS OF OUR DAY

The Committee decided that the staff be asked to study and report on this vital question in the light of the report of the committee on evangelism, keeping in mind the following essential considerations: (1) the Y.M.C.A. is a missionary Movement; (2) our message is the sovereign claim of Christ; (3) the personal relation to Christ must be at the center of our work; (4) the personal example of the leadership of the Movement determines the effectiveness of its work; (5) the special needs and problems of the boy age must receive careful attention; (6) the experience already gained in various countries in evangelistic methods at boys religious conventions and summer camps must be utilized to the greatest possible extent. It further decided that special Bible courses and pamphlets for boys be prepared in the light of this study.

Y.M.C.A. BOYS' WORK AND RELIGIOUS EDUCATION CARRIED ON BY THE CHURCHES AND SCHOOLS

The Committee decided that those carrying on Y.M.C.A. boys' work continue their policy of co-operation with the Churches in religious education, while at the same time maintaining their autonomy, and that they take advantage of every opportunity of extension into untouched fields. It further decided that a study of the effect of recent theological tendencies on religious education be made, with a view to maintaining the timeliness and effectiveness of the work in this field.

VI. YOUNG MEN'S WORK

The Committee decided:

To accept with thanks the report of the study of "Membership in the Y.M.C.A." and to invite the national alliances to co-operate further with the Committee and staff by furnishing the information and comment called for at various places in the report;

To request the national alliances to co-operate particularly in providing much fuller and more exact information about (1) membership and participation in Y.M.C.A. life by women and girls; (2) how membership and activities are being affected by new legislation and publicly supported programs in different countries; and (3) how membership is affected by the various forms of relationship to and co-operation with the Churches;

To continue the publication of yearly statistics of membership based upon the questionnaire used hitherto, but modified to show the number of members eighteen to thirty, also to show, if possible, the number of new members each year;

To request the staff to study the replies and comments received from national alliances as a result of this report, with a view to publishing them as information material and to devising an improved form of records to be introduced in 1940 or 1941.

Y.M.C.A. AND Y.W.C.A. RELATIONSHIPS

The Committee decided:

To urge the national alliances and local Associations to give further study to the question of relationships between the Y.W.C.A. and the Y.M.C.A., and to suggest the circulation and utilization of the memorandum accepted by the Executive Committees of the two World Movements in 1937 as an aid to this study;

To request the staff to report, as information becomes available, on how this study is carried out and on new forms of co-operation in various parts of the world.

WORLD CONFERENCE OF CHRISTIAN YOUTH

The Committee decided:

To urge each national Movement to provide for the appointment of the full quota of delegates to the World Conference of Christian Youth permitted to the Y.M.C.A., for the training of delegates in advance, and for inclusion among the delegates and advisers of a number of competent leaders of group worship and discussion;

To give its hearty approval to the policy of forming united committees of the Churches and the other movements involved in the Conference to plan together for appointment and training of national delegations.

VII. LEADERSHIP

The World's Committee emphasized the importance of constant concern on its own part and on the part of National Councils with respect to challenging the highest type of young men to consider Y.M.C.A. service, secretarial or lay, either as a life vocation or as an opportunity for the most sacrificial use of available time.

To this end the World's Committee itself and the National Councils should keep in the closest possible touch with the World's Student Christian Federation and with the Student Christian Movements in the various countries. They should also maintain close contact with rising leadership among workers and in workers' movements, among youth in independent movements, in the Churches, and elsewhere, to the end that these and other groups may be aided in playing their part in the life and membership of the Association Movement. The Committee also suggested that the National Councils should have in mind the possible call of one or more of their secretaries at some later date to the World's Committee staff, and that they should provide for the training of secretaries with this possibility in view.

The World's Committee: (1) was convinced that one of its specific tasks is to foster throughout the world brotherhood a clear understanding of the present needs and opportunities for Christian leadership, both within the membership and in the community at large; (2) it considered as an essential part of the training of all secretaries and leaders the acquisition of a thorough knowledge of the meaning and purpose of a world Christian Movement, such as ours, as a part of the universal Christian Church; (3) believed that Christian education for better understanding of national, international, and interracial relationships can best be acquired by practical experience and direct study, and should be designed to help men and boys to put into practice in all their relationships the spirit of love as taught by Jesus Christ; and accordingly decided:

To urge all national committees to make such study and practical experimentation an integral part of any scheme for secretaries and lay leaders;

To request the staff to call the attention of all training agencies to this recommendation;

To request the staff, as soon as time and personnel permit, to put at the disposal of national alliances and of training agencies any outline study material and practical suggestions which may help to achieve this end.

The Committee, viewing the question of leadership in relation to the work of extension urged the following qualifications for those who are selected to go to other lands:

A strong sense of vocation;

Experience or training in Association work;

Intellectual training, a marked capacity for intellectual and spiritual growth, and ability to inspire respect among the educated classes in the country where they are going to work;

The ability to understand those among whom they are to work and to present the claims and the message of Christ in terms intelligible to those whom they seeek to serve;

Adaptability to changing conditions;

A spirit of humility, and a willingness to listen and learn as well as to teach.

The Committee felt that in general too little provision is made for the maintenance of the spiritual life of leaders, and recommended that national alliances should endeavor to meet this need by arranging for periodic retreats where in fellowship with other leaders they may renew their spiritual life.

VIII. MIGRATION

The World's Committee, having studied the report presented on the migration problem, expresses its unanimous approval of the work which has been accomplished. It is of the opinion that, though for various reasons the movement of peoples has been very much restricted in recent years, there still exists a field of need, both among those voluntarily traveling to and from various parts of the world and among the thousands of those who are homeless refugees. The Committee feels that service in this field is an integral part of the work of the World's Alliance, and that it should be maintained, not only because it has a value in itself, but also because it preserves a nucleus of work capable of immediate expansion, whenever migration on a large scale is resumed as a result of the removal of restrictions now in existence.

The Committee approves the plan of action set out in the report and requests the staff and the Committee on Migration to carry it out.

Note.—The plan of action referred to reads as follows:

1. That the attention of all national committees, and through them the mindfulness of all local Associations, be drawn to this important field of operation.
2. That steps be taken to obtain the co-operation of national committees which are directly concerned with this problem, in order that the needs of migrants may be met in a practical way.
3. That greater attention be given to the problem of migrants:

   (1) in Y.M.C.A. periodicals;
   (2) during training courses of leaders and secretaries;
   (3) in regional conferences;
   (4) in the whole Association program.

4. That the Committee on Migration be reappointed and requested to take steps deemed advisable or necessary to meet the contingencies of the moment.

5. That the transfer of Mr. Karl Schmid from Bremen to Geneva be approved as being instrumental in allowing the World's Committee to grant more effective assistance to national alliances which have to face the responsibility of practical work in harbors, as set forth in this report.

IX. LITERATURE

INFORMATION BULLETIN

The World's Committee agreed to arrange for the issuing of an information bulletin in English, French, and German which should aim to supplement *World's Youth* by providing:

1. News from the life of local Association and national Movements;
2. Notes on topics of current interest to the Y.M.C.A.;
3. Notices and reviews of books bearing on the Y.M.C.A. program;
4. A reference to the contents of the current issue of *World's Youth,* and to the availability of any part of these contents on request in any of the three official languages.

CENTENARY HISTORY

The Committee authorized the officers' committee to initiate the project of producing a suitable history of the Movement for the Centenary in 1944, inviting the co-operation of all national alliances in the preparation of the necessary historical material.

X. REPORT OF THE EXECUTIVE

The World's Committee has received with much pleasure and sincere gratitude the report of its Executive on the work done in the period since the Mysore Conference. In view of the limitations under which we still labor, it is gratifying to note that the staff has been able to do so much and that the results have been presented in such an able and attractive record. Many of the matters referred to in the report are covered by the Resolutions passed on the recommendation of the various committees.

Mention should, however, be made of an important change in the staff through the resignation of Mr. W. W. Gethman, for health reasons, from his position as general secretary, before the Mysore

Conference. It was with the greatest regret that the World's Committee accepted his resignation. It desires to set on record its high appreciation of the great service which Mr. Gethman's wise leadership as general secretary has rendered to the whole World's Alliance. It recalls that it was he who led the Movement, first in the days of expansion after Helsingfors, and then during the period of depression when the very existence of our World Movement and a number of our national Movements was threatened, and when the maintenance of the work involved great sacrifice and strain. It rejoices that after a prolonged illness he is able to render an invaluable service through study, writing, and counsel, and it earnestly desires and prays that increasing health and strength may be given him to carry forward this work.

THE MYSORE CONFERENCE

The Committee recognizes its obligation to carry forward the important convictions and actions of the delegates to the 1937 World's Conference held in Mysore, India, a conference which marked a turning point in the history of the organization and will for many years to come affect the life of the Movement. It is profoundly grateful to God for the manifestation of His Spirit in that meeting and in the intervening days, and for the new unity of spirit and purpose that has been created, made real to us, and symbolized.

The present meeting of the Committee has devoted primary attention to certain aspects of the large program dealt with at Mysore:

> The question of evangelism,
> The problem of relations with the Churches, and
> The extension work of the Movement.

We call the attention of ourselves, both as members of the World's Committee and as workers in our own national Movements and local Associations, and we also call the attention of our national alliances to the important and timely pronouncements at Mysore on other matters. The objectives and proposals for Association effort in the field of interracial relations, international appeasement, economic and social progress, and duty to nation and state are before us as a Movement, to be pursued until measurably achieved or modified. Events in the life of our Movement and the world about us make many of our convictions of even greater importance today than when they were recorded in Mysore early in 1937.

We therefore urge upon ourselves and upon the Movements we represent renewed attention to the policies set forth in the last World's Conference Report.

XI. Staff Appointments

In the spirit of the decision of Dr. Mott to continue in office for a time if the Movement took a forward step in the spirit of Mysore and carried out the Mysore decisions to add four members to the staff of the World's Committee and to encourage young leadership in the Movement, the World's Committee made the following decisions in plenary session:

The World's Committee approved the recommendation of the Executive that a call be extended to Mr. Finn Hov, of Norway, to join the staff of the World's Committee as a boys' work secretary. In view of Mr. Hov's eminently successful work as national boy's work secretary of Norway, where he has created a significant boys' work Movement and developed a strong group of Christian leaders, and in view of his contacts with youth and leaders of other countries through international camps and his studies in Springfield, Massachusetts, U.S.A., the Committee was confident that he will bring to the staff not only the wholehearted support of the Scandinavian countries, but will enable the Committee to serve more effectively the various national Movements in their work with boys.

The World's Committee approved the recommendation of the Executive to call to the staff, beginning on June 1, 1938, Reverend Denzil G. M. Patrick, of Scotland, for literary work and general services to the Committee. The Committee believed that Mr. Patrick, because of his literary ability to interpret the deepest aspect of our Christian faith and obligations as expressed in different nations and different confessions, can render an invaluable service to the work of the World's Committee.

The World's Committee approved the action of the Executive in extending a call to Professor Benjamin E. Mays, Dean of the School of Religion at Howard University, U.S.A., to join the staff. It learned with great satisfaction that Dean Mays is ready to come in September of 1939 for a period of two years. The Committee approved the plan of the officers that he carry on studies on racial relations and on the content of our Christian faith; that in his travels he visit especially Africa and Europe and to some extent other areas; that during the two years he help the World's Alliance to determine its policy and responsibility towards the Negro youth of the world; and if it seems feasible and desirable, help to secure, train, and find the support for a permanent successor.

The World's Committee approved the recommendation of the Executive that Dr. Mott, Dr. Datta, and Mr. Strong be authorized to secure the services of Mr. D. T. Niles, of Ceylon, for a period of at least one year. It will be recalled that Mr. Niles attended the World's Conference at Mysore and served as a member of the Commission on Evangelism. During recent years he has rendered in the field of evangelism an outstanding service in Ceylon and amongst the Christian forces in India, especially with the Student Christian Movement. It is believed that Mr. Niles will greatly strengthen at this time the services of the Worlds Committee to the Alliance as it places a greater emphasis upon evangelism.

XII. Finance

It recorded its profound thanks to the many individual friends and national alliances who have continued their support of the work throughout the year so as to enable the Committee to close its books with the small surplus of Swiss francs 224.19. It further desired to express its appreciation to those national Movements which have found it possible to make their remittances on a quarterly or monthly basis or early in the year, as this has relieved the Committee of considerable borrowing at the banks with the consequent heavy interest burden. It agreed that this practice be continued and that other national Movements consider the possibility of following this procedure.

ENDOWMENT FUND

The Commitee read with deep interest and satisfaction a letter from the Treasurer's Committee pointing out the desirability of securing an endowment fund, in view of the increasing difficulties of maintaining support for an international organization. The Treasurer's Committee believed that the 1944 Centenary offers a unique opportunity to give a stable base to the World's Committee finances and to insure in the future not only the maintenance but also the development of the work. The World's Committee resolved that, in view of the world-wide celebration of the Centenary of the Young Men's Christian Association Movement in 1944, the occasion be taken for the provision of a capital fund of $500,000 (Swiss francs 2,150,000), as a partial endowment of the work of the World's Committee. It further urged the representatives present to give unanimous and enthusiastic support to the launching of a five-year plan for securing this much-needed fund, and to accept quotas to be laid before their National Councils after a careful study by the Officers' Committee, in order that the fund may be completed by the year 1943.

As has already been noted in the prologue, the Committee received with acclamation Dr. John R. Mott's decision to continue his presidency for some time longer. It must be noted that Dr. Mott qualified his acceptance by insisting on the necessity for being on the watch for a younger successor. The decision he made, however, caused universal pleasure and satisfaction.

MEMBERS OF THE OFFICERS' COMMITTEE

Dr. John R. Mott, President, U.S.A.,
Dr. S. K. Datta, Vice-President, India,
John Forrester-Paton, Vice-President, Scotland,
John B. Frosst, Vice-President, Canada,
Dr. A. Kœchlin, Vice-President, Switzerland,
Dr. C. T. Wang, Vice-President, China,
Pierre Lombard, Treasurer, Switzerland.

CHAIRMEN OF STANDING COMMITTEES

Hugo Cedergren, Sweden,
J. E. Sproul, U.S.A.,
Yataro Kobayashi,[3] Japan,
F. W. Ramsey, U.S.A.

TWO MEMBERS-AT-LARGE

Dr. E. Stange, Germany,
H. Lightbody, Scotland.

LETTER OF THE PRESIDENT TO THE PRESENT AND FORMER MEMBERS OF THE WORLD'S ALLIANCE OF THE YOUNG MEN'S CHRISTIAN ASSOCIATIONS

National Council Bulletin, DECEMBER, 1943

DEAR FRIENDS:

As President of he World's Alliance of Young Men's Christian Associations, I write to convey a most hearty message of greeting to the present and former members of the World's Committee and, through them, to the leaders and members of the various national Movements, including the National Councils in process of formation. We are living in a time and under conditions which render the work of our world-wide Association brotherhood of increasing importance. This is due to the ever-widening area and ever-deepening depth of

---

[3] Mr. Yataro Kobayashi, chairman-elect, has not yet finally accepted the post. Mr. Charles R. Hemingway, honorary chairman of the Boys' Work Committee, remains acting chairman until Mr. Kobayashi makes his final decision, and as such remains a member of the Officers' Committee.

human need. The continued shrinkage of the world, due to manifold inventions, has set the nations and races to acting and reacting upon each other with startling directness, power, and virulence. The present terrible world conflict is without parallel in the history of mankind. Significantly, along with this alarming manifestation of divisive forces and influences, there are multiplying evidences of the ecumenical spirit, that is, the growing awareness that there is such a reality as a world-wide Christian community or fellowship which transcends all barriers.

These and other considerations accentuate the vital importance of the Young Men's Christian Association in both its extensive and its intensive aspects. Here is a Divinely inspired Movement which, far more than any other society of youth, weaves together in aspiration and purpose, and increasingly in helpful activity, the young men and boys of the various nations, races, and Christian communions across the breadth of the world. The one thing they have in common is the supremely important fact and factor, the Central Figure of the Ages, the Lord Jesus Christ.

Although the present tragic world convulsion precludes our coming together in our customary conferences, fellowship, and concerted action, there are matters of truly front-line importance with which we in common can and should occupy ourselves:

1. With a sense of greater need than ever, we can serve the young men and boys within the range of our influence in their conflicts with present-day temptations and perils, and in their development of vital faith and Christlike character and helpfulness.

2. We can and should wage a more effective and relentless warfare against influences which tend to blast character and undermine faith.

3. In recognition of the indubitable fact that man's extremity is God's opportunity, and likewise man's opportunity, we should press the advantage which such a time affords.

4. We should ascertain and follow the mind of Christ as to how to prevent a recurrence of the present world struggle, and how to bring in the new day wherein dwelleth justice, righteousness, and love.

5. Let the Associations of different lands bear in mind and give effect to the action of the World's Committee at the meetings in Mysore, Stockholm, and Geneva regarding the Centennial Anniversary of the London Association, founded June 6, 1844. Although the difficulties render it impossible to bring together a large and fully representative gathering, each national alliance should seek to make worthy recognition of this historic event.

6. We should afford financial aid to the World's Committee in its large and constantly expanding program on behalf of the millions of prisoners of war on both sides of the present conflict, and for its significant part in the overwhelming task of repatriation and rehabilitation.

7. Because of the demand for augmenting the leadership of the Association forces in our different countries, due to war conditions, and this at a time of widening need and opportunity, it is essential tht we bring to bear with greater faithfulness Christ's method—that of praying the Lord of the harvest that He thrust forth laborers into His harvest. In this connection, let us recall in grateful memory the passing on into their heavenly reward during recent months of a number of truly great leaders of our brotherhood (great in the sense that "he who would be greatest among you shall be the servant of all")—Dr. Karl Fries, for years the general secretary of the World's Committee, Dr. S. K. Datta, Oliver H. McCowen, Dr. Paul Des Gouttes, and Henry Lightbody.

8. Let us without fail promote the observance of the Week of Prayer, the oldest, most vital, and most potential of the many helpful agencies and practices fostered by our World's Committee.

9. At a time of alarming evidences of hatred and bitterness it is well that we bear in mind the practice of Christ in praying for His enemies, and His high-priestly prayer that all His disciples might be one.

JOHN R. MOTT

RETROSPECT AND PROSPECT

THE CALL TO THE CENTENARY WEEK OF PRAYER OF THE YOUNG MEN'S CHRISTIAN ASSOCIATION, GENEVA, SWITZERLAND, NOVEMBER 13 TO 19, 1944

As President of the World's Alliance of Young Men's Christian Associations, I hereby call upon our entire brotherhood throughout the world to observe, in accordance with our well-established practice, the days November 13 to 19, 1944, as a Week of Prayer. Let us all join in making this occasion memorable as a period of thanksgiving, of dedication, and of intercession.

In many respects this observance is the most significant in all our history, coming as it does at the close of the first hundred years of our life as an organization and on the threshold of a new century. It is fitting, in the language of the Scriptures, that we should "abundantly utter the memory of Thy great goodness," and that we should also catch a vision of the greater things which God has in store for us in the years to come.

I. *Our First Century.* Our first century has been one of pioneering, of pathfinding, and of adventure. It has been a period of opening and entering doors.

This century has also been a period of secure foundation laying. There follow many periods of rearing the edifice, but, I repeat, only one foundation-laying period in the life of an organization. In this case, generally speaking, the foundations laid have been broad, deep, solid, and capable of sustaining a great superstructure.

It has been a century of seed-sowing, and watering, at times with tears; also of diligent cultivation, and, as a result, on all continents, there have been ripened fields and marvelous harvests.

What a century it has been of unwearying proclamation of the eternal evangel, that is, the confronting of successive generations of youth with the Central Figure of the Ages, the Lord Jesus Christ. Herein we find the hiding as well as the releasing of the spiritual power and fruitfulness of the Young Men's Christian Association Movement.

This, our first century, has likewise been an epoch of character building—dealing with youth in the vision-forming years, the habit-forming years, the years of determining life attitudes and tendencies, the years of discovery, of invention, of creation. This alone would explain the highly multiplying spiritual power and influence of the Young Men's Christian Association.

The century has been one of ceaseless conflict with the agelong enemies of mankind—ignorance, poverty, disease, strife, and aggression. We have come to grapple closely, the world over, with these forces that oppose, and, notwithstanding discouragement here and there, the Association has waged a triumphant warfare.

The secret of our victories has been the evolution of a program and a wonderful technique, making possible the building of symmetrical manhood and the generating of the spirit of unselfish service. The Association Movement has developed new and truly creative professions, at the same time maintaining its distinctive mission—that of training and liberating a great and ever increasing lay force both in the Orient and in the Occident.

Across the century the Young Men's Christian Association has afforded conditions for the fostering of significant, vital, and truly creative movements; for example, the Student Volunteer Movement for Foreign Missions, the World's Student Christian Federation, the Inter-Seminary Missionary Alliance, the Men and Religion Movement. Archbishop Söderblom of Sweden, who did so much to promote the modern ecumenical movement, has borne testimony that he derived his vision of Christian unity at a conference of the North American Student Young Men's Christian Associations, and had it expanded later at the World's Conference of the Young Men's Christian Association held in Northfield, Massachusetts, in 1890, and in Amsterdam in 1891.

It would be difficult to overstate the extent and value of the contribution of the Association Movement in drawing together, notably in the last fifty years, the nations and races of mankind, as well as the various Christian Communions.

II. *Our Second Century.* Let us turn to the second century. We hand on to this new era a vast, expanding, vital Christian brotherhood —a brotherhood with 10,000 branches planted in sixty-eight nations, with a membership of over 2,000,000, not counting past millions of older men who were members and were influenced in their youth and young manhood, blending most of the races of mankind, and acknowledging one Leader, the Lord Jesus Christ, and rendering unto His Church their unswerving loyalty.

As the Young Men's Christian Association enters upon its second century, it is with the conviction that our best days lie in the future. This must be so. What could be more dishonoring to the wonderful century behind us than to assume that it had not prepared the way for something which will far transcend in opportunity and achievement that which lies behind? Therefore, in devout and grateful recognition of what God has accomplished through this agency in the past, let us ask ourselves with searching of heart and courageous obedience, why the new century in the life of the Association Movement should not transcend what we are leaving behind us.

By far the best days of the Young Men's Christian Association lie in the future because of the larger knowledge and priceless experience, much of it acquired at infinite cost, which we bring to bear upon the tasks of the new country.

Think also of the vastly greater numbers with which we confront the exacting demands of the fateful period before us, in contrast with the small, unacknowledged and inexperienced bands which pioneered the work of the brotherhood in virtually every field. Surely this not only awakens great expectations but also makes possible our going from strength to strength.

Then let us remind ourselves of the organization which has been built up across the world. What is organization? It is the means of distributing force most advantageously. Here we have evolved what is in reality a blend of the best constructive genious and experience of all national and racial groups. This great resource is at our disposal to be brought to bear upon the baffling situations which confront us in our ministry to the young manhood of the world.

We carry forward another priceless asset—momentum. This is in reality the habit and the contagious power of achievement, of conquest, of victory. Like the rising tide, what does it not make possible in contrast with an ebbing or falling tide?

Each of the past ten decades has witnessed the opening of new doors to the unselfish action of the Association, but none comparable in extent and significance to those that now confront us. It would be difficult to name any considerable area of the world which is now closed to the friendly and constructive ministry of Christ in His outreach to the young manhood and boyhood of the nations.

Moreover, the Association the world over is confronting the greatest array of major unsolved problems which we have ever been called upon to meet. Coming simultaneously with our greatly enlarged opportunities, one is reminded of the word of St. Paul under similar circumstances, "A great and effectual door is opened unto me, and there are many adversaries,"—that is, besides the open doors or opportunities we have the added challenge or attraction of adversaries. Surely the unparalleled situation occasioned by the present global war, and the accompanying world-wide upheaval with its stern economic, social, interracial, and international problems, presents to our great brotherhood an irresistible challenge. This is calculated to call out all our hidden powers and to throw us back on the all-sufficient superhuman forces. It brings to mind the words of Martin Luther: "Before every great opportunity God sent to me some special trial." May it not be in the case of our world-wide Christian brotherhood that the period of serious, unexampled testing through which we are now passing is to be used by God to usher us into our greatest opportunities for unselfish Christlike achievement. And how true it is that the class who constitute our primary and chief obligation, the youth of our day, are in reality the key to the situation which is to confront us in the coming day. Think of their limitless possibilities. Think of their numbers—tens of millions of them in the fighting forces, in the hospitals, in prisoner-of-war camps; other tens of millions behind the fighting lines, still other tens of millions of tender youth—boys in the years of adolescence. I repeat it, all these constitute our special field and incomparably our principal concern.

Above and beyond all, our best days are before us because we have a larger Christ. Not a new Christ, for He is the same yesterday, today, yea and forever. Larger in the sense that associated with us up and down the wide world in all nations and among all races are so many more interpreters of Christ—men with an authentic, firsthand, indubitable experience of His wonderworking power.

JOHN R. MOTT
President of the World's Alliance
of the Young Men's Christian Association

LET US PRAY

First Day

LOOK ON THE FIELDS

PRAY FOR THE PEOPLES OF WESTERN AND NORTHERN EUROPE:

Pray that, as the Association Movement enters upon its second century, it seek to extend its helpful and indispensable ministry to the youth of lands where it has not been established; for example, many of the countries of Latin America, the eastern, western, and central areas of Africa, and the great land of Russia.

> "Say not ye, There are yet four months, and then cometh harvest? Behold, I say unto you, Lift up your eyes, and look on the fields; for they are white already to harvest."
>
> (John IV:35)

Second Day

PRAY FOR LABOR

PRAY FOR THE PEOPLES OF EASTERN AND SOUTHERN EUROPE:

Pray for a greater liberation of the latent lay forces of all the Churches throughout the world, not only as to numbers but also as to their time, money, service, and influence, and for the relating of these forces to the expanding plans of the Kingdom of God.

> "Saith He unto His disciples, The harvest truly is plenteous, but the laborers are few; Pray ye therefore the Lord of the harvest, that He will send forth Laborers into His harvest."
>
> (Matt. IX:37, 38)

Third Day

ENTER THE OPEN DOOR

PRAY FOR THE PEOPLES OF ASIA:

Pray for the enlargement of plans and of efforts on behalf of the millions of men and women returning from the tragic experiences of the World War.

> "A great door and effectual is opened unto me, and there are many adversaries."
>
> (I Cor. XVI:9)

Fourth Day

THE CALL OF YOUTH

PRAY FOR THE PEOPLES OF AFRICA:

Pray for greater concentration of attention and sacrificial effort on behalf of the youth of the world during the adolescent period.

> "Remember now thy Creator in the days of thy youth, while the evil days come not, nor the years draw nigh, when thou shalt say, I have no pleasure in them."
>
> (Eccles. XII:1)

Fifth Day

THE GOOD FIGHT

PRAY FOR THE PEOPLES OF THE AMERICAS:

Pray for better conceived and more heroic warfare, in the fateful period right before us, against the great evils and perils threatening youth in every part of the world, for example, the dangerous reaction following the World War, the alarming lowering of the moral standards the world over, as well as against the agelong enemies—ignorance, poverty, disease, and strife.

> "Fight the good fight of faith."   (1 Tim. VI:12)

> "Wherefore take unto you the whole armor of God, that ye may be able to withstand in the evil day, and having done all, to stand."
>
> (Eph. VI:13)

Sixth Day

"I HAVE OVERCOME THE WORLD"

PRAY FOR THE PEOPLES OF AUSTRALASIA AND THE PACIFIC ISLANDS:

Pray that the Young Men's and Young Women's Christian Associations in every land may take advantage of the widening opportunity, the more vivid realization of the depths of human need, and the humble recognition the world over that Jesus Christ, and He only, can make the world a safe place and flood it with good will.

> "In the world ye shall have tribulation; but be of good cheer; I have overcome the world."   (John XVI:33)

> "Thine is the kingdom, and the power, and the glory, forever."
>
> (Matt. VI:13)

Seventh Day

THAT THEY ALL MAY BE ONE

PRAY FOR THE WORLD CHRISTIAN MOVEMENTS INCLUDING THE YOUNG MEN'S CHRISTIAN ASSOCIATION, THE YOUNG WOMEN'S CHRISTIAN ASSOCIATION, THE WORLD'S STUDENT CHRISTIAN FEDERATION, THE INTERNATIONAL MISSIONARY COUNCIL, AND THE PROVISIONAL COMMITTEE OF THE WORLD COUNCIL OF CHURCHES:

Pray that the growth of the ecumenical movement may be wisely fostered and carried to full fruition by drawing together in fellowship, in sharing of knowledge and experience as well as of burdens and hopes, and in planning for united action on the part of all who acknowledge the Lordship of Christ.

"That they all may be one . . . . that the world may believe that Thou hast sent Me."

(John XVII:21)

INDEX

ligious Emphasis, with Leaders of the Churches, 555-558; reports of committee of delegates and of John R. Mott at series of world conferences prior to Helsingfors, 1033-1167; Richmond, 455; Transportation (Washington, D. C., 1935), 640; Triennial International Conference and Jubilee Celebration of the Young Men's Christian Associations, 139-141; War Work (Garden City, 1917), 743-751; White House, on the Worldwide Expansion of the Young Men's Christian Association, 261-320; World, of Association Workers with Boys (Pörtschach), 469, 604; World's (Basel, 1898), 1033-1037; World's (Christiania, 1902), 1037-1042; World's (Cleveland), 376, 381, 382, 385, 1101-1124, 1128; World's (Helsingfors, 1926), 328, 557, 718, 1056-1060, 1061, 1071, 1072, 1077, 1079, 1080-1097; World's (Mysore, 1937), 1125-1134, 1155, 1156; World's (Paris, 1855), 1075; World's (Stockholm, 1888), 1143; World's Student Christian (Northfield), 141; World's Young Men's Christian Association (Cleveland), 376, 381, 382, 385; World's Young Men's Christian Association (Helsingfors), 328, 1071, 1072, 1074, 1076
Conferences, student, 71-72; theological seminary, 160, 204
Confronting Young Men with the Living Christ, 552, 984
Confucianism, 47, 260, 282
Congo, 1128
Congregational Theological Seminary (Foochow), 248
Constantinople, 279, 313, 360, 361, 364, 877
Constitution of the National Council of the Young Men's Christian Associations of the United States and Canada, 942-952
Constitutional Convention, 509-510, 519, 909-917, 918, 926, 939, 942, 961; Addresses, 913-917
Constructive and Destructive World Forces, 870-878
Constructive Plans for Meeting the Critical Russian Situation, 894-899
Continuation Committee, 397, 399, 401, 407
The Contribution of Physical Education to the Kingdom of God in the World, 654-658

Contribution of the Young Men's Christian Association to World Christianity, 365-372
Convention, Constitutional, 509-510, 519, 909-917, 918, 926, 939, 961; International (See International Convention); Representation and Rules, 457, 477; thirtieth annual, of the Young Men's Christian Associations of Illinois (1902), 651; World (Amsterdam, 1891), 1017
Cook, John W., 399, 480, 747, 748
Cooke, R. W., 912, 918
Coolidge, Calvin, 963, 985
Cooper, Clayton S., 43, 56-61 *passim*, 63, 88
Cooper, William Knowles, 399, 912, 917
Co-operating Commission on the Foreign Work, 441
Co-operative relations of the Student Movement and other Christian organizations, 184-185
Copec Conference (Manchester), 516
Copeland, Mr., 119
Copenhagen, 1089
Copernicus, 867
Coptic Church, 381
Cornelius, Chester, 114
Cornell, Ezra, 4
Cornell University, 3-7 *passim*, 11-15 *passim*, 22, 23, 24, 32, 91, 116, 129, 151, 271, 407, 669, 732, 970, 991, 992, 995, 998, 1016
Corvallis, 127
Cossum, W. H., 36
Costa Rica, 1098
Cotton, Arthur N., 833
Coulter, L. A., 461
Council of National Defense, 804
Council of North American Student Movements, 401
Couper, E. J., 459, 490
Coyle, Dr., 134
Crane, Charles R., 335
Cranston, Earl, bp., 757
The Crisis of Missions, 217
Criticism of the War Work of the Young Men's Christian Association, 817-829
Criticisms of the War Work Answered, 808-817
Crosby, W. H., 492, 835, 838, 839
Crossett, L. A., 437, 757, 776, 777, 831, 835, 836
Crowder, Enoch, General, 788
Crowe, H. J., 424
Cuba, 239, 255, 286-287, 290, 313, 361, 363, 370, 769, 805

sponse to Address of Welcome by the
Maharajah of Mysore (1937), 1136-
1137; Response to the Call of the Na-
tional Council, 937-940; student days
at Cornell University, 3-7; Testimonial
Dinner (Chicago, 1928), 971-1001;
Trustee of the War Fund, 836; visit
to Poland, 350-354; Vote of Thanks
(Mysore, 1937), 1133-1134; See also:
General Secretary of the International
Committee
Mott, Mrs. John R., 328, 727, 737, 973,
986-988
Moule, H. C. G., bp., 193, 997
Mt. Allison College, 117
Mount Hermon, Massachusetts, 5, 8, 9
Mount Hermon Conference, 7-12, 22, 114,
996
Mueller, C. A., 74
Mukden, 282
Müller, Max, 215
Munn, Dr. J. P., 411
Muramatsu, Mr., 271
Murray, Andrew, 193
Murray, W. D., 396, 411, 424, 463, 494,
517, 621, 831
Mysore, 298, 318, 1125, 1133-1138 passim,
1142, 1160; Maharajah of, 1133, 1134-
1137

Nagasaki, 269, 270
Nagpur, 471
Nanking, 249, 251
Nanking University, 248
Napa College, 125
Napoleon Bonaparte, 264, 630, 771, 883
Nashville, 60, 61, 64, 70, 74, 424, 553,
758; Southern Association College, 513
National Athletic Federated Committee,
416
National Board of Certification, 933
National Catholic War Council, 781-784
passim, 790, 807
National Committees of the Young Men's
Christian Associations of the United
States and Canada, 3, 1120
National Intercollegiate Athletic Asso-
ciation, 416
National Council of Young Men's Chris-
tion Associations, 333, 509-510, 519,
528, 701, 702, 703, 733, 909-1030, 1094;
Agreement with the International Com-
mittee and the Canadian National
Council, 940-942; Constitution, 942-
952; Fifth Annual Meeting, 942; First
Meeting (1924), 917-918; Second An-

nual Meeting, 942; Sixteenth Meeting
(1941), 1001
National War Work Council, 433, 444,
453, 457, 470, 473, 492, 504-505, 833,
834, 835, 850, 883, 893, 1010; Administrative and General Activities Ex-
penses at General Headquarters in
New York, 849; classes of men served,
744; Disposition of Balance, 841; Dissolution, 835-839; Expenditures in the
United States, 845-846; Expenditures
Overseas, 846-847; Extracts from the
Minutes of the First Meeting (New
York, 1917), 752-758; Final Report,
839-850; Financial Statement, 843-845;
Launching, 743-758; Meeting with
Federal Council of Churches, 756-757;
Religious Work Bureau, 756; State-
ment of Independent Auditors, 850;
Statement of Operations of Post Ex-
changes and Canteens, 847-848; State-
ment of Reserves, Liabilities and
Adopted Budget for 1921, 842; See
also: United War Work Campaign;
War Work.
Near East, 206, 317, 340, 341, 359, 360,
365, 374, 431, 440, 452, 458, 459, 463,
472, 490, 495, 517, 518, 643, 695, 860,
861, 936, 997, 1012, 1098
Near East Relief, 345
Nebraska, 82, 553, 701
Neesima, J. H., 217, 221, 876
Negro students, 163
Netherlands; See: Holland
Netherlands Indies; See: Dutch East
Indies
Nevada, 100
New Brunswick, 116; University of, 116
New Caledonia, 889, 1128
New England, 31, 34, 43, 82, 84, 86, 115,
116, 122, 126, 264, 278, 344, 548, 550,
552, 585, 776, 777, 985
New Hampshire, 424
New Haven, 194, 204, 757
New Jersey, 82, 552
New Mexico 553
New Orleans, 501
New Renaissance (China), 589, 695, 696
New Thought Movement (China), 589,
695
The New World and the New Day, 658-
669
New York, 3, 4, 6, 12, 13, 22, 32, 63, 64,
74, 79, 89, 113, 114, 116, 149, 150, 172,
174, 190, 235, 274, 277, 279, 297, 298,
302, 310, 321, 330, 358, 370, 404, 405,